Sexual Types

Sexual Types

Embodiment, Agency, and Dramatic Character
from Shakespeare to Shirley

Mario DiGangi

PENN

UNIVERSITY OF PENNSYLVANIA PRESS

PHILADELPHIA

Published by
University of Pennsylvania Press
Philadelphia, Pennsylvania 19104-4112

Printed in the United States of America on acid-free paper
10 9 8 7 6 5 4 3 2 1

Library of Congress Cataloging-in-Publication Data
DiGangi, Mario
    Sexual types : embodiment, agency, and dramatic
character from Shakespeare to Shirley / Mario DiGangi. —
1st ed.
        p. cm.
    Includes bibliographical references and index.
    ISBN: 978-0-8122-4361-1 (hardcover : alk. paper)
    1. English drama—Early modern and Elizabethan,
1500–1600—History and criticism. 2. English drama—17th
century—History and criticism. 3. Sex in literature. 4.
Characters and characteristics in literature. 5. Typology
(Psychology) in literature. 6. Stereotypes (Social
psychology) in literature. I. Title
PR658.S39 D54   2011
822'.309353—dc23   2011022664

Contents

Illustrations

Introduction

Deformation of Character

And no society can properly function without classification, without
an arrangement of things and men in classes and prescribed types.
This necessary classification is the basis for all social discrimination,
and discrimination, present opinion to the contrary notwithstanding,
is no less a constituent element of the social realm than equality is
a constituent element of the political. The point is that in society
everybody must answer the question of *what* he is—as distinct from
the question of *who* is he—which his role is and his function, and
the answer of course can never be: I am unique, not because of the
implicit arrogance but because the answer would be meaningless.
   —Hannah Arendt

Grandma
You look familiar.

Young Man
Well, I'm a type.
   —Edward Albee, *The American Dream*

In Shakespeare's *1 Henry IV*, Hotspur uses a curious rhetorical strategy to convince the king of his loyalty: he provides a remarkably detailed portrait of the appearance, mannerisms, and speech of an affected courtier. King Henry has accused Hotspur of deliberately withholding his prisoners of war, which by right belong to the monarch. Denying this charge, Hotspur offers the narcissistic courtier as his excuse:

My liege, I did deny no prisoners;
But I remember, when the fight was done,
When I was dry with rage and extreme toil,
Breathless and faint, leaning upon my sword,
Came there a certain lord, neat and trimly dressed,
Fresh as a bridegroom, and his chin, new-reaped,
Showed like a stubble-land at harvest-home.
He was perfumèd like a milliner,
And 'twixt his finger and his thumb he held
A pouncet-box, which ever and anon
He gave his nose and took't away again—
Who therewith angry, when it next came there
Took it in snuff—and still he smiled and talked;
And as the soldiers bore dead bodies by,
He called them untaught knaves, unmannerly
To bring a slovenly unhandsome corpse
Betwixt the wind and his nobility.
With many holiday and lady terms
He questioned me; amongst the rest demanded
My prisoners in your majesty's behalf.
I then, all smarting with my wounds being cold—
To be so pestered with a popinjay!—
Out of my grief and my impatience
Answered neglectingly, I know not what—
He should, or should not—for he made me mad
To see him shine so brisk, and smell so sweet,
And talk so like a waiting gentlewoman
Of guns, and drums, and wounds, God save the mark!¹ (1.3.28–55)

By this point in Hotspur's speech, the logic of his excuse is evident: exhausted and aching from his wounds, he neglected to heed the words of a garrulous courtier who slighted the sacrifices of soldiers and trivialized the horrors of war. Yet the reasonableness of Hotspur's excuse also renders gratuitous his elaborately detailed portrait of the courtier. Couldn't Hotspur simply blame his impatience on the need to attend to his injuries? Or might he not just admit that the courtier's impertinent chatter angered him? What purpose is served by his finely observed account of the courtier's dress, gestures, linguistic mannerisms, and even smell?

To raise these questions is to begin to address the complex dramatic and ideological functions of the theatrical figure I am calling a sexual type. As I will argue in this book, while dramatic representations of sexual types might be humorous or titillating, they are also motivated by ideological concerns. In the case of the narcissistic courtier from *1 Henry IV*, the workings of gender and sexual ideologies are fairly transparent because the sexual type is not embodied in a dramatic character but called into being through the language of a character with particular motives and values. Depending on one's interpretation, Hotspur might have very good reason to evoke, at this precise moment, the type of the narcissistic courtier: to veil his political or economic motives for denying the king's request; to displace blame for miscommunication from himself to another; to remind the king of his loyal service and sacrifices in war; to excuse his rudeness by implying that his "masculine" soldiership justifies belittling the lord's "effeminate" courtiership; to embarrass the king for having sent such an inappropriate representative on a military errand, and so on. In all these ways, signifiers of gender and (more subtly) of sexuality serve to convey arguments about political loyalty, military ethics, and aristocratic comportment.

To begin with gender, the narcissistic courtier is evidently a figure of effeminacy, in that he demonstrates a "feminine" daintiness and refinement at odds with the "masculine" stoicism suited for warfare. Hotspur scornfully attributes the lord's effeminacy to his status as one of the leisured nobility who serve in courtly offices. Paradoxically, however, even as Hotspur paints the lord as the epitome of an idle aristocrat, he associates the lord with the figure of the milliner: a citizen of middling social rank who is rendered "effeminate" through his trade in "fancy wares, accessories, and articles of (female) apparel" (*OED*, milliner, *n.* 2). According to Hotspur's masculinist ideology, what arbitrarily links the idle lord with the industrious milliner is perfume, a sign of the feminine refinement that disqualifies either man from wielding a sword in combat. Hotspur's condemnation of the narcissistic courtier for being at once too aristocratic and too common (an association that also emerges in the comparison to "a waiting gentlewoman") provides a lesson in the political utility of the sexual type: a familiar figure that can be strategically deployed to convey arguments about social categories such as masculinity and nobility.

Whereas Hotspur overtly manipulates gender signifiers such as "lady" and "waiting gentlewoman" to excuse his gruff treatment of the courtier, sexual signifiers function more subtly in his narrative. To describe the lord, Hotspur turns from an unadorned description of his own actions on the battlefield to the resources of figurative language: through simile, he describes the lord as "Fresh as a bridegroom" and compares his shaved chin to a cropped field at the end of harvest. In this way, Hotspur links effeminate mannerisms with heteroerotic desire: the courtier is like a "fresh" young bridegroom eagerly anticipating a first night of passion with his bride.[2] At the same time, since the beard signifies male sexual potency, the shaved beard hints at the impotence of this castrated ("trim" and "reaped") lord, an implication strengthened by the allusion to the harvest-home celebration of late September, when all the crops have been cut down and barren winter approaches.[3] Hotspur's assessment of the courtier's effeminacy also derives from witnessing the courtier's interactions with other men. For Hotspur, true manhood is forged through affectionate, communal bonds with other men, in this case the soldiers with whom he has braved the perils of war. The lord's callous disregard for male camaraderie, particularly his objectification of other men as "unhandsome corpses" and "good tall fellows," earns him Hotspur's contempt. What makes the narcissistic courtier legible as a reviled sexual type, then, is his social isolation from other men, including those men—such as the "good tall fellows"—to whom, arguably, he reveals an erotic attraction.

Far from serving simply as scapegoat figures, sexual types can also function to expose and critique the ideologies that make them intelligible. Whereas Hotspur presents the narcissistic courtier as his degraded antithesis, a perceptive reader or playgoer might detect similarities between the two men. Ironically, Hotspur speaks copiously in denouncing the courtier for his copious speech. "Popinjay," Hotspur's insulting moniker for the gaudy and garrulous courtier, resonates with "paraquito," the word Hotspur's wife uses to reprimand her husband for his capricious chattering (2.4.78). Perhaps most telling in terms of Hotspur's affinity with the courtier is his joke about the courtier's nose taking the perfume box "in snuff": a pun on "to snuff" as "to inhale" and "to take in snuff" as to take offense at something. Diverted by his own wit, Hotspur indulges the same impertinent "holiday" language of which he accuses the frivolous lord (1.3.45). These parallels suggest that the particular traits for which Hotspur vilifies the narcissistic courtier are not, in fact, limited to one type of person. Consequently, even as the sexual type functions as an easily recognizable figure representing socially abject or deformed modes of gender and erotic comportment, his very participation in familiar social relations can expose the ideological interests that draw the boundaries between the normative and the monstrous, the appropriate and the transgressive.

The paradoxical embodiment of the strange or deformed in a familiar form is at the heart of this study. In early modern drama, sexual and gender transgressions commonly regarded as "abominable," "diabolical," "unnatural," and "monstrous" are often embodied in characters who, in the words of my second epigraph, "look familiar." These characters look familiar not because they (necessarily) represented people likely to be encountered in the daily lives of early modern English men and women, but because they were readily identifiable as *types*: recognizable figures of literary imagination and social fantasy. From among the many early modern sexual types that might be discussed in a study such as this (e.g., the cuckold, the widow, the prostitute), I limit my analysis to six figures that reveal in particularly compelling ways, both individually and collectively, how sexual transgressions were understood to intersect with social, gender, economic, and political formations. These six types are the sodomite, the tribade, the narcissistic courtier, the citizen wife, the bawd, and the monstrous favorite.

The very notion of a "sexual type," of course, begs the question of how sexuality informs the broader notion of a social type or stereotype. What does it mean to identify these six figures as *sexual* types? How does the "sexual" component of each type intersect with other defining features such as gender, profession, and rank? Is sexuality a more salient feature of some types than others? An additional set of questions pertains specifically to the sodomite and tribade, sexual types that appear in early modern texts and discourses but that do not correspond to social identities in the same way as the four other sexual types I consider. Unlike the courtier, citizen wife, bawd, and favorite, the sodomite and the tribade do not appear in seventeenth-century character books, which provide detailed descriptions of contemporary social and professional types.[4] If, as I claim, the sodomite and tribade constitute recognizable sexual types in early modern drama and culture, what might explain their absence from character books? Put another way, do representations of sodomites and tribades have any correspondence with actual persons?

In addressing such questions below, I hope to demonstrate that the broad concept of a sexual type is capacious enough to accommodate figures whose defining features might vary greatly in terms of rank, wealth, age, and profession, and who might typically appear in different kinds of texts, including sermons, legal statutes, travel narratives, anatomy texts, court satires, urban comedies, and political tragedies. Despite this variety, sexual types consistently function to reveal conflicts over sexual agency as symptomatic of conflicts over gender, social, economic, or political agency. My emphasis on the ideological work performed by representations of satirical or "deformed" sexual

types is not meant to imply that early modern culture recognized no posi-
tively inflected figures that might be defined as sexual types, such as amorous
shepherds or romantic heroines. Nonetheless, my concern is to understand
how sexual figures primarily found in urban and courtly venues function as
sites through which skirmishes over the boundaries of social legitimacy and
illegitimacy are fought. Thus I define the sexual type not as the bearer of a
sexual identity or subjectivity, but as a familiar cultural figure that renders
sexual agency intelligible as a symptom of the transgression of gender, social,
economic, or political order.[5] The condition of intelligibility for a sexual type
might be called "deformation of character," in that the sexual type becomes an
easily recognized figure for vilified forms of embodiment and agency.

As easily legible, familiar figures, sexual types correspond to the concept of "social persons" proposed by Elizabeth Fowler in *Literary Character:
The Human Figure in Early English Writing.* Fowler defines social persons as
"familiar concepts of social being that obtain currency through common use.
. . . As conventional kinds of person, social persons are very much like literary
genres, because they depend upon the recognition of convention" (2). According to Fowler, a literary character (e.g., the Knight in Chaucer's *Canterbury
Tales*) emerges from a reader's apperception of the cues provided by the text's
evocation of multiple, potentially contradictory, social persons (e.g., the *cru-
sader*, the *mercenary soldier*, and the *pilgrim*). In short, "Social persons are, by
definition, simple and thin; positioned among a number of them, a character takes on complexity and weight" (9). Whereas Fowler's aim is to analyze
how a "weighty" literary character is generated from the reader's cognitive
negotiations among a multitude of social persons drawn from many cultural
discourses, I explore how the definitive traits of a particular sexual type (e.g.,
the courtier, the bawd) are embodied in dramatic characters whose sexual
transgressions are linked to transgressions against gender, social, economic, or
political order. Approaching sexual types in the drama as symptoms of ideological conflicts that extend beyond sexuality, I share Fowler's conviction that
"by referring to social persons, single characters are able to convey arguments
about larger social structures" (14). I argue, for instance, that in the type of
the narcissistic courtier the "effeminacy" embodied in self-loving mannerisms
and excessive consumption becomes intelligible as a sign of social and political
illegitimacy.

At the same time, I argue that when a sexual type is embodied in a dramatic character, the character's own strategies for resisting the constraints of
dominant social and sexual ideologies can disturb the logic of the reductive

and vilified associations imposed by the type. Thus a particularly dissident instantiation of the type can put the type itself under scrutiny, suggesting its partiality or inadequacy as a standard for classifying and evaluating the social practices of an individual.[6] Moreover, I would argue that this critical exposure of the type's regulatory and disciplinary authority is much more likely to occur in drama than in genres such as verse satire or the prose character description, in which character types are relatively fixed. Through the social, verbal, and corporeal interactions that constitute drama, characters are able to exercise an agency that might exceed the parameters implied by the dominant type. When embodied in dramatic characters, then, sexual types are more likely to resemble the unruly bodies of which feminist theorist Elizabeth Grosz writes: "Bodies are not inert; they function interactively and productively. They act and react. They generate what is new, surprising, unpredictable" (xi). Through their unpredictable interactions and assertions, bodies in the drama have the capacity "to always extend the frameworks which attempt to contain them, to seep beyond their domains of control." Moreover, in the dramatic embodiment of any character, even a character restricted by the limitations of a familiar stock type, the actor's body in performance exerts its own unpredictable agency.[7] A guiding premise of this study, then, is that sexual types in the drama provide rich sites for both the assertion and the demystification of disciplinary ideologies.[8] By inserting sexual types into dynamic, unpredictable social scenarios, playwrights can generate compelling forms of critical knowledge.

Of the six types in my study, the sodomite and the tribade are those who are most indisputably defined by their sexual practices. Although same-sex practices are the sine qua non of the sodomite and tribade, both types are composed of discursive strands that engage categories of nationality, religion, status, and economics, as well as sexuality. The sodomite is not a distinct social type in early modern England, in that the concept of sodomy did not serve to organize one's primary sense of self or to situate persons in a particular structure of relations within the family, neighborhood, or polity. Rather, the sodomite is a composite type, a hybrid figure comprised of elements from common social types such as the prodigal, the epicure, the "good fellow" (a gamester or drunkard), and the friend. In early modern theological and moral texts, any of the familiar vices associated with these various social types (such as idleness and drunkenness) might be cited as the source and manifestation of "sodomitical" transgression. Moreover, in early modern social life sodomites were sometimes "recognized"—if not explicitly named as "sodomites" or overtly accused of engaging in anal intercourse—when same-sex disorder occurred in the context of everyday gender, social, or economic transgressions. Consequently, those theological, moral, or legal texts that identify the sodomite as a threat to civil society can be shown to contain the contradictory recognition that "sodomitical" practices are not, in fact, a manifestation of almost unimaginable crimes against the monarch, nature, and God, but rather a function of everyday social and economic relations. By violating the definitional boundary between the familiar and the strange, the sodomite exposes the incoherent early modern conceptualization of male same-sex relations.

Likewise, the tribade exposes the incoherent conceptualization of female same-sex relations in early modern patriarchal culture. English patriarchal norms defined female sexuality in terms of gender-differentiated, conjugal reproductive intercourse. The tribade's sexual practices were generally regarded as so alien to this norm of English femininity that this figure appears neither as a social type in character books nor as a subject of sodomy statutes: rather, she most often appears in travel narratives, anatomical treatises, and imaginative texts that locate her in exotic realms associated with strange sexual customs. Travel and anatomical texts usually define the tribade as a "masculine" woman who imitates the "male" role in heteroerotic relations, in that she is the seducer and sexually dominant partner of a more "feminine" woman. However, the indeterminate, contradictory descriptions of sexual acts between women in these texts permit the alternative conclusion that female-female relations might not be modeled after hierarchical male-female relations after all, but might instead be erotically egalitarian and symmetrically gendered (e.g., consisting of two "masculine" female partners). Alternatively, these texts suggest that if female same-sex relations are indeed hierarchically organized, they might be organized by differences of age, beauty, and status that do not correspond to the terms of binary gender structuring conventional male-female relations. The tribade, then, can be understood as an "imitative" sexual type, but one that simultaneously reasserts and resists an absent standard (the male position in heteroerotic sex). Together, the sodomite and the tribade expose the limitations of the very logics of classification that constitute any sexual type.

The narcissistic courtier and working wife are both sexual types in that their modes of economic agency and corporeal self-display are linked with particular kinds of erotic transgression. An indiscriminate consumer, the narcissistic courtier collects fragments of manners, languages, and fashions, which he uses to gain access to an elite culture of which he is unworthy. As I suggested in my reading of *1 Henry IV*, the courtier's "effeminate" self-regard causes him to reject "masculine" forms of aristocratic association as well as socially productive homoerotic and heteroerotic relations. The working citizen wife, an active producer and seller of goods, is suspected of using her domestic authority and mobility in the public marketplace to obtain access to illicit sexual pleasures. Consequently, the working wife's exertion of social, economic, and sexual agency complicates the distinction between the categories of "chaste wife" and "whore." As with the sodomite and tribade, these types unsettle the taxonomical thinking that produces them: through his embodiment of courtly civility, the narcissistic courtier troubles the difference between legitimate ("masculine") and illegitimate ("effeminate") forms of elite male display and association. Through her public industry and economic authority over her husband, the working wife troubles the difference between legitimate (profitable) and illegitimate (sexual) forms of female labor. More importantly, both figures can be shown to function as symptoms of the ideological ruptures that accompanied early modern England's gradual and uneven development from a land- and status-based economy to a proto-capitalist economy. Products of what Arendt calls a constitutive "social discrimination," these ridiculed types thus perform significant ideological work in "explaining" the larger cultural transformations whose disruptive consequences they are made to embody.

In that the distinction between "masculine" and "feminine" forms of elite male display is central to my discussion of the narcissistic courtier, it should be clear that gender as well as sexuality is a crucial analytical category in my study. Throughout the book, I use "gender" to refer specifically to the cultural manifestations of masculinity, femininity, and their variants (i.e., male "effeminacy" or mannishness in women); I use "sexuality," "sexual," or "sex" to refer to erotic fantasies, desires, and acts. In my analysis of figures such as the tribade and the narcissistic courtier, I sharply distinguish gender from sexual signifiers as a way to demonstrate that "homosexuality" fails to explain the complex and multiple power relations in which these figures are engaged. However, at a broader theoretical level, I also want to acknowledge that categories of gender and sexual meaning are impure, variable, and overlapping. In this I take my cue from Judith Butler's discussion in "The End of Sexual Difference?" of the critical and political value of retaining the openness and the contestedness of concepts such as *gender, sexuality, sexual difference,* and *feminism* (*Undoing Gender,* 177–92). For Butler, the point of doing critical and political work in feminist and queer arenas is to keep alive the questions of how gender and sexual meanings continue to operate differently for different individuals and communities across time.

The last two types I consider, the bawd and the monstrous favorite, are sexual types in that they function as intermediaries or agents in fashioning illicit heteroerotic relationships. The bawd and the favorite are agents of perverse displacement: they appropriate the authority derived from age, experience, or position to establish illicit sexual alliances that advance their own social, economic, or political interests. In early modern plays and character books, bawds are often depicted as old women who, by exploiting same-sex intimacies, seduce younger women into sexual relationships with men. The decrepit body of the bawd signifies the loathsomeness of sexual commerce and the corruption of the ideal of female chastity. Nonetheless, the bawd's success in seducing younger women indicates the appeal of her strategies for selling sex, and her appropriation of proverbial wisdom to defend her profession demystifies condemnatory moral authority as an equally tendentious rhetorical performance. Whereas the bawd deploys proverbial wisdom and everyday forms of same-sex intimacy to guide other women into whoredom and adultery, the favorite uses the authority bestowed by his position to ally himself through marriage with a noble or royal family, thus aggrandizing his own power at his prince's expense. Dramatic representations of the favorite's sexual and political scheming convey the dangerous consequences of his intimacy with the prince, even as the language of monstrosity typically applied to the favorite exaggerates the power that any single man could possess. The consistency of this hyperbolic language of monstrosity suggests that the abuses of authority blamed on the favorite can be traced back to larger systemic causes lodged in absolutist rule. The acute loathing directed against the deformed bodies and sexual practices of the bawd and favorite thus exists in uneasy tension with the recognition that their effective seductive strategies draw upon authorized forms of moral knowledge and political association.

My analysis of the dramatic and ideological function of sexual types builds on the groundwork laid by Renaissance scholars of different theoretical stripes during the last thirty years. Previous studies of sexual types have largely examined the theatrical representation of stereotypical characters in the context of early modern gender and sexual norms. In the 1980s, feminist Shakespeare critics began to analyze how female characters such as the virgin, whore, shrew, patient wife, and lusty widow conformed to or challenged patriarchal definitions of proper female comportment.[9] Similarly, scholars who have written on dramatic representations of Moors, Africans, Spaniards, Italians, and Turks have addressed sexual stereotyping as one aspect of the theatrical production of racial, national, and religious otherness.[10] Genre criticism, particularly of London city comedy, has provided another avenue for the study of sexual types. In *The City Staged*, Theodore Leinwand explores how city comedy offered urban audiences the opportunity to assess the accuracy of social prejudices manifested in types such as the sexually predatory gallant, the jealous citizen husband, and the lascivious citizen wife. Jean Howard's *Theater of a City* offers a feminist analysis of the whore as a multiply layered signifier for the place of women in London's multinational economy. These studies provide valuable perspectives on the ways in which theatrical representations engage social attitudes and ideological struggles. However, these studies do not offer a sustained account of how the sexual type functions as a site of ideological contradiction. That is, they do not approach the sexual type as a familiar cultural artifact through which sexual ideologies are reproduced but also exposed as inadequate explanations for complex forms of social agency.

My understanding of sexual types such as the sodomite, tribade, courtier, and favorite is also indebted to lesbian, gay, and queer Renaissance scholarship.[11] Throughout the book I situate my arguments in relation to the relevant scholarship in these fields, but a brief account of three studies that have fruitfully examined early modern same-sex types should clarify some key points of my own methodology. I begin with Bruce Smith's *Homosexual Desire in Shakespeare's England* (1991), which offered the first comprehensive account of male-male sexual types in early modern literature and culture. Smith's conceptualization of homosexual character types and motifs as "myths" suggests that his interests lie in identifying broad cultural narratives that impose structure and coherence upon the multiple forms of same-sex experience. This quest for narrative unity is corroborated by Smith's citation of Denis De Rougemont's claim that a "myth makes it possible to become aware at a glance at certain types of *constant relations* and to disengage these from the welter of everyday appearances" (qtd. Smith, *Homosexual* 19). Whereas Smith emphasizes the large stories that make same-sex relations culturally intelligible despite the centrifugal energies of "everyday appearances," I emphasize how "everyday" social relations can offer an angle of resistance to the imposition of the dominant cultural narratives that constitute a type.

Simon Shepherd's essay, "What's So Funny About Ladies' Tailors? A Survey of Some Male (Homo)sexual Types in the Renaissance" (1992) explicitly takes up the problem of sexual types in early modern historiography. In opposition to the strict Foucauldian position that homosexuals did not exist before the nineteenth century, Shepherd argues that since "dominant ideologies, perhaps at all historical conjunctures, need their distinct types of sexual deviance," it makes sense to posit that early modern England also recognized certain "homosexual types," which functioned to define the boundaries between normative and non-normative sexual practices (18). Discussing types such as the ladies' tailor, fop, and favorite, Shepherd links dominant sexual ideologies, particularly those associated with an emergent bourgeoisie, to dominant ideologies of gender and economics, according to which male extravagance in sexual passion, spending, or attire was considered "effeminate." Particularly germane to my own approach is Shepherd's understanding of how types allow social and economic transgressions to be expressed in terms of sexual transgressions. What is most compelling and trickiest about Shepherd's argument is the notion that the Renaissance homosexual type need not be defined primarily by sexual object choice: the ladies' tailor is a "homosexual type" not because he has sex with men, but because he threatens the norms of patriarchal masculinity and sexually monogamous marriage by gossiping, encouraging wives' indulgent appetites, and producing extravagant apparel. In the broad outlines of his brief essay, Shepherd cannot offer a more developed account of the complex articulation of gender and sexuality that informs sexual types. I intend to pursue this line of inquiry in discussing figures such as the sodomite and narcissistic courtier, who are defined as figures of gender and sexual deviance. Moreover, Shepherd's belief that homosexual types are essentially products of dominant ideology does not leave space to explore the struggle between the assertion and resistance of dominant cultural forms, which is at the core of my project.

In *The Renaissance of Lesbianism in Early Modern England* (2002), Valerie Traub focuses on the antithetical sexual types of the tribade and friend to support a diachronic argument about how and why the meanings of female homoeroticism changed during the seventeenth century.[12] Before this change took effect, Traub argues, the figure of the "masculine" tribade was sharply distinguished as a "mode of embodiment" from the figure of the "feminine" chaste friend or "femme." Through a process she calls the "perversion of lesbian desire," the "erotic potential" of the femme became more visible in cultural representations during the course of the seventeenth century, and consequently the once clear difference between the innocent femme and the unnatural tribade began to collapse, thus rendering a greater range of female-female bonds subject to suspicion and derogation (231). Like Traub, I am interested in the "rhetorics of desires and acts" through which female same-sex desire was rendered intelligible in early modern England (169). However, in my analysis of the tribade as an embodiment of these rhetorics, I am not concerned to trace large-scale historical transformations in the meanings and representation of female same-sex desire. Instead, I concentrate on a narrower historical moment, and ask how the sexual type operates as a site for the assertion and resistance of cultural beliefs that were dominant at that time. To illuminate the dynamics of this ideological struggle, I focus on contradictory representations of the tribade and her imagined sexual partners, which vacillate from scenarios implying erotic equality and mutuality to scenarios implying erotic hierarchy and aggression.

Perhaps the most obvious difference between my study and previous work on sexual types is my inclusion of both male and female sexual types, operating within both homoerotic and heteroerotic scenarios. I hope that this inclusiveness will represent a salutary critical move in going beyond the male/female and homo/hetero divisions that continue to structure a good deal of scholarship on early modern sexuality.[13] Although there are good reasons for such divisions—not least among them being the gender separatism of much early modern social life—there is also new knowledge to be produced by working across these boundaries. For instance, the sodomite and tribade have rarely been studied alongside each other, even though they play analogous roles in early modern culture as the male and female embodiments of "unnatural" sexuality. The critical difference of gender means that the sodomite and tribade do not embody transgressive same-sex practices or their social consequences in the same way; nonetheless, I hope to show that as sexual types they reveal the definitional incoherence that informs early modern understandings of male-male and female-female relations alike. Although differently positioned in terms of gender, rank, and profession, the narcissistic courtier and the working wife reveal how sexual types function as symptoms of the incomprehensible social and economic changes transforming both the city and the court. Finally, by exploring how the bawd and monstrous favorite use authorized forms of same-sex intimacy to promote illicit heteroerotic alliances, we can think across the homoerotic/heteroerotic boundary—a boundary that these character types eagerly violate in attempting to accomplish their political, financial, and erotic ends.

This book is organized in three parts, each comprised of a pair of chapters that address comparable dramatic types and social issues from different angles. In each part, one chapter features a female sexual type and the other features a male sexual type; consequently, gender is the most obvious differential in my analysis of sexual relations, but differences of status and genre are also important throughout. The different mode of argumentation that characterizes each of the three parts reflects my desire to explore different ways of situating sexual types among literary and cultural discourses in an effort to understand the complexity of their functioning. In the first part, diverse texts drawn from the realms of law, anatomy, travel, and so on are examined alongside the drama; in the second part, each chapter proceeds through a detailed reading of a single play (a city comedy and a court comedy); in the third part, each chapter traces the transformation of a particular set of social and sexual conflicts as they travel through a range of plays, primarily tragedies and tragicomedies. Although I might have made similar arguments using different texts, the plays I have chosen represent in particularly intense and revealing ways the sexual and social conflicts embodied through my six character types. Read individually as well as in conversation with each other and with the texts that serve as their sources and contexts, these plays also repay close attention to the linguistic and formal details that provide indispensible access to social and ideological meaning.[14] Whenever possible, I use visual images to illuminate how particular sexual types are represented as embodied personae.

Part I, "Sexual Types and Necessary Classifications," serves as the foundation of this study. It foregrounds the social consequences of the contradictory and incoherent schemes of classification that early moderns used to fix the sodomite and the tribade: male and female same-sex types that occupied complementary positions as the embodiments of alien and threatening sexual practices. In addition to a variety of cultural discourses in which the sodomite and tribade typically appear, I also examine the allusive presence of the sodomite and tribade in three plays of Shakespeare. One of my aims in this part of the book is to take "nonliterary" (or quasi-literary) texts—such as crime pamphlets, legal commentaries, medical treatises, and travel narratives—that purport to report the "truth" of early modern sexuality and to subject these texts to an interrogative reading that unfolds the ideological consequences of rhetorical and linguistic style.

Chapter 1, "Keeping Company: The Sodomite's Familiar Vices," examines how a variety of early modern texts—including plays, sermons, depositions, diaries, and pamphlets—deploy the figure of the sodomite to define by contrast norms of sexual, gender, and social behavior.[15] Even as the sodomite is evoked to define the parameters of communal order, the proximity of the sodomite's transgressive practices to those familiar practices that constitute everyday social relations can unsettle those definitions, exposing the logic of the type to critical scrutiny. I detect this alternating current of discipline and resistance in sermons as well as in Shakespeare's *Troilus and Cressida*. I conclude the chapter with a reading of a remarkable crime pamphlet, *The Arraignement . . . of Humfrey Stafford* (1607), which records one of the extremely rare instances in early modern England in which a private man suffered death under the sodomy statute. Through this text I demonstrate how the sodomite, the epitome of the alien, unnatural, and treasonous, can, in the guise of a Protestant English gentleman, look oddly familiar.

Chapter 2, "Fulfilling Venus: Substitutive Logics and the Tribade's Agency," scrutinizes the typical definition of the tribade as a masculine woman who imitates the "male" role in sexual relations with women. I begin by revisiting oft-cited English and continental medical texts—by Helkiah Crooke, Thomas Bartholin, and André Du Laurens—and travel narratives—by Nicholas de Nicolay and Leo Africanus—that represent the tribade as a substitute figure for a phallic male. At the same time, I argue, these texts contradict the imitative thesis by acknowledging the ways in which sexual relations between women are not necessarily analogous to sexual relations between men and women. Turning to the drama, I argue that Titania in *A Midsummer Night's Dream* and Paulina in *The Winter's Tale* function as types of the tribade who challenge the imitative logic of that category in different ways. Unlike the tribades described in anatomical and travel texts, Titania and Paulina exert agency in defining and defending their same-sex relations. Titania paradoxically resists Oberon's patriarchal control both by imitating that patriarchal control in her own domination of the votaress and by rejecting it in her depiction of female-female relations as erotically mutual and egalitarian. In *The Winter's Tale*, Leontes attempts to defame Paulina's intimacy with his wife by associating her with the tribadic figure of the "mankind witch." Nonetheless, Paulina's triumphant "resurrection" of Hermione in the final scene of the play affirms the tribade as an embodiment of restorative physical intimacies and social allegiances between women.

Part II, "Sexual Types and Social Discriminations," examines the boundary between authorized and transgressive forms of economic and sexual agency through the types of the narcissistic courtier and the citizen wife. In each of these two chapters, I focus primarily on a single play. I provide a detailed reading of that play in order to demonstrate how a theatrical text (and its performance) might reproduce dominant sexual ideologies, even as the dialogic action of the play exposes the incoherence of those ideologies as ways of explaining the transgressive practices of courtiership and urban commerce.

The central text of Chapter 3, "Mincing Manners: The Narcissistic Courtier and the (De)Formation of Civility," is Jonson's satiric court comedy *Cynthia's Revels*, which critiques "effeminate" apparel, speech, and manners as violations of normative male aristocratic comportment. Although a number of plays, including *Hamlet*, might have made appropriate subjects for the analysis of courtly effeminacy, I selected *Cynthia's Revels* for several reasons. First, the play includes several embedded character sketches that illuminate the early modern rhetoric of social and sexual types; one editor of *Cynthia's Revels* has described its second act as "the first English character book" (Judson lxviii). Second, with its evocation of Narcissus as a kind of ur-type of the self-loving courtier, *Cynthia's Revels* demonstrates how a familiar mythological type might be employed in the service of topical satire against social, gender, and erotic vices. Finally, Jonson's detailed examination of excessive courtly pastimes, fashions, and manners piercingly affirms an absent ideal of modest civility, even as it paradoxically suggests how difficult it is to distinguish legitimate from illegitimate forms of courtiership.

Centering on Middleton and Dekker's city comedy *The Roaring Girl*, Chapter 4, "Calling Whore: The Citizen Wife and the Erotics of Open Work," considers how the imputation of sexual impropriety constitutes a strategy for disciplining the economic as well as sexual agency of women who participate in an urban market economy. Unlike the neglected *Cynthia's Revels*, *The Roaring Girl* has been the subject of countless readings by feminist, queer, and materialist scholars since the 1980s. Whereas these readings tend to privilege the outlandish cross-dressing Moll Cutpurse, I focus on the outwardly more respectable citizen wives as sexual types who are publicly shamed for appropriating domestic authority and threatening household credit. I argue that the mechanisms of sexual slander that define and discipline Moll Cutpurse operate less overtly but more potently to define and discipline the wives for asserting authority in erotic and financial affairs. A more complex understanding of the ideological work performed by *The Roaring Girl* around issues of gender and sexuality thus requires a fuller account of its representation of the citizen wives in their roles as shopkeepers, spouses, and rivals with Moll.

Part III, "Sexual Types and Intermediary Functions," focuses on two character types—the female bawd and the male court favorite—who exploit same-sex intimacy to orchestrate illicit heteroerotic relationships that advance their own agendas. In these two chapters, I consider how several different playwrights use sexual types to address the imagined social, economic, and political threats that can arise from the abuse of familiar intimacies. Chapter 5, "Making Common: Familiar Knowledge and the Bawd's Seduction," scrutinizes the logic of the anti-bawd rhetoric found in character books, moral treatises, and plays. Whereas these texts typically represent the deformed old bawd as a wicked mentor who morally poisons a younger woman, the dramatic bawd exerts her seductive powers on women in ways that belie the simple metaphors of instruction and infection. Strategically evoking moral commonplaces, dramatic bawds seduce women into illicit relations that are made to seem both appealing and familiar. Discussing four plays by different authors—Fletcher's *A Wife for a Month*, Dekker and Webster's *Westward Ho*, Middleton's *Women Beware Women*, and Shakespeare's *Pericles*—I explore the different degrees of agency enjoyed by bawds who manipulate common knowledge and the common spaces of same-sex intimacy for their own pleasure and profit.

Focusing on Caroline drama, Chapter 6, "Making Monsters: The Caroline Favorite and the Erotics of Royal Will," considers a cultural milieu and set of dramatic texts by Massinger, Killigrew, and Shirley that are still overwhelmingly neglected in early modern studies. Using as evidence a number of plays—primarily Massinger's *The Maid of Honor* and *The Great Duke of Florence*; Killigrew's *Claricilla*; and Shirley's *The Royal Master*, *The Duke's Mistress*, and *The Traitor*—I argue that the dominant type of the favorite shifted in the early seventeenth century from the alluring Ganymede to the monstrous favorite, a figure of sexual and political mediation who functions to convey the abuses and failings of royal will. By scheming to marry into a noble or royal family, the favorite abuses his position as mediator between prince and subjects, thus betraying his master's trust. Types of sexual and political treachery, the favorites are the overt villains of these plays, but their villainous actions also implicate princes who govern through rash assertions of sexual and political will.

If, as I will consider in a brief conclusion, character studies have made a comeback in early modern dramatic scholarship, I hope that development brings with it a renewed sense of the possibilities for the historical analysis of sexuality and gender. And I hope that analysis is not limited to the work of Shakespeare. In contrast to the touted humanity of Shakespeare's characters, who have often been promoted to the status of real "persons" or "individuals," the characters created by Shakespeare's contemporaries have often been slighted as deformed or deficient.[16] No less than Shakespeare's characters, however, the characters of Fletcher, Middleton, and Shirley contribute to our understanding of how the early modern theater might have deployed sexuality to articulate and to mediate social, economic, and political conflicts. The lessons of post-structuralist theory, historicism, and political criticism—including, but not limited to, feminist and queer theory—invite us to return to the study of character in ways that acknowledge the complexity and vitality of dramatic types as indexes of social and ideological change.[17]

Part 1

Sexual Types and Necessary Classifications

Chapter 1

Keeping Company

The Sodomite's Familiar Vices

> his death might be a warning to all others, to beware how they gave
> up themselves to wine, swearing, and companie keeping with such
> as he tearmed good fellowes, which from his youth hee had greatly
> delighted in . . .
> — *The Arraignement . . . of Humfrey Stafford*

In *Homosexual Desire in Shakespeare's England* (1991), Bruce Smith presents
an important argument about the "personalization" of English sodomy laws
during the course of the sixteenth century. Examining the rhetorical framing
and punitive scope of the sodomy laws from their initial formulation under
Henry VIII in 1533–1534 through their final iteration under Queen Elizabeth
in 1562, Smith demonstrates that sodomy shed its metaphysical associations as
it came to be understood as a matter of what individual bodies did in familiar
domestic spaces.[1] According to Smith, in the course of only twenty-eight years
the legal discourse of sodomy had narrowed its view of the crime from a form
of "religious heresy" to a matter of personal morality within the family (47).[2]
Smith's analysis represents an important departure from a dominant thesis
of Alan Bray's enormously influential *Homosexuality in Renaissance England*
(1982). Having traced the pervasiveness of the early modern theological discourse of sodomy, which conceived of "homosexuality" not as "part of the
created order" but as "part of its dissolution," Bray concluded that sodomites
were "not the stuff of daily life but of myth and legend" (19, 25). Whereas
Bray's focus on hyperbolic religious rhetoric convinced him that the sodomite

was a myth, Smith's focus on legal rhetoric suggested instead that the sodomite was a man whose criminal behaviors could be discovered and punished through the evidentiary practices of secular authority. Despite the volume of scholarly work produced on sodomy in the twenty years since Smith's book appeared, the impact of this historical shift from the understanding of sodomy as an offense against God to the understanding of sodomy as an offense committed within and against social institutions has yet to be fully explored.

In this chapter, I will argue that a variety of early modern texts—including plays, sermons, depositions, diaries, and pamphlets—deploy the type of the sodomite in the interests of defining the limits of proper sexual, gender, and communal relations. Attempts to depict the sodomite as a recognizable sexual type whose behavior places him outside the boundaries of a normative community can have the paradoxical effect of revealing the proximity of the sodomite's transgressive practices to those familiar practices that constitute the normative community, thus opening the norms themselves to scrutiny. We might read a scene from Marlowe's *The Jew of Malta* as an allegory of this dynamic: the ruling Christians mistake the drugged Barabas for dead and happily throw him over the walls of the city; awaking outside the boundaries of civilization, Barabas strikes a deal with the invading Turkish forces, guiding his new allies back into the city through secret passages. Howsoever exiled from the boundaries of civil life, once the sodomite is accorded recognition as a social actor, the actions that constitute his "sodomy" are available to interpretation not as a manifestation of metaphysical evil, but rather as a function of the material relationships that constitute families, communities, and the nation. The sodomite's habits of same-sex association—eating and drinking with male companions; participating in riotous camaraderie; nurturing same-sex friendships; sharing intimacies with bedfellows—might therefore be recognized as the same activities that constituted authorized masculine relations.[3] As a sexual type, therefore, the sodomite can serve both to establish definitions of orderly community (through representations of his practices as antithetical to social norms) and to destabilize those definitions (through unsettling revelations of the proximity of his "sodomitical" practices to those very norms).[4]

I will pursue this argument in three stages. First, I will consider how previous scholarship has overlooked the sodomite's function as a familiar sexual type in early modern English culture, either because he is regarded as a figure of absolute otherness or because he is read deconstructively as a trope, a destabilizing linguistic effect rather than a social actor. Building on recent work by Bruce Smith and Mary Bly, I will consider the possibility that early moderns could, in fact, recognize sodomites as social actors, whether on the stage or on the street. Nonetheless, evidently little effort was made to identify and punish sodomites, either through slanderous language, shaming rituals, or legal prosecutions. To explain the paucity of sodomy trials, some scholars have claimed that the sodomite was so alien a figure as to be unrecognizable in the person of a neighbor or acquaintance, whereas others have claimed that the English law simply made it too difficult to discover and to prosecute men who had committed anal intercourse. Although I find the latter theory more plausible to explain the paucity of sodomy trials, I will argue that sodomites were in fact "recognized"—if not explicitly named as "sodomites" or overtly accused of engaging in anal intercourse—in circumstances when same-sex disorder occurred in the context of gender, social, or economic transgressions. In local contexts involving household members, neighbors, or fellow citizens, "sodomites" were not regarded as felons or traitors accountable to the civil law that required their death; however, they could still be disciplined through the shaming mechanisms or misdemeanor laws commonly used to correct smaller social and moral infractions within local communities. Sermons as well as stage plays such as Shakespeare's *Troilus and Cressida* provide insight into attempts to identify and shame sodomites through the implication that they have violated norms of sexual, gender, or communal comportment; these texts likewise reveal how those disciplinary attempts might be thwarted by recognition of the sodomite's consonance with social norms. Finally, I will consider the remarkable case of a London gentleman hanged for sodomy in 1607—one of the rare circumstances in which a private man came under the purview of the sodomy statute. Even in the case of a man publicly identified and executed by the state as a sodomite, the associations of sodomy with the alien, unnatural, and treasonous sit uneasily with the recognition of the sodomite as a familiar type, an English Protestant gentleman who enjoyed "good company."

*   *   *

Previous treatments of the sodomite have largely regarded him either as the alien figure constructed by legal and theological discourse, or as a figure of textual instability through which dominant discourses of gender and sexuality might be deconstructed. In *Homosexuality in Renaissance England*, Alan Bray posits that, in early modern England, the sodomite was not someone whom you knew. Through his analysis of court records, Bray discovered that "for the great majority of people homosexuality . . . was overwhelmingly something which took place between neighbours and friends" (43); the sodomite, how-ever, was a dark figure not of "daily life" but of "myth and legend" (19). In short, Bray unearthed a kind of cognitive paradox: same-sex practices were the stuff of daily life, arising from the otherwise unremarkable intimacies between a master and his apprentice, a barber and his neighbor's son, or a clergyman and his young parishioner (48, 43). At the same time, same-sex practices were the stuff of fantasies about outlandish and legendary bugbears such as sorcer-ers, heretics, papists, and traitors (19). The "sodomite," conceptually speaking, was not the man who cut your hair, made your shoes, or cured your soul, but a shadowy figure encapsulating all that was foreign and threatening to social, moral, and religious order.[5] According to Bray, sodomy trials were so rare in the early modern period because it was so difficult for people to recognize the monstrous sodomite in the actual persons of their barbers or bakers. Bray, in short, posits a stark binary between the alien sodomite and the familiar neigh-bor, master, or friend.

Focusing on the imaginative possibilities of homoerotic subjectivity in early modern poetic texts, Paul Hammond argues in *Figuring Sex Between Men from Shakespeare to Rochester* that a contemporary reader could not have identified with the sodomite, because the sodomite represented not a subject of erotic desire but a profoundly subversive other.[6] Hammond claims that homoerotic literature in Renaissance England "offered a gamut of imaginative possibilities, a range of social and erotic roles which a reader might try out in the private world of his imagination, and thence, perhaps, in the shared tex-tual and physical spaces of sexual intimacy" (10–11). The range of sexual roles a reader might imaginatively "try out" encouraged a "discontinuous identity, resources for temporary and shifting modes of self-definition" (11). Hammond insists, however, that one role a reader could not identify with, one mode of self-definition that was not available to him, was that of the sodomite. Sod-omy's "translation of desire into subversion denies the individual a plausible subjectivity, moving him out of the kind of narrative or social space which readers could imagine themselves inhabiting" (8–9).[7] For Hammond, the alienness of sodomy—its association with "un-English" and "un-Christian" figures—offered a starkly "punitive definition" of same-sex relations, in sharp contrast with the "fluid, productively indefinite vocabulary for intensely affec-tive male relationships at home" (21, 28).

For deconstructive critics such as Gregory Bredbeck and Jonathan Gold-berg, the sodomite functions primarily as a textual effect of the discursive category of sodomy. As the title of Bredbeck's book suggests, *Sodomy and*

Interpretation aims to reveal how Renaissance homoeroticism is "a slippery category that is at once both a type of sexual meaning and an effacement of sexual meaning" (21). Bredbeck argues that the figure of the sodomite—Patroclus in Shakespeare's *Troilus and Cressida*, Edward II in Marlowe's *Edward II*, the speaker of Shakespeare's *Sonnets*—is constructed in and through language. This linguistic construction in turn allows the critic "to create a hermeneutic" that can demonstrate the ideological workings of social, political, and sexual discourses (48). Thus, when Bredbeck asks if we can "speak of the sodomite" in early modern sonnets, his answer comes via the operations of grammar. We can indeed find the sodomite within the "linguistic practices of the culture," but not as a subject who signifies sodomy, or male-male desire (143, 145); in Shakespeare's sonnets, the sodomite generates a "range of subjective possibilities" intended not to construct the meaning of sodomitical desire, but to critique the signifying capacities of gendered and sexual language (184).

Although Goldberg insists that his approach to sodomy as "a site for deconstructive reading" should not be taken as a denial of the "worldly effects" of sodomy—including the executions of men who were labeled as sodomites in the early modern period—his primary emphasis falls not on "the sodomite per se" but on the "relational structures precariously available to prevailing discourses" (*Sodometries* 20).[8] In his analysis of Marlowe's *Edward II*, Goldberg identifies King Edward and Gaveston as "sodomites" because in advancing an unworthy favorite the king becomes the "site of legitimation and transgression at once" (123). Yet in the broader sense of the term as "the explosion of the marital tie, *sodomy* is the name for all behavior in the play"; hence, the adulterous Queen Isabella and rebellious Mortimer are also "sodomites" (123). Regarding sodomy as a "defoundational site" or "a deconstitutive locus" (125–26), Goldberg concludes that the "identity that Marlowe gives to the sodomite is a fully negativized one against which there is no positivity to be measured" (124). In short, for Goldberg the sodomite constitutes not a distinct type of person but rather a radically oppositional position that "glimpses the destruction of the social" by undermining the "categorical oppositions"—male and female, masculinity and femininity, homoeroticism and heteroeroticism— that ground gender and sexual meaning (129, 136).

In *Homosexual Desire in Shakespeare's England*, Bruce Smith treats the sodomite primarily as a juridical subject, a construction of sixteenth-century sodomy laws (41–53). These laws defined the act of sodomy so narrowly (as, essentially, anal intercourse), that early modern English juridical power rarely captured actual "sodomites." Nonetheless, sodomites populate literary texts with juridical and "political" motives (162), particularly social satires and related works such as Marlowe's *Edward II* that explore how same-sex relations threaten social order. Smith argues that the shift in English law from "sodomy as a species of heresy to sodomy as . . . a matter of personal morality" influenced the satirical depiction of the sodomite as an agent of illicit desire: "it was the legally defined sodomite who emerged as a recognizable *type*" (165–66). Smith's definition of the type of the sodomite as an idle, debauched aristocrat is borne out by my readings below. However, Smith's dual emphasis on ancient Roman satirists' disgust at "effeminate" male sexual passivity and on the Christian discourse of the crime against nature paints the early modern sodomite as an alien, virtually soulless, figure, even as it downplays how the details of everyday life in Renaissance satires serve to make the sodomite familiar. In John Donne's first satire, for instance, the satiric persona reviles his sodomitical companion's taste for whores, expensive silk clothing, and dancing boys; yet even in his disgust he describes not the alien "sodomite" of religious discourse but a familiar acquaintance with familiar appetites that can be satisfied in a recognizable urban landscape. Likewise, John Marston's disparagement of a sodomite who has sex with boys and goats in the London suburb of Hogsden seems less to limn "a graduated descent down the great chain of being" than to hyperbolically link illicit sexual agency to the excesses of urban consumption (Smith 180). In Marston's vivid fantasy, if a "bawdy-house of beasts" indeed stands in Hogsden, it is because the proprietor has identified a profitable market for buggery (Marston, qtd. Smith, 179). Smith might be correct in stating that early modern satirists could not imagine that the sodomite possessed an identity or subjectivity, but satirists do attribute to the sodomite a recognizable, if grotesquely exaggerated, set of social habits and familiar appetites (185).[9]

In *Shakespeare and Masculinity*, Smith modifies his earlier account of the sodomite as a figure who typifies aristocratic vices by positing a "continuum" of male-male relations ranging from romanticized friendship on one end, to excoriated sodomy on the other (124). Citing Bray's influential distinction between the friend and the sodomite, Smith explains that what "a Renaissance man most aspires to be is another man's friend; what he most abhors to be is a sodomite," and this is because sodomitical desire epitomizes the indulgence of passion that early modern culture regarded as antithetical to manly virtue and self-control (123). Yet, Smith intriguingly suggests, the ambiguous friendships in Shakespeare's plays would have presented a male playgoer with an epistemological problem: how is masculinity defined in relation to homoeroticism in a play such as *The Merchant of Venice*? Where does Antonio fall on the continuum from friend to sodomite? Such ambiguities, Smith posits, opened up an opportunity for "approaching the sodomite, despite his being a dreaded other" (126). Whereas Hammond believes that it would have been impossible for a male reader to identify with the sodomite, Smith implies that a male playgoer might have understood his own masculinity in a complex, shifting, and perhaps not completely self-conscious relation to a set of behaviors, emotions, and sexual desires that could be legible as attributes of the sodomite. For different playgoers, then, Shakespeare's Antonio could be a site of active identification (as an ideal friend), of active disidentification (as a loathsome sodomite), or of a more complicated engagement with an impure figure who "flirt[s] with sodomy without declaring it" (125).[10]

Mary Bly goes even further than Smith in broadening the meaning of "sodomite" beyond the overwhelmingly negative associations attached to sodomy by early modern legal discourse. In *Queer Virgins and Virgin Queans on the Early Modern Stage*, Bly argues that the managing syndicate of the Whitefriars Theater, active during 1607–1608, realized the profit to be made from marketing satirical, bawdy plays to male playgoers with a taste for the homoerotic. Whitefriars plays feature transgressive sexual puns that typically yoke the figure of the desiring boy to that of the desiring woman. In the "bonds of shared laughter" among male playgoers who appreciated such flaunting of conventional morality Bly finds the "space for identification as a sodomite in early modern culture" (20). What Bly seems to be getting at is not a *criminal* sexual subjectivity implied by the legal category of "sodomy," but something like the concept of an overtly transgressive or "queer" sexual subjectivity, for which no name existed in the period. The "sodomites" in the audience at Whitefriars would presumably not have identified themselves with the demonized figure of the sodomite condemned in contemporary religious or satiric discourses, but instead formed "a self-aware homoerotic community" that took pleasure in the witty representation of same-sex desire (6). Because, as I argue more fully below, I consider the sodomite a composite type that conjoins the sexual practices of "sodomy" to the moral and social sins typically attributed to the biblical Sodomites, I am skeptical of Bly's claim that early modern sodomites constituted an "erotic minority," which implies a social identification based primarily on sexual practices or preferences (16). Nonetheless, Bly, like Smith, productively suggests that the London stage made available to male playgoers avenues of identification with "sodomites": men who enjoyed dissonant forms of male-male intimacy, even if they were not the alien, unnatural figures of satirical, legal, and theological discourse.

In what follows, I first pursue the question implicitly raised by Smith's understanding of the sodomite as an "approachable" social type and by Bly's account of the possibility of a sodomitical community in early modern London. If the sodomite was recognizable as a kind of person, then why were there evidently so few instances in which sodomites came under the purview of social and legal discipline in early modern England? If, as Bly claims, one London theater company deliberately catered to sodomites, why did these sodomites appear to escape the notice of authorities who should have taken an interest in restraining their subversive pleasures? The contrast with witchcraft is instructive. Like the sodomites of legal and religious discourse, witches embodied frighteningly alien forms of sexual, gender, and religious deviance. But witches were also familiar figures: one's neighbor might be publicly accused of witchcraft, tried, and executed. Published accounts of witchcraft trials and the popular literature drawn from those accounts expose the social mechanism by which a witch might be identified. For instance, in Dekker, Ford, and Rowley's *The Witch of Edmonton* (1621), a tragicomedy based on an actual case, Elizabeth Sawyer's neighbors are quick to accuse her of witchcraft. A local Justice's skepticism—"Fie! To abuse an aged woman!"—provokes a neighbor to insist on Sawyer's abject identity: "Woman? A she-hellcat, a witch!" (4.1.35–36). The play in fact represents Sawyer as a witch, but at the same time gives her the insight to explain how envious neighbors might push a marginalized figure to commit transgressive acts: "I am none. None but base curs so bark at me. I am none. Or would I were! If every poor old woman be trod on thus by slaves, reviled, kicked, beaten, as I am daily, she, to be revenged, had need turn witch" (4.1.76–79). Why don't we find analogous scenes in early modern drama in which neighbors identify some abject or alienated member of their community as a sodomite?

In *Homosexuality in Renaissance England*, Bray observes that despite the harsh condemnation of sodomy in the written law, the courts rarely prosecuted it in actual practice.[11] Bruce Smith's detailed analysis of the sodomy laws in *Homosexual Desire in Shakespeare's England* supports Bray's findings: describing sodomy indictments as statistically insignificant, Smith points to a single conviction for sodomy during the sixteenth century, in a case involving the rape of a five-year-old boy (48). To explain the infrequency of sodomy trials in early modern England, Bray posits a general inability to recognize in everyday homosexual behavior the exaggerated theological account of sodomy as a monstrous sin of cosmic proportions. Smith, approaching the issue from the opposite direction, concludes that the increasing precision of the legal definition of sodomy—as, essentially, anal penetration—left all other kinds of male-male sexual activity (and *all* kinds of female-female sexual activity) outside the scope of juridical detection.[12] Like Smith, Kenneth Borris attributes the rarity of sodomy trials to features of the English judicial system that had nothing to do per se with social attitudes about sodomy. "English legal proceedings against sodomy were necessarily rare," Borris argues, "because certain unique characteristics of English common law inadvertently entailed major difficulties of establishing proof in the case of this consensual and ordinarily private sex crime" (*Same-Sex*, 82). For instance, English law forbade the use of investigative judicial torture, by which suspected sodomites might otherwise have been forced to confess their crimes. Because consensual anal intercourse was difficult to prove, "sex between males could only come before English courts under certain exceptional conditions," such as the 1631 trial of the Earl of Castlehaven (83). If Smith and Borris are right, we might speculate that male-male sex (including but not limited to anal intercourse) took place in everyday life in early modern England, and that some people knew that it was taking place in their neighborhoods or communities, but that it was understood to have been generally immune from prosecution under the sodomy statute.

One implicit challenge to the theory that sodomy could be recognized as an everyday practice comes from social historian Laura Gowing's analysis of slander depositions from London's church courts. According to Gowing, despite the fact that slander depositions of nearly 6,000 English men and women survive for the period between 1572 and 1640, and despite the sharp increase in defamation suits heard in London between 1600 and 1610, none of the depositions "feature any allegations of homosexual behaviour" (*Domestic* 32, 65).[13] Gowing provides two "[e]qually important" explanations for the absence of defamation cases involving same-sex conduct. First, because sodomy was a secular crime, it was not a "technically actionable allegation" at the church courts that heard defamation suits (65).[14] Surviving sixteenth- and seventeenth-century legal records involving sodomy derive not from the church courts, but from the secular Assizes, which handled serious felonies, and from the Quarter Sessions, which handled lesser felonies and misdemeanors (Bray, *Homosexuality*, 38–50); the case I discuss at the end of this chapter was heard in the King's Bench Court, the highest common-law court in England. Gowing's second explanation for the absence of same-sex slander litigation adopts Bray's theory regarding the paucity of sodomy indictments in

Renaissance England: "Renaissance thought pictured sodomy through distant metaphors, not the realm of daily life; and it was daily life with which these defamers were most concerned. Their insults focused around the street, the market, and the household" (65). Gowing's line of reasoning requires us to conclude that in early modern England sodomy was not visible in "the street, the market, and the household."

Nonetheless, other evidence suggests that sodomy could be recognized in the social and sexual relations of the street, the market, or the household. This impression is confirmed by the definition of "sodomitrie" in Robert Cawdry's 1604 dictionary: "when one man lyeth filthylie with another man" (sig. H6v). Strikingly, Cawdry intended his dictionary to assist "Ladies, Gentlewomen, or any other unskilfull persons" in understanding hard words they might encounter "in Scriptures, Sermons, or elsewhere, and also be made able to use the same aptly themselves" (title page). That Cawdry includes "sodomitrie" in a relatively brief dictionary (of 122 small pages) as a word important enough for gentlewomen to know and use themselves implies that men "lying filthily" with other men was a common enough practice—or, at the least, a common enough concept—to merit discussion among ladies. Another example of the familiarity of sodomy is found in the diary of Josias Bodley, which records a journey through Ireland in 1602–1603. According to Bodley, one morning some of the young men on the journey "greeted their companions the back way, which was not—to my way of thinking—very decent, although some say that it is good for the loins; but nothing is amiss which is not taken amiss" (qtd. P. Hammond, 29). Perhaps in order to avoid any strife, these young men chose not to make a fuss about the indecency of some of their fellows; and, in any case, such activities might well promote good health![15] Though possibility indecent, this same-sex behavior might well be ignored in the absence of any more serious transgressions of social, moral, or economic order.[16]

If same-sex relations did openly break into socially disruptive behavior, such behavior could have been identified and corrected by appropriate disciplinary methods far milder than the fatal exactions of the sodomy statute. For instance, the smaller secular courts attempted to control disorderly alehouses, which were blamed for keeping servants and apprentices from work and for functioning as brothels. Yet when the brewer William Firthe was reported to a court of hundred in 1582 because he "keeps apprentices, boys, and servants in his house at night," the perception of his inappropriately intimate congregation with young men arises as a contributing factor to the charge of misconduct (qtd. McIntosh, *Controlling Misbehavior*, 76).[17] Likewise, in 1597–1598 a

Norfolk innkeeper was reported for allowing four men "to keep bad gover-
nance at night time in his said house to the great disturbance of his neighbors"
(qtd. McIntosh, 79 n.79). Another target of local discipline, nightwalking, was
sometimes linked to sexual misconduct, as in the 1576 presentment of John
Baker and William Newton for "leading a lascivious [*liciviosa*] life and being
'common night watchers'" (qtd. McIntosh, 67). Describing an unusually explicit case of 1609 in which a London merchant was called before the Quarter
Sessions for abusing his servant and "correcting him unreasonably with whip-
cords, being quite naked," Alan Bray remarks that "the courts were apparently
unconcerned with sexual relations between masters and servants unless a scandal was involved or an illegitimate child was produced" (*Homosexuality*, 50).
If we can read male-male "sodomy" into these assertions of local discipline,
the sodomite who emerges is not the antisocial monster of legal and religious
rhetoric but rather a figure guilty of recognizable, even commonplace, excesses
and indiscretions.[18]

For a fuller understanding of how the sodomite was recognizable as what
I am calling a composite sexual type, we can turn to a variety of religious
texts on the destruction of Sodom.[19] The most helpful place to start is Robert
Milles's sermon *Abrahams Suite for Sodome* (1612), which carefully parses the
sexual and social sins that Sodomites came to embody in early modern England.[20] Milles explicates the four primary sins of Sodom mentioned in Ezekiel:
pride, fullness of bread, idleness, and contempt of the poor.[21] The fifth, "nameless," sin of Sodom lurks in the shadows, even as the four primary sins themselves are described in terms of sodomitical companionship: the "capitall vices
of *Sodom* had many fellowes, many followers and partners, like trait'rous *Absa-
lon* and *Achitophel*, which by their flattery drew many mens hearts after them"
(sig. C5r). To begin with the sin of pride, the archetype of the proud man who
seeks high authority is that chief "Sodomite" and "Divell," the pope, a figure
commonly associated with sodomy in Protestant polemics (sig. C6v). Whereas
the proud man rejects "brotherly love" or orderly male-male relations (sig.
C7r), the glutton seeks raucous companionship: "I fear me, Blessed Brethren,
that we have in these daies many Sodomites, boone companions, and sensual
good fellows quite drowned and overwhelmed in this sinne of *fulnesse of bread
and drink*" (sig. C7v). Although Milles praises the industriousness of Londoners, he discovers the Sodomitical sin of idleness in the "close back wings
and obscure angles" of the city among gamesters, epicures, coney-catchers,
and the "licentious Poet and Player" (sigs. D4r, D5v). Gamesters and epicures are akin to those "sensual good fellows" who indulge in food and drink;

coney-catchers will "embrace a man" with a courtly greeting and then cut his throat; poets and players prefer the sexually corrupt practices of the stage to religious instruction (sigs. C7v, D5r). To illustrate the fourth Sodomitical sin, contempt of the poor, Milles narrates how Faith, Hope, and Charity sought three earthly husbands: Faith took Abraham, Hope took David, and Charity, rejected, still searches for her mate. Thus Milles understands all four of the ostensibly nonsexual sins of Sodom in terms of wicked same-sex companionship and non-(re)productive social, economic, and marital practices. When Milles does finally acknowledge his fear that "the horrible and namelesse sinne of *Sodom* hath poisoned some" Londoners (sig. E5r), his metaphor of sodomy as poison returns us to the logic of his account of Sodomitical pride, idleness, and gluttony as sins that spread among so "many followers and partners," "boone companions," and "sensual good fellows" (sig. C7v). Despite his reluctance to name or explicitly discuss sodomy, Milles provides quite a full portrait of the sodomite as a composite sexual type.[22]

Milles's elaboration of the constituent traits of the sodomite allows us to discover the sodomite in places we might not expect to find him. It is precisely to the point that Francis Lenton's *Characterismi* does not include the sodomite among its character portraits, but does include characters who might be taken for sodomites under different guises: the prodigal, the common drunkard, and the ordinary gamester. Just as Milles renders male-male sodomy legible as a symptom of the Sodomites' social, moral, and economic sins, so the vices of Lenton's characters place them in a particular relationship to virtuous or debauched male same-sex communities. Lenton's Prodigal proudly rejects honest company for the flattering caresses of knaves: "His carriage is very courteous, yet somewhat quilted with singularity (the secret pride of Prodigals,) fooles are his admirers, and knaves his soothers" (sig. D8v). Like the Sodomite full of bread and drink, Lenton's Common Drunkard "either spues himselfe out, or gives occasion to be spurnd out of all civill Company" (sig. F1r). Milles's gamester, who consorts with other idle men, is matched by Lenton's Ordinary Gamester, who is "somewhat too prodigall of other mens purses" and who "preposterously alters the course of Nature, as he alters the Cards; sleeps all day, and plays all night" (sigs. E7v–8r). The male "purses" that the gamester spends too prodigally might refer either to money or to genitalia (testicles), and "preposterously" carries the familiar early modern connotation of sodomitical inversion. Even Lenton's character of the True Friend might be considered an inverted image of the Sodomite who pursues the affection of "sensual good fellows": "Love and amity hath so knit him to you, that 'tis a question whether you be two or one, reciprocally answering each other in affection, and are equally sensible of each others defects or disturbances" (sig. H1v). In the common figures of the "sensual" prodigal, drunkard, and gamester, and even perhaps in the figure of the "sensible" friend, a contemporary reader might have recognized the familiar outlines of the sodomite.

It is significant in this regard that despite casting his glance back to the ancient city of Sodom, Milles recognizes the sodomite as a familiar, and even a familial, contemporary figure. Just as Abraham sued for the preservation of the Sodomites, Milles enjoins, when "wee see our brethren sunke in sinne, loose in life," we should pray for them and "use all meanes to covert them" (sig. G6r). The sodomite is not an alien simply to be extruded from the community; like the "prodigall brother," he is a sinner who should be reformed and reabsorbed into the community (sig. G6v). Nonetheless, Milles seems to conclude his sermon on a note of doubt regarding the success rate of conversions. Recalling that God destroyed Sodom because he could not find even ten good men there, Milles recommends that "populous Cities" ensure "that there may alwaies bee found among them a righteous *Lot*, and above the number of tenne" (sig. G6v). Unrepentant sodomites, Milles implies, might remain in our midst, surfeiting, contemning the poor, and enjoying sex with each other; yet if enough of us are righteous God might still preserve our communities from destruction.

As we have seen, Milles parses the composite type of the sodomite as a way to illustrate a series of wicked behaviors that his parishioners are to avoid or reform. William Storre, a minister of Market Rasen who was murdered following a sermon about Sodom in 1602, evidently offered too precise an account of the sodomites residing in his local community. An anonymous pamphlet, *The Manner of the Cruell Outragious Murther of William Storre* (1603), reports how the sermon precipitated Storre's murder at the hands of one of his parishioners, Francis Cartwright. According to the pamphlet, the minister and the hotheaded young Cartwright had previously clashed, on which occasion Cartwright had verbally abused Storre. Subsequently, Storre delivered a sermon drawn from Isaiah 1: 9: "*Except the Lord of Hosts had reserved unto us, even a small remnant, we had bin as Sodom, and like unto Gomorah.*" Storre delivered out of his biblical text "many points of necessary doctrine," yet Cartwright "wrested al things he heard into the worse sense, as purposely spoken against him, and after that, more, and more thirsted for revenge" (sigs. A2v–3r). Despite the assumption of a universal condition of sinfulness in Storre's biblical text—"*we* had bin as Sodom"—Cartwright apparently concluded that the allusions to Sodom and Gomorrah were meant to single him out for public humiliation. Cartwright, that is, believed that the minister was identifying him as a Sodomite. Although the pamphlet does not relate the specific content of the sermon, it seems likely that the sodomite's function as a composite type contributed to Cartwright's paranoia, in that Storre's discussion of any of the five vices commonly attributed to Sodomites (pride, idleness, surfeit, contempt of the poor, or unnatural sex) might have convinced Cartwright that his characteristic behavior, presumably known to his neighbors, was being targeted for communal shaming.

As in Milles's and possibly Storre's sermons, an Elizabethan ballad "Of the Horrible and Wofull Destruction of Sodome and Gomorra" (1570) offers the composite Sodomite as a warning against a variety of sins, but its emphasis on sexual vice unexpectedly implicates women more overtly in what the Sodomite might be made to signify. From the start, the ballad identifies the Sodomites as both men and women:

> The Scripture playne doth show and tell,
> How Lot in Sodome Towne did dwell
> Amongst the Sodomites vile:
> He did rebuke their noughty lives,
> Both yong and olde, both men and wives, . . .

The Sodomites are "noughty" because they scorn the poor and indulge in drunkenness, but also because "In filthy sinne they wallowed all, / As filthy Swyne in Myre." Although the word "filthy," as Bruce Smith corroborates, is frequently attached to sodomy, it is also general enough in this context to encompass a range of sexual and moral transgressions that might be committed by either men or women (*Homosexual* 217).[23] Recounting the suffering of infants, children, and mothers when the wicked cities were destroyed, the ballad implies that God targeted for punishment more sins than just male-male intercourse:

> Both man and Beast were burnd to Mucke,
> And Babes in Mothers lap:
> And eke the Chyldren that did sucke
> On Mothers tender Pap:
> With Fier were they burned,
> O woful grievous sight,

They cryed, and shryked,
To healpe no boote it might.

Only Lot and his household are spared such suffering, because "Lot hymselfe was counted just." Yet the story continues. Lot was counted just until "his Doughters tempted hym to lust":

Loe, wanton Girles whiche so doth burne,
In Venus pleasant games.
If that they may content their turnes,
And eake their youthfull flames,
They do desire their Fathers Bed,
The cankred flesh to please:
Alas that ye so wanton bee,
That you wyll never cease.

The flames that consumed Sodom have been transformed to the wicked flames of lust; having left Sodom behind, Lot's daughters have carried on its fleshly sins in the form of incest. Consequently, the ballad suggests that the Sodomites have not been destroyed: wantons will "never cease" their efforts to satiate the flesh. The ballad ends by widening its address from "ye" to the entire nation:

O England thou like Sodome art,
In filthy sinne doth play thy part,
What sinnes are found in thee?
Thou dooest exceede Sodome in sinne,
Thou carest not for Lots preaching: . . .

Ultimately, the ancient city of Sodom, consumed for its proud, idle, and "filthy" sinners, has been reconstituted in the men and women of England.

An even more explicit depiction of the "filthy" sexual vices of the Sodomites appears in a sequence of three woodcuts from Claude Paradin's *Quadrins Historiques de la Bible*, translated into English by Peter Derendel in 1553. The first woodcut depicts Abraham's prayer for the Sodomites; the second, the Sodomites' attempt to rape the male angels residing with Lot; and the third, the destruction of the city (see Figures 1, 2, and 3). Unlike the other religious texts I have discussed, Paradin emphasizes the sexual sodomy in

GENESIS   XVIII.

Of Sodomis the thre Aungels forʃai,
To Abraham the fearful euerʃion:
For their ʃtraunge vice he doeth vnto god prai:
Wherof he hath pitie nor compaʃſion.

Figure 1. Abraham praying for the Sodomites, from Claude Paradin (trans. Peter Derendel), *The true and lyvely historyke purtreatures of the woll Bible* (1553). By permission of the Folger Shakespeare Library.

Sodom. There are at least two reasons for the occlusion of the composite social and economic vices of the Sodomites detailed in texts such as Milles's sermon and the Elizabethan ballad. First, Paradin narrates the story of Sodom's destruction found in Genesis; he does not incorporate the commentaries on the Sodomites' multiple vices found in Ezekiel (as in Milles's sermon) or in Isaiah (as in Storre's sermon). Second, the constraints of the emblem format, in which the story is told through a series of visual images and brief verses,

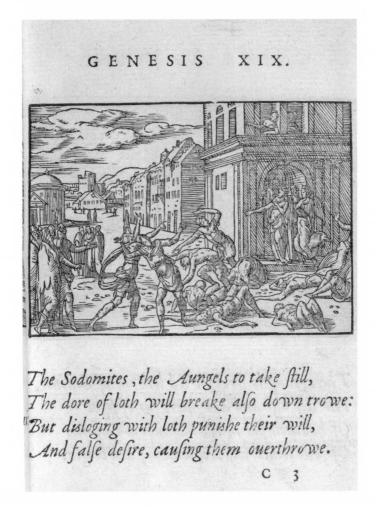

Figure 2. The angels punishing the Sodomites, from Claude Paradin (trans. Peter Derendel), *The true and lyvely historyke purtreatures of the woll Bible* (1553). By permission of the Folger Shakespeare Library.

requires an economy of form that militates against elaborating on the multiple vices conventionally attributed to the Sodomites.

Even as it foregrounds the "strange vice" of the Sodomites, however, Paradin's account embeds that sexual vice in an explicitly communal, public, setting that recalls more expansive accounts of Sodomites as debauched men who transgress moral, social, and economic codes of civility. For instance,

GENESIS   XIX.

The Aungels ſtraight led loth out of Sodome,
His wif alſo and daughters far of ſight
Of heauens fire that Sodomites conſomme:
Of ſalte lothes wif becommeth ſtatu bright.

Figure 3. The destruction of Sodom, from Claude Paradin (trans. Peter Derendel), *The true and lyvely historyke purtreatures of the woll Bible* (1553). By permission of the Folger Shakespeare Library.

Paradin's images distance Abraham and Lot from the "strange" (both foreign and unnatural) sexual vice of the Sodomites by placing the just men outside the boundaries of the city or, in the case of the central emblem, by placing Lot safely in his doorway behind the angels, who smite a group of Sodomites in a public square. Nonetheless, in each of the three images the imminent or immediate punishment of the Sodomites is subject to a public, even sympathetic, witnessing that suggests recognition in their fate of a common condition of human sinfulness. In the first image, Abraham is located far outside Sodom but faces toward the city in a futile effort to stir God's compassion through his own empathy with the citizens. The central emblem depicts the angels punishing the Sodomites in a square outside Lot's house; the text does not specify the reactions of the citizens who witness this gruesome "overthrow" of "false desire," yet the image allows us to read their gestures as signs of astonishment, righteous indignation, horror, pity, and so on. In the final image, Lot turns away from the burning city, severing all bonds with his former community; nonetheless, his wife has been transformed into a statue of salt for looking back at Sodom. Paradin's woodcuts suggest a range of attitudes English readers might take toward sodomites in their own communities: like Abraham, they might pray for their reformation; like the citizens of Sodom, they might react with satisfaction, horror, or pity at the prospect of their punishment; like Lot's wife, they might identify with their pleasures. One's attitude toward local sodomites would depend, in part, on which aspects of the composite type one chooses to see.

Having explored these overtly didactic deployments of the sodomite to define norms of sexual, social, and economic relations, we are in a better position to understand the workings of the sodomite as a character type in early modern drama. Because the sodomite is a composite type, he does not appear as a distinct character type in the drama, any more than he appears as a distinct character type in the early seventeenth-century "character" genre. Consequently, playwrights do not represent situations in which one character accuses another of being a "sodomite." Nevertheless, we do find dramatic episodes in which an accusation of sexual transgression renders the composite type of the sodomite intelligible as an agent of social, economic, or gender transgression. In such instances, we can perceive how the accusation of sodomy reaffirms social norms even as the revelation of the proximity of "sodomitical" behaviors to those norms blurs the boundaries of communal inclusion and exclusion.

In Shakespeare's *Troilus and Cressida*, Thersites's slandering of Patroclus as Achilles's "male varlet" and "masculine whore" has served as a touchstone for understanding the disciplinary workings of sodomy in early modern England. In Gregory Bredbeck's reading, Thersites functions as a satirist who employs base language to scourge base practices, such as the sexual deviance he attributes to Patroclus. Bredbeck argues that "the juxtaposition of Thersites' sodomitical Patroclus" to the more heroic Patroclus described elsewhere in the play "begins to suggest a critique of satire and its strategies of social hierarchicalization" (39). Bruce Smith compares Thersites's slander to urban satires that ridicule the effeminacy of "sodomites in the streets of London"; yet whereas the satires present their critiques in "moral" terms, Thersites understands sodomy as a matter of "social" and "political" power differentials between men (*Homosexual* 198). Even as these critics use Thersites's accusation of sodomy to illuminate the "political terms" (198) or "complicated network of political meanings" (Bredbeck 45) through which *Troilus and Cressida* examines same-sex relations, they underestimate, in my view, the degree to which Thersites's language engages the braiding of sexual, social, economic, and moral norms that make up the composite type of the sodomite. That is, the play does not simply explore "sodomy" (same-sex relations) through the discourse of "politics"; rather, it reveals that the sodomite can be effectively deployed in political conflicts because of the familiarity of the social, economic, gender, and sexual transgressions that make him intelligible as a figure of communal exclusion.

To begin with, Shakespeare foregrounds the contingent social conditions that make Patroclus intelligible as a sodomite in that Thersites does not directly accuse Patroclus of anything, but rather claims to be repeating a rumor. The source of the rumor and the precise meaning of the "preposterous discoveries" ostensibly brought to light by that rumor are occluded (5.1.19):

> **Thersites:** Prithee be silent, boy. I profit not by thy talk.
>   Thou art thought to be Achilles' male varlet.
> **Patroclus:** "Male varlet," you rogue? What's that?
> **Thersites:** Why, his masculine whore. (5.1.13–16)

As Keith Botelho observes in his study of rumor and early modern masculinity, a passive construction such as "It is reported" (or, here, "Thou art thought to be") is a sign of the circulation of "unauthorized information" (13).[24] Botelho argues that rumor "has the potential both to destabilize and to bolster an individual, a community, or a nation" (13). In *Troilus and Cressida*, Thersites clearly attempts to silence and degrade Patroclus as a "boy" by voicing a scurrilous rumor about behavior unworthy of a solider, but it is less clear what exactly that behavior is thought to be. As I have argued, the composite type of the sodomite usually works through such layered indirection: to be Achilles's "male varlet" might involve several kinds of "preposterous" disorders, not just that of sodomitical sexuality.

In this regard, it is crucial to note that "male varlet" is a blatantly cryptic insult, since in early modern (and Shakespearean) usage, a varlet is by definition male. Had Thersites simply called Patroclus Achilles's "varlet," the insult to Patroclus's status as Achilles's friend would have been unmistakable, as "varlet" denoted a personal attendant or groom. In the first line of *Troilus and Cressida*, Troilus calls for his "varlet"—a servant or page—to unarm him (1.1.1). Elsewhere in Shakespeare, "varlet" is used in the same sense, for instance in *2 Henry VI*, in reference to Shallow's servant Davy (5.3). The subordinate status of the personal servant apparently gave rise to the negative meaning of "varlet" as a person of "low, mean, or knavish disposition" (*OED*). Most often in Shakespeare, "varlet" is used to insult a social inferior or servant by imputing to him a base or roguish character: the word is used this way by Agrippa against the Volscian watchman in *Coriolanus* (5.2.74), by Kent and Lear against Oswald in *King Lear* (2.2.24, 2.4.181), by Elbow against Pompey the bawd in *Measure for Measure* (2.1.150), and by Prospero against Caliban and his co-conspirators in *The Tempest* (4.1.170). Alternatively, "varlet" can be used to disgrace a social superior who behaves dishonesty: Pistol and Mistress Page refer to Falstaff as a varlet in *Merry Wives of Windsor* (1.3.84, 4.2.86), and Dogberry calls Conrade a varlet in *Much Ado about Nothing* (4.2.65). At the end of the scene in which he insults Patroclus as a "male varlet," Thersites uses the word in this distinctly moral sense in referring to Diomedes as one of the many "incontinent varlets" involved in the war (5.1.88–89). In specifying that Patroclus serves as Achilles's varlet, Thersites seems to use the word "varlet" in its occupational meaning instead of its moral meaning, but his anomalous addition of the adjective "male" shifts that meaning in a direction that evokes the sodomite.

Responding to Patroclus's understandable confusion about the meaning of "male varlet," Thersites translates the phrase as "masculine whore," a formulation that makes evident the gendered logic of the original insult. "Masculine" simply means "male" (not "manly"); since whores are typically female, "masculine whore" specifies a whore who is atypically male.[25] By analogy to "masculine whore," then, "male varlet" implies that a varlet, like a whore, is typically female, and that in this anomalous instance the specification of "male" is necessary to render intelligible an atypically gendered varlet.[26] Yet since a varlet, unlike a whore, is in fact typically male, Thersites's insult renders preposterous the orderly male-male service usually signified by "varlet" by tainting it with effeminacy. In this way the male varlet, so to speak, opens the door to the type of the sodomite.

For Thersites's rant about Patroclus's "effeminate" vanity, Shakespeare seems to draw from the catalogues of the urban sodomite's vices found in the satires of Donne or Marston (Smith, *Homosexual* 198): "Thou idle immaterial skein of sleave-silk, thou green sarsenet flap for a sore eye, thou tassel of a prodigal's purse thou! Ah, how the poor world is pestered with such water-flies! Diminutives of nature" (5.1.25–29). This character portrait of Patroclus draws not only on the mockery of debauched, fashion-conscious, sodomites in urban satires, however, but also on the typical sins of the Sodomites as recounted in religious discourses such as Robert Milles's *Abrahams Suite for Sodome*: Patroclus is "idle" and "prodigal," and there might even be an allusion to the Sodomites' contempt for the poor in the allusion to the "poor world" pestered by such useless men. Thersites's exposure of Patroclus as a sodomite, of course, serves to reflect on Achilles's pride (the fourth Sodomitical vice), which violates the communal norms of the Greek army. In an earlier scene, ironically enough, Shakespeare has Patroclus himself warn Achilles not to be "an effeminate man / In time of action" (3.3.211–12). Just a few lines after Thersites's rant, as if to confirm the connection between effeminacy and military dishonor, Achilles places his passion for the Trojan Polyxena before his loyalty to his countrymen: "Fall, Greeks; fail, fame; honour, or go or stay. / My major vow lies here; this I'll obey—" (5.1.38–39).[27]

Troilus and Cressida makes Patroclus a more substantial character than the diminished sodomite Thersites makes him out to be here. Patroclus resists this satirical imposition of sodomitical typology by identifying his critic's motives as envy and spite. But what really belies Thersites's deployment of the sodomite as a symptom for social dissolution is the play's revelation of the ways in which the social norms of Greeks and Trojans alike are compromised by "sodomitical" vices. If Patroclus is indeed Achilles's "masculine whore," the impact of his sexual corruption of the Greek hero pales in comparison to the destruction occasioned by the Trojan authorization of Helen's status as Paris's "whore." According to Thersites, the war was occasioned by a quarrel over "a whore and a cuckold" (2.3.65). For most of the play before Act 5, during the period of Achilles's and Patroclus's "sodomitical" idleness, the Greek and Trojan princes are not fighting heroic battles but scheming, speechifying, proclaiming, seducing, and indulging petty rivalries. As Gary Spear observes, the play "draws attention to the effeminacy and emasculation of nearly every central male figure," including Troilus, Ajax, Paris, and Achilles (412). Thersites's diminishment of Patroclus's military value through references to "prodigal" expenditures and to the vanity of silk and sarsenet fineries recalls the debate about Helen's value in the Trojan council. Countering Hector's argument that Helen is not worth the lives lost in her defense, Troilus insists that she "is a pearl / Whose price hath launched a thousand ships / And turned crowned kings to merchants" (2.2.80–82). Helen, Troilus claims, is worth the prodigal expense of her possession. As an idle, proud, prodigal, and sexually transgressive sodomite, then, Patroclus seems to behave in ways consonant with the dominant social values of the play.[28]

Turning from the representation of the sodomite on the London stage to an actual case in which a sodomite was executed on a London scaffold, it is easy to be less sanguine about the way in which rhetorical deployments of the sodomite seem to expose their own ideological contradictions. Sodomy was a capital offense under English common law. Technically speaking, as Kenneth Borris reminds us, "the lives of all those who consensually engaged in a main means of sexually consummating masculine love were legally forfeit," and for this reason he contests the view that "sexual love between males" was regarded with "civic acceptance" or tolerance in early modern England (*Same-Sex* 80). Borris demonstrates his point about the rigor of the English law by citing the denunciation of sodomy by legal commentators Anthony Fitzherbert, William Lambarde, Edward Coke, and Michael Dalton, the latter of whom defines "buggery" as a felony and "sin against God, Nature, and the Law" (qtd. Borris 80). Moreover, Borris reproduces an excerpt from a fascinating and little-known text that reports the hanging of a London gentleman for sodomy on June 10, 1607. Evidently capitalizing on the rare scandal of a state execution for sodomy, an account of the case was published later that month under the title *The Arraignement, Judgement, Confession, and Execution of Humfrey Stafford Gentleman.*[29]

In some ways, *The Arraignement* is typical of the many sensationalistic crime pamphlets published in early modern England, a genre Peter Lake has exhaustively discussed in *The Antichrist's Lewd Hat. The Arraignement* contains several of the conventional features of these pamphlets, including a description of the crime, an account of the trial and imprisonment of the accused, and a moralizing scaffold speech. But unlike virtually all the pamphlets discussed by Lake, *The Arraignement* focuses on the crime and punishment not of a murderer, but of a sodomite. More important, *The Arraignement* provides a fascinatingly complex account of the sexual and nonsexual vices that characterize the sodomite who is identified and seized by the law. Instead of elaborating on this London gentleman's sexual outrages or riotous lifestyle, *The Arraignement* separates out the component strands of the sodomite, allowing Stafford both to repent for his sins *and* subtly to deny his guiltiness under the technical terms of the English sodomy statute. I want to argue that the composite type of the sodomite accounts for the remarkable agency the text affords Stafford in distinguishing familiar habits of socialization described as "keeping company" from the sodomitical crime described as using "unlawful company." [30] If, as I have argued, the composite type of the sodomite can be used to define male-male sex as transgressive by linking it to a host of social, gender, and economic vices, then the composite type of the sodomite can also be used to disarticulate transgressive male-male sex from those other vices: to suggest, in short, that those familiar nonsexual vices constitute the extent of the sodomite's antisocial behavior. Strangely enough, of all of the texts that I have treated in this chapter, the one that reports the actual execution of a sodomite does the most to disarticulate the act of sodomy from the component vices with which the sodomite is usually associated. It does so, I will argue, not from any good will toward the sodomite, but in an attempt to use the familiar sodomite to identify a much greater threat to the English Protestant community.

What makes *The Arraignement* so intriguing as a record of the detection and punishment of an actual sodomite is the absence of the sensationalistic depiction of wild young gentlemen that is so characteristic of popular crime literature. When *The Arraignement* does explicitly place other men in Stafford's company, they are not the drinking companions of his sinful days, but sober family members and religious figures who charitably "beare him company" to the scaffold: his brother; his kinsman, Master William Stafford; the minister of St. George's Church; and the "reverend Preacher" Master Paget (sigs. B3r–v). When *The Arraignement* alludes to Stafford's wider social networks as his "much companye keeping," it is difficult to determine if this means that he had a long habit of maintaining illicit relationships with many men, or if he had a few illicit relationships that became widely known due to his habit of gentlemanly hospitality: "As he was a Gentleman of good birth, so his much companye keeping could not chuse but make his vitious life knowne to manye thousands, unto whome happily the report of his repentant death, might never come, it being as great and just a cause of his friendes joy and comfort, in that he made so godlye an end, as it was a cause of griefe and sorrowe in that he lived so ungodly a life" (sigs. A3r–v). Whatever the scope of Stafford's vicious life, his social habits as a gentleman of good birth made his vices widely known.

The Arraignement's description of Stafford's actual crime is strikingly prosaic and clinical, especially given the proclivity of crime pamphlets to attribute supernatural influences to the commission and the detection of crimes. Typically, early modern murder pamphlets relate Satan's temptations of the weak into performing wicked deeds, which are eventually brought to light through miraculous or providential means. In *The Arraignement*, there is no demonic temptation and no providential discovery, just the reports of two adolescent boys who apparently had to explain to their parents why they needed the services of a surgeon.[31] *The Arraignement* reports that on May 3, 1606, Humfrey Stafford

> unnaturally and feloniously, contrarie to the lawes of God and the King, used unlawfull company with two Boyes, & had them carnaly knowne, the one of them named *Richard Robinson*, the other *Nicholas Crosse*, the one about the age of xvii yeares, the other of xiii or xiiii yeres. . . . The two boyes upon their oathes did directly charge him with the fact, and the particulars therof: as the time when, the place where, the manner how, the circumstances both precedent and consequent (which here for modestye sake I over passe). The man and the Woman [the father of one boy and the mother of the other boy] testified onelye some matters ensuing upon the fact, for confirmation of the truth of the Boies allegations, shewing that the boyes had received hurt therby, & that they were forced to use the helpe of a Surgion for their cure. (sigs. B1r–v)[32]

Despite citing modesty as his motive for omitting details of the crime, the anonymous author of the pamphlet seems less concerned to convey the "unnaturalness" of sodomy than to report the fairness of the legal proceedings against Stafford. Moreover, although it is likely that parental complaint brought the case to judicial notice, in the pamphlet the parents serve merely as witnesses of the boys' physical injuries, not as voices of moral indignation.

The relative absence of moral and theological rhetoric in *The Arraignement* is even more striking when we compare the account of the Stafford case in Edward Coke's *Book of Entries* (1614), a collection of pleadings. Coke reinserts the condemnatory trope of "demonic" influence missing from *The Arraignement*:

> H.S., knight, lately of London, having not God before his eyes nor respecting the order of nature, but led astray by the instigation of the Devil, on the twelfth of May last year, in the parish of St. Andrew, High Holborn . . . specifically in the house of one M., did with force and with arms assault a certain R.B., a lad of about 16 years of age. And at that time, he did wickedly, and in a manner diabolical, felonious, and contrary to nature, have sexual relations with the same R.B., and did

at that time have carnal knowledge of the same R., and did wickedly, and in a manner diabolical, felonious, and contrary to nature, commit and perpetrate with the same R. that detestable and abominable sin of sodomy, . . . to the great displeasure of almighty God, and to the dishonor of the whole human race, against the King's peace, and his crown and dignity, and against the form of the statute published and provided for this case. (qtd. Borris, *Same-Sex* 95–96)

Even as he simplifies the circumstances of the sodomitical crime by omitting mention of one of the two boys and by unambiguously representing Stafford as a rapist, Coke widens the purview of sodomitical disorder by indicating that the crime took place "in the house of one M." and by condemning Stafford's crime as an offense against God, the king, the law, and "the whole human race." The ambiguity in Coke's report regarding the complicity of "M" potentially raises the specter of a conspiracy of sodomites. Did this "M" know that Stafford was raping a boy in his house? Was this boy a member of the household or a stranger? Had this happened before?

Instead of evoking the hyperbolic rhetoric of the "detestable and abominable sin of sodomy," *The Arraignement* euphemistically describes Stafford's crime as "us[ing] unlawful company." Having introduced this locution, moreover, *The Arraignement* surprisingly does not push "unlawful company" into a gripping narrative about the illicit behavior of a group of vicious London gentlemen. It seems odd that a crime pamphlet about the execution of a gentleman for sodomy would not exploit the opportunity to tell this story of sodomitical debauchery and decline. In *Meanings of Manhood in Early Modern England*, Alexandra Shepard remarks that early modern moralists often associated "the corrupting influence of bad company" with the youthful vices of drink, sex, and violence (27).[33] As I argued above, theological accounts of the destruction of the Sodomites typically warn against the sins of gluttony, idleness, pride, and sexual incontinence that flourish among wicked companions.[34]

Early modern historical writings also draw lessons about the social and political dangers of "unlawful company" by suggesting that noble men are derogated through physical contact with inferiors. According to Holinshed, King Edward II "was suddenlie so corrupted" by the "companie and societie" of Gaveston, that "he burst out into most heinous vices; for then using the said Peers as a procurer of his disordred dooings, he began to have his nobles in no regard. . . . and to helpe them forward in that kind of life, the foresaid Peers . . . furnished his court with companies of jesters, ruffians, flattering parasites, musicians, and other vile and naughtie ribalds" (qtd. Forker, 329). In Shakespeare's *1 Henry IV*, King Henry articulates a similar critique when describing how King Richard II

> Mingled his royalty with cap'ring fools,
> Had his great name profanèd with their scorns,
> And gave his countenance, against his name,
> To laugh at gibing boys, and stand the push
> Of every beardless vain comparative;
> Grew a companion to the common streets,
> Enfeoffed himself to popularity,
> That, being daily swallowed by men's eyes,
> They surfeited with honey, and began
> To loathe the taste of sweetness, whereof a little
> More than a little is by much too much. (3.2.63–73)

To appreciate the full impact of this condemnation, we have to perceive the figurative exchange of bodily fluids in Henry's description of the "mingling" of royal and common bodies. Jonathan Goldberg (*Sodometries* 152–75) and Richard Corum have explored the sodomitical implications of Hal's tavern fellowship, but it is enough for my purposes to recall that Falstaff, playing the part of King Henry, can call up an axiomatic warning against the infectious proximity of "unlawful company": "This pitch, as ancient writers do report, doth defile. So doth the company thou keepest" (2.5.377–78).[35]

The notion of "unlawful company" as status debasement through physical intimacy with commoners also informs popular crime literature. *The Bloudie Booke*, a crime pamphlet published in 1605, intriguingly uses the tropes of sodomy to signal the degeneration of a once respected Devonshire knight, John Fitz. Fitz's criminal career is initiated through a betrayal of male friendship:

> Amongst many, to (whom in the linkes of perfect friendshippe he was ingaged) one Gentleman moste especially in all rightes of love, and reguarde tendered him, (and as it seemed) was muche of hym agayne respected, his name was Maister *Slanning*, a worshipfull Esquire and a proper Gentlemanne, of goodly living, and deserved credite, of whome most menne coulde but speake well, since of all menne he was generally reputed wise, and courteous. Thys Gentleman ever inwardlye affected Sir *John Fites*, so that the Countrey noted them, for firme and mutual love,

to be unfained friendes, and so indeede they were untill mishap (ever fatall to Sir *John* his proceedings) crossed their affectionat association with this mischance. (sig. A3v–4r)

At a communal meal, the writer goes on to report, Slanning claimed that Fitz owed him rent on a piece of land. His manhood challenged by the implication that he was financially dependent on another man (Shepard, *Meanings* 16), Fitz gave Slanning the lie; later, he ambushed and murdered him. Having fled to France, Fitz eventually repented and returned to England, but it is not long before he slides back into crime:

> [Fitz] did not onely proceede in unlawfull courses of abuse, but would oftentimes glory in his former execrable fact, and being now in a manner prest in the highway of all abhomination, hee beganne to roote his thoughts to plotte nothinge but mischiefe, insomuch as firste, he by little and little lothed his lawful bed (a manifest argument of a vitious mind) turning his pleasures to lawlesse desires, neyther could the sweet remembrance of his wives earnest affection, withdraw him from consorting himselfe with loose prodigals. (sig. B1v)

In early modern England, "abomination" is a code-word for sodomy. The English statute defines buggery as "a detestable and abominable sin," a phrase that derives from Leviticus: "You shall not lie with a male as with a woman; it is an abomination" (qtd. Borris, *Same-Sex* 97). Although *The Bloudie Booke* does not accuse Fitz of sodomy, it pointedly accounts for his criminal deviance in terms of his abandonment of the conjugal bed. With his gang of "dissolute and desperate" associates, led by one "*Lusty Jacke*," Fitz recklessly indulges in drink, prostitutes, and violent brawls (sig. B2r).

In contrast to *The Bloudie Booke*, *The Arraignement* does not imply that in keeping "unlawful company" Stafford abandoned the social habits of a gentleman. Even when the narrative appears to be leading to a tale of prodigal expenditure followed by criminal behavior—the tale of a prosperous gentleman's trip down a "highway of abomination"—*The Arraignement* fails to deliver on that expectation. In his scaffold speech, Stafford confesses that "hee had consumed much in riottousnesse, and abhorred living, which might have relieved many a poore creature, and done many thousands good" (sigs. C1v–2r).[36] Although contempt for the poor is one of the sins of Sodom, Stafford's confession of riotous consumption does not generate a narrative about his

Of Gluttonie.

Where murther is suffered not scene to in time,
There mischiefe encreaseth and bringeth to woe:
All such as to Bacchus doth honour diuine,
Shall soone bee bereft their goods to forgoe.

¶ The signification.

These which are fightyng, signifieth incontinence : he
which is slaine hazarde : and death : and the one which
goeth out with hys sword in hys hand audax, one past grace,
or a murtherer,

Figure 4. An emblem of gluttony, from Stephen Batman, *A christall glasse of christian reformation* (1569). By permission of the Folger Shakespeare Library.

decline into "abhorred living." In this respect, Stafford's confession goes nowhere. Moralists conventionally linked idleness and drunkenness to the graver sins of adultery and murder, as in an emblem "Of Gluttonie" from Stephen Batman's *A christall glasse of christian reformation* (1569), in which the incontinent worship of "Bacchus" turns good fellowship into murderous hostility (see Figure 4). The escalating chain of sins depicted in this emblem was a commonplace; it is given particularly sharp articulation in John Taylor's murder pamphlet, *The Unnatural Father*: "For sloth is linked with drunkenness, drunkenness with fornication and adultery and adultery with murder and so of all the rest of the temptations, suggestions, and actions wherewith miserable men and women are ensnared and led captive into perpetual perdition" (qtd. Lake 47). Stafford's scaffold speech implicitly short-circuits this chain of sins and its emplotment of a teleological narrative linking sloth to drunkenness to fornication to perdition. Instead, Stafford is reported to have spoken as if his passion for fancy neckwear *directly* materialized the halter that encircled his neck: "The Halter being put about his necke, come (saide he), This Halter is more welcom unto mee then ever was Ruffe or falling Band" (sig. C2r). It is as if the visual analogy between ruff and rope revealed the destiny that was always hiding within those luxurious and serpentine folds of cloth.[37]

The Arraignement also gives Stafford significant agency in contesting more openly the conventional linkage of drunkenness with fornication. At his trial, Stafford admits to drunkenness, but denies carnal knowledge of the boys, "affirming and protesting that hee was guiltlesse therein, excusing himselfe, that if he had offended it was in wine" (sig. B1v). On the scaffold, he sticks to his story:

> Then saide [the preacher] M[aster] *Paget*, "I pray you that you will satisfie the world for this fact, for which you are now to dye, I desire not the particulars of it." M[aster] *Stafford* replyed with a lowde voice, "I acknowledge that I have deserved death but yet I could not performe mine intention"; whereat hee bowed towards the Preacher, and other his friendes, adding with a very lowe voice "For I could not put it in Execution for drunkennesse."[38] (sig. B4r)

Stafford's delivery of that excuse might be heard as an unintentionally comical aside reminiscent of Marlowe's Jew of Malta, whose *sotto voce* gloating frequently undercuts his openly pronounced moral platitudes. One wonders what readers of *The Arraignement* familiar with the drunken Porter in *Macbeth* might have thought about Stafford's analysis of drink as an equivocator with male sexual performance. In any case, Stafford affirms that, with him, the chain of sin ended with drunkenness:

> lifting up his voice to the people, [he] prayed that his death might be a warning to all others, to beware how they gave up themselves to wine, swearing, and companie keeping with such as he tearmed good fellowes,

which from his youth hee had greatly delighted in, but especially he wished that all men would have a care never to delight in making of men drunk, which, as it should seeme, was the sin his soule then chiefly stood guiltie of. (sig. C1r)

As Alexandra Shepard reminds us, early modern moralists regarded drunkenness as a very serious offense. Taking away the rational self-control that was essential to masculine identity, drink incited men to all kinds of bestial, riotous behavior (*Meanings* 27). Remarkably, *The Arraignement* allows Stafford to take the moralists at their word by admitting to drunkenness as the "sin his soule then chiefly stood guiltie of" while exonerating himself from the crime of sodomy, which he claims he could not commit.[39]

Yet even as Stafford admits to his wicked "delight in making of men drunk," he replaces the sodomitical imagery of unlawful company with the positive language of good fellowship that was commonly associated with moderate drinking as "a marker of accord and friendship between men" (Shepard, *Meanings* 101). Writing to John Chamberlain in 1613, Dudley Carleton evokes the insouciant mischief of "good fellowship" to introduce a tale of drinking and bed sharing. Carleton reports the arrival in Venice of his cousin, Phil Lytton, who has evidently been busy carousing with his drinking companions. Carleton writes:

Yesterday was the first time I saw him, and this night he enters commons with us both at bed and at board, which will hinder him of much good fellowship abroad, there being a strange Dutch humor crept into our English gallants to drink themselves friends in place of all other caresses. Two of them (whereof one hath been formerly named unto you) finding better wine abroad than in my house tumbled lately into one bed in a house where they never lay before, and one of them had all his clothes taken away or hooked out of the window with a good stock of doubloons in his pocket before he wakened; if his bedfellow's clothes had been fastened upon he had been in danger to have lost *corpus cum causa*, for he lay in them all night. I hear you cry out, *o tempora, o mores*; but to our former purpose. (Lee, ed., *Carleton* 152–53)

Carleton takes a bemused attitude toward the potential risks of drunken good fellowship, such as losing one's clothes (or one's body) out the window. Stafford's valorization of his company keeping with "such as he tearmed good fellowes," is, of course, subject to a much darker ironic reading, in that so-called good fellows and drinking companions were frequently condemned in didactic literature as fair-weather friends.[40] *The Arraignement* fails to mention if any good fellows accompanied Stafford to the scaffold to hear him confess the delight he had taken in their company. Nonetheless, through its representation of Stafford's evasions of the charge of sodomy, *The Arraignement* suggests that legal, moral, and theological discourses of "unlawful company" can provide only partial, contestable, accounts of the proper boundaries of gentlemanly association.

Why would *The Arraignement* work so hard to represent a convicted sodomite not as a "diabolical" and "abominable" criminal (in the words of Coke), but as the rather familiar figure of an idle London gentleman too much given to drink, fine clothing, and male companionship? The answer is found in what I regard as the key scene of the pamphlet, which Kenneth Borris omits in the version of the text he includes in *Same-Sex Desire in the English Renaissance*. In the omitted passage, a group of recusant Catholics imprisoned with Stafford attempts to convert him. The activism of imprisoned Catholics is not surprising, but their role as potential corruptors of Stafford's loyalty to the Anglican Church is crucial to understanding what is at stake in *The Arraignement's* representation of the sodomite and his participation in male communities.[41] Here is that crucial scene:

> During the time of his being in Prison, the knowledge of his fact, and the report of the sentence pronounced against him, coming unto some Recusants in the King's bench prison, they studied much how they might separate him from the bodie of our Church, being a Gent. of good descent, unto which end they wrote a certain Letter unto him in Latine, which was closely conveyed unto him, therein perswading him that there was no Salvation in our Church, and that he should not admitte of any of our Ministers to conferre with him, but that he should be Confessed by some Seminarie Priest. (sig. B2r–v)

The text implies that the recusants consider Stafford's sodomy a promising sign of his susceptibility to Catholic conversion. Writing to him secretly in Latin, the recusants try to ease Stafford from membership in one Latin-literacy group—educated English gentlemen—to another Latin-literacy group, Roman Catholics (Dolan, *Whores* 25–26). That the recusants appear so confident in their ability to pervert religious faith seems intended to contrast the author's own premise—clearly a fantasy in the England of 1607—that the national Church constitutes a unified, integral body.[42] The text grants Stafford membership in this sacred national body despite his status as a convicted sodomite. In the king's prison, then, the unlawful company that threatens religious and political loyalties is not the act of sodomy, but rather the "close" intimacies of activist Catholics.

The association between Catholicism and sodomy in post-Reformation England is well known. Alan Stewart and Frances Dolan have documented the strategies used by English Protestant writers from the Reformation through the Restoration to brand Catholics as sodomites.[43] In *The Arraignement*, the stigma of "unlawful company" remarkably expands from its initial reference to a sodomite's sexual crime to encompass the religious activism of an entire Catholic community:

> the world may see how the Papists seeke by al means possible, both in prison & out of prison, to withdraw his Majesties Subjects from the truth of Religion, unto the acknowledgement of the false Doctrine of the whore of *Babylon*, and that they more especially labour with, and aime at men of great birth and calling, rather then meane Personages, whereby may be gathered that they doe it more of policy than for Conscience sake.[44] (sig. B2v)

Unlike the Papists, who place policy over conscience, Stafford remains "in conscience perswaded of the truth of our Religion" and rebuffs his Catholic seducers. Moreover, explains the author of *The Arraignement*, Stafford's denunciation of the Romish faith was "witnessed by the presence of some others, . . . some of them being men of reverend esteeme, who with their owne mouthes reported it unto me, which makes me presume of the truth thereof, they being men of known good report, and as such as I verilye thinke, make conscience of speaking the least untruth wittinglye" (sig. B2v). The devotion to truth that Stafford and his esteemed witnesses collectively demonstrate is thus referred to the purity of conscience enjoyed by loyal English gentlemen, even if one of them happens to be a sodomite. By contrast, the filth of corporeality—of carnal temptation, of secretive and vigorous labor on behalf of the Whore of Babylon, of bonds of treacherous and unlawful company—belongs to Roman Catholic traitors. A grotesque image from Stephen Batman's *The new arival of the three gracis, into Anglia. Lamenting the abusis of this present age* (1580) stunningly renders Protestant anxieties about the pope's "wicked government" over

Figure 5. Anti-papal satire, from Stephen Batman, *The new arival of the three gracis, into Anglia* (1580). © The British Library Board. Shelfmark C.57.c.8, f.3v.

his Catholic subjects (sig. E3v) (see Figure 5). Inspired by depictions of the Whore of Babylon riding a seven-headed beast, this woodcut portrays a hideous seven-headed female beast giving anal birth to a pope, as a former pope and a prelate grasping a moneybag roast in flames.[45] *The Arraignement* thus not only drives a wedge between the sexual and the nonsexual characteristics (idleness, drunkenness) that typify the sodomite, it also minimizes the stigma of Stafford's conviction for keeping "unlawful company" by associating the most dangerous forms of unlawful company with Catholic seducers.

Significantly, in repudiating his Catholic tempters and affirming his faith in Christ, Stafford, recently convicted of raping two boys, comes to resemble not those biblical Sodomites who attempted to rape the two angels staying with Lot, but Lot himself, who escapes from Sodom before its destruction. *The Arraignement* reports that the minister who was present at Stafford's execution actively encouraged Stafford to conceive of his redemption in terms of a sudden deliverance from fiery death. At the scaffold, Master Paget directed Stafford to "pray that thou mayest bee that *brand taken out of the fire*, hee replyed that he hoped he was, and that his sparke of joy was turned into a flame" (sig. B4v). Paget here alludes not to the story of Sodom in Genesis, but to an image from Zachariah 3:2: "Is not this a brand, snatched out of the fire?" In 1607, that image from Zachariah had wider cultural resonance: it had served as the scriptural text for a sermon preached by William Barlow before the Privy Council and "the grave Judges of the Law" on November 5, 1606, and published in 1607 as *A Brand* (title page). Barlow's universal application of the text from Zachariah affirms that Christians are "by nature and sinne *Brandes*, ready for *Hellfire*: and our *spirituall Redemption* by *Christ*, dispatching us so *strangely* from that *fire*" (sigs. B2v–3r).

It is significant, of course, that Barlow's sermon was first preached on November 5, the anniversary of the Gunpowder Plot. When applying his scriptural text to that historical event, Barlow explicates the brands not as universal Christian sinners, but as the "*Great* and *Excellent* men" who were the objects of the Gunpowder conspirators' "*fierie* designements" (sig. B3r). Just as a brand is more likely to burn than a green stick, Barlow reasons, so eminent men are more subject to Satan's rage than men "of *meane birth*, of *obscure place*, of no *imploymentes*" (sig. C1v). Similarly, the author of *The Arraignement*, explaining Stafford's appeal to his Catholic seducers, argues that Papists strive to convert men of "great birth and calling, rather then meane Personages" (sig. B2v). Not surprisingly, Barlow also connects Parliament's deliverance from the Gunpowder Plot to Lot's deliverance from Sodom, observing that the destructive ferocity of fire "requireth more then an ordinary deliverie, it had neede of a *Rapuit* (for so the *Angels snatcht Lot out of Sodoms fire* . . .)" (sig. E4r).

Only two years after the Gunpowder Plot, *The Arraignement* takes the occasion of an English gentleman's trial and execution for sodomy to demonize Roman Catholics as a community of opportunistic seducers, always seeking and laboring to destroy His Majesty's subjects. The visual depiction of the Gunpowder conspirators in the popular engraving by Crispijn van de Passe the Elder suggests the cohesiveness and vigorous energy of the traitors by

Figure 6. Crispijn van de Passe the Elder, *The Gunpowder Plot Conspirators* (1605); National Portrait Gallery, London.

densely packing them into a frame that can hardly contain them (see Figure 6). The conspirators seem to be wrangling over an important point of strategy, perhaps demonstrating the persuasive powers that the Catholic recusants in the King's Bench prison deployed unsuccessfully with Humfrey Stafford. Curiously, the horizontal arrangement of the eight heads closely resembles the arrangement of the seven heads in the image of the pope-birthing monster discussed above (see Figure 5). In each image, moreover, pairs of heads face each other—two on the left, two in the middle, and two on the right—as if to suggest that Catholics never cease plotting with or attempting to seduce their neighbors. If we grant the cultural resonance in 1607 of these narratives of Catholic treachery, it is even more plausible to imagine some readers of *The Arraignement* placing Stafford not in the unlawful company of the Sodomites, but in the good company of those worthy individuals who merit salvation from fiery destruction.

Aside from the Gunpowder Plot, another local, if less directly topical, context for reading Stafford's trial and execution is provided by the London theater. By displacing the moral, political, and theological connotations of "sodomy" from Stafford onto Catholic recusants, *The Arraignement* discourages its readers from establishing a direct correlation between the gentlemanly activity of keeping company with "good fellows" and the criminal act of keeping "unlawful company" with adolescent boys. Mary Bly argues that in 1607 the Whitefriars Theater syndicate was also distancing the criminality of sodomy by deliberately promoting a same-sex community of "good fellowship" centered on the pleasures of language, performance, and sex. Bly argues that a theater "specializing in queer puns suggests that homoeroticism was not always associated with an alloy of criminal acts" (5); it is even possible that these plays afforded male playgoers the opportunity to fashion a kind of nonce homoerotic community.[46]

Edward Sharpham's *Cupids Whirligig* (1607), one of the Whitefriars plays Bly discusses, beautifully illustrates this disjunction between homoerotic fellowship and sodomitical culpability. "One of the primary threads of humour" in Sharpham's play, Bly observes, "is an emphasis on the paedophiliac aspect of early modern pedagogy" (82). In the following scene, the pedant Master Correction conducts a Latin lesson with one of his "prettie" schoolboys in the presence of a visitor:

M[aster] C[orrection]: What part of speech is *Mentula*?

[Boy] 1: A nowne Adjective.

M[aster] C[orrection]: And why a nowne adjective?

[Boy] 1: Because it stands not by himselfe, but it requires an other word to be joyned with it.

M[aster] C[orrection]: Marke you Syr, I teach both substance and meaning. . . . (sig. I4r).

Mentula is Latin for "penis," which the boy knows "stands not by himselfe."[47] The implication of pederasty in this pedagogy is underscored by the witty visitor, who remarks to Master Correction, "I thinke yee spend most of your time with your Schollers heere: yee keepe little other companie" (sig. I4v). Master Correction is certainly an object of mockery, but he might also be admired as a man who gets what he wants: no one suggests that he desist from using his "mentula" as a pedagogical tool. Even if the Whitefriars audience laughed at this pederastic pedant, in so doing, Bly suggests, they might also have been expressing through "the bonds of shared laughter" an appreciation for the pedant's ability to indulge his homoerotic desires for pretty boys—the same pretty boys who were displaying their bodies and wit on the Whitefriars stage for the appreciation of a paying audience (20).[48] Sharpham's play was printed in late June 1607, and, according to its title page, had been performed "sundry times" before (126). Humfrey Stafford was executed on June 10, 1607. In the same month, then, it would have been possible for a Londoner both to take pleasure in the company of boys at the Whitefriars and to witness the execution of a London gentleman who had taken pleasure in the company of boys.

As I have argued, *The Arraignment*, despite its obvious indebtedness to the legal and theological discourses of sodomy, registers the counter-claim of a valorized notion of gentlemanly "good fellowship." If *The Arraignment* permits the convicted sodomite to claim the privilege of good fellowship, it does so in the interest of exposing the threat of Catholics who form communities of association, working collectively to seduce, infiltrate, and destroy. In the England of 1607, it does not yet seem possible to imagine the analogous horror of a community of sodomites.[49] Indeed, for all Stafford's admitted "delight" in "company keeping" with good fellows, *The Arraignment* gives us very little sense of how his life was textured by the pleasures of erotic intimacy, the comforts of reciprocal friendship, or even the more fleeting camaraderie of shared group activities, such as going to the theater or tavern.[50] To the author of *The Arraignment*, a solitary sodomite is clearly less frightening than a community of Catholics.

By the late seventeenth century, as Alan Bray and Randolph Trumbach have shown, a community of sodomites had emerged in London, associated with particular social rituals and institutions such as the molly house. Bray concludes *Homosexuality in Renaissance England* with a chapter on "Molly" in which he contrasts the "socially diffused homosexuality of the early seventeenth century" to this "continuing culture" in which "clothes, gestures, language, particular buildings and particular public places . . . could be identified as having specifically homosexual connotations" (*Homosexuality* 92). Consequently, these newly visible sodomites "attracted to themselves persecution on a scale and of an immediacy unknown before," as large groups of men were identified and arrested (89).[51] The question that emerges in *The Arraignment* over whether the sodomite's conduct represents a mode of gentlemanly "good fellowship" or of "unlawful company" no longer seems relevant a century later, as the sodomite comes to be understood as a distinct social type: an easily identifiable member of a community of sodomites.

If the eighteenth-century sodomite takes on a new kind of social visibility and familiarity, we cannot conclude that the early seventeenth-century sodomite was therefore a figure of alien otherness, his image impossibly distanced from "an image that one might normally apply to oneself, to one's neighbor or one's friend" (Bray, *Friend* 218), his behavior unrecognizable as anything that might commonly take place in "the street, the market, and the household" (Gowing, *Domestic* 65). Along with the evidence from sermons, plays, and other cultural texts I have presented in this chapter, *The Arraignement*'s representation of Stafford as a Protestant English gentleman indicates that this account of the metaphysically evil sodomite is simply not true. The composite type of the sodomite worked to render theologically and legally demonized same-sex practices intelligible in terms of familiar gender, social, and economic transgressions that could be practiced—by oneself, one's neighbors, or one's friends—in any street, market, or household.

Chapter 2

Fulfilling Venus

Substitutive Logics and the Tribade's Agency

those wanton-loined womanlings, Tribades, that fret each other by
turns, and fulfil Venus even among Eunuchs with their so artful
secrets
　　—Robert Burton, *Anatomy of Melancholy*

As sexual types, the sodomite and tribade organize social fantasies about what
is alien to dominant early modern ideologies of marriage, reproduction, and
patriarchal authority. In the previous chapter, I argued that representations
of the sodomite, whose habits of communal affiliation slip across the definitional boundary between the familiar and the strange, reveal an incoherence
in the early modern conception of male same-sex relations. I turn now to the
tribade, a figure whose purported sexual practices bring into focus a different
kind of disturbance in the early modern social logics of same-sex relations. As
a sexual type, the tribade reveals an incoherence about the conceptualization
of sex between women in a patriarchal culture that organized female sexuality
around the norm of gender-differentiated, conjugal, reproductive intercourse.[1]
　　Early modern discourses typically define the tribade as imitating the
"male" role in a hierarchical model of heteroerotic relations that takes the
man to be the agent of seduction and the sexually dominant partner.[2] Yet in
representations of the tribade, I will argue, that imitative thesis, while present,
is often unsettled by terminology or narratives that imply that sexual relations
between women are symmetrically gendered and erotically egalitarian, or, alternatively, that they are structured by differences that cannot be described

in the terms of binary gender.[3] Narrative accounts of tribadism in particular often introduce differentials of age, beauty, and status among women that fail to map clearly onto any hierarchically gendered model of heteroerotic relations. The tribade thus enacts a logic of substitution that reasserts an absent norm (the male position in heteroerotic sex that she ostensibly imitates) but also challenges the priority of that norm by demonstrating that it fails to provide a reliable template for female-female relations structured by other forms of difference or by gender symmetry and mutual sexual agency.

Here my argument resembles that of Valerie Traub, to whose discussion of the tribade in *The Renaissance of Lesbianism in Early Modern England* I am indebted throughout this chapter. Traub argues that "both gynecological tribadism and statutory sodomy [which, in France, could be proven by women's use of a dildo] depend upon a logic of supplementarity for their condition of possibility, with tribadism functioning through anatomical rather than artificial means" (194). The tribade who uses her clitoris to take pleasure from another woman is understood to "*take the part* of a man" (195). Although she acknowledges the cultural dominance of this rhetoric of supplementation, Traub resists it in her own critical practice by insisting on women's "erotic autonomy," particularly their ability to render their own homoerotic practices meaningful in ways that are not determined by the patriarchal logic of imitation (195). Like Traub and other scholars of early modern sexuality, I find heuristic value in a deconstructive reading practice that can reveal how "the tribade displaces and supplements masculine privilege, exposing it as nothing more (or worse) than a simulacrum" (197).[4] Traub deconstructs anatomical discourses about the clitoris by reading them through "the angle of female specificity" instead of through the dominant logic of male imitation (197). I go about a similar project of articulating the tribade's agency via a different route: by putting pressure on how these texts imagine or occlude the specific dynamics of gendered, sexual, and social power between the tribade and her sexual partner.

Elucidating the relationship between the tribade and her partner in the drama is a challenging task, since of all the sexual types I explore in this book the tribade is the least recognizable as a distinct social type that one might have identified on the streets of London or on the London stage.[5] Nonetheless, the tribade can be recognized in the substitutive logics of female characters who imitate, appropriate, or displace male sexual agency. Appropriately, the trope of metonymy, in which one thing is associated with or substitutes for another thing, can help to reveal how the type of the tribade functions in early modern drama. As various critics have argued, unusually assertive expressions of gender/sexual agency characterize several early modern female types who appear in the drama and other kinds of texts: the Amazon (Schwarz); the witch, the hermaphrodite, the cross-dresser, and the nun (Traub 24, 43, 46, 57, 63); the virago and the changeling (Bruster, *Shakespeare* 133); and the "queer virgin" who resists the imperatives of patriarchal marriage (Jankowski, *Pure Resistance*). All these figures might be regarded as metonymic versions of the "tribade," who at once constitutes an imitative version of and an alternative to patriarchal masculinity.

A good example of this metonymic logic can be found in the Induction to Marston's *Antonio and Mellida* (1599), in which the actor who portrays Antonio complains about having to disguise himself as an Amazon. He scornfully describes his role as that of "an hermaphrodite, two parts in one" (68), and a fellow actor recommends that he use a "virago-like" voice (73). The figure of the Amazon here slides effortlessly into the hermaphrodite and the virago. The actor further worries that "when use hath taught me action to hit the right point of a lady's part, I shall grow ignorant, when I must turn young prince again, how but to truss my hose" (77–79). Simply put, once he has become used to playing a woman, he will forget how to play (or to be?) a man. But this complaint also carries a bawdy innuendo that activates the tribadic logic subtending the Amazon-hermaphrodite-virago linkage: once the habit of playing an Amazon has taught him how to gain sexual access to ("hit the right point of") a lady's part (i.e., his mistress's vagina—or clitoris?), he will forget how to play a normative male sexual role ("truss my hose"). The tribadic Amazon both imitates and displaces male heteroerotic aggression. The metonymic chain is further extended by the names of two of the play's pages: Catzo (penis) and Dildo, the dildo being frequently cited as a penis substitute employed by tribades. Through the metonymic Amazon, Marston makes the tribade visible.

Metonymy can also serve as a productive critical practice for reading female homoeroticism in early modern texts. Madhavi Menon opens her chapter on metonymy in *Wanton Words* with a reading of John Donne's "Sappho to Philaenis," which, she argues, associates male-female sexuality with metaphor and female-female sexuality with metonymy, even though "metonymy is unable to extricate itself fully from a metaphoric register" (38). Surveying treatments of metonymy in early modern English rhetorical handbooks, Menon finds that its ability to "pass undetected in tropological schematization and to be frequently misrecognized as something other than itself also bears a startling resemblance to understandings of early modern homosexuality," particularly, I would add, to the understanding of female-female homoeroti-cism as "invisible" (39).[6] Because metonymy "depends on an *affinity* between two things rather than an *innate* link between two terms" (Menon 41), an interpretative practice based on metonymic association can bring to visibility the often unnamed, occluded, or oblique presence of female-female homo-eroticism in dramatic texts.

My argument will proceed first by examining references to female homo-eroticism in early modern anatomy books and travel narratives, which "with their shared cartographical impulse to chart the bodies of both self and other . . . revived the category of the tribade and invested it with new implications in England" (Traub 217). With their graphic accounts of the tribade's exces-sive body and desires, these texts present her as a figure who transgressively imitates or appropriates male sexual agency. But a closer reading reveals alter-native logics of female homoeroticism that depart from the patriarchal model of male-female relations in terms both of the particular power differentials between women, and of the mutuality and equality sometimes attributed to female-female communities. I then consider less overtly sexual accounts of intimacy between women in Shakespeare's *A Midsummer Night's Dream* and *The Winter's Tale*. In arguing that Titania in *A Midsummer Night's Dream* and Paulina in *The Winter's Tale* are types of the tribade, I employ a metonymic reading method that both uncovers and unsettles the substitutive logic of trib-adism, thus opening up space for resistant female sexual and social agency.

*   *   *

In many early modern texts, a signal difficulty in interpreting the power at-tributed to the tribade is the ambiguity and occlusion that surrounds the rep-resentation of her sexual partner. Continental legal texts represent a significant exception to this pattern. On the continent, prosecutions of female sodomy (which was not criminalized in England) clearly distinguished between "ac-tive" and "passive" partners: the woman accused of penetrating her partner with a dildo or with her clitoris was typically identified as the sodomite or tribade. Because the tribade's seeming appropriation of the masculine role was regarded as particularly abhorrent, the more "feminine" woman "involved with a tribade generally was perceived as the not-altogether-innocent victim of another woman's lust" (Traub 182). Perhaps the most famous example of the masculine tribade, discussed by Stephen Greenblatt in his influential essay "Fiction and Friction," is Marie le Marcis, who was discovered by French authorities to have adopted a male appearance, social identity, and name (Marin) in order to marry a conventionally gendered woman. Although both women were convicted of sodomy, only Marie was defined as a tribade and as such was sentenced to a significantly harsher punishment (Greenblatt 74).[7] The harsher punishment of tribades and female husbands was based on the substitutive logic in which a "masculine" woman was excoriated for taking the male role in a sexual relationship with a "feminine" partner.

The kind of sexual role attributed to the tribade in early modern anatomy books and travel narratives is harder to assess, because these texts do not depict her as part of a *couple*. Travel writers claim that tribadic lust finds expression in the social customs of African witches or emerges from the collective eroticism of Turkish baths. Anatomy books focus on the tribade as the singular possessor of an enlarged clitoris that can offer non-procreative pleasures; they do not suggest that the masculine tribade necessarily forms a conjugal relationship with a more feminine partner. Like the early modern anatomists she reads so insightfully, Valerie Traub typically discusses "the tribade" as a singular figure. When Traub considers women in couples, it is usually to elucidate the "femme-femme love" shared by traditionally gendered women such as Hermia and Helena in *A Midsummer Night's Dream*. Traub's focus on the femme-femme couple is part of a deliberate strategy to make visible the erotic desires of a type—the "chaste" female friend—who has often been rendered invisible or insignificant, precisely because of her normative gender performance. In the historical record and in contemporary criticism, the femme has often signified only as "the invisible, if antithetical, complement to a masculinized tribade" whose transgressive gender performance renders her remarkable (230). Traub's formulation of the femme's invisibility is telling, however, because it posits that when early modern writers are silent or vague about the tribade's partner—thus rendering her "invisible"—they nonetheless imagine her as a woman with a gender identity "antithetical" to that of the tribade. In other words, Traub seems to believe that dominant discourses did not conceive of the tribade outside of a paradigm of asymmetrical gender, in imitation of traditional male-female coupling.[8] That Traub regularly refers to "femme-femme" desire but not to "tribade-femme" or "tribade-tribade" desire implicitly acknowledges the difficulty of determining what early modern writers believed about the kind of gender agency and erotic pleasure the tribade enjoyed in relation to her partner.

The critical debate over lesbian historiography that followed the 1996 publication of Bernadette J. Brooten's *Love Between Women: Early Christian*

Responses to Female Homoeroticism crystallizes the theoretical issues at stake in attempting to determine precisely what premodern cultures found transgressive about the tribade's sexual relationship with another woman. On one side of this debate, Brooten argues that ancient Romans generally understood female same-sex partners as adult women who were alike in gender identity, status, and agency. Consequently, she claims, the ancients recognized "a category of persons . . . having a long-term or even lifelong homoerotic orientation" (8–9), and that they had a difficult time classifying female-female sexuality in terms of an active (penetrating) partner and a passive (penetrated) partner, a model more readily applicable to male-female and male-male sexuality. Whereas some ancient authors used the term *tribas* to refer only to the "masculine" woman who sexually penetrated other women (and sometimes boys), Brooten finds it significant that other authors used *tribas* to refer to both women in a same-sex couple (24). Additionally, whereas some ancient authors condemned only the penetrating woman in a female-female couple, remaining silent about the moral culpability of the penetrated woman, others condemned both women equally (322). Brooten therefore concludes that what ancient writers found transgressive about female homoeroticism was not the "phallic" woman's violation of gender norms, but the refusal of both women to accept sexual subordination to a man.

On the other side of the debate, David Halperin and Ann Pellegrini argue against Brooten that ancient texts condemn only the masculinized, penetrating woman in a female-female couple, not the penetrated woman who acted according to conventional gender norms by taking a submissive sexual role. What is at issue in condemnations of the *tribas*, they propose, is not homoerotic desire but gender transgression: the *tribas* was a "masculinized, phallic wom[a]n" (Halperin) or a "butch" (Pellegrini) who violated the cultural norms of female passivity ("Lesbian Historiography" 565, 582). Whereas Brooten claims that female same-sex partners possessed a *similarity of sexual agency* that violated social norms, Halperin and Pellegrini counter that female same-sex partners were distinguished by a *difference of gender agency*, with only the "masculine" woman perceived to violate social norms. In short, Brooten posits the social significance of tribade-tribade sex, Halperin and Pellegrini of tribade-femme sex.

When we turn to accounts of the tribade in early modern anatomical texts, it is in fact difficult to determine if what is being described is tribade-tribade sex or tribade-femme sex—or some kind of illicit same-sex relationship that fails to conform to any consistent mapping of gender performance.

According to Traub, early modern anatomists commonly attribute to the tribade an enlarged clitoris that "either propels her to engage in, or is itself the effect of" her illicit sexual behavior with other women (207). But they are much less precise about distinguishing "carefully between specific sexual acts: vaginal or anal penetration, rubbing of clitoris on thigh or pudendum, and autoerotic or partnered masturbation" (195). Because these writers focus on the clitoris as the metonymic source or sign of the tribade's transgressive sexual desires and practices, it perhaps seems beside the point to provide further details about which particular sexual acts the tribade might commit with which sexual partners. That is, in defining tribades as women who take homoerotic pleasure from the clitoris, anatomists fail to specify if they understand a tribade to require a "feminine" woman to penetrate or to rub, or if a tribade might take pleasure from another symmetrically "masculine" woman. This obfuscation returns us to the theoretical impasse reached in the debate between Brooten, who posits the social significance of tribade-tribade sex, and Halperin and Pellegrini, who posit the social significance of tribade-femme sex.

For a rich illustration of this hermeneutic problem, we can consider English anatomist Helkiah Crooke's definition of the clitoris as the part "which those wicked women doe abuse called *Tribades* (often mentioned by many authours, and in some states worthily punished) to their mutuall and unnaturall lustes" (238). Crooke's mention of the punishment of tribades in other states evokes France, where particularly severe legal sanctions were taken against the "masculine" female sodomite who penetrated a more "feminine" partner with her clitoris or a dildo. Yet Crooke's specification of the "mutual" lust of "tribades" contradicts the juridical recognition of the tribade's relatively innocent "feminine" partner, as does his broad definition of tribades as "wicked women" who "abuse" the clitoris. Evidently, a tribade is a woman who abuses her clitoris, "which groweth to a rigiditie as doth the yarde of a man," by rubbing it on another woman. But might the woman rubbed *by* that clitoris, thus "abusing" or perverting its "natural" function in reproductive sexuality, also be considered a "tribade"? Given the generality of Crooke's language, might a tribade be *any* woman who uses her clitoris or another woman's clitoris in same-sex acts, whether rubbing clitoris on clitoris, rubbing the clitoris on the thigh, using the clitoris to penetrate the vagina, etc.? Does Crooke's emphasis on the "mutual" lusts of tribades open the possibility of imagining two phallic tribades rubbing or penetrating each other?[9] If so, the assumption of a putative gender distinction between a "masculine" tribade and a "feminine" partner—and with it the notion of the tribade as decisively imitating the male partner in a patriarchal model of male-female intercourse—seems to dissolve.[10]

That accounts of clitoral abuse do not always clearly specify whether they are describing penetration or rubbing further complicates representations of the relative sexual agency of the tribade and her partner. As Traub rightly notes, the distinction between penetrating and rubbing is itself difficult to maintain (both during sexual acts and in the descriptions of those acts) as an "enlarged clitoris could be an instrument of friction or entry or something in between" (213). Yet to the degree that these practices can be distinguished, clitoral penetration most closely imitates the gendered dynamics of male-female sex, in which penetration is understood as "a definitively masculine privilege" (212). Clitoral rubbing less effectively maps on to the ancient binary of active (masculine) and passive (feminine) sexual roles. Brantôme, a French courtier and author of *Lives of Fair and Gallant Ladies* (ca. 1585), insists that the non-penetrative activity of clitoral rubbing, which he calls the "little exercise" of "friggings and mutual frictions," does not provide women the satisfaction of full phallic penetration with a man: "all they do get of other women, 'tis but appetizers to whet them to go feed a full meal with men" (qtd. Borris, *Same-Sex* 305).

Unable to depend upon the familiar active/passive binary implied by sexual penetration, early modern medical writers render ambiguous whether the sexual friction between tribades replicates the hierarchical structure of male-female sex or replaces it with a more symmetrical, mutual practice distinctive to a same-sex relationship. In the *Anatomy of Melancholy* (1621), for instance, Robert Burton refers to "those wanton-loined womanlings, Tribades, that fret each other by turns, and fulfil Venus even among Eunuchs with their so artful secrets" (qtd. Traub 168). Burton seems to imagine tribades who take turns "fretting" each other, an alternating "active" or "top" partner presumably generating pleasurable friction against the body of her "passive" partner; hence the active tribade can even get pleasure from rubbing against a eunuch's body. By contrast, Swedish anatomist Thomas Bartholin's reference to "*Confricatrices* Rubsters" in *Bartholinus Anatomy* (1668) suggests the simultaneous production of erotic friction (76): the "con-" prefix, as Jeffrey Masten has shown, is the linguistic sign of mutuality in Renaissance discourses of male friendship (35). Likewise, French anatomist André Du Laurens describes as "*tribades*" or "*fricatrices*" those women who "mutually rub each other" (qtd. Andreadis 41).[11]

Although travel writings evince a similar indeterminacy regarding whether the tribade imitates the "masculine" sexual role in a heteroerotic relationship or participates in a gender symmetrical, erotically mutual same-sex relationship, their more detailed scenarios of same-sex seduction further complicate questions of sexual agency by introducing differences of age, appearance, and status among women. Nicholas de Nicolay's account of a Turkish bathhouse in *The navigations, peregrinations and voyages, made into Turkie* (translated into English in 1585) offers contradictory indications about whether or not women who wash each other experience mutual erotic desire:

> somtimes they do go 10 or 12 of them together, & somtimes more in a company aswel Turks as Grecians, & do familiarly wash one another, wherby it cometh to passe that amongst the women of Leva[nt] ther is very great amity proceding only through the frequentation & resort to the bathes: yea & somtimes become so fervently in love the one of the other as if it were with men, in such sort that perceiving some maiden or woman of excellent beauty they wil not ceasse until they have found means to bath with them, & to handle & grope them every where at their pleasures, so ful they are of luxuriousnes & feminine wantonnes: Even as in times past wer the Tribades, of the number wherof was Sapho the Lesbian which transferred the love wherwith she pursued a 100 women or maidens upon her only friend Phaon. (60r)

Although Nicolay initially attests to the mutual desires of women who wash one another and consequently fall "in love the one of the other," he goes on to indicate different degrees of erotic agency among the bathers, some of whom aggressively seduce or force themselves upon others noted for their "excellent beauty." Stressing the invasiveness of these seductions, Nicolay claims that the women will not cease until they have satiated their passion by handling and groping their objects of desire "every where at their pleasures."

Ultimately, however, it is difficult to determine which women Nicolay considers to be the counterparts of ancient "tribades." Are the tribades *only* those putatively "masculine" women who, like Sappho, aggressively pursue the putatively "feminine" women noted for their beauty? Or are the women who grope and the women who get groped—or allow themselves to be groped—equally tribadic? Perhaps all the women who participate in the "very great amity" of communal bathing should be considered tribades. Nicolay's claim that some women desire other women "as if it were with men" further thwarts any clear delineation of gender roles, since its substitutive logic posits that a woman inappropriately occupies the place of a man in another woman's affection; at the same time, the pursuing woman, motivated by "feminine wantonnes," paradoxically appropriates the agency of a conventionally male sexual aggressor.

Because of its richly descriptive language, the passage above has become a commonplace in studies of early modern lesbianism.[12] But no prior critic, including myself, has discussed the passage that follows, which stresses the status differences among women at the baths. The acknowledgement of status differences complicates the fantasy of an undifferentiated group of women taking collective erotic pleasure with one another at the baths. Distinctions of status between women, however, do not seamlessly map onto conventional gender distinctions, so that the difference in sexual agency between an elite woman and a servant woman becomes analogous to the difference between a "masculine" tribade and her "feminine" partner. According to Nicolay, "women of estate" are accompanied to the baths by one or two slaves, a social ritual striking enough to merit a woodcut (see Figure 7). The slaves are responsible for carrying luxury items and washing their mistresses' bodies:

> Nowe beyng come to the place of bathing, the coverlet is spread abrode, upon the which they uncloth them selves and lay downe their garments and jewels: for their preparation and order is suche, that going to the bathes whither they be Turks or Christians, the better to be liked the one of the other, they set forth them selves with their richest apparell, and most precious tablets: and being thus uncloathed upon the carpet, they turne the vessell wyth the mouth downewardes and the bottome upwards for to sit the more easily, and then the slaves the one of the one side, and the other on the other side, do wash and rubbe the bodye untyll it doe suffyce: and then do goe to repose them selves in a small chamber being indifferently hot. In which meane space, and during this repast, the slaves doe washe one another. (60v)

Nicolay imagines that the elite women wish "to be liked the one of the other," and are therefore motivated by the pursuit of mutual homoerotic desire. Setting forth their richest apparel and most precious jewels, these women, however, provoke that mutual desire through a differential display of wealth and status, manifested in the use of servant women to rub their bodies. This cross-status sensuality, represented as a kind of vigorous labor for the slaves, evidently takes place in the open bath. As such, Nicolay imagines that these elite women both enjoy and provoke homoerotic scopophilia: a pleasure in

Figure 7. "A woman of Turkie going to the Bathe," from Nicholas de Nicolay, *The navigations . . . made into Turkie* (1585). By permission of the Folger Shakespeare Library.

observing naked female bodies that might also reflect the voyeuristic plea-sure of the reader elicited by the text (Toulalan 148–49).[13] Having displayed their pampered bodies in the open bath, the elite women assert their exclusive social status by withdrawing "to repose them selves in a small chamber." If in the much-cited earlier passage on Turkish baths Nicolay wavers in repre-senting the tribade's sexual agency as both gender-differentiated (in terms of her "masculine" aggression) and as gender-symmetrical (in terms of the "very great amity" among women), in the latter passage he wavers in representing the tribade's sexual agency as both status-differentiated (in terms of her assertion of wealth and privilege) and as status-symmetrical (in terms of the elite women's desire to be "liked the one of the other").

As I suggested above, the ambiguities of Nicolay's language allow us to define the "tribades" in his account of the Turkish baths more or less broadly: tribadism might be narrowly understood as an attribute only of sexually aggressive women, or it might be capaciously understood as characterizing an entire roomful of women who share erotic pleasure. Approaching the problem of definition from this angle ratchets the distinction between unequal and mutual sexual agency into a larger social register, as the tribade might be identified as an anomalous type (Sappho the Lesbian) within a larger group of women, or as a typical member of a larger group of women (the hundred women or maidens Sappho pursued).

Visual illustrations of female bathhouses from this period confirm that we can recognize the tribade's sexual agency in terms either of individual aggression or of collective pleasure. In Jean Mignon's engraving of a bathhouse from a drawing by Luca Penni (ca. 1540), all of the women are naked, young, and of a similarly "feminine" morphology, with the exception of a single clothed older servant (see Figure 8).[14] No less than in Nicolay's description of Turkish baths, voyeuristic fantasies doubtless inform this depiction of generically beautiful naked women luxuriating in each other's company.[15] A particular generic convention present in this image might, however, specify tribadism not as a collective female eroticism, but as an imitation of the gender difference that structures heteroerotic relations. According to Leo Steinberg, the "slung leg" motif visible in the couple seated at the right foreground is "invariably a token of marital or sexual union, of sexual aggression or compliance" (343). Groping the inner thigh of her companion with one hand as she draws her closer with her other hand, the woman on the left might be read as a sexual aggressor; the companion might be understood as resisting this seduction as she pushes away the arm that gropes her thigh. Then again, the companion might be directing her friend's hand to her thigh. Furthermore, both women are smiling and appear to be giving equal attention to the woman to the left holding a stringed instrument, a typical symbol of female sexual pleasure, including autoerotic and homoerotic varieties.[16]

A similar indeterminacy about whether tribadism signifies through a distinct amorous gesture or through part of a larger group dynamic informs the illustration of a bathhouse in the early seventeenth-century English woodcut,

Figure 8. *Women Bathing*, by Jean Mignon after Luca Penni (ca. 1540). By permission of the Albertina Museum, Vienna.

Tittle-Tattle; Or, the Several Branches of Gossipping (see Figure 9). In this image, as the accompanying verse explains, a group of naked young women congregate at "the Hottehouse" in order to make "rough skin smooth." As in the Penni illustration, one woman in the bath remains clothed, but since she is just entering the bath from the dining room to the left, it appears that she has not yet had time to remove her robe. Alternatively, she might be a servant, the counterpart to the robed woman who is serving food to the bare-chested women seated at the table. Even apart from this clothed figure, the wood-cut thwarts any clear reading of gender and sexual agency among the naked women in the bath. In the group of four figures to the right, the woman in the foreground gestures and moves more actively, perhaps even aggressively, than the others. With her right hand, she holds another woman's hand, and with her left hand she reaches out as if to welcome the new arrivals. Yet the intimation of zeal in this woman's kinetic movement is tempered by the symmetrical hand gesture of the woman to the left: the two raised hands, framed by the large central window, suggest a friendly greeting. Still, a tribadic groper might be present: the woman in the left foreground appears to place her outstretched

Figure 9. Women in a bathhouse, detail from *Tittle-Tattle; Or, the several Branches of Gossipping* (ca. 1600). © Trustees of the British Museum.

hand on the thigh of a woman whose head is turned the other way, suggesting that she has not invited such attention. Given the difficulty of determining perspective in the image, it is possible that this woman's hand occupies a plane in the foreground of the image and does not make contact with her neighbor's thigh. Nonetheless, her head is angled downward, her line of sight precisely fixed on the thigh that she appears to be caressing. This woodcut, like Nicolay's description and Penni's drawing of female baths, offers the sexual titillation of observing tribadism in action through contradictory metonymic logics: the singularly aggressive tribade takes the place of a male seducer in a conventionally gendered heteroerotic relationship; at the same time, the group dynamic of tribadism suggests the equality among symmetrically gendered women who take mutual erotic pleasure in each other's company.

For a final example of how the metonymic logic of tribadism can obfuscate our ability to interpret sexual agency, we can turn to Leo Africanus's *A geographical historie of Africa* (1600), as translated into English by John Pory. Activating the metonymic association between the tribade and the witch, Africanus identifies female diviners in Fez as "women-witches" who actively seduce and deceive innocent women:

> But the wiser and honester sort of people call these women *Sahacat*, which in Latin signifieth *Fricatrices*, because they have a damnable custome to commit unlawfull Venerie among themselves, which I

cannot expresse in any modester termes. If faire women come unto them at any time, these abominable witches will burne in lust towardes them no otherwise than lustie yoonkers [young men] doe towards yoong maides, and will in the divels behalfe demaunde for a rewarde, that they may lie with them: and so by this meanes it often falleth out, that thinking thereby to fulfill the divels command they lie with the witches. (sigs. N2v–3r)

The apparent witch is known by "wiser and honester" people to be a "frica-trice" (or "rubster" in English) who preys upon the fair women who come to her for spiritual assistance.[17] As in Nicolay's account of the Turkish baths, a beautiful young woman provokes the uncontrollable passion of a presumably less feminine woman who asserts her erotic agency like a "lusty" man. Africa-nus's distinction between witches and fair women, Kim Hall remarks, seems roughly analogous to Traub's distinction between tribades and femmes (36).

Yet immediately following this condemnation of experienced fricatrices who coerce young women into committing "unlawfull Venerie," Africanus concedes that there are some women who, "allured with the delight of this abominable vice, will desire the companie of these witches." Such women, he explains, deceive their husbands,

and faining themselves to be sicke, will either call one of the witches home to them, or will send their husbands for the same purpose: and so the witches perceiving how the matter stands, will say that the woman is possessed with a divell, and that she can no way be cured, unlesse she be admitted into their societie. With these words her silly husband being persuaded, doth not onely permit her so to doe, but makes also a sumptuous banket unto the damned crew of witches: which being done, they use to daunce very strangely at the noise of drums: and so the poore man commits his false wife to their filthie disposition. Howbeit some there are that will soone conjure the divell with a good cudgell out of their wives: others faining themselves to be possessed with a divell, wil deceive the said witches, as their wives have been deceived by them. (sig. N3r)

In this scenario, the married woman actively seeks out a witch who initiates her into the collective tribadic rituals of her "damned crew." Whereas Africa-nus begins by describing the tribade as a witch who aggressively deceives and seduces a fair woman, he ends by describing tribadism as a "filthie disposition" shared by a group of women who seek mutual erotic pleasures. When tribades are identified as a collectivity, the salient distinction is not between the masculine witch and the feminine wife, but between a "societie" of transgressive women and the neglected husband who responds with naïve credulity or jealous rage to their sequestered revels.

In moving from anatomical texts to travel texts (and related voyeuristic images of group baths), I have stressed that the indeterminacy about the tribade's sexual and gender agency in the former—what does she do with her clitoris, and to whom?—broadens out to encompass an indeterminacy about the tribade's social agency, whether she is understood as a distinct type (a "masculine" aggressor pursuing a more feminine woman) or as one among a larger group of women who pursue collective erotic pleasure. Descriptions of tribadism in anatomical and travel writings might offer voyeuristic pleasures, but they also serve a disciplinary function in defining a type of woman who "abuses" her body in nonreproductive sexual practices or who or embodies an inappropriately masculine, foreign form of "luxuriousness."

In dramatic texts, social classifications also serve to discipline female characters who are associated with or accused of anti-patriarchal forms of same-sex intimacy. However, in dramatic texts the tribade also exerts a degree of agency in defining and defending her same-sex desires, motives, and loyalties. In what follows, I propose that Titania's recollection of her votaress in *A Midsummer Night's Dream* constitutes a kind of imaginative "first-person" elaboration of anatomical and travel writers' accounts of tribadic agency. Like anatomical discourses that occlude the sexual agency of the tribade's partner, Titania's account of her votaress makes it difficult to determine if what is being described constitutes a "tribade-femme" partnership that imitates a gender asymmetrical, heteroerotic organization of sexuality or a "tribade-tribade" partnership that rejects such a hierarchical model. Like the travel narratives with which it has much in common generically, Titania's narrative also offers contradictory indications about whether the tribade acts as a sexual aggressor against a more vulnerable woman or as a participant in a female alliance sharply distinguished from an oppressive patriarchalism. Through a metonymic reading, I unpack the richly imagistic, associative language with which Shakespeare endues Titania to argue that the tribade can assert an anti-patriarchal agency both by imitating and by eschewing a model of sexual partnership structured on heteroerotic norms.

In *The Winter's Tale*, what I will describe as a direct confrontation between the tribade and her accuser has no equivalent in the monological writings of anatomists and travelers. Attacking Paulina as a "mankind witch" and "bawd" for defending the sexual honesty of his wife Hermione, Leontes metonymically evokes the figure of the tribade. Through Leontes's wrath, the play reveals how the citation of a sexual type can function to discipline perceived deviations from gender and sexual norms, but through Paulina's resistance to Leontes's authority it also explores how these classificatory logics might backfire or stall. In a theatrical application of the metonymic logic we have come to associate with the tribade, Paulina ultimately appropriates the discourses of tribadism and witchcraft in a way that affirms instead of diminishes the value of female same-sex intimacy.

Titania's account of her Indian votaress appears to conflate rhetorical traits that Harriette Andreadis has identified as antithetical in the period's discourses of lesbianism: the male-authored language describing exotic, sexually transgressive, tribades and the "erotically charged yet shadowed" language used by the female poet to articulate feelings of same-sex love (103). In Titania's fond recollection of her votaress, of course, Shakespeare does not purport to describe an overt sexual encounter between women, as do writers of anatomical and travel texts: neither mutual friction nor aggressive groping has any place in this elegiac lyric. Nonetheless, Titania's recollection of her sequestered same-sex intimacy with a pregnant Indian woman seems to emerge from the same voyeuristic imaginary of anatomical and travel texts that represent wanton tribades enjoying each other's bodies in the absence of men.[18] Titania's symbolic connection with the Amazon Hippolyta (probably realized in the play's original performances by casting the same male actor in both roles) further aligns her with the type of an exotic, "masculine" tribade. At the same time, and in its immediate dramatic context, Titania's romantic lyricism rhetorically elevates the image of physical contact between women in an attempt to convince Oberon of her inalienable bond with the son of her deceased friend:

> Set your heart at rest.
> The fairyland buys not the child of me.
> His mother was a vot'ress of my order,
> And in the spicèd Indian air by night
> Full often hath she gossiped by my side,
> And sat with me on Neptune's yellow sands,
> Marking th'embarkèd traders on the flood,
> When we have laughed to see the sails conceive

And grow big-bellied with the wanton wind,
Which she with pretty and with swimming gait
Following, her womb then rich with my young squire,
Would imitate, and sail upon the land
To fetch me trifles, and return again
As from a voyage, rich with merchandise.
But she, being mortal, of that boy did die;
And for her sake do I rear up her boy;
And for her sake I will not part with him. (2.1.121–37)[19]

Crucially, and in contrast to anatomy books and travel narratives, the contradictory indications of mutuality and hierarchy between women in this passage are organized not around sexual practices (i.e., simultaneous rubbing vs. aggressive groping, experienced fricatrices vs. naïve maids), but around distinctions of power. Through a metonymic reading that identifies the social, economic, corporeal, mythological, and sexual associations that animate this passage, I will suggest that Titania resists Oberon's patriarchal authority in two seemingly contradictory ways. Titania imitates and hence appropriates Oberon's patriarchal authority by providing an account of her own power over the votaress; she also rejects patriarchal authority by advocating a more harmonious model of mutual desire centered on female-female loyalty.

Given the elegiac tone of the speech, as well as its immediate dramatic context—a salvo in the ongoing, sharply gendered, conflict with Oberon over the right to possess the changeling boy—it is perhaps easier to read Titania's account of her love for the votaress as a pointed rejection of her husband's coercive and unequal model of patriarchal power. We might even regard her speech as a kind of "fairy tale": a fantastic story, typically delivered by an old female servant, that served to display her authority and "psychological power" over a socially privileged audience, the children of her master (Lamb 282). Although the truth claims of Titania's Indian fairy tale can be neither proved nor disproved, its rhetorical purpose is to deploy the votaress as a positive figure of reproductive femininity: the good, self-sacrificing, mother who authorizes Titania's surrogate motherhood of the boy. Puck, of course, claims that Titania acquired the boy illicitly, stealing him from his father and then holding him captive in her forest bower. Puck's counter-narrative reveals how Titania's narrative of same-sex friendship might also function to legitimize what could otherwise be perceived as a transgressive act of tribadism, in much the same way that English people told fairy stories as "white lies" to explain theft, illicit pregnancy, or the death of a child (Lamb 283–94).

By recalling how the votaress often "gossiped at [her] side," Titania further validates their friendship as a form of privileged same-sex association. "Gossip," derived from Old English godsib (spiritual kin), originally meant a godparent of either gender; the votaress's pregnancy suggestively places Titania in the familiar role of the female gossip who was present during childbirth and provided companionship for the recovering mother during the lying-in period. "Gossip" came to mean a close female friend, and as such the "evolution of the term reflects the fundamental importance of childbirth in women's lives, and a recognition that the supportive networks manifested in the delivery room played an equally important part in their everyday lives" (Capp, *Gossips* 51). Through these associations, Titania's recollection of her votaress imparts to "gossiping" a positive value as a form of privileged, communal female conversation and support. It is worth recalling that although the act of gossiping has primarily negative connotations for us, gossip in early modern England "had a respected function in the community as a means of enforcing canons of morality and neighbourliness" (Mendelson and Crawford 215).

The very importance of the gossip network could give rise to male anxieties that "unsupervised female sociability posed a threat to the order and values of patriarchal society" (Capp, *Gossips* 50). Contemporary literary texts often lampoon the festive gathering of childbed gossips through satiric portraits of drunken, tattling women who abuse and dislodge poor husbands (Cressy 84–87). Depictions of "gossips' meetings," such as the one in Samuel Rowlands's *Tis Merrie when Gossips meete* (1602) typically represent women as heavy drinkers who invade male preserves such as the tavern, waste time and money in idle chatter, badmouth men, and exchange advice on how to dominate husbands (Woodbridge 224–43). Crucially, however, both the natural setting and the marked solitude of Titania's gossiping with the votaress distance this tableau from the unruly spectacles of childbed gossips who noisily usurp the marital bedchamber or of inebriated tavern gossips who bemoan their husbands' shortcomings. Titania's reminiscence of her "gossips' meeting" is relentlessly antisocial, even mythical in its idyllic circumscription of same-sex intimacy.[20]

In this regard, Titania's memory of gossiping together on the yellow sands of India paints a seductive imaginative scene, a kind of displaced pastoral sexual invitation on the order of Marlowe's "Passionate Shepherd to his Love." The pastoral invitation conventionally comprises a catalogue of sensual pleasures, and here Titania mentions only the "wanton wind," "yellow sands," and "spicèd Indian air." Yet that single olfactory image of spiced air does copious metonymic work in evoking a sensual landscape. Edible spices such as pepper and ginger were among India's staple exports to Europe, but "'spices' could also refer to a dizzying array of drugs (including opium, camphor, and cannabis), cosmetics, sugar, [and] waxes" (Brotton 172–73). *An historicall description of the most famous kingdomes and common-weales in the worlde*, the 1603 English translation of Giovanni Botero's *Relationi Universali*, cites the "sweet savour" (i.e., fragrance) of agalloch trees as a typical manifestation of Asian sensuality: "In India and Cambaia they use it at the burial of great Lords, in bathes and in other wantonnes" (200). A scene from Barnabe Barnes's *The Divils charter* (1607), in which Pope Alexander woos a young man, includes exotically spiced air among the many sensual enticements offered to sweeten the sexual encounter: "Thy bed is made with spice and *Calamus*, / With Sinamond and Spicnard, Arabick, / With Opobalsam and rich gums of Ægipt" (sig. E2v).[21] Titania's rhetorical evocation of eastern spices is intended not to seduce the absent votaress, of course, but to recreate for Oberon the pervasive sensual landscape in which she enjoyed the votaress's intimacy.

Male figures are notably absent from that intimate scenario. Titania's allusion to "Neptune's yellow sands" testifies to the physical absence of the patriarchal sea god; Neptune is present only as a metonymy, a figure for the sea whose pulsing rhythm, we might imagine, harmonizes with the rising and falling rhythms of female gossiping and laughter.[22] Advising her husband to "Set [his] heart at rest," Titania uses a metaphor of physiological agitation not only to underscore Oberon's anxiously unfulfilled yearning for the changeling boy, but also to mark his exclusion from the pleasurable agitation of the heart she claims to have shared with her votaress, as they laughed together at the "big-bellied" sails (2.1.121).[23] In his *Treatise on Laughter* (1579), Laurent Joubert defines laughable subject matter as that which provokes simultaneous pleasure and sadness; in laughter, the heart both "expands," as it does in the experience of joy, and "shrinks and tightens," as it does in the contrary experience of sadness (44).[24] According to Joubert's theory, imagining sails as impregnated with the wind could provoke laughter because there is something mildly "deformed" or indecorous, though pleasantly titillating, in the fantasy of a ship becoming pregnant:

> What we see that is ugly, deformed, improper, indecent, unfitting, and indecorous excites laughter in us, provided we are not moved to

compassion. Example: if perchance one uncovers the shameful parts
which by nature or public decency we are accustomed to keeping
hidden, since this is ugly yet unworthy of pity, it moves the onlookers to
laughter. (21)

By laughing at the pregnant ships, Titania and the votaress transform public
signs of national economic power into private signs of the "shameful" acts "we
are accustomed to keeping hidden."[25] Especially because the votaress died in
childbirth, Titania's recollection of sails that conceive with wind suggests the
advantage of a same-sex eroticism that produces no physical consequences
(2.1.128).[26] In Donne's poem "Sappho to Philaenis," Sappho advocates female
homoeroticism along just these lines:

> Men leave behind them that which their sin shows
> And are as thieves traced, which rob when it snows.
> But of our dalliance no more signs there are
> Then fishes leave in streams, or Birds in air. (qtd. Borris, *Same-Sex* 339)

The indivisibility of water and air figures a same-sex "dalliance" that does not
divide sexual partners into actor and acted upon, sinner and sinned against,
leaver and left behind.

As the travel narratives analyzed above suggest, however, Titania's narrative of a same-sex companionship in India might also evoke the type of the
tribade as a sexual aggressor against a less experienced or powerful woman,
and as such complicates a "Romanticized, idealized, even sentimental" reading of her relationship with the votaress (Walen 153). Ania Loomba associates
the luxurious Indian votaress with African tribades and Amazons as common
types of foreign women's sexual and familial deviance "conjured up" by European observers "to assist in the formation of an alternative family structure
shaped by the ideological imperatives of both mercantilism and colonialism"
("Indian" 179).[27] Along with Hippolyta's Amazonian past and the girlhood
friendship of Hermia and Helena, Loomba argues, the play evokes Titania's
memory of "female bonding" in order finally to displace these histories of
female homoeroticism with scenarios of women's "willing subjection" to the
"heterosexual couplings" of patriarchal marriage ("Indian" 179, 181).

Although the votaress's pregnancy might appear to signify her "willing
subjection" to "heterosexual coupling," the suggestion of Titania's magical,
witch-like, agency in this exotic all-female setting throws the Indian king's

sexual agency into doubt. Whereas Traub argues that the changeling boy "is the manifest link of a prior affection between women that is associated with their shared fecundity and maternal largess" (68), we might also say that the child is the sign of a connection between women that is at once maternal *and* paternal, since the passage admits the possibility that Titania herself somehow "fathered" the child. Referring to the votaress's womb as "rich with my young squire," Titania erases the reproductive agency of a biological father, just as Theseus elides the reproductive agency of Hermia's biological mother in the fantasy of male parthenogenesis he delivers in the first scene of the play (2.1.131).[28] In the period's "gendered opposition between masculine spirit and female flesh" (Rackin 76), Titania, ontologically speaking, represents the masculine spirit to the votaress's female flesh. More precisely, Kathryn Schwarz claims that Shakespeare's account of the changeling's birth "in the absence of men" recalls early modern "speculations about amazonian parthenogenesis": one account of Magellan's voyage describes an island inhabited by women who "become mothers by the wind" (228). Avicenna, an eleventh-century Persian physician, claimed that mares could be impregnated by the wind (Lochrie 76). Titania is associated with the impregnating "wanton wind" that makes "big-bellied" signs out of the trading ships, for it is her superior power that inspires the votaress to imitate the ships by "sail[ing] upon the land" to collect gifts for her mistress (2.1.129, 132).[29] In her seeming appropriation of patriarchal fatherhood, Titania emerges as the "masculine" tribade who takes the man's part in relation to the more "feminine" votaress.

Along with Titania's double role as the changeling's "mother" and "father," the status difference between Titania and her nameless votaress cuts across any attempt to categorize their relationship definitively in terms of an egalitarian friendship.[30] Whereas the relationship between Helena and Hermia comprises a symmetrical friendship sealed by "sisters' vows" (3.2.199), the votaress is a subordinate who has vowed herself to Titania's "order." We might expect that the pregnant votaress, like the pregnant Duchess in Marlowe's *Dr. Faustus*, would be the recipient of exotic delicacies.[31] Instead, the votaress fetches "trifles" for her mistress. In contemporary economic discourse, "trifles" were worthless foreign "fashion goods" that could be sold at great profit to feminized native consumers, such as New World Indians (Linton 84). For Ania Loomba, the account of an Indian woman who tenders Titania vain "trifles" as well as her precious son evokes the stereotypical image of the naïve African or New World native who offers gifts to European visitors ("Indian" 169). Thus the Indian boy himself serves to represent "the human or material traffic of

'India'" that becomes the site of a proprietary struggle between Oberon and Titania in their "tussle over colonial goods" ("Indian" 167, 170).[32] No less than Oberon, Titania might recognize that the display of the changeling boy, a precious foreign commodity, adds symbolic capital to her "order."

I would go even further than Loomba in arguing that in Titania's discourse of India the votaress herself functions as a kind of exotic commodity through which Titania justifies her possession of the boy. Drawing from the richly allusive material of Titania's speech, a metonymic reading might venture a connection between Titania's nostalgic portrait of her deceased Indian votaress and the lament over a deceased Indian female parrot in Ovid's *Elegy* 2.6. As translated by Marlowe, the elegy opens with the speaker announcing the death of the parrot he had given to his mistress, Corinna: "The parrot from east India to me sent, / Is dead, all fowls her exequies frequent" (*Ovid's Elegies* 1–2). Just as Titania fondly recalls how her votaress gossiped by her side and cleverly mimicked the passing ships, Ovid's speaker recalls the parrot's imitative vocal skills—"No such voice-feigning bird was on the ground" (23)—and commemorates its same-sex devotion to a turtledove:

Full concord all your lives was you betwixt,
And to the end your constant faith stood fixt.
What Pylades did to Orestes prove,
Such to the parrot was the turtle dove. (13–16)

According to Morgan Holmes, who identifies Ovid's elegy as a precedent for the female homoerotic lament in Andrew Marvell's *The Nymph Complaining for the Death of her Faun*, the friendship between Pylades and Orestes "stands as a homoerotic precedent for the love between the parrot and the turtle-dove, and, by extension, the parrot and Corinna" (84). Yet whereas the love between parrot and turtledove, as between Pylades and Orestes, depends on "concord" or equality, the love between Corinna and her parrot is based on difference of species as well as status.[33] Ovid's speaker gave the parrot "to please [his] wench," as its epitaph confirms: "I pleased my mistress well" (19, 61). If the association of Titania's speech with Ovid's *Elegy* is at all plausible, it is because we can imagine how representing the Indian votaress as a beloved domestic pet might serve to advance Titania's propriety claim to the votaress's offspring.

The association between the votaress and the parrot, of course, diminishes the votaress by taking away her human agency and elevated social status. According to Bruce Boehrer, medieval Europeans originally identified parrots

Durum telum necessitas.

N ECESSITIE doth vrge, the Popiniaye to prate,
And birdes, to drawe their bucketts vp, and picke theire meate
    through, grate:
Which warneth them, whoe needes muſt eyther ſerue, or pine:
With willing harte, no paines to ſhunne, and freedome to reſigne.

Terent. In
Adel. 4. 7.

Placet tibi factum mitio? M 1. *non ſi queam*
Mutare : nunc, cum nequeo, æquo animo fero.

Inimi.

Figure 10. A caged parrot, from Geffrey Whitney, *A choice of emblemes* (1586). By permission of the Folger Shakespeare Library.

with Asia and imparted to them a "quasi-mythical status" (*Shakespeare* 121), but during the early sixteenth century parrots come to be identified with the New World, from which they were brought back to Europe as examples of marvelous beasts. Increasingly available as domestic pets, parrots "undergo a swift process of trivialization" in the late sixteenth century (114). The talkative birds become associated with "subordinate and ostensibly inferior men" and "artists regularly elide them with servants, children, and decorative trinkets of various kinds, while sometimes presenting them, in the process, as ornamental backdrops or counterpoints to the portraiture of aristocratic subjects" (101).[34] In Geffrey Whitney's *A choice of emblemes* (1586), a caged parrot (or "Popinjaye") that prates by "necessitie" is an emblem of servitude (see Figure 10). When regarded as one who "needes must . . . serve," the votaress primarily functions in Titania's account neither as an intimate same-sex partner to be lovingly commemorated nor as the source of a precious foreign gift to be guarded and cherished. Instead, she functions as a domestic servant the product of whose labors is to remain in her mistress's ownership.

Titania's tribadism thus comes to signify both as a rejection of patriarchal agency over women and as an imitation of patriarchal agency over a particular woman. Through her rhetorical deployment of the votaress, Titania resists Oberon's authority by representing the value of women's erotic mutuality as an alternative to gender asymmetrical, patriarchal domination, and also by claiming her own right to patriarchal domination over a woman who variously fulfills the roles of fertile wife, religious devotee, exotic pet, and domestic servant. Oberon eventually takes revenge on Titania by translating her insubordinate tribadic agency into an involuntary bestiality that humiliates and degrades her even as it offers erotic pleasure.[35]

In *The Winter's Tale*, Paulina's resistance to Leontes's patriarchal and sovereign authority calls down his immediate wrath in the form of an indirect—that is to say, metonymic—accusation of tribadism. During Hermione's imprisonment, Paulina acts as her mistress's defender and substitute in confronting Leontes. Hoping to mitigate Leontes's jealousy by presenting him with his newborn daughter, Paulina adopts the roles of symbolic midwife and substitute mother, roles that Leontes associates with the transgressive intimacies of the "mankind witch," "intelligencing bawd," and "callet" or strumpet, as well as the scolding wife (2.3.67–68, 90). Both the witch, as I have argued above, and the bawd, as I will demonstrate more fully in Chapter 5, can be associated with the tribade as aggressively masculine figures who pursue illicit bodily intimacy with other women.[36] Witches were typically believed to murder infants; consequently, a witch might be understood as a perverse mother, midwife, or gossip (Willis 35).[37] Leontes activates these gruesome associations to delegitimize not only Paulina's testimony regarding his paternity of the infant, I would argue, but also her same-sex intimacy with Hermione, and the belligerently "masculine" act of substitutive advocacy that intimacy has authorized. In short, Leontes metonymically evokes the type of the tribade to overwrite Paulina's aggressive substitution of herself for the silenced Hermione.

Despite Leontes's metonymic deployment of the tribade to punish Paulina's agency, a different series of metonymic substitutions woven into the language of the play critically exposes the tendentious rhetorical foundations of Leontes's misogyny. In the absolutist kingdom of Sicilia, Leontes's monarchical word is law, yet in the linguistic texture of the play, Leontes's word is subject to critical imitation and displacement. The ironic operations of metonymy are especially evident in Paulina's first scene, in which she comes to visit Hermione at the prison and is informed by the jailer of the "express commandment" he has received not to admit her (2.2.8). That several women already attend the queen in prison suggests that Leontes has a particular reason for keeping Paulina away from Hermione, just as he tears Mamillius away from Hermione on the grounds that her moral turpitude might infect him: "Bear the boy hence; he shall not come about her" (2.1.59). Ridiculing Leontes's insistence on sequestering his wife, Paulina fumes, "Here's ado, to lock up honesty and honour from / Th'access of gentle visitors" (2.2.9–10). As Stephen Orgel points out in his edition of the play, the words "honesty and honour" recall Leontes's complaint that Hermione is "honourable" but not "honest" (2.1.68). To express the essence of Hermione's virtue, Paulina unknowingly calls up precisely those concepts that Leontes had used to express his absolute conviction of Hermione's guilt, a coincidence that renders ironic Leontes's confidence in the truth of his observations. Paulina, in fact, uses these words as a kind of personification of Hermione: she is "honesty and honour" perversely sequestered from the ranks of the gentle.

In Paulina's subsequent complaint, "Here's such ado to make no stain a stain / As passes colouring" (2.2.18–19), the image of dyeing recalls Leontes's earlier remark about female deception: "women say so, / That will say anything"; they are as "false / As o'er-dyed blacks" (1.2.129–31). Whereas Leontes had compared excessively stained fabrics to false women, Paulina more pointedly compares the *effort* of excessive staining to Leontes's effort to create a moral stain where none exists—"coloring" also connoting rhetorical embellishment or misrepresentation. Moreover, Paulina's repeated phrases "Here's ado" and "Here's such ado" metadramatically evoke *Much Ado About Nothing*, Shakespeare's earlier comedy about a jealous man who slanders an innocent woman. The metonymic connection between the plays' differently situated slanderers—the easily manipulated young bachelor of *Much Ado* and the ostensibly wiser king and husband of *The Winter's Tale*—only underscores the folly and recklessness of Leontes's jealousy.[38] Overall, these linguistic substitutions have the effect of rendering ironic and exposing the tendentiousness of Leontes's subsequent use of classifications such as "witch" and "bawd."

Leontes's failed attempt to discipline Paulina as witch and tribade only enhances Paulina's assertion of agency in the final scene of the play, in which she uses theatrical magic to animate Hermione's statue as well as to demonstrate her loyalty to the queen. In an analysis of Hermione's sixteen-year cohabitation with Paulina, Theodora Jankowski argues that their prolonged homoerotic intimacy elevates Paulina from a servant to a kind of spouse. Jankowski finds evidence for the egalitarian or "coterminous" relationship between Paulina and Hermione in the way that Hermione, though socially superior, appears to obey Paulina's commands to descend from the pedestal ("Lesbian Void" 306). Building on Jankowski's reading, I would argue that because Paulina's affection for Hermione "creates" the statue and then makes it "come to life," her metonymic connection to Pygmalion in the Ovidian myth to which the scene alludes activates yet another tribadic association.[39] Paulina's ability to "stir" Leontes's desire to kiss and touch the statue might also convey her familiarity with the contours of Hermione's body (5.3.74). Moreover, even as Paulina worries that Leontes will conclude that she is aided by "wicked powers" and engaged in "unlawful business," she overtly aligns herself with sorcery in declaring that her "spell is lawful" (5.3.91, 96, 105).

Paulina thus comes to embody the "masculine" tribade in a more affirmative mode than seemed possible in the social and sexual logics of anatomical texts, travel narratives, or even *A Midsummer Night's Dream*. Admittedly, Shakespeare, unlike anatomical or travel writers, does not purport to describe an overtly sexual relationship between Paulina and Hermione; from the outset, Paulina is protected from the orthodox condemnation of "unnatural" clitoral abuses attributed to the tribade. As I have already argued, however, Leontes's allusions to the masculine witch and bawd metonymically associate Paulina with the tribade. Moreover, Paulina's husband Antigonus links female sexual transgression to the clitoris through a metonymic association typical of anatomical accounts of the tribade. In a remarkable (but largely unremarked) passage, Antigonus defends Hermione's honor by claiming that if she is false, then "every inch of woman in the world, / Ay, every dram of woman's flesh, is false," including the flesh of his wife (2.1.137–38). Antigonus's hyperbolic location of sexual dishonesty in the smallest "inch" or "dram" of woman's "flesh" appears to invert the logic of anatomists who exaggerated the length of the clitoris when representing it as "the disturbing emblem of female erotic transgression" (Traub 205).[40] Furthermore, if Hermione, and thus all womankind, proves to be false, Antigonus promises to "geld" his three daughters, who are five, nine, and eleven years of age, to keep them from having bastards (2.1.147). "Geld" means to spay or remove the ovaries so as to prevent procreation, but here it also resonates with early modern anatomists' common recommendation of "genital amputation" as a surgical response to tribadism (Traub 216). Removing the clitoris would also prevent reproduction, as it was the source of sexual pleasure necessary for women to ejaculate "seed" for conception.

Particularly since Antigonus launches his defense of Hermione by declaring that were she to prove unchaste he would treat his own wife as an animal to be kept in the "stables" (2.1.134), it is possible to regard his bizarre surgical threat against his prepubescent daughters as a displaced threat against his wife. As a rhetorical substitute for Hermione in Antigonus's impassioned defense, Paulina is caught up in the metonymic associations that link both clitoral abuse and bestiality to the tribade's sexual agency.

By the end of the play, however, it is as if the tribade, depicted by anatomists as an unnatural abuser of her body with other women and by travel writers as a participant in non-reproductive sexual "customs," has been given the opportunity to speak a different language about the aims of physical intimacies and social allegiances between women. Unlike the lusty Turkish women who grope each other in bathhouses, the African witch who cuckolds husbands and seduces wives, or the rebellious Titania who spurns her husband's sovereign authority in memory of her Indian votaress, Paulina publicly affirms her sixteen-year intimacy with Hermione as a legitimate expression of same-sex allegiance, restorative witchcraft, and monarchical service. It might be that what makes this homoerotic affirmation possible in *The Winter's Tale* is Paulina's apparent abandonment of the tribade role once she "returns" Hermione to Leontes and to her conjugal role. Nonetheless, the moment of Hermione's restoration to her roles as mother, wife, and queen is also the moment that we discover that Hermione has been living exclusively with Paulina for sixteen years. The substitutive logic that has informed Paulina's protection of and intimacy with Hermione therefore suggests that, in certain cases, the metonymies that govern the representation of the tribade can undermine as well as bolster the "necessary classifications" and disciplinary norms that serve the status quo.

Part 2

Sexual Types and Social Discriminations

Chapter 3

Mincing Manners

The Narcissistic Courtier and the (De)Formation of Civility

> . . . some mincing marmoset / Made all of clothes and face
> —*Cynthia's Revels*

Ben Jonson's *Cynthia's Revels* satirically explores the social and political implications of narcissism as a form of elite male embodiment. Representing the Elizabethan courtier as a narcissist, Jonson draws together two strains of contemporary satiric discourse: critiques of effeminate fashions and manners at court, and interpretations of the Narcissus myth that associated self-love with gender and sexual transgressions. Jonson, of course, is not alone in his theatrical critique of courtly vices—as witnessed by Marlowe's *Edward II* and Shakespeare's *Richard II*, *1 Henry IV*, and *Hamlet*—yet *Cynthia's Revels* is worthy of extended attention not only because it is a less familiar play than these, but also, and more importantly, because it uniquely represents the courtier by using the generic resources of Ovidian mythology and the prose character description. More than any other play of its age, *Cynthia's Revels* demonstrates how a mythological framework might be brought to bear as an instrument of courtly satire.[1] Even though Narcissus never appears as a character in the play, the myth provides Jonson with vivid material for exposing the transgressive bodily practices of unauthorized courtiers, especially through Amorphus ("the deformed"), whose affected manners and speech violate orthodox prescriptions for male aristocratic comportment.[2]

Moreover, the play's embedded character portraits conceive of courtly types in terms of fragmentation: the clothes, manners, idioms, and habits that make up an incomplete "parcel of man" (2.1.23). Ironically, even as Jonson represents bodily fragmentation as the deformed sign of courtly narcissism, his satirical strategy of mincing the courtier's body and gestures dramatically enacts that fragmentation.

With its episodic, fragmented structure, *Cynthia's Revels* is a profoundly tedious play.[3] Although it might have fared better on stage, especially as performed by the witty children who first presented it in 1600, Jonson does not spare his audience a full airing of the trivial and inane courtly pastimes that dominate the action.[4] These pastimes fill up several dilated prose scenes: a courtier teaches an aspirant how to woo a lady (3.5); the ladies fantasize about what they would do if granted the power to transform themselves (4.1); the courtiers and ladies play language games called "substantives and adjectives" and "a thing done and who did it" (4.3); and the courtiers engage in a combat at four "cunning weapons of court-compliment" (5.3.83): the bare accost, the better regard, the solemn address, and the perfect close. These scenes gather more thickly at the latter end of the play, when the audience's "gracious silence" and "sweet attention" might well be flagging (Prologue 1). Offering a kind of ascetic relief from these tableaus of court folly are scenes of high moral instruction (5.1, 5.5–5.6, 5.8), in which authority figures such as Mercury, Cynthia, and Crites (a Jonson-style scholar) deliver platitudes in blank verse. The play finally ends after the presentation of two allegorical masques (5.7, 5.9–5.10), which deliver the narcissistic courtiers and ladies to Cynthia's censure (5.11). Like the courtiers it satirizes, the overall effect of the play itself one of incoherence, artificiality, and tedious excess.

Jonson's satiric method meticulously anatomizes Amorphus as a type "so made out of the mixture and shreds of forms that himself is truly deformed" (2.3.77–78). Representing Amorphus as a collection of affected gestures, dispositions, and styles, Jonson, we might say, deploys a "mincing" dramatic strategy against the figure of the "mincing" courtier (3.4.22).[5] In early modern England as today, "mincing" could refer to effeminate gender comportment, such as "speaking, walking, or behaving, in an affectedly dainty or refined manner" (*OED*, mincing *adj.* 1.b).[6] Yet whereas for us "mincing" is likely to evoke the stereotype of an effeminate gay man, in Jonson's culture male effeminacy existed in a more oblique relationship to homoerotic and heteroerotic desires.[7] Amorphus's immediate attachment to a new male acquaintance, whom he narcissistically attempts to mold in his own courtly image, does not impugn all forms of same-sex affection, but implies that deficient manhood requires the support of a narcissistic reflection. Moreover, even though the play's narcissistic courtiers woo women, they appear no more masculine for that, because Jonson represents narcissism as a rejection of socially and sexually productive bonds. As Crites observes, the ladies' rhetorical mincing of the courtiers they admire does not enhance the courtiers' manhood as objects of female desire but rather exposes their insubstantial and deformed natures:[8]

> . . . you shall hear one talk of this man's eye;
> Another of his lip; a third, his nose;
> A fourth commend his leg; a fifth his foot;
> A sixth his hand; and everyone a limb:
> That you would think the poor distorted gallant
> Must there expire. (3.4.75–80)

For Jonson, the "distorted" gallant's collection of ill-fitting parts connotes an effeminacy that violates aristocratic standards of "civilized" masculine comportment, and hence of social and political legitimacy.[9]

Nonetheless, through his proficiency with courtly practices the narcissistic courtier in *Cynthia's Revels* ends up troubling the distinction between legitimate and illegitimate forms of elite male self-display. This category trouble impacts the play's resolution through a masque that requires each courtier to portray a courtly virtue that tempers or inverts his characteristic vice. For instance, the "deformed" Amorphus portrays "the commendably-fashioned gallant, Eucosmos," whose name might be translated as "good order" or "pleasing adornment" (5.9.18). Before doling out punishments and restoring order, Cynthia accuses the masquing courtiers of having deceptively "mix[ed] themselves with others of the court" who are worthy of her presence (5.11.53). However, the nuances of the masque indicate that, absent Cynthia's divine powers of discrimination, stark antitheses such as orderly/deformed provide poor tools for determining the worth of courtiers. Confronted with the baffling "mixture and shreds of forms" that constitute courtly practices—and the representation of those practices through the type of the narcissistic courtier—discerning observers might well reach different conclusions as to what distinguishes legitimate from illegitimate courtiership.

*   *   *

To satirize the deformity of courtly bodies and manners, Jonson draws on the myth of Narcissus as told by Ovid and as interpreted and refashioned by subsequent mythographers, translators, and poets. *Cynthia's Revels* was originally entered in the Stationer's Register as *Narcissus, or the fountain of self-love*, and is the only play in which Jonson makes "extended use of Ovidian material" (Wiltenburg 5–6). Jonson's uncharacteristic recourse to Ovid suggests his recognition of the Narcissus myth's theatrical viability as a vehicle for courtly satire; he was doubtless familiar with the Ovidian epyllia of the 1590s, in which Narcissus often functions as the epitome of "failed masculinity" (Ellis 110).[10]

The Narcissus myth had developed an extended, complex, cultural legacy by 1600, and it is important to understand the general outlines of this legacy before considering Jonson's use of it in *Cynthia's Revels*. In medieval and renaissance moralizations of Ovid, Narcissus typically represents the "folly of loving an image" (Vinge 76). Arthur Golding's influential 1567 translation of *The Metamorphoses*, for instance, interprets the myth as warning against the folly of pride and vanity.[11] Emblematist Geffrey Whitney elaborates on the social consequences of Narcissus's inflated self-image (see Figure 11):

> Narcissus lovde, and liked so his shape,
> He died at lengthe with gazinge there uppon:
> Which shewes selfe love, from which there fewe can scape,
> A plague too rife: bewitcheth manie a one.
>   The ritche, the pore, the learned, and the sotte,
>   Offende therein: and yet they see it not. (149)

Whitney's emblem significantly departs from the Virgil Solis woodcut of Narcissus that graced several Latin and German editions of Ovid printed in the late sixteenth century.[12] Whereas the Solis woodcut depicts Narcissus alone at the fountain (see Figure 12), Whitney shows in the background one of the many men Narcissus rejected. In Golding's rendition, one of these suitors, "miscontent / To see himselfe deluded so," raises his hands to heaven and prays that Narcissus "may once feele fierce Cupids fire / As I doe now, and yet not joy the things he doth desire" (3.503–6). The poem attached to Whitney's emblem does not mention the rejected suitor; nonetheless, it remarks the wider social consequences of self-love, which "makes us judge too well of our desertes, / When others smile, our ignorance to see."

NARCISSVS loude, and liked so his shape,
He died at lengthe with gazinge there vppon:
Which shewes selfe loue, from which there fewe can scape,
A plague too rife: bewitcheth manie a one.
  The ritche, the pore, the learned, and the sotte,
  Offende therein: and yet they see it not.

This, makes vs iudge too well of our desertes,
When others smile, our ignorance to see:
And whie? Bicause selfe loue doth wounde our hartes,
And makes vs thinke, our deedes alone to bee.
  Whiche secret sore, lies hidden from our eyes,
  And yet the same, an other plainlie sees.

What follie more, what dotage like to this?
And doe we so our owne deuise esteeme?
Or can we see so soone an others misse?
And not our owne? Oh blindnes most extreme.
  Affect not then, but trye, and prooue thy deedes,
  For of selfe loue, reproche, and shame proceedes.
                    T 3   *Nusquam*

Ouid.Metam.lib.3.

Anulus in pict.
poëf.
Narcissus liquidis for-
mā speculatus in vndis,
Contemnent alios, arsit
amore sui, &c.

Terent. And.2.&4.
Verum illud verbū est,
vulgo quod dici solet
Omnes sibi malle me-
lius esse, quàm alteri.

Suum cuique pul-
chrum est, adhuc
neminem cognoui
poëtam, qui sibi nō
optimus videretur,
sic res habet, me de-
lectant mea, te tua.
Cicer. 5. Tuscul.

Figure 11. Narcissus as emblem of self-love, from Geffrey Whitney, *A choice of emblemes* (1586). By permission of the Folger Shakespeare Library.

Figure 12. Virgil Solis woodcut of Narcissus, from Johann Spreng, *Metamorphoses Illustratae* (1563). Watkinson Library, Trinity College, Hartford, Connecticut.

In his moralization of the myth, George Sandys similarly reads Narcissus as the archetype of those who reject full participation in social life. Narcissists "sequester themselves from publique converse and civill affaires, as subject to neglects and disgraces, which might too much trouble and deject them: admitting but of a few to accompany their solitarinesse; those being such as only applaud and admire them, assenting to what they say, like as many *Ecchos*" (sig. N3v). Despite Sandys's emphasis on solitariness, the synoptic illustration to his Book Three aggressively socializes Narcissus by placing him in the company of the other, mostly male, figures who share his narrative space (see Figure 13). Most of these figures, who might aptly be illustrated in isolation, are also placed in broader social contexts: Cadmus submits to the command of Athena (above) as the armed Spartoi (eventual founders of Thebes) engage in battle; Diana transforms Actaeon into a stag for intruding on her all-female community; Tireseas strikes the snakes that will transform his sex from male to female and back to male; disguised as a nurse, Juno treacherously advises Semele to receive Jove in his divine form; Bacchus punishes Acetis's sailors for

Figure 13. Narcissus among other figures from the Third Book of the *Metamorphoses*, from George Sandys, *Ovids Metamorphosis Englished* (1632). By permission of the Folger Shakespeare Library.

falsely swearing to transport him home; and the Bacchantes destroy Pentheus for spying on their sacred rites. In this composite illustration, Narcissus's self-love is imagined not as an affliction of those who sequester themselves from public converse and civil affairs, but rather as a solipsistic self-regard in the midst of spectacular conflicts over social value, authority, and legitimacy.

If Renaissance mythographers and emblematists regard narcissism as an aggressive rejection of the social construction of value, Renaissance poets and playwrights tend to represent narcissism in terms of the scornful rejection of sexual and social relationality, whether in the form of failed homoerotic courtships, heteroerotic courtships, or both. In Golding's translation, Narcissus proudly rejects both men and women who admire his adolescent beauty:

> For when yeares three times five and one he fully lyved had,
> So that he seemde to stande beetwene the state of man and Lad,
> The hearts of dyvers trim yong men his beautie gan to move
> And many a Ladie fresh and faire was taken in his love.
> But in that grace of Natures gift such passing pride did raigne,
> That to be toucht of man or Mayde he wholy did disdaine. (3.437–42)

After one of his male suitors prays for revenge, Narcissus mistakes his own reflection in the water for the face of a beautiful youth who apparently disdains his touch: "He would be had. For looke how oft I kisse the water under, / So oft againe with upwarde mouth he riseth towarde mee. / A man would thinke to touch at least I should yet able bee" (Golding 3.565–67). Having given his "passing pride" tyrannical reign, Narcissus disdains the social and sexual relationality that comes with being touched of man or maid, and thus dies alone.

In Richard Brathwaite's elegy *Narcissus Change* (1611), Narcissus rejects male suitors because he believes that his beauty is worthy of only the gods. Admitting that "Bright-eide Alexis is beyond compare," Narcissus recognizes the beauty of other men; he also recognizes their desire for him: "*Damon* hath told me oft, I was most faire" (sigs. D4v–5r). Yet, spying his reflection in the fountain, Narcissus takes the "conceit" of his "beauteous forme" to a preposterous conclusion (sig. D4v):

> *Narcissus* gemme, for who can ere compare
>   With the surpassing beautie of his face?
> Which intermixed is with red most faire,

> Resembling *Io*, whose admired grace
> Strucke such a love in *Jupiters* high brest,
>   That he protested, he lov'd *Io* best. (sig. D5v)

Even as he compares himself to the beautiful women admired by Jupiter and Apollo, Narcissus seems unaware that, unlike himself, these gods deigned to love mortal youths such as Ganymede and Hyacinth. Ultimately punished for indulging "soaring thoughts" of "his owne beautie fitter for Gods then men" (sig. D7v), Narcissus might have avoided tragedy, Brathwaite implies, had he accepted the affection of an Alexis or Damon. Narcissus's effeminate vanity perilously removes him from the common circuits of same-sex evaluation and socialization.

Whereas Brathwaite portrays Narcissus's disastrous avoidance of same-sex relations, Thomas Edwards's poem *Narcissus* (1595) shows how Narcissus's effeminate self-love derails his participation in heteroerotic relations. Edwards represents Narcissus, who is as "nice as any she alive," as feminine in his pride (39). Although Narcissus scorns his female suitors, he accepts their gifts, which baubles ultimately complete his transformation into a state of womanish vanity:

> I took the Jewels which faire Ladies sent me,
> And manie pretie toies, which to advance
> My future bane, unwillingly they meant me,
> Their whole attire and choice suites not content me;
>   But like a lover glad of each new toy,
>   So I a woman turned from a boy.
>
> Which once perform'd, how farre did I exceed
> Those stately dames, in gesture, modest action,
> Coy lookes, deep smiles, faining heroique deeds,
> To bring them all under my owne subjection,
> For as a woman tired in affection,
>   Some new disport neare thought on is requir'd,
>   So now I long'd to walke to be admir'd. (48)

Once transformed into a "woman," Narcissus takes a seemingly homoerotic pleasure in the company of other women: "thus we like to wanton wenches were, / In severall sports best pleasing and delightfull" (49).[13]

Consequently, when Narcissus spies his image in the water he mistakes it for the face of an actual woman.

In an astute analysis of Edwards's poem, Jonathan Gil Harris observes that the ostensibly "heterosexual" attraction Narcissus feels for the female figure in the water would be more accurately described as homoerotic, since "its origin and object [are] disclosed as male": Narcissus actually desires himself ("Narcissus" 414). Concluding that what generally passes for male heterosexual desire might be fundamentally motivated by male homosocial, homoerotic, or narcissistic energies, Harris fails to account for the importance of *female* homoerotic desire in the poem's climactic scene. Discovering his error, Narcissus chastises himself for a double absurdity, for not only has he become a woman, he has become a woman homoerotically attracted to her own image:

> Fie wanton, fie, know'st not thou art a boy,
> Or hath a womans weeds, thee sinful elfe,
> Made wilfull like themselves, or how growen coy?
>   Wer't thou a woman, this is but a shaddo,
>   And seldome do their sex themselves undo. (59)

Edwards's poem seems concerned less to expose male heteroerotic desire as fundamentally homoerotic than to explore a common cultural fantasy about the susceptibility of manhood to various forms of emasculation. Whatever the truth of the claim that women seldom "undo" (i.e., sexually ruin) other women, the poem aims to demonstrate how effectively women can undo a boy who succumbs to conventionally "effeminate" behaviors.

Finally, in *Narcissus, A Twelfe Night Merriment*, performed at Oxford in 1602, the Narcissus myth is mined for the comic potential of scenes of disorderly homoerotic and heteroerotic courtship. The confusion begins when two rustic men, overcome by Narcissus's beauty, incompetently address him in the language of a Petrarchan blazon: "O thou whose cheeks are like the skye so blewe, / Whose nose is rubye, of the sunnlike hue" (341–42). Jonathan Sawday has described the blazon as a courtly homosocial competition in which the "female body may have been the circulating token, but it was male desire which valorized the currency" (192). An anomalously gendered "token," Narcissus fails to understand his position within a male circuit of exchange:

> Nor sunne, nor moone, nor twinkling starre in skye,
> Nor god, nor goddesse, nor yet nimphe am I,

And though my sweete face bee sett out with rubye,
You misse your marke, I am a man as you bee. (354–57)

Undeterred, his suitors retort that like will to like: "A man thou art, Narcisse, &
soe are wee, / Then love thou us againe as wee love thee" (366–67). The rustic
men's seduction is absurdly ineffective because it burlesques the status and gender
conventions of elevated courtship rhetoric. Here and elsewhere, the play generates
"merriment" from incongruous and inept seductions, culminating in Narcissus's
futile wooing of the "delicate pretty youth" he spies in the water (719).

In *Cynthia's Revels*, Jonson presents the moral, sexual, and social transgressions associated with Narcissus through two distinct generic modes: Echo's
opening monologue to the absent Narcissus; and, subsequently, the actions of
the courtiers and ladies who drink from the Fountain of Self-Love. For Echo's
monologue, Jonson draws heavily on the moralizing interpretations of narcissism as delusional self-regard while allowing for the wider social, economic,
and political applications of narcissism that inform the play's depiction of
courtiership.[14] Echo laments that

> self-love never yet could look on truth
> But with bleared beams; sleek flattery and she
> Are twin-born sisters, and so mix their eyes
> As if you sever one, the other dies. (1.2.36–39)

Affiliating self-love with the quintessential courtly vice of flattery, Echo's critique clearly applies to politics as well as epistemology. Her complaint also
touches on the economic implications of self-consuming narcissism. Apostro-
phizing Narcissus, Echo recalls that he

> with starved and covetous ignorance,
> Pined in continual eyeing that bright gem,
> The glance whereof to others had been more
> Than to thy famished mind the wide world's store:
> 'So wretched is it to be merely rich'.
> Witness thy youth's dear sweets, here spent untasted,
> Like a fair taper with his own flame wasted. (1.2.47–53)

Echo's accusation of miserliness seems to contradict the Induction's account
of Narcissus as a "pretty foolish gentleman [who] melted himself away"

Figure 14. An emblem of pride, from Stephen Batman, *A christall glasse of christian reformation* (1569). By permission of the Folger Shakespeare Library.

(45), a likely allusion to the much-noted phenomenon of gentlemen frittering away their estates through extravagant expenditure (Haynes 51–68). Hoarding and prodigality, however, can both be understood as unproductive financial practices that misrecognize the function of exchange within a larger economy. As Echo complains, Narcissus wastefully "spent" the "sweets" of his beauty instead of allowing them to be productively consumed by others.

Echo's critique might be understood as a more lyrical rendering of the satire against pride in Stephen Batman's *A christall glasse of christian reformation* (1569). Batman's emblem of "Pride" associates inflated self-worth with the rejection of social obligations (see Figure 14). The illustration features a fashionably dressed courtier scorning a beggar, and the "Signification" beneath the illustration identifies the "rich man" as "a proude man covetous, such a one as careth for no poore man, but for such as hym lyketh (to many such are not good in a common wealth)" (sig. H4r). Batman's economic critique of pride strikingly cites the danger to the commonwealth of too many wealthy narcissists, who care for other men according to personal likes, not according to a principle of universal Christian charity.

In sum, Echo's complaint accords with traditional commentaries on the disastrous social, political, and economic consequences of self-love. Narcissism isolates and alienates: others see what the narcissist cannot (Whitney); narcissists avoid public life (Sandys); narcissists keep from others what they possess in abundance, whether their beauty's "dear sweets" (Jonson), or their money (Batman). Even before the courtiers arrive on stage in *Cynthia's Revels*, Echo's complaint prepares us to evaluate their behavior through the logics of misrecognition, privation, and disconnection.

What Echo's complaint does not convey, however, is the function of narcissism as a mediator of social relationships in a courtly milieu. In this emphasis the play resembles those contemporary verse and dramatic treatments of the Narcissus myth that explore how effeminately self-regarding behaviors generate social conflict by thwarting bonds of affection and erotic attraction. The first of these conflicts in *Cynthia's Revels* arises when Amorphus accosts Echo, who, having completed her monologue, has reverted to her reduced linguistic capacities. Offended by the apparent rudeness of Echo's clipped replies and hasty departure, Amorphus drinks from the Fountain of Self-Love and immediately delivers an elaborate self-portrait defending his excellent qualities:

> If my behaviours had been of a cheap or customary garb; my accent
> or phrase vulgar; my garments trite; my countenance illiterate; or
> unpractised in the encounter of a beautiful and brave-attired piece;
> then I might, with some change of colour, have suspected my faculties:
> but, knowing myself an essence so sublimated and refined by travel;
> of so studied and well exercised a gesture; so alone in fashion; able
> to tender the face of any statesman living; and to speak the mere

extraction of language; one that hath now made the sixth return upon venture; and was your first that ever enriched his country with the true laws of the duello; whose optics have drunk the spirit of beauty in some eight score and eighteen princes' courts where I have resided and been there fortunate in the amours of three hundred forty and five ladies, all nobly, if not princely descended, whose names I have in catalogue; to conclude, in all so happy as even admiration herself doth seem to fasten her kisses upon me: certes, I do neither see, nor feel, nor taste, nor savour the least steam or fume of a reason that should invite this foolish fastidious nymph so peevishly to abandon me. (1.3.23–41)

The remarkably accretive syntax of this sentence both manifests and generates narcissism by pulling its speaker deeper and deeper into solipsistic reflection. Like Sandys's image of Narcissus fixated on his reflection while the world heaves violently around him, Amorphus performs "mimic tricks" of self-regard as if he "practised in a pasteboard case, / And no one saw the motion but the motion" (1.5.58, 60–61). The narcissist behaves as if he were a puppet performing alone and unseen in his own little theater, when, from the perspective of a discerning spectator such as Crites, he disrupts orderly social relations by aggressively "woo[ing]" vice, with her "loathed and leprous face" (1.5.47, 50).

Before going on to examine the ideological work done by the type of the narcissistic courtier in *Cynthia's Revels*, it is important to acknowledge the difficulty of precisely defining the courtier's role in Jonson's culture. In Elizabethan England, the "court" was not so much a distinct group of persons as a fluid social and political network comprised of office-holders, royal household members, elite visitors, marginal aspirants, and hopeful patronage-seekers. As David Starkey observes, "The court was not only a machine of government; it was also a machinery for conspicuous expenditure" (2), and as such it was difficult in practice to distinguish "statesmen" from those "courtiers" who served a more ceremonial role at court or who came there to seek patronage from the monarch or members of the nobility.[15] No less than "courtiers," Starkey adds, "councillors" were "aspirants for power" who sought the monarch's favor (13). In his *Characterismi*, Francis Lenton describes the "Gallant Courtier" as "the outside of a Statesman a little more gaily trimd up, and as he is repleat with internall indowments, so this is compleat with externall Complement" (sig. B2v). Although Lenton distinguishes the statesman's internal qualities from the courtier's external qualities, he also implies that, aside from the courtier's gayer trimmings, they might be difficult to tell apart.

Courtiers were also members of a social network beyond the immediate vicinity of the monarch. In his analysis of the social tropes of Elizabethan courtesy theory, Frank Whigham usefully reminds us that although patronage centered on the monarch, it was not limited to the monarch. "Most actions of self-presentation," Whigham writes, "flowed between individuals of *adjacent* ranks, seeking and awarding patronage at all levels of intimacy and degrees of distance from the throne at the heart of the court" (12). Elaborating on the fluid social, political, and spatial boundaries of the court, Malcolm Smuts explains that many "English peers and gentlemen normally lived away from the court but still paid it occasional visits and maintained relations with a court patron" (4). Moreover, "No firm social or geographic boundaries ever separated the court from other fashionable milieus in the capital, since court society was never contained within a single building or confined to a narrow coterie" (55). In sum, Starkey, Whigham, and Smuts all describe a court milieu that accommodated occasional, marginal, and unattached "courtiers": those whom Jonson's Cynthia rather too absolutely identifies as "imposters."

The problem of defining the "courtier" in *Cynthia's Revels* becomes evident in the way that many characters not explicitly identified in the text as courtiers nevertheless participate in courtly practices. In the Induction, the four primary male characters are identified and their Greek and Latin names translated into English: "Hedon, the voluptuous, and a courtier"; "Anaides, or the impudent, a gallant"; "Amorphus, or the deformed; a traveller"; and "a citizen's heir, Asotus, or the prodigal" (48–57). Although all four characters are associated with the court, only Hedon is explicitly identified as a "courtier." Unlike the powerful minister-favorites discussed in Chapter 6, however, Hedon is a courtier with no political office and no access to the monarch. Consequently, he is not represented as a politician who might be accused of typical abuses such as taking bribes, accumulating monopolies, engrossing grain, or promoting faction.[16] Instead, Hedon seems to be a "marginal courtier" with "no formal connection" to the royal household or government (Smuts 56). Posing as Hedon's page, Mercury explains that his master is "a courtier . . . during this open time of revels, and would be longer, but that his means are to leave him shortly after" (2.1.25–27). Although Hedon's status as courtier seems dependent on his limited finances, Mercury goes on to provide an elaborately detailed portrait of his courtly "graces":

> He doth, besides me, keep a barber, and a monkey: he has a rich
> wrought waistcoat to entertain his visitants in, with a cap almost
> suitable. His curtains and bedding are thought to be his own: his
> bathing-tub is not suspected. He loves to have a fencer, a pedant, and
> a musician seen in his lodging a-mornings. . . . himself is a rhymer,
> and that's a thought better than a poet. He is not lightly within
> to his mercer, no, though he come when he takes physic, which is
> commonly after his play. He beats a tailor very well, but a stocking-
> seller admirably: and so consequently anyone he owes money to, that
> dares not resist him. He never makes general invitement, but against
> the publishing of a new suit, marry then you shall have more drawn
> to his lodging than come to the launching of some three ships; . . .
> He's thought a very necessary perfume for the presence, and for that
> only cause welcome thither: six milliners' shops afford you not the like
> scent. He courts ladies with how many great horse he hath rid that
> morning, or how oft he hath done the whole, or the half pomado in a
> seven-night before. (2.1.33–53)

As this embedded version of the prose character genre indicates, Hedon is a social type ridiculed for his accumulation of servants, clothes, furnishings, smells, and social gestures. Nonetheless, if only for his fine smell, he is welcome to the presence. Likewise, Crites later scorns Hedon as "a light voluptuous reveller," thus diminishing his contribution to the court even as he associates that contribution with the titular revels commanded by Cynthia (3.3.25).

Companions of courtiers, Anaides and Asotus are not courtiers themselves. Hedon's friend Anaides, explains Mercury, is no courtier despite possessing "two essential parts of the courtier, pride and ignorance; marry, the rest come somewhat after the ordinary gallant" (2.2.71–73).[17] Unlike the more refined Hedon, Anaides is an impudent gallant who presides over the "ordinary" or tavern. Asotus, the son of a citizen, enjoys wealth but not status. He attaches himself to Amorphus to gain access to courtly pleasures, but fails to make the transition from the humbler urban idiom of his upbringing to the refined mannerisms of the court.

Although identified as a "traveller," Amorphus is associated with the figure of the courtier in several ways. According to Cupid, he always walks with his clove and picktooth, just like those "perfumed courtiers" who carry "casting-bottles, picktooths, and shuttlecocks" (1.1.62–63). Declaring himself a "master of the noble and subtle science of courtship" (5.3.79–80), Amorphus adopts Asotus as his protégé. According to Crites, Amorphus's courtiership is superficial but deeply informed. Such a "mincing marmoset" (22) as Amorphus

> Hath travelled to make legs, and seen the cringe
> Of several courts and courtiers; knows the time
> Of giving titles and of taking walls;
> Hath read the court commonplaces; made them his:
> Studied the grammar of state, and all the rules
> Each formal usher in that politic school
> Can teach a man. (3.4.29–35)

To the degree that learning the arts of courtliness promoted by courtesy theorists makes one a "courtier," Amorphus is a courtier, and though he is presumably lying when he boasts of having resided in the courts of 178 princes (1.3.34), he clearly has access to Cynthia's court. Taking advantage of this access, Amorphus escorts Asotus to a private room "in regard of the presence" (2.3.1), and promises to introduce his friend to "gallants" such as Hedon and Anaides (1.4.155).

Early on in his courtly instruction of Asotus, Amorphus delivers a lesson on types of faces that perfectly illustrates the relationship between bodily deformity and social deformity in Jonson's conception of the narcissistic courtier. Amorphus endeavors to disabuse Asotus of the notion that the face is "the index of the mind" (2.3.13). In early modern Europe, the belief that the face revealed the mind was grounded in the scientific theory of the humoral body. Physiognomic books interpreted particular facial features as the index of particular mental and emotional dispositions. For instance, Thomas Hill's 1571 translation of Bartolommeo Cocles's 1504 treatise on physiognomy includes the observation that the "face appeering leane, doth argue a carefull person, and sometimes a betrayer," whereas the very fleshy face "doth indicate a sluggishnesse of actions, foolishnesse, and the great desire of covating" (85r–85v; see Figure 15). Amorphus associates facial types not with innate mental and emotional dispositions but with social types that can be identified and imitated. Although Amorphus identifies himself as a traveler and courtier, he holds that a truly "politic creature" will manipulate the face in order to pass as any "species of persons, as your merchant, your scholar, your soldier, your lawyer, courtier, etc." (2.3.13–16):

Figure 15. Two facial types, from Bartolommeo Cocles, *The Contemplation of Mankinde* (1571). By permission of the Folger Shakespeare Library.

> First, for your merchant, or city-face, 'tis thus, a dull plodding face,
> still looking in a direct line, forward: there is no great matter in this
> face. Then have you your student's, or academic face, which is here, an
> honest, simple, and methodical face: but somewhat more spread than
> the former. The third is your soldier's face, a menacing and astounding
> face, that looks broad and big: the grace of this face consisteth much in
> a beard. The anti-face to this is your lawyer's face, a contracted, subtle,
> and intricate face, full of quirks and turnings, a labyrinthean face, now
> angularly, now circularly, every way aspected. (2.3.19–28)

Amorphus goes on to anatomize the statist's face, as well as three sorts of
courtier's face: the "elementary, practic, and theoric" (2.3.33–34).

Demonstrating his ability to "mince" various professions into their characteristic faces, Amorphus exposes his true nature to Mercury and Cupid, who
are spying on his private lesson with Asotus. Mercury scoffs that Amorphus
is "so made out of the mixture and shreds of forms that himself is truly deformed" (2.3.77–78). Amorphus does not add up: the multiple languages, fashions, skills, and objects he amasses through his travels and attendance at court
have nothing to stick to. For instance, like a "perfumed courtier," Amorphus

Figure 16. <a, b> Silver casting bottle (English, 1540–1550) and enameled gold toothpick (English, ca. 1620). Photo © Victoria and Albert Museum, London.

carries typical accoutrements such as "casting-bottles" (used to store perfume) and "picktooths" (Figure 16), but Crites recognizes in these objects only the "painted beauties" and "airy forms" of vanity (1.1.62–63, 1.5.21–22, 26). Rather than productively ornamenting Amorphus's body and thereby declaring his high social status, these objects function as prosthetic parts that gender his body as feminine (Fisher, *Materializing* 24–32). Similarly, Amorphus's attempts at self-expression fail to manifest an authoritative masculine subjectivity. Mercury comments, "his face is another volume of essays. . . . He speaks all cream, skimmed, and more affected than a dozen of waiting women" (2.3.80–82). A monstrous hybrid of the excessive—he speaks "all cream," like "a dozen"

Figure 17. Deformed man, from Stephen Batman, *The new arival of the three gracis, into Anglia* (1580). © The British Library Board. Shelfmark C.57.c.8, f.iv.

women—and of the deficient—the cream is "skimmed," the women only ser-vants—Amorphus becomes difficult to visualize as an actual stage character.

If we were to picture Amorphus as an emblem of deformity, however, he might look something like the monstrous gallant portrayed in Stephen Batman's moral treatise *The new arival of the three gracis into Anglia* (1580) (Figure 17). An explanatory legend underneath the poem allegorically minces the monster's body, rendering it as a composite of vices: "the long schull be-tokeneth Craftie imagination: The pleasant countenaunce, Flattery: The long necke, Excesse in eating and drinking: The right arme being shorter then the left, betokeneth small Devotion: The bagge of money Covetousnesse: The left arme, Wilfulnesse: The sworde Crueltie: The straunge disguising in apparell, Pride" (sig. F1v). Like Amorphus, this morally "deformed" gentleman is both excessive (in gluttony, craft, and pride) and deficient (in faith and generosity). Moreover, the prophetic verse preceding the image associates this figure of monstrous gentility with a threat to English national identity. The proph-ecy warns that a monster will appear when "divers fashions in apparell are worne," and when "Glandene" [England] "will be the whole world it selfe, / A Spaniarde, Italian, French, Flemmishe and else" (sig. F1r).[18] Like Batman's multinational monster, Jonson's Amorphus is a traveler who has been served "Greek wine" from "the hand of an Italian antiquary" (1.4.13, 23–24); eats "an-chovies, macaroni, bovoli, fagioli, and caviare" (2.3.93–94); and speaks "choice remnant[s]" of Spanish, "parcels of French," and "some pretty commodity of Italian" (1.4.70, 3.5.80). Amorphus boasts that his hat was a gift from "a great man in Russia" and that he has "enriched his country with the true laws of the duello" (1.4.172, 1.3.32–33), presumably from Italy or Spain.

Even closer in spirit to Jonson's satiric mincing of Amorphus is the repre-sentation of a gallant's funeral as a parade of clothes in *The Funeral Obseques of Sir All-in-New-Fashions*, a print issued around 1630 (Figure 18). As Malcolm Jones explains, this engraving, which closely copies a German print of 1629, does not accurately depict contemporary English fashion. Nonetheless, the English engraver translates certain details into a London idiom, such as speci-fying that the gallant's clothes can be viewed as trophies in "Hounsditch" or "Long Lane."[19] Like Jonson's portrait of Amorphus, the image of the funeral procession minces the gallant into his constituent parts, suggesting that his identity comprises no more than the "mixture and shreds of forms" (2.3.77). With these fashionable "toyes" from "forreyne Lands," Sir All-in-New-Fash-ions "used to swagger" proudly. The verse punctures the gallant's inflated social and economic worth first by claiming and then by denying that his tailors,

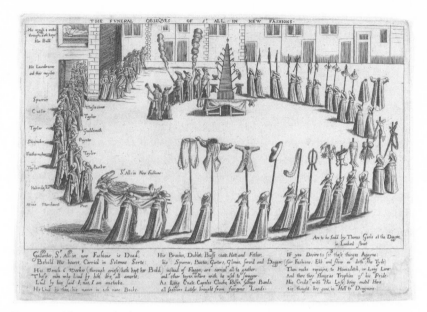

Figure 18. *The Funeral Obseques of Sir All-in-New-Fashions* (1630). Ashmolean Museum, University of Oxford.

spurrier, feathermaker, haberdasher, and other tradesmen "Livd by him." Instead, we discover, Sir All-in-New-Fashions "Livd by them: his names in each mans Booke." Indebted to the men who created his minced forms, the gallant truly lived only as figures in their account books.

As these satiric portraits of monstrous gallants make particularly evident, the narcissistic courtier resembles the mythical Narcissus in his transgressive social behaviors but not in his physical beauty. Although narcissistic ladies do not escape censure in *Cynthia's Revels*, Jonson reserves the "deformed" name of Amorphus for a male character, and male bodies are especially noted for physical deformity throughout the play. Crites's satiric catalog of courtiers ridicules various male "forms" (3.4.10): the "proud and spangled sir, / That looks three handfuls higher than his foretop" (12–13), the "mincing marmoset / Made all of clothes and face" (22–23), the "subtle Proteus" who "Can change and vary with all forms he sees" (42–43), the "neophyte glazing of his face, / Pruning his clothes, perfuming of his hair" (55–56), and so on. The inappropriate display of the male body in *Cynthia's Revels* epitomizes the follies of courtly narcissism. What happens, then, when these deformed male bodies get together? What is the relationship between courtly narcissism and male-male desire in *Cynthia's Revels*?

Adopting Rebecca Bach's notion of the "collective masculinity" at work in Shakespeare's history plays, we can better understand how courtly effeminacy might signify as a violation of authorized, and potentially homoerotic, same-sex relations. According to Bach, whereas masculinity in the history plays is manifested through the formation of collective, loving bonds among men at court or on the battlefield, effeminacy is manifested as an orientation toward "personal advancement at the expense of service ties, ties to God, and kinship links between men" (221).[20] In Shakespeare's *1 Henry IV*, Hotspur's report of a battlefield confrontation between himself and the "neat and trimly dressed" lord acting as the king's messenger associates narcissistic effeminacy with the violation of masculine military fellowship (1.3.32). Using "holiday and lady terms" on the battlefield, the lord refers to the soldiers who have died in the king's service as "slovenly unhandsome corpse[s]" that offend his sensibilities (1.3.43, 45). The lord never appears on stage; that he speaks only through Hotspur's mocking ventriloquism foregrounds Hotspur's political motives for censuring King Henry's courtly representative. Hotspur's ridicule of the effeminate lord can be interpreted as a lesson to the king about his own "effeminate" ingratitude toward the Percies, who fight on his behalf. Just as the lord worries only about his own safety and comfort, so King Henry, Hotspur implies, maintains his political security at the expense of the loving bonds that should link the sovereign to his peers.

Although in *Cynthia's Revels* the political stakes are not as high as they are in *1 Henry IV*, Amorphus's narcissistic friendship with Asotus violates the ethos of a "collective masculinity" that would strengthen the moral and social foundations of a well-governed court. Having drunk from the Fountain of Self-love and grown "dotingly enamoured" of himself, Amorphus admires the reflection of himself he sees in Asotus, a "pretty formal young gallant" (1.2.104, 1.4.30). Flattering Asotus, Amorphus perverts the Renaissance convention of friendship as a virtuous and loving bond between social equals: "I think I shall affect you, sir. . . . your sweet disposition to travel, I assure you, hath made you another myself in mine eye, and struck me enamoured of your beauties" (1.4.111, 119–21).[21] Amorphus's language recalls the "effeminate" affectations of speech criticized by Thomas Wright in *The passions of the minde in generall* (1604): "I cannot moreover excuse most of these persons from certaine effeminat affections, because such speeches especially were invented to tickle women and gallants eares, that by alluring wordes they might win the credit of wittie, and so beguile the weaker mindes" (112). Evidently tickled by Amorphus's alluring words, Asotus declares his new friend "ravishing" (1.4.57).[22]

Amorphus and Asotus seal their acquaintance not, as Renaissance friendship theory requires, through the mutual and properly "masculine" sharing of minds, souls, and bodies, but through the unequal exchange of hats. While Crites derides the ridiculous, erotically charged, intimacies of this "brace of butterflies" (1.4.67), Amorphus manipulates Asotus into giving up his fashionable new beaver hat[23]:

> **Amorphus:** Good faith, this hat hath possessed mine eye exceedingly; 'tis so pretty and fantastic: what? Is't a beaver?
>
> **Asotus:** Aye, sir, I'll assure you 'tis a beaver, it cost me eight crowns but this morning.
>
> **Amorphus:** After your French account?
>
> **Asotus:** Yes, sir.
>
> **Crites:** [*Aside*] And so near his head? Beshrew me, dangerous.
>
> **Amorphus:** A very pretty fashion, believe me, and a most novel kind of trim: your band is conceited too!
>
> **Asotus:** Sir, it is all at your service.
>
> **Amorphus:** Oh, pardon me.
>
> **Asotus:** I beseech you, sir, if you please to wear it, you shall do me a most infinite grace.
>
> **Crites:** [*Aside*] 'Slight, will he be praised out of his clothes?
>
> **Asotus:** By heaven, sir, I do not offer it you after the Italian manner; I would you should conceive so of me.
>
> **Amorphus:** Sir, I shall fear to appear rude in denying your courtesies, especially being invited by so proper a distinction: may I pray your name, sir?
>
> **Asotus:** My name is Asotus, sir.
>
> **Amorphus:** I take your love, gentle Asotus, but let me win you to receive this, in exchange— [*They exchange hats*]
>
> **Crites:** [*Aside*] Heart, they'll change doublets anon.
>
> **Amorphus:** And, from this time, esteem yourself in the first rank, of those few whom I profess to love. What make you in company of this scholar, here? I will bring you known to gallants, as Anaides of the ordinary, Hedon the courtier, and others whose society shall render you graced and respected: this is a trivial fellow, too mean, too cheap, too coarse for you to converse with.
>
> **Asotus:** [*Aside*] 'Slid, this is not worth a crown, and mine cost me eight but this morning.

Crites: [*Aside*] I looked when he would repent him, he has begun to be sad a good while.

Amorphus: Sir, shall I say to you for that hat? Be not so sad, be not so sad: it is a relic I could not so easily have departed with but as the hieroglyphic of my affection. (1.4.130–65)

In exchange for Asotus's costly hat, Amorphus offers his "affection" and access to gallants. Amorphus cannot, of course, fulfill his promise to render Asotus "graced and respected" at court, since only Cynthia or her deputies can vouchsafe grace and respect to a courtly aspirant. Flattery, ambition, and an illegitimate desire to appropriate Cynthia's political prerogative mark the friendship between Amorphus and Asotus as an effeminate rather than a masculine same-sex bond.[24]

The narcissistic courtiers of *Cynthia's Revels* fare no better at the decorous management of heteroerotic courtships than they do at homoerotic courtships. Hedon practices oaths, compliments, salutations, prophecies, and riddles to be delivered to his mistress "in the presence," where others can approve his wit and invention (2.2.12). Cataloguing the "prodigies of men" he has observed at court, Crites describes one fetishistic courtier who "Plays with his mistress' paps, salutes her pumps, / Adores her hems, her skirts, her knots, her curls, / Will spend his patrimony for a garter, / Or the least feather in her bounteous fan" (3.4.21, 67–70). In the next scene, Amorphus teaches Asotus a highly artificial method for courting his lady:

First, you present yourself, thus: and spying her, you fall off, and walk some two turns; in which time, it is to be supposed, your passion hath sufficiently whited your face: then, stifling a sigh or two, and closing your lips, with a trembling boldness and bold terror, you advance yourself forward. (3.5.6–11)

Amorphus's advice amounts to an acting lesson in playing the courtly lover, and so it comes as little surprise when Amorphus offers to take the part of the lady so that Asotus might practice his lines. This metadramatic turn would have reminded Jonson's audience that all the women in *Cynthia's Revels* were played by boys, and that any such courtship between a gallant and a lady in the play potentially carried a homoerotic charge. When Amorphus praises Asotus's courtship style by gushing, "Why, this was ravishing" (3.5.119), he also evokes the homoerotic banter of the boy player in the

Induction, who jokingly asks if his fellow players are about to "ravish" or "rape" him (84, 87).

These metadramatic gestures underscore Jonson's use of *Cynthia's Revels* to display his own credentials as a proper servant of the court, and as such prompt us to ask what is finally at stake in his ridicule of the courtly narcissist. Certainly, an increased preoccupation with refined courtly manners has been identified as one effect of what Norbert Elias has named "the civilizing process" in Renaissance Europe. In an analysis of the early modern courtesy literature that contributed to this process in England, Anna Bryson observes a new emphasis on describing manners "as dramatic 'representations' of personal qualities," so that the body became "a text from which good or bad character could be read" (108, 100). Gentlemen, in particular, were expected to "exemplify and direct the manners of society," displaying the civility that would "promote social harmony and the overall peace of the community" (70). Narcissism was clearly incompatible with the promotion of social harmony based on good manners. Rather, Bryson explains, early modern courtesy texts insisted that the civil gentleman "must be constantly aware of the reactions of others and must anticipate their view of himself. He must scrutinize himself in the constant awareness of a social audience whom he may offend" (111). To be sure, in many of his writings Jonson is greatly concerned with the relationship between manners and morals, and his plays are "full of studies of social gestures, the small arts of everyday life" (Haynes 46).

From a more narrowly political perspective, *Cynthia's Revels* addresses the role of the courtier as the representative of the nation's rulers, one who circulates as a visible sign of the social and economic interests being served at the political center of the kingdom. The proliferation of "male deformities" at Cynthia's court directly engages early modern discourses regarding the public comportment and sartorial display appropriate to the courtier (5.11.113).[25] In an analysis of Renaissance courtly ideology, David Kuchta argues that in the "sartorial regime" of the early modern court "the act of self-display was not itself given a gender" (26). The courtier's gendering as "masculine" or "effeminate" was instead determined by the degree of correspondence between the wearer and his clothes:

> In this hierarchy, dress was meant to make one's social position visible by a one-to-one correspondence between one's rank and one's purse, by the analogy between one's internal worth and external wealth. . . . In the

old sartorial regime, rich clothing proclaimed gentility, represented it, manifested it, and made it conspicuous. (21, 23)

Displaying a "natural, unaffected attitude" to sumptuous dress, the masculine courtier complied with a royalist ideology in which "the crown determined what clothing meant, who was allowed to wear what, and how it could be purchased" (Kuchta 25, 28). Effeminacy was defined as "dressing out of place, as the affected misuse of sartorial signs by those who did not merit their noble significance" (21).[26] Effeminate courtiers undermined the legitimate "aristocratic aesthetic of conspicuous consumption" that was a source of the court's ideological power (27).

In the dedication to the court that he included in the Folio version of *Cynthia's Revels*, Jonson articulates through the conventional image of the fountain the ideal correspondence between the virtuous courtier and the virtuous court:

> Thou art a bountiful and brave spring: and waterest all the noble
> plants of this island. In thee, the whole kingdom dresseth itself,
> and is ambitious to use thee as her glass. Beware, then, thou render
> men's figures truly, and teach them no less to hate their deformities
> than to love their forms: for, to grace there should come reverence;
> and no man can call that lovely which is not also venerable. It is
> not powdering, perfuming, and every day smelling of the tailor that
> converteth to a beautiful object: but a mind, shining through any
> suit, which needs no false light either of riches, or honours to help it.
> (Dedication 1–10)

At once a "bountiful and brave spring" for the nobility and a "glass" for the kingdom, the court should present only truly virtuous "figures" as models of behavior.[27] The true courtier appears "lovely" not because of a rich "suit" but because of the virtuous mind that shines through his graceful "form." By contrast, those courtiers obsessed with powdering and perfuming are "deformities," their riches and titles comparable to the "false light" a merchant uses to mask defective goods. To avoid becoming a "Spring of Self-love," the court must reject such deformities (Dedication 13).

The difficulty with this imperative, as Mercury recognizes, is in making apparent to all observers the difference between those courtiers who do and those who do not "represent" the fountain of virtue at the center of the kingdom. Mercury reassures Crites that when the unworthy courtiers are finally exposed and humiliated, those courtiers who know themselves to be virtuous will find their merit affirmed by this spectacle of punishment:

> The better race in Court
> That have the true nobility, called virtue,
> Will apprehend it as a grateful right
> Done to their separate merit: and approve
> The fit rebuke of so ridiculous heads,
> Who with their apish customs and forced garbs
> Would bring the name of courtier in contempt,
> Did it not live unblemished in some few
> Whom equal Jove hath loved, and Phoebus formed
> Of better metal, and in better mould. (5.1.30–39)

But how are legitimate and illegitimate courtiers to be recognized from the outside? If courtiers who flaunt their "apish customs and forced garbs" reveal themselves to be illegitimate—and even this problematically assumes that one can easily distinguish between courtly manners that are "ridiculous" and those that are just courtly—then legitimate courtiers can presumably be recognized by the absence of such affectations. It is much easier, however, to spot "deformities" than to apprehend ideal "forms": particularly abstract "forms" such as the "better race" and "true nobility" that inhere in virtuous courtiers. Moreover, if Mercury is able to identify the truly noble as those whom Jove has loved and Apollo has formed of "better metal," how are mere mortals supposed to detect the presence of such divine gifts?

Even assuming that the deformed and "unblemished" courtiers can tell each other apart, the noble few are burdened with safeguarding the virtue of the court from the relentless influx of undeserving upstarts:

> And good men, like the sea, should still maintain
> Their noble taste, in midst of all fresh humours
> That flow about them to corrupt their streams,
> Bearing no season, much less salt of goodness.   (5.1.13–16)

According to this elaborate conceit, good courtiers must maintain their "noble taste," or the "'civil' virtue" on which "the 'civil' order of the whole polity depended" (Bryson 69), in the face of "fresh humours," or faddish manners, just as the sea maintains its saltiness against the influx of freshwater streams. By exaggerating the deformity of courtiers such as Amorphus and Hedon, and contrasting them to the ascetic scholar Crites, Jonson makes this ongoing work of filtration seem a lot simpler than even his own language of fluid infiltration suggests. Discussing Jonson's similar critique of effeminate social climbers in *Every Man out of His Humour*, Gail Kern Paster argues that sartorial "affectation is not merely narcissism in a socially conspicuous form—indeed narcissism *for the sake of* conspicuous form—but colossal misrecognition of one's place in the world" (*Humoring* 198).[28] But is one's place in the world—or, as in *Cynthia's Revels*, one's place in the court—always so self-evident or so inert? How does an Amorphus "recognize" his proper place in a social milieu that functions precisely through ever-shifting negotiations over favor, access, and value?

The most evident symptom of this intractable epistemological problem in *Cynthia's Revels* is the masque that resolves the plot by humiliating Amorphus and his associates, even as it further dissolves the distinctions between worthy and unworthy courtiers. Significantly, Jonson does not employ here the antithetical structure of a false anti-masque followed by the true masque, as he would in the Jacobean masques he produced later in his career. In *The Masque of Queens*, for instance, a disorderly coven of witches, played by professional male actors, gives way to the true masque of queens, played by the queen and her ladies. In *Cynthia's Revels*, each of the courtiers and ladies performs in the masque "disguised" as an emblematic virtue that translates his or her dominant flaw into a positive register. Hedon, Amorphus, Anaides, and Asotus portray the "four cardinal properties without which the body of compliment moveth not" (5.9.7–8). For instance, Hedon, the voluptuous courtier, portrays Eupathes ("fine humour"), a "gallant that, without excess, can make use of superfluity: go richly in embroideries, jewels, and what not, without vanity, and fare delicately without gluttony" (5.9.26–28). The "deformed" Amorphus portrays "the commendably-fashioned gallant," Eucosmos ("elegant"), whose "courtly habit is the grace of the presence, and delight of the surveying eye" (5.9.18–19). These allegorical idealizations demand an extremely fine discrimination of the "surveying eye" to tell the difference between voluptuous "excess" and making virtuous "use of superfluity." The same insistence on fine discriminations of taste informs Thomas Gainsford's character sketch of the Courtier in *The Rich Cabinet* (1616): "A courtier must needs be hansome in apparell; neither over-garish, nor over-plaine: but orderly comely, and extraordinarily fashionable" (sig. D3r-v). Jonson's staging of this boundary in the doubled persons of Hedon/ Eupathes and Amorphus/Eucosmos foregrounds the dilemma of discerning proper forms from deformations.

Consequently, it appears that only the goddess Cynthia possesses the discernment necessary to reform courtly deformities. When the nymph Arete ("virtue") commands Crites to provide a masque for Cynthia's pleasure, Crites despairs at organizing the narcissistic courtiers into the concord that the masque form requires. Pointing out Crites's error, Arete affirms Cynthia's power to tame eccentricities; moreover, she reassures Crites, most of the masquers, being "either courtiers, or not wholly rude, / Respect of majesty, the place, and presence, / Will keep them within ring" (5.5.23–25). Given the play's relentless mincing of courtly deformity, it is remarkable to learn that Cynthia regards the narcissistic courtiers as fundamentally civilized. Cynthia, in fact, has countenanced the presence of the narcissistic courtiers at her revels as a tactic of reformation:

> holding true intelligence what follies
> Had crept into her palace, she resolved
> Of sports and triumphs, under that pretext
> To have them muster in their pomp and fullness;
> That so she might more strictly, and to root,
> Effect the reformation she intends. (5.5.41–46)

As a sign of the virtue of Cynthia's political authority, the narcissistic courtiers will not be expelled but rather exposed, reformed, and properly "incorporate[d]" into a newly civilized courtly body (5.5.29).

To understand the early modern equation between civil manners and civil order should be to appreciate more fully the serious ideological work Jonson performs by mincing the narcissistic courtier in *Cynthia's Revels*. In early seventeenth-century England, as a rising merchant class was competing with the traditional landed aristocracy for economic, social, and political power, an ideology of civilized courtly manners served to justify the aristocracy's "natural" fitness to rule. Presenting himself as the servant of the true aristocracy, Jonson delegitimizes those ill-mannered courtiers who undercut its representational strategies and thus demystify its exercise of power.

In the very process of reforming courtly deformities, however, Jonson stages for public consumption "the narcissist": not the neurotic persona of psychoanalytic invention but a disorderly sexual type reflecting seventeenth-century anxieties about the power and reputation of the court.[29] Such anxieties are hardly dispelled by the ritual purgation that concludes *Cynthia's Revels*. In a gesture of comic resolution, Amorphus and his fellow narcissists are dismissed from Cynthia's presence, commanded to drink from "the well of knowledge, Helicon," and thus "become / Such as you fain would seem," at which point they may return and serve Cynthia (5.11.153, 155–56). Yet the Fountain of Self-love seems to be a permanent fixture at Cynthia's court, for no mention is made of its destruction or purification. The endurance of the symbolically dominant Fountain of Self-love quietly acknowledges the difficulty of banishing deformation from courtly forms.

Chapter 4

Calling Whore

The Citizen Wife and the Erotics of Open Work

> Her husband's ship lay gravelled
> When hers could hoise up sails;
> Yet she began, like all my foes,
> To call whore first; for so do those—
> A pox of all false tails!
>   —*The Roaring Girl* (4.1.119–23)

In the previous chapter, I examined through Jonson's *Cynthia's Revels* the "social discriminations" brought to bear around definitions of legitimate and illegitimate courtiership in early modern culture. Those discriminations define the illegitimate courtier as a narcissist who displays effeminate speech and manners, rejects socially productive homoerotic and heteroerotic relations, and fails to recognize that a courtier's value derives not from his external accomplishments but from his worthiness to represent the virtue of the truly noble. However, *Cynthia's Revels* betrays ideological fissures in its critique of the narcissistic courtier, I argued, not only because it reveals that differences between legitimate and illegitimate courtiership are very difficult to discern, but also because the play's formal qualities paradoxically seem to imitate the "deformity" the play excoriates. Through his satiric anatomy, Jonson minces the courtier's minced manners; by melding diverse mythical and courtly materials into a hybrid dramatic form, Jonson exposes the hybrid deformities of the courtier's body.

In this chapter, I examine a similar paradox in the production of social discriminations around the sexual legitimacy of urban women's economic labor. Focusing on Middleton and Dekker's *The Roaring Girl*, I argue that the mechanisms of sexual slander that operate to define and discipline the transvestite Moll Cutpurse operate less overtly but perhaps more potently to define and discipline citizen wives who assert authority in erotic and financial affairs. Whereas the play exposes the viciousness and hypocrisy of the more conventional characters who slander Moll, including the wives themselves, it also engages in a form of social discipline by representing working women as wielders of a sexual and economic agency that threatens household credit.

Although feminist and materialist scholarship on London city comedy has illuminated the early modern association between women's sexual and economic agency, in readings of *The Roaring Girl* the play's outsized title character has usually left the citizen wives in the critical shadows.[1] This marginalization of the citizen wives remains constant across the different critical approaches to the play that have emerged since Mary Beth Rose's influential 1984 essay, "Women in Men's Clothing: Apparel and Social Stability in *The Roaring Girl*."[2] With some simplification, it is possible to group scholarship on *The Roaring Girl* into three large areas of concern. Variously influenced by feminist theory, queer theory, and new historicism, many critics writing from the mid–1980s through the mid–1990s examined how *The Roaring Girl* engaged contemporary discourses of gender, sexuality, and marriage.[3] More recent scholarship has discussed the play's representation of a criminal underworld as well as the historical Moll Frith's career as a cutpurse and broker of stolen goods.[4] A third approach has ventured even further beyond the dramatic and historical Molls by analyzing the languages and structures of mercantile exchange, consumption, and credit in the play.[5] Somewhat surprisingly, even these economic critics do not significantly engage with Middleton and Dekker's representation of the citizen wives as participants in an urban economy.[6]

A more complex understanding of the ideological work performed by *The Roaring Girl* around issues of women's sexual and economic agency requires a fuller account of its representation of citizen wives in their roles as shopkeepers, spouses, and rivals with Moll. By participating in the pervasive sexual defamation of Moll, Mistress Openwork and Mistress Gallipot publicize their own legitimacy as chaste and economically productive women. Invested in the values and associational habits of the middling sort, the citizen wives do not recognize a common cause with Moll as women vulnerable to sexual slander.[7] At the same time, to compensate for the decline in status and wealth they suffered by marrying citizens, these gentle-born women risk their reputations as chaste wives by pursuing intimate relationships with gallants. Consequently, even as the play initially distinguishes the citizen wives as more respectable than Moll in terms of birth, profession, traditional gender role, and marital status, it gradually emerges that the wives are no less susceptible than Moll to the disciplinary mechanisms of sexual shaming.

*   *   *

One of the pleasures of reading *The Roaring Girl* is the proliferation of prurient rumors that circulate about Moll's anatomy, morality, and sexual habits. An "astounding number of pejorative terms" are used throughout the play to identify and shame Moll as a "disorderly" woman (McNeill, *Poor* 122).[8] The worst offender, Sir Alexander Wengrave, identifies Moll as a "blazing star" and an "infamous" subject of "discourse in ordinaries and taverns" (1.2.134; 2.2.141–42). Mistress Gallipot observes that "Some will not stick to say she's a man, and some, both man and woman" (2.1.209–10). Although the "two-leaved tongues of slander or of truth / Pronounce Moll loathsome," Sebastian asserts that he will judge her by his own eyes (2.2.10–11). On several occasions Moll defends herself against all those "slanderers" and "foes" who "call whore first," staining her with a "black ill name" (3.1.114, 4.1.121–22, 5.1.342). As Moll reminds her detractors, appearance and reputation do not always correspond to true character: "How many are whores in small ruffs and still looks? / How many chaste whose names fill slander's books?" (5.1.344–45).

On this point, Middleton and Dekker appear to agree with Moll, for the play regularly exposes the malicious motives of the "foul mouth[ed]" detractors who record Moll's name in slander's books (5.1.313). According to Kenneth Gross, in the early modern period slander was usually understood as "the product of a fallen, rebellious will, linked to failures of charity, sinful pride, anger, and despair"; it is often described as "a kind of projection, at once conscious and unconscious" (17). In an urban setting pervaded by the "volatile, diffuse energy of rumor" (Gross 51), Moll serves as a kind of scapegoat onto which her accusers project their own fears, desires, anxieties, and faults.[9] Although Moll bears the burden of overt slander, by the end of the play she also enjoys the satisfaction of seeing her nemesis, Sir Alexander, discredited for having voiced foul opinions of her and shamed for having set "trains of villainy" against her life (5.1.16).

Unlike Moll, the citizen wives in *The Roaring Girl* are not overtly slandered for sexual misconduct, yet they are subject to a more subtle form of sexual defamation that generates a constant aura of suspicion around their activities as shopkeepers and tradeswomen. Social historians Martin Ingram and Laura Gowing have demonstrated that in early modern England calling a woman a "whore" or "quean" was the most frequent catalyst of litigation for sexual slander (Ingram 302; Gowing, *Domestic* 62–67). Yet the imperative to maintain an honest reputation meant that even a generally worded glance against a woman's chastity could have led to legal action. Moreover, the spreading of "slanderous tales and rumours" could be particularly insidious in a society in which gossip served "as an informal means of social control" (Ingram 305). Regarding the definitional slipperiness of slander, M. Lindsay Kaplan emphasizes the "incredible instability of the categories of legitimate and illegitimate speech" in early modern England (9). For instance, although slander was primarily defined as "the false imputation of a crime or other shameful behavior/status," the "very problem with defamation is its ability to be believed and thus inflict damage on its victim" (Kaplan 13). Consequently, "words can be defamatory whether they are true or false, depending on the consequences" (18).

The Roaring Girl reveals how, short of overt slander, sexual innuendo and insult could function to discipline women who were active workers in an urban market economy. The position of the play's citizen wives can be illuminated by Marjorie McIntosh's conclusions about working women in her comprehensive study *Working Women in English Society, 1300–1620*. McIntosh explains that "Although a larger proportion of all women may have been working to generate an income in 1620 than during the fifteenth century, they were generally found within just two categories." The first category comprised "women active in trades or craftwork," usually "wives or daughters who assisted their male relatives in running a business"; the second category comprised women who worked as servants, "did piecework at home, worked in alehouses/inns, or sold goods on the streets, rendering them vulnerable to sexual advances and social disapproval" (252–53).[10] The citizen wives in *The Roaring Girl* appear to straddle these categories: they are tradeswomen who work with their husbands in shops, but through their public sale of goods they become vulnerable to sexual slander.[11] As a result, the wives face an ideological contradiction: they contribute to the household economy through the production and sale of goods, yet they are regarded with suspicion and anxiety due to their public mobility and economic agency.[12]

This ideological contradiction can be succinctly illustrated through the overlapping early modern meanings of "housewife" and "huswife." Whereas a

"housewife" was a thrifty, productive woman, a "huswife" was a hussy or prostitute (Crane 212–17). Behind the double meaning of "housewife"/"huswife"
Douglas Bruster finds the threatening implication that a "woman who controlled the household economy . . . seemed more likely to control her own
sexual economy" (*Drama* 51). In *Othello*, Iago activates this implication when
he berates women for being "Players in your housewifery, and hussies in your
beds" (2.1.115). Rebuking Iago as a "slanderer," Desdemona speaks more truth
than she realizes (2.1.116). More importantly for my purposes, however, this
exchange demonstrates that sexual slander does not always operate by explicitly categorizing women as "chaste wives" or "whores." Iago's defamation of
housewives as hussies suggests how easily the distinction between the "chaste
wife" and the "whore" can be made to collapse (Crane 216–17).[13]

The representation of working women in *The Roaring Girl* likewise complicates the distinction between the "chaste wife" and the "whore." Before
turning to a reading of the play proper, however, I want to argue that its
Prologue and Epilogue limn the sexual type of the citizen wife by critiquing
London women's fondness for playgoing. Promising a personal stage visit by
the real Mary Frith, the Epilogue, which was most likely spoken by the actor
who played Moll, shrewdly capitalizes on its subject's notoriety: "The Roaring
Girl herself, some few days hence, / Shall on this stage give larger recompense"
(35–36). A record of Frith's appearance before the London diocese ecclesiastical court in 1612 indicates that she did, in fact, grace the stage of the Fortune
Theater. According to the court record, Frith "sat there uppon the stage in
the publique viewe of all the people there presente in mans apparrell & playd
uppon her lute & sang a songe." She also "told the company there present that
she thought many of them were of opinion that she was a man, but if any of
them would come to her lodging they should finde that she is a woman &
some other immodest & lascivious speaches she also used at that time" (qtd.
Mulholland 262). This remarkable incident of the early modern theater's implication in sexual transgression and official discipline has generated much
critical commentary.[14] Sitting cross-dressed on a public stage, playing the lute,
and inviting audience members to discover the female body underneath her
male apparel, Frith—"The Roaring Girl herself" as the Epilogue would have
it—performed a version of her celebrity persona to complement (or to surpass
or even contradict) the version just performed by a cross-dressed boy on that
very stage. I am less interested here in the meaning of Frith's actual stage appearance than in the metatheatrical resonance of the Epilogue's promise to
exhibit the "real" Roaring Girl to an audience that has been watching, and is

still watching, a theatrical representation of the Roaring Girl. In other words, it is not simply that the "real" Moll can be said to have occupied the "fictional" space of the stage; rather, the Epilogue foregrounds for the audience how fluid the boundary between off-stage and on-stage performance, between exhibition and mimesis, can be.[15]

The Prologue's satire of stereotypically extravagant wives also blurs the boundary between offstage and onstage worlds, but in a way more directly relevant to the play's depiction of female types in contemporary London. The Prologue distinguishes the eponymous "roaring girl" from two other types of roaring girl: "suburb-roarers" or prostitutes, and the "civil, city-roaring girl" or citizen wife, "whose pride, / Feasting, and riding, shakes her husband's state, / And leaves him roaring through an iron grate" (21–24). Moll, the Prologue assures us, "flies / With wings more lofty" than either the prostitute, who "sells her soul to the lust of fools and slaves," or the citizen wife, whose reckless spending lands her husband in debtor's prison (25–26, 20). Linking London wives with suburban prostitutes, the Prologue encourages playgoers to judge the women among them against what Theodore Leinwand has called the "exaggerated, comic figures" of contemporary stereotypes and "self-conscious urban roles" (12, 10). A similar interpellation of the audience occurs in the second scene of the play, when Sir Alexander, ostensibly describing the portraits in his gallery, refers to the playgoers who fill the galleries of the Fortune Theater as "men and women, mixed together / Fair ones with foul" (1.2.17–18). Presumably, such "foul" women in attendance might include not only prostitutes, but also those wives whom the Prologue has reproached for squandering their husbands' money on consumer pleasures. Citizen wives in the audience thus found themselves in a contradictory position: having paid for the right to act as critical *subjects*, to judge for themselves the merits of Middleton and Dekker's play, including its representation of citizen wives, they found themselves exhibited by the Prologue as *objects* of public scrutiny.

In *Epicene* (1609), a contemporary city comedy generally regarded as more overtly misogynist than *The Roaring Girl*, Ben Jonson similarly targets urban wives as objects of public knowledge. The Prologue to *Epicene* distinguishes among female audience members as "ladies," "waiting-wench[es]," "city wires," and "daughters of Whitefriars" (22–24). Significantly, whereas "ladies" and "waiting-wenches" clearly designate social rank, the metonymic designations "city-wires" and "daughters of Whitefriars" are overtly satiric rather than descriptive. "City-wires" are spendthrift London wives who use wire to hold up their fashionable ruffs; "daughters of Whitefriars" are prostitutes who frequent

that notorious London district. Jonson thereby associates the economic transgressions of city wives with the sexual transgressions of prostitutes. Furthermore, the image of the licentious "city-wire" surfaces early in the play, when
Truewit, urging Morose not to marry, details the horrifying financial, sexual,
and intellectual promiscuity of London wives. Such a monster, he warns, will
require her husband to maintain

> embroiderers, jewellers, tire-women, sempsters, feathermen, perfumers;
> while she feels not how the land drops away, nor the acres melt; nor
> foresees the change when the mercer has your woods for her velvets;
> never weighs what her pride costs, sir, so she may kiss a page or a
> smooth chin that has the despair of a beard . . . or so she may censure
> poets and authors and styles, and compare 'em, Daniel with Spenser,
> Jonson with the tother youth, and so forth. (2.2.107–18)

By including himself among those authors voraciously consumed by the
proud city wife, Jonson indicts such women in his own audience, much as
the Prologue to *The Roaring Girl* implicitly reproaches the "city-roaring girls"
who have come to the Fortune Theater to see the "loftier" roaring girl staged
by the playwrights. Though loftier in status and wealth, the Prologue implies,
the citizen wives in attendance might not be as lofty in virtue.

Unlike the citizen wives at the Fortune Theater, the citizen wives in the
play, Mistress Openwork and Mistress Gallipot, are represented primarily as
producers, not consumers, of London goods. Nonetheless, there is a connection between the citizen wives in the play and those described in the Prologue.
Revealing their familiarity with *Westward Ho* (1604), a city comedy by Dekker
and Webster, Mistresses Openwork and Gallipot attest to the consumer pleasures enjoyed by London tradeswomen in their leisure time (4.2.137–38).
More significantly, the Prologue's linkage of the citizen wife who promiscuously spends and the prostitute who promiscuously "sells" articulates a more
general distrust of the economic and sexual agency of citizen wives (20). It is,
of course, quite difficult to assess the impact that such representations might
have had on the socially heterogeneous audience of the Fortune Theater. Ap-
ropos the "equivocal and confusing characterizations" in *The Roaring Girl*,
Theodore Leinwand judiciously argues that by "exaggerating the worst traits
of gentry and merchants alike, city comedy distanced its audience, and it enforced the discrepancy between spectators' perceptions of themselves and their
socially conditioned perceptions of others" (76). This might well be true; yet

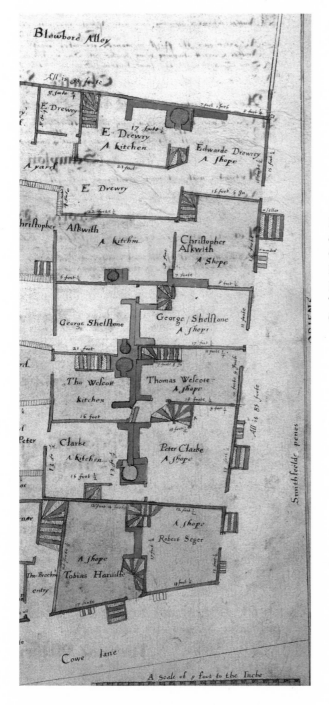

Figure 19. Shops
on Cow Lane,
Clothworkers' Hall
Plan Book, 41.
By permission of
The Clothworkers'
Company.

Figure 20. Merchant shops, from Johann Amos Comenius, *Orbis Sensualium Pictus* (1659). © The British Library Board. Shelfmark 627.b.9, p. 256.

by drawing playgoers' attention to the complementary exaggerated types of "city-roaring girls" and "suburb-roarers," Middleton and Dekker establish that urban women are to be judged primarily in terms of their use and abuse of financial and sexual power.

It is thus significant that the citizen wives make their first appearance in a public market scene. Middleton and Dekker's uniquely detailed stage direction requiring "*three shops open in a rank*" (2.1. *sd*), as Leslie Thomson notes, is "the visual and thematic context for all that happens in this long scene" of commercial exchange (154). A sense of the intimate "ranking" of the citizens' shops is provided by a drawing of West Smithfield (a livestock market) by the London surveyor Ralph Treswell (see Figure 19); the activity of the market and the general appearance of the shops, with their windows open to the street, are suggested by Johann Comenius's mid-seventeenth-century image of "Mercatura," or Merchandizing (see Figure 20). As the scene begins, Mistress Openwork stands at her stall hawking her wares to the passing gallants: "Gentlemen, what is't you lack?" (2.1.1). The hawker's cry is conventional; yet in this context it recalls an earlier bawdy pun on the name of the gallant Laxton, or "lack-stone," meaning "missing a testicle" (1.2.56). That Mistress Openwork's seemingly innocent sales-pitch should generate a bawdy innuendo is not surprising, since Jacobean city comedies regularly satirize shopwives' flirtatious methods for attracting customers. Garrett Sullivan cites a pertinent instance from *The Family of Love*: "he that tends well his shop, and hath an alluring wife with a graceful *what d'ye lack?* shall be sure to have good doings, and good doings is that crowns so many citizens with the horns of abundance" (qtd. Sullivan 26; cf. Cahn 61).[16] By implicitly offering the consumer her body as well as her merchandise, the shopwife's industrious hawking produces economic profit or "abundance" for her husband, but at the price of crowning him with cuckold's horns (Sullivan 26; see also Miller 13). Mistress Openwork's attempt to lure gentlemen customers by announcing the desirability of her openwork stitchery likewise activates the pun on sexual openness in her name.

In the event, Mistress Openwork's industrious hawking attracts only her rival Moll, and the ensuing conflict activates a similar range of puns linking merchandizing and illicit sexuality. Suspecting Moll of being her husband's whore, Mistress Openwork fiercely asserts the moral purity of her business:

Moll: Let me see a good shag ruff.

Openwork: Mistress Mary, that shalt thou, i'faith, and the best in the shop.

Mistress Openwork: How now?—Greetings! Love terms, with a pox between you! Have I found out one of your haunts? I send you for hollands, and you're i'the low countries with a mischief. I'm served with good ware by th'shift that makes it lie dead so long upon my hands, I were as good shut up shop, for when I open it, I take nothing.

Openwork: Nay, and you fall a-ringing once, the devil cannot stop you; I'll out of the belfry as fast as I can.— Moll.

Mistress Openwork: Get you from my shop!

Moll: I come to buy.

Mistress Openwork: I'll sell ye nothing; I warn ye my house and shop.

Moll: You, goody Openwork, you that prick out a poor living
And sews many a bawdy skin-coat together,
Thou private pandress between shirt and smock,

I wish thee for a minute but a man:
Thou shouldst never use more shapes; but as th'art,
I pity my revenge. (2.1.222–42)

Mistress Openwork conveys the intensity of her moral outrage by banning Moll from the building that serves as her family's house as well as shop; in so doing, she reminds her husband and neighbors that she works modestly at home, whereas Moll, like an idle gentleman, freely wanders about the market buying goods and chatting with acquaintances. Hugh Alley's drawing of New Fish Street from his manuscript account of London markets provides a visual equivalent of the distinction Mistress Openwork draws between the "house and shop" in which she works, and the open market through which Moll walks (see Figure 21). Mistress Openwork sharply draws the boundary that defines the community of honest working wives from outsiders such as Moll, who occupies the marginal "haunts" and distant "low countries" visited by her errant husband.[17] Pertinent here is Laura Gowing's observation that the "competitive confrontation between strange whores and lawful wives was very often the foundation on which women defamed each other: as they defined other women as whores, they proclaimed themselves models of honesty" (*Domestic* 87). Gowing cites a case from 1608 in which Winifred Bland attacked Elizabeth Hollinshed, saying, "I never rode 12 myles on a bare horseback nor ever carried a payer of sheetes out of dores to Ned Bird . . . Bes Bes when I have any children I will have but one father to them" (qtd. *Domestic* 76).[18]

Regarding herself as a model of sexual as well as financial honesty, Mistress Openwork blames any business losses on her husband's susceptibility to Moll's erotic enchantments, his "haunt[ing]" of her "low countries" (2.1.226–27). According to the densely punning language of Mistress Openwork's complaint, Master Openwork's neglect of his responsibility to serve her with "good ware" (quality cloth/a fully functioning penis) produces failure in the bed as well as at the market, for the goods he offers her "lie dead so long upon my hands, I were as good shut up shop, for when I open it, I take nothing" (2.1.228–30). Diverting Master Openwork from his financial and conjugal responsibilities, Moll deprives Mistress Openwork of the profit and the pleasure she believes are her due as a legitimate wife.[19] Significantly, in describing her capacity (however thwarted) to run the family business in her husband's absence, Mistress Openwork touts her housewifely thrift and relative economic independence. The competence with which Middleton and Dekker endow her markedly contrasts with the helpless stance taken by the wife in John Taylor's *Juniper Lecture*

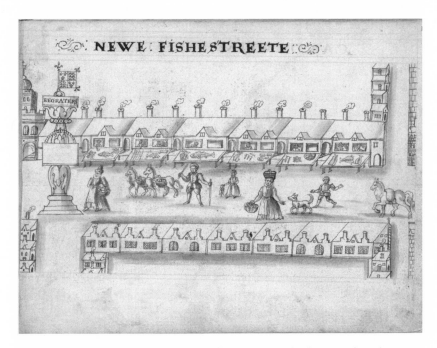

NEWE FISHE STREETE

Figure 21. London markets, from Hugh Alley, *A Caveatt for the Citty of London* (1598). By permission of the Folger Shakespeare Library.

(1639) who also complains of the "ill Husbandry" of a husband who "never keep[s] at home": "Do you think I can sell your Wares or know the prices of them when your Customers come? Let them look to your shop that will, for I will not. Keep your shop, and then it will keep you, I say" (qtd. Henderson and McManus 292). Despite her lack of "good ware," Mistress Openwork declares that she fulfills her productive role in the domestic economy.

However, by complaining that when she "open[s]" shop she "take[s] in nothing"—neither money from customers nor, in a sexual double entendre, her husband's erection—Mistress Openwork blurs the distinction between the "chaste wife" and the "whore" on which her slander of Moll depends. That is, she inadvertently evokes a connection between the shop-woman and the sexually open woman that informs contemporary city comedies and verse satires. For instance, Henry Parrot's epigram of 1608, "*Ostendis Haedera Vinum*" ["You advertise wine by means of ivy"], represents the Cheapside prostitute as a kind of urban shop-woman displaying her goods:

A scoffing mate, passing along Cheapside,
Incontinent a gallant lass espied;
Whose tempting breasts (as to the sale laid out)
Incites this youngster thus to 'gin to flout.
"Lady," quoth he, "is this flesh to be sold?"
"No Lord," quoth she, "for silver nor for gold;
But wherefore ask you?" (and there made a stop).
"To buy," quoth he, "if not, shut up your shop." (qtd. Manley 244–45)

That Cheapside was in this period "one of the great thoroughfares and commercial centers of London" perhaps explains why the young man suspects the lass' self-display to be a sexual marketing strategy (Howard, *Theater* 136). Refusing to sell her flesh for "silver" or "gold," the lass defends her reputation by referring to Cheapside's fame as a street of prosperous goldsmiths and moneychangers. So far, the poem has seemed to strike a balance between aggressive male scoffing and defensive feminine virtue. The syntactic and grammatical ambiguity of "incontinent" in the poem's second line, moreover, allows us to assign lack of restraint to either the "scoffing mate" or the "gallant lass." The mate, however, gets the last word in the poem, and his chastisement of the lass' self-display suggests that she is guilty of both sexual and financial incontinence.

The incontinent citizen wife shows up as well in Thomas Gainsford's character book, *The Rich Cabinet* (1616). In his portrait of the "Citizen," Gainsford defines the citizen wife as more "trouble" than help to her husband's financial welfare. The wife's assistance in luring customers to the shop seems to produce the unintended consequence of augmenting her agency as a voracious consumer of urban pleasures:

A citizen is more troubled with his wife, then his wares: for they
are sorted, locked up, and never brought out, but by constraint for
the profit of their master; but his wife is decked, adorned, neatly
apparrelled, sits for the gaze, goes at her pleasure, and will not be
restrained from any sights or delights, or merry-meetings; where they
may show their beauties, or riches, or recreate themselves. (sig. E4r)

In Gainsford's syntax, the wife's function as an alluring object of display—she is "decked," "adorned," and "apparrelled"—makes her equivalent to the merchant's wares, which are "sorted," "locked up," and "brought out" by their master at his will. But the wife's apparent passivity modulates seamlessly into action when she "sits for the gaze" of clients, and even more so when she "goes at her pleasure, and will not be restrained" from spending her husband's profits on London's "sights and delights." Although Gainsford does not accuse the wife of sexual promiscuity, he implies an erotic liberty in her eagerness to detach the urban pleasures of seeing and being seen from any consideration of financial profit.

Perhaps due to its reiteration in city comedy and satire during the first decades of the seventeenth century, the type of the sexually loose shop-wife seems to have become so commonplace that Francis Lenton includes a full portrait of the "Sempster Shopkeeper" in his *Characterismi* of 1631:

> Shee is very neatly spruc'd up, and placed in the frontispice of her shop, of purpose, (by her curious habit) to allure some Custome, which still encraseth and decreaseth as her beauty is in the full, or the wane. Shee hath a pretty faculty in presenting herselfe to the view of Passengers, by her roling eyes, glancing through the hangings of Tiffany and Cobweb-lawne, that the Travellers are suddenly surprized, and cannot but looke backe, though but to view babbies in her face, and in affection to her comelinesse, must needs cheapen her commodity, where they are wrapt into a bargaine by her beauty, and doe kisse the Nurse for the childs sake, which shee kindely accepts, and desires them as they like that, she may have more of their Custome. (sigs. E3v–E4v)

Whereas Lenton at first seems to praise the seamstress's business acumen in donning a "curious habit" to call attention to the fabric she sells, it quickly becomes clear that her sales depend on her beauty. Evidently aware of this connection, the seamstress strategically displays herself in a way that proves irresistible to customers, who are "wrapt" into a purchase. "Wrapped" connotes a state of being "deeply absorbed" in a person or thing as well as "absorbed or engrossed in thought."[20] The association of the latter meaning with "rapt," as in "transported with joy" or "intense delight," hints that when the seamstress, having been kissed by her clients, requests more of their custom, she is making an overtly sexual offer.

In the remainder of the passage, Lenton's use of sewing terms generates double entendres that implicate the seamstress in illicit forms of production and consumption such as prostitution, drink, and theft:

> In her trade shee is much troubled with stitches; amongst which, backe-
> stitch is the most ordinary, easie, and pleasant to her; and if you cannot
> bargaine for her Ruffes in her shop, shee will fit you with choyce at your
> Chamber, so you pay her well for her paines: She is well acquainted with
> hemming too, which sometimes makes her leave her Needle to drinke
> a cup of Canary, to breake her stitch; nor is shee ignorant of Cutworke
> and Pursework but hath her particular patterns for them too. (sigs.
> E4v–E5r)

To be "troubled with stitches" ostensibly means to be pricked or stabbed with
pain, but the seamstress' preference for the "backe-stitch," in which the needle
enters behind the previous stitch, perhaps implies her pleasure in being penetrated from behind.[21] Because of the round shape of a lace ruff, the act of bar-
gaining for the seamstress' ruff in a private chamber euphemistically describes
a negotiation for sexual services. "Hemming" refers to sewing a border and
to clearing the throat, which might lead to a cup of canary.[22] "Cutworke" is a
"kind of openwork embroidery," but the proximity of "Cutworke and Purse-
work" apparently means that the seamstress enhances her income by cutting
purses.[23] Tellingly, Lenton follows the character of the "Sempster Shopkeeper"
with that of the "Prostitute or Common Whore."

In *The Roaring Girl*, it is this association between the open shop and the
open female body that Moll so shrewdly turns against Mistress Openwork.
By redefining Mistress Openwork's "private" (domestic) labor of needlework
as the "private" (secretive) labor of pandering, Moll debases her rival as the
proprietress not of a shop but of a brothel, an implication discernable in
her insulting admonition to Master Openwork: "Prithee tend thy shop and
prevent bastards!" (2.1.390). Moll implies that any citizen's house "might be
a covert whorehouse, a place where loose women perform versions of respectable femininity in order to conduct their trade" (Howard, *Theater* 126).
Interpreting the seamstress' ostensibly respectable labor of "pricking" and
joining pieces of cloth as a sign of illicit sexuality, Moll deflates the social,
economic, and moral pretensions of the ostensibly more respectable citizen
wife.[24] To borrow a bawdy turn of phrase from Shakespeare's Mercutio, Moll
"pricks" Mistress Openwork for her labor of "pricking," in that she uses sharp
words "to sting" her rival "with sorrow or remorse" (*Romeo and Juliet* 1.4.28;
OED, prick *v.* 2). Moll's "pricking" of her rival might also implicate Mistress
Overdone in the rumors about transgressive homoeroticism that contribute
to Moll's own marginal status. As Fiona McNeill observes, Sir Alexander's

defamatory claim that "nature hath brought forth" Moll "to mock the sex of woman" (1.2.127–28) paints Moll as hermaphrodite or tribade (*Poor* 117). In a sense, then, the conflict between the outwardly "unnatural" Moll and the outwardly more respectable, "feminine" citizen wife replays in the arena of public shaming the struggle over sexual agency between the overtly "masculine" tribade and her more ambiguously gendered female partners I examined in Chapter 2.[25]

Consonant with the ambiguous gendering of the tribade's sexual partners, Moll suggests that the outwardly "feminine" Mistress Openwork actually behaves in a transgressively masculine manner. Since Moll regards women as unworthy partners in combat, she wishes that Mistress Openwork were a man whom she could thrash for having "use[d] . . . shapes," or lied. By imagining Mistress Openwork in a man's shape, Moll obliquely indicts Master Openwork for having relinquished his domestic authority to a domineering "masculine" wife. Moll's revenge fantasy, then, betrays the desire to turn against her accuser the common slanders of herself as an ambiguously gendered being, both male and female, with "two shadows to one shape" (1.2.132). Attacking Mistress Openwork for "using shapes," in other words, Moll deflects public attention away from her own vulnerable condition as an unmarried cross-dressing woman.

Diane Willen's study of poor working women in early modern England suggests why Moll might benefit from such a deflection:

> city fathers prohibited single women from living on their own, assuming they would come to no good. . . . Time and again, the mayoralty court of Norwich ordered a female "lyvinge idely at her own hand" either to be retained in service, usually within a fortnight, or be committed to Bridewell, where work would be provided for her. (185)

The historical Mary Frith had been sent to work in Bridewell for various acts of public indecency, including her performance on the Fortune stage. Curiously, however, Moll in *The Roaring Girl* neither works as a domestic servant nor engages in any recognizable form of steady labor that would allow her to support herself while maintaining her chastity, as the play insists she does. How, then, does the play account for Moll's financial solvency and personal freedom as a chaste single woman, the remarkable set of circumstances that provokes Mistress Openwork's distrust and slanderous speech?

The woodcut on the title page of the 1611 quarto seems to raise precisely this question: the caption "My case is alter'd, I must worke for my living"

Figure 22. Title page of *The Roaring Girle* (1611). By permission of the Folger Shakespeare Library.

appears alongside the image of a cross-dressed, pipe-smoking, Moll (see Figure 22).[26] Why does this particular phrase, which has no verbal parallel in the play, serve as Moll's defining "motto," and what does it mean? Aside from a possible allusion to the similar comic intrigues of Ben Jonson's *The Case is Altered*, the motto's "altered case" might refer to the actual Mary Frith's incarceration in Bridewell, where she would have been forced to work for her living.[27]

However, the phrase might also speak to the contrasting economic statuses of the unmarried Moll and the citizen wives, who technically might not be understood to "work for their living." In early modern England, a wife's labor was subsumed into the occupational identity of her husband, whose work "within the family economy was the recognised and defining labour of the household" (Bennett, "Medieval" 152).[28] "Case" in early modern usage commonly designated the female genitalia, and, less often, the male genitalia (Bly 62–66); hence, "altered case" aptly describes the blurring of gender and sexual boundaries produced by Moll's cross-dressing and "masculine" behavior. Having "altered" her "case" by abandoning traditionally feminine clothes and behavior for a more masculine appearance and freedom, Moll refuses financial dependence on a husband: she must work for her own living.

How, then, does Moll support herself?[29] Although she appears to be financially comfortable, Moll earns money only sporadically and incidentally, on two occasions in which gentlemen solicit her unique services as a single, independent, woman. The sexual connotations of the service Moll provides to these gentlemen are on the one occasion implicit, and on the other explicit, yet during both encounters Moll succeeds in refuting any affront to her chastity.

Moll flirts with sexual impropriety in helping Sebastian to marry Mary against the wishes of his father. Posing as a music teacher, Moll is invited by Sebastian to play the viol, the placement of which between the legs evokes bawdy connotations (Howard, "Sex" 184–85). Sebastian attempts to defuse the sexual charge of Moll's performance by attributing any such imputation of indecency to the hypocritically puritanical women whom he imagines censoring her: "there be a thousand close dames that will call the viol an unmannerly instrument for a woman, and therefore talk broadly of thee, when you shall have them sit wider to a worse quality" (4.1.95–98). Sebastian here employs Moll's own characteristic strategy of slandering the slanderers, thus delegitimizing their moral authority. Viol between her legs, Moll likewise sings about loose and hypocritical city wives:

> I dream there is a mistress,
>> And she lays out the money;
> She goes unto her sisters;
>> She never comes at any.
> She says she went to th'Burse for patterns;
> You shall find her at Saint Kathern's,
>> And comes home with never a penny. (4.1.102–8)

Instead of going to the New Exchange to purchase clothing patterns, this wife spends all her husband's money in "a former nunnery-turned-brothel district," visiting the "sisters" who, according to a common epithet, might well be prostitutes (McNeill, *Poor* 127–28).

Moll's next satiric target is a woman who commits adultery while her husband languishes in prison, presumably for debt:

> Here comes a wench will brave ye,
>   Her courage was so great,
> She lay with one o' the navy,
>   Her husband lying i' the Fleet.
> Yet oft with him she cavilled;
>   I wonder what she ails:
> Her husband's ship lay gravelled
>   When hers could hoise up sails;
> Yet she began, like all my foes,
> To call whore first; for so do those—
>   A pox of all false tails! (4.1.113–23)

This wife might be complicit in her husband's bankruptcy—the graveling of his merchant ship—since his enforced absence frees her to "hoise up" her skirts for a sailor: when his sales go down, her "sails" go up (120). Alternatively, Moll's contrast between the husband's grounded ship and the wife's seaworthy ship might indict the wife for laying with the sailor instead of selling merchandise to raise the money needed to redeem her husband. Either way, Moll suggests that city wives spread false tales of her looseness in order to cover up their own economic and sexual misdeeds: the adulterous use of their pox-ridden "tails" (McNeill, *Poor* 128). Rather than wasting money and engaging in illicit sex, Moll chastely *earns* money. Sebastian gives Moll forty shillings for facilitating his marriage to Mary and, through her viol performance, for exposing the sexual promiscuity of seemingly respectable citizen wives.

Notably, the other occasion on which Moll profits from chaste labor indirectly involves a citizen wife, Mistress Gallipot, who habitually gives Laxton money in an effort to win his affection. When Laxton offers Moll the ten angels Mistress Gallipot has just given him, she challenges him to a duel for treating her as a "hired whore" (3.1.121). For Moll, Laxton's presumption of her sexual availability is akin to slander: "How many of our sex by such as thou / Have their good thoughts paid with a blasted name / That never deserved loosely or did trip / In path of whoredom beyond cup and lip?" (3.1.81–84). Moll indignantly defends the chaste women like herself who wrongly suffer from a "blasted name"; however, she also takes the opportunity to distinguish herself from those women who turn to prostitution out of financial desperation (Krantz 10):

> Distressèd needlewomen and trade-fallen wives—
> Fish that must needs bite, or themselves be bitten—
> Such hungry things as these may soon be took
> With a worm fastened on a golden hook:
> Those are the lecher's food, his prey. He watches
> For quarreling wedlocks and poor shifting sisters:
> 'Tis the best fish he takes. (3.1.95–101)

Although Moll speaks sympathetically of impoverished spinsters and wives, she once again deflects slander against her own chastity by publishing the sexual transgressions of wage-earning women. Working neither in prostitution nor in an orthodox "feminine" trade like needlework, Moll earns money—Mistress Gallipot's money, no less—by defeating Laxton in a duel that justifies her formal declaration of sexual honor.

Moll's comments about women's financial reasons for yielding to sexual temptation reinforce the importance of social and economic status as a motive in the citizen wives' intimacies with gallants. Mistress Openwork and Mistress Gallipot are neither the "poor shifting sisters" nor the "trade-fallen wives" whom Moll empathetically describes as resorting to prostitution for economic survival. In fact, the play suggests that it is their relative prosperity and sense of entitlement that motivates these wives' usurpation of their husbands' authority and their liaisons with sexually treacherous gallants. Mistress Openwork boasts that she is a "gentlewoman born," though married to a citizen.[30] During a routine business discussion with her husband, she expresses a superior attitude that we might attribute to pride in her lineage and resentment at her diminished status as a laboring wife:

> **Openwork:** Mass, I had quite forgot!
> His honour's footman was here last night, wife:
> Ha' you done with my lord's shirt?
>
> **Mistress Openwork:** What's that to you, sir?
> I was this morning at his honour's lodging
> Ere such a snail as you crept out of your shell.

Openwork: O, 'twas well done, good wife.

Mistress Openwork: I hold it better, sir,
Than if you had done't yourself.

Openwork: Nay, so say I;
But is the countess's smock almost done, mouse?

Mistress Openwork: Here lies the cambric, sir, but
wants I fear me.

Openwork: I'll resolve you of that presently.

Mistress Openwork: Heyday! O audacious groom,
Dare you presume to noblewomen's linen?
Keep you your yard to measure shepherd's holland!—
I must confine you, I see that. (2.1.158–71)

Not only does Mistress Openwork assume greater responsibility for the smooth operation of the family business, but her impulse to "confine" her husband seems to arise from a suspicion about his inclination for social climbing as well as sexual wandering. In her jealous imagination, her husband's sexual transgression—applying his "yard" [penis] to a woman's smock—is of a piece with his social transgression. A man accustomed to handling coarse "shepherd's holland" would have to be an "audacious groom" to aspire to fine "noblewoman's linen."

Mistress Openwork's eagerness to credit Goshawk's slanderous report of her husband's infidelity evidently stems from resentment at Master Openwork's middling status. Goshawk craftily manipulates this resentment to seduce Mistress Openwork:

Goshawk: Nay, more, I tell you in private, he keeps a whore i'th'suburbs.

Mistress Openwork: O spittle dealing! I came to him a gentlewoman born: I'll show you mine arms when you please, sir.

Goshawk: [*Aside*] I had rather see your legs, and begin that way!

Mistress Openwork: 'Tis well known he took me from a lady's service where I was well-beloved of the steward. I had my Latin tongue and a spice of the French before I came to him, and now he doth keep a suburbian whore under my nostrils.

Goshawk: There's ways enough to cry quit with him—hark in thine ear. [*Whispers*]

Mistress Openwork: There's a friend worth a million. (2.1.327–41)

When Mistress Openwork discovers Goshawk's treachery later in the play, she joins with her husband to trap him in his own lie. Yet because this trap requires Mistress Openwork to maintain the role of the indignant wife, she once again has an opportunity to complain about her disadvantageous marriage: "Did I for this lose all my friends? Refuse / Rich hopes and golden fortunes to be made / A stale to a common whore?" (4.2.151–53). To convince Goshawk of her sincerity, Mistress Openwork's complaint must be plausible, and her previous statements suggest that it contains some truth. In the personal history Middleton and Dekker construct for her, Mistress Openwork could have married a steward and established herself in a noblewoman's household; instead, she has relegated herself to a modest citizen existence and to the occasional privilege of visiting a noble household to deliver work. Despite Goshawk's failure to seduce Mistress Openwork, what emerges from this episode is the potential for infidelity and conjugal disorder when a gentlewoman perceives that she has traded fortune and status for the drudgery of a citizen life.

Mistress Gallipot, another born gentlewoman married to a citizen, comes close to realizing this threat of infidelity. According to Laxton, Mistress Gallipot is a "gentlewoman born, . . . though it be her hard fortune now to shred Indian pot-herbs" (2.1.9–10). By attributing to Mistress Gallipot a decline into "hard fortune," Middleton and Dekker hint at her discontent with her citizen husband and sense of entitlement to his money, both of which fuel her affair with Laxton. On several occasions, the play suggests that Mistress Gallipot's sexual and economic agency threaten her husband's financial solvency. Receiving ten angels from her, Laxton smugly comments that she "has wit enough to rob her husband, and I ways enough to consume the money" (2.1.92–93); he later explains that she "cozens her husband to keep me, and I'll keep her honest, as long as I can, to make the poor man some part of amends" (2.1.142–44). When Master Gallipot catches his wife with a letter from Laxton, her feigned distress at the apparently horrific news contained therein tellingly leads him to suspect some financial disaster:

> **Gallipot:** Heavens bless me! Are my barns and houses
> Yonder at Hockley Hole consumed with fire?—
> I can build more, sweet Prue.

> **Mistress Gallipot:** 'Tis worse, 'tis worse!

> **Gallipot:** My factor broke? Or is the *Jonas* sunk?

> **Mistress Gallipot:** Would all we had were swallowed in the waves,
> Rather than both should be the scorn of slaves! (3.2.95–100)

Claiming that Laxton demands financial redress for their previous engagement, Mistress Gallipot costs her husband the thirty pounds Laxton had originally requested in the letter, and an additional fifteen pounds later (4.2.260). Mistress Gallipot puts an end to Laxton's extortion only after he demands the ruinous sum total of one hundred pounds. Having nearly brought upon her husband the financial disaster that he feared, Mistress Gallipot has little choice but to confess her sexually motivated theft: "Husband, I plucked— / When he had tempted me to think well of him— / Gelt feathers from thy wings, to make him fly / More lofty" (4.2.289–92).

The suggestion that a citizen wife might use her sexual agency to manage her resentment about a loss of status, money, or opportunity through marriage appears in a different but highly suggestive form in a satiric pamphlet from 1595, Oliver Oat-meale's *A quest of enquirie, by women to know, whether the tripe-wife were trimmed by Doll yea or no*. *A quest* reports how one Doll Philips posed as a fortune-teller to scam a wealthy London widow, the owner of a tripe shop in St. Nicholas Shambles. Admitted to the widow's home, Doll requests a snippet of the widow's pubic hair in order to divine which of her suitors she should marry. A remarkable illustration of this incident appears in another contemporary pamphlet about Doll Philips' criminal activities (see Figure 23). In this illustration, the widow's finger, positioned directly over her vagina, evokes the clitoris, which was sometimes described as comparable in length to "half a man's finger" or a "little finger" (Traub, *Renaissance* 209). The notorious instrument of offense against the widow's modesty, Doll's scissors might even be imagined as a kind of dildo: Doll grasps the scissors so that their handles form a kind of head. Once she has established a homoerotic intimacy with the widow, Doll proceeds to steal her money and jewels (P. Brown 150–151). Publically shamed by the discovery of her financial and genital "trimming"—one mocking jig in *A quest* crows that "you were trimd unwomanly, / and in most shamefull sort" (Oat-meale, sig. CIv)—the widow hastily marries the only suitor who will still take her, Nick Trickes, who "proves to be a milksop husband, ineffectual and outmaneuvered by his wife" (P. Brown 172). The Tripe-Wife bitterly complains to her husband of the happier days she spent as an independent shopkeeper:

> Ah were we seated in a sowce-tubs shade,
> Over our heads of tripes a canopie:
> Remembrance of my past joy-thriving trade,
> Would somewhat ease my present miserie,
>
> But since I trotted from my trotter stall,
> And figd about from neates feete neatly drest:
> I finde no pleasure nor content at all,
> But live disdaind, despisde, abusde, distrest . . .
>
> Accurst was I to leave the Butchers fees,
> How base so ere, they brought in golden gaine,
> The mistres Tripe-wives name by thee I loose:
> That losse, their lacke, I ceaselesse doe complaine.
>   (Oat-meal, sigs. A3v, A4v)

The Tripe-Wife's lament about her poor choice of husband, and the implication that before marriage she enjoyed greater "name," "gaine," and sexual independence (as witnessed by her intimacy with Doll as well as with her suitors) chimes with the complaints of the gentle-born citizen wives in *The Roaring Girl*.[31]

Although *A quest* treats the issue of a wife's sexual and economic agency farcically, it joins *The Roaring Girl* in drawing upon contemporary anxieties about women's appropriation of domestic authority. Criticism of the shrewish wife is commonplace in popular literature of the period; however, a domineering wife might also be blamed for meddling in her husband's business affairs. Samuel Rowlands's popular 1617 poem "The Bride" admonishes the wife to avoid such "boldness":

Figure 23. The Tripe-Wife and Doll Philips, from *The brideling, sadling and ryding of a rich churle . . .* (1595).

> When as the husband bargains hath to make,
> In things that are depending on his trade,
> Let not wife's boldness power unto her take,
> As though no match were good but what she made:
>> For she that thus hath oar in husband's boat,
>> Let her take breech, and give him petticoat. (Aughterson 87–88)

Alternatively, a wife's undue appropriation of her husband's authority might derive not from belief in her superior business acumen but from pride in her superior wealth or lineage. Marriage manuals such as Robert Cleaver's popular *A Godly Form of Household Government*, first published in 1598, typically warn male readers to seek "no match in marriage above thy degree" (qtd. Wright 214). A socially superior woman might be inclined to reject her inferior status as wife, as William Whately acknowledges in *A Bride-Bush* (1617):

> Wherefore, O thou wife, let thy best understanding be to understand
> (that, that makes for thy peace) that thine husband is by God made thy

governor and ruler and thou his inferior, to be ruled by him. Though he be of meaner birth and of lesser wit, though he were of no wealth nor account in the world before thou didst marry him, yet after the tying of this knot God will have thee subject, and thou must put upon thyself a willingness to confess thyself so to be. (259–60)

In *The Flower of Friendship*, a popular dialogue on marriage published in seven editions between 1568 and 1587, Edmund Tilney describes the misery of the husband who marries a social superior:

Marry not a superiour, saith *Plutarch*. For in so doing, in steede of kinsfolkes, thou shalt get thee maisters, in whose awe thou must stande, and a riche woman, that marieth a poore man, seldome, or never, shake off the pride from hir shoulders. Yea *Menander* sayth, that suche a man hath gotten in steed of a wyfe, a husband, and she of him a wyfe, a straunge alteration, a wonderfull metamorphosis. (108)

Tilney's account of the disorderly marriage dominated by a superior wife deploys the same language of bodily "metamorphosis" used in *The Roaring Girl* to stigmatize Moll as a strangely "alter[ed]" hermaphroditic creature. When Mistress Gallipot circulates the rumor that Moll is "both man and woman" (2.1.210), she thereby verifies Moll's complaint that her slanderers project their own transgressions onto her, for if Moll literally wears men's breeches, Mistress Gallipot does so metaphorically as a domineering wife. Middleton and Dekker even have Mistress Gallipot complain about her husband's uxorious behavior: "Thou dost not know how to handle a woman in her kind. . . . I cannot abide these apron husbands: such cotqueans!" (3.2.26–27, 32–33).

Although Middleton and Dekker suggest that Mistress Gallipot resents her husband, they also show that she is aware of the need to protect his reputation. Mistress Gallipot's awareness of her vulnerability to slander underscores the callousness with which Laxton jeopardizes her reputation in order to repair his own reputation as an effeminate coward and impoverished gentleman. When Goshawk comments that Mistress Gallipot, who sells tobacco, is typical of wives who "begin with pipes and set up again" after their husbands go bankrupt, Laxton bawdily responds, "And indeed the raising of the woman is the lifting up of the man's head at all times" (2.1.12–15). Seemingly praising Mistress Gallipot's industriousness, Laxton echoes the gallant from Marston's *The Dutch Courtesan* who defends a wife's turn to prostitution: "A poor, decayed mechanical man's

wife, her husband is laid up; may not she lawfully be laid down when her husband's only rising is by his wife's falling?" (1.1.101–4). Laxton eagerly points out
to his companions the sexual connotations of Mistress Gallipot's preparation of
a tobacco pipe: "The pipe's in a good hand, and I wish mine always so" (2.1.50).
Understandably, Mistress Gallipot urges Laxton to be "not forgetful; respect my
credit; seem strange" (2.1.56–57). One of the most complex, multivalent terms
used in court defamation cases, "credit" variously referred to "good neighbourliness, trustworthiness, financial independence, sexual virtue, and social class"
(Gowing, *Domestic* 128). Mistress Gallipot also expresses concern about her
credit when she considers pawning her "childbed linen" to supply Laxton with
the thirty pounds he requests (3.2.71); she decides against selling the linen when
she realizes that her husband will be thought "bankrupt" if her "mark" is recognized on the cloth (3.2.74, 72). Despite Mistress Gallipot's continual vigilance
about her credit, Laxton compromises it on several levels: when he boasts that
his "credit" at her shop "may take up an ounce of pure smoke," Goshawk understands him to mean that his sexual credit with the tradeswoman "May take up
an ell of pure smock!" (2.1.22–24).

Among those in the play's original audiences, Goshawk might not have
been alone in assuming that Laxton's public access to Mistress Gallipot's
"smoke" signified his private access to her "smock." In a sermon preached
at Whitehall in 1607, Robert Wilkinson explored the contemporary association between imported luxury goods and female promiscuity. Published as *The
merchant royall*, the sermon constitutes an extended gloss on the definition of
a virtuous woman in Proverbs 31:14: *Shee is like a Merchant's shippe; shee bringeth her food from afarre*. Wilkinson is at pains to demonstrate that the good
woman resembles a ship in qualities such as gravity, balance, frugality, and
profitability, but not in many other qualities: multiple ownership ("one ship
may belong to many merchants, . . . yet neither may one woman divide her
love to many men" [11]); mobility ("it is a note of the unchast woman, that her
feete cannot abide in her house" [12]); inconstancy ("a ship of all things is move-
able and carried with the winde, but so must not a good woman be" [12]); or
"too much rigging": "with her French, her Spanish, and her foolish fashions,
. . . with her plumes, her fannes, and a silken vizard, with a ruffe like a saile,
yea a ruffe like a rainebow, with a feather in her cap like a flag in her top, to
tel (I think) which way the winde will blow" (13). Returning several times to
the wife's consumption of luxury goods, Wilkinson blames the destruction of
her husband's credit on "French Hoods, Ruffes, Lawnes and Looking-glasses"
(23) and contrasts the profitable household management of industrious wives

with the wastefulness of those who "must have bread from one countrie, and drinke from another, and . . . meate from Spaine, and sauce out of Italy: and if wee weare any thing, it must be pure Venetian, Romane, or Barbarian; but the fashion of all must bee French" (25–6). The picture that emerges from this sermon, paradoxically, is that the good woman is most like a profitable merchant ship when she is most firmly grounded at home, not gadding about London buying luxury goods or even "run[ning] to the shop or to the s[t]ore" to buy necessary food and clothing, but making it herself (27). In Wilkinson's nostalgically ahistorical conflation of proto-capitalist mercantilism with feudal household production, the consumption of foreign "toyes and trifles" signifies a promiscuity of appetite that is gendered female (24).

By making Mistress Gallipot a purveyor of tobacco, a controversial import from the New World (Peck, *Consuming* 115), Middleton and Dekker suggest not only that she participates in a promiscuous new consumer economy, but also that she might be using a luxury item to entice her lover.[32] According to Laura Gowing, in defamation cases luxury food frequently "prompts and sustains illicit liaisons" outside the household (*Domestic* 91). In a case from 1619, for instance, Sisley Wayte accused a neighbor as follows: "Thowe didst ride behind Henry Goodwyn from Storeford faire, and he tooke thee by the geere fortie tymes, and thowe still . . . wilte entice him . . . for pies or cakes to be naught with him" (qtd. Gowing, *Domestic* 91). Although Laxton has no intention of being naught with Mistress Gallipot, he admits that by accepting her enticements of tobacco and money he functions as a kind of "whoremaster" to her (2.1.145). For her part, Mistress Gallipot naively believes that she has successfully purchased her lover's fidelity. Consequently, when Laxton employs a door-to-door saleswoman to deliver a letter to her, Mistress Gallipot fails to recognize the parallel between herself and this "masterless" working woman, who might well have been regarded by authorities as a prostitute (McNeill, *Poor* 154–58). Instead, Mistress Gallipot misrecognizes herself as the heroine of a fabliau: "Would any husband suspect that a woman crying, 'Buy any scurvy-grass,' should bring love letters amongst her herbs to his wife? Pretty trick! Fine conveyance! Had jealousy a thousand eyes, a silly woman with scurvy-grass blinds them all" (3.2.46–50). The discrepancy between the romantic fantasy of lovers blinding a jealous husband and Laxton's bald request for thirty pounds reveals Mistress Gallipot's own blindness to being treated like a whore, a mere instrument of Laxton's financial desires. As she later admits to Mistress Openwork, all her efforts on Laxton's behalf resulted in her being "frumped at and libelled upon" (4.2.66–67).

Despite the mutual culpability of Mistress Gallipot and Laxton in robbing and deceiving Master Gallipot, the resolution of this plot indicates that the wife represents a greater threat than the gallant to the citizen's reputation as a good householder and shopkeeper. In a complex argument about the social and ethical crises brought about by an emergent proto-capitalist culture in late sixteenth-century England, Lorna Hutson has argued that an ideology of "good husbandry" or *oikonomia* served to justify the "masculine power" of the householder in his role as a self-interested manipulator and arranger of his possessions (*Usurer's* 31). Fundamental to the achievement of *oikonomia* was the husband's ability to "manage people and situations," an ability "pre-eminently expressed in the fiction of the husband who could 'fashion' his wife" (87). The policing of female sexuality, particularly of a daughter or wife, thus emerged as the "secret of moderation and discipline" essential for achieving good husbandry (201). In *The Roaring Girl*, Sir Alexander alludes to the discourse of good husbandry when he praises his son as "No city monster neither, no prodigal, / But sparing, wary, civil, and— though wifeless— / An excellent husband" (1.2.118–20). Ironically, this encomium is belied by Sir Alexander's conviction that his son's reputation as an "excellent husband" has been jeopardized by his courtship of Moll, a "city monster" if ever there was one.

Whereas Sebastian has no intention of risking his reputation by husbanding Moll, the economic and sexual misconduct of Mistress Gallipot does call into question her husband's management of household and shop. Middleton and Dekker's conclusion to the citizen plot suggests that to regain his credit as a "good husband" Master Gallipot must establish his ability to "fashion" or control his wife. Instead of graciously pardoning Mistress Gallipot when she protests that she "never wronged" their marital bed, Master Gallipot cynically replies that she could as easily have cuckolded him in their shop, and indicates his fear that she might do so in the future: "A shop-board will serve / To have a cuckold's coat cut out upon; / Of that we'll talk hereafter" (4.2.296–99). Evidently improvising, Laxton attempts to excuse his inappropriate intimacy with Mistress Gallipot by explaining that their relationship began over a debate about marital fidelity and sexual slander:

> The first hour that your wife was in my eye,
> Myself with other gentlemen sitting by
> In your shop tasting smoke, and speech being used

That men who have fairest wives are most abused
And hardly 'scaped the horn, your wife maintained
That only such spots in city dames were stained
Justly, but by men's slanders; for her own part,
She vowed that you had so much of her heart,
No man by all his wit, by any wile
Never so fine spun, should yourself beguile
Of what in her was yours. (4.2.303–13)

Scorning to be braved by a "she-citizen" (4.2.317), Laxton claims that he put Mistress Gallipot's declaration of chastity to the test: "Therefore I laid siege to her: out she held, / Gave many a brave repulse, and me compelled / With shame to sound retreat to my hot lust" (4.2.318–20). With this colorfully pious tale, Laxton successfully passes off his seduction of Mistress Gallipot as a "merriment"; consequently, Master Gallipot commends his sexual restraint: "I am beholden—not to you, wife,— / But Master Laxton, to your want of doing ill" (4.2.333, 337–38).

As Master Gallipot's cutting response indicates, Laxton's exculpatory tale casts Mistress Gallipot as the type of undisciplined, indiscreet, wife whose loose speech and behavior threaten the householder's attainment of "good husbandry." Ardently protesting against "men's slanders," she makes herself an object of slander. The scene ends as Master Gallipot condescendingly enjoins his wife to beware indiscreet talk that will soil her reputation: "Wife, brag no more / Of holding out: who most brags is most whore" (4.2.342–43). The vehemence of this public reprimand reveals the severity of the threat posed not simply by the citizen wife's sexual agency, but also by her predominance in the shop and her control over household finances (Capp, "Separate" 126–27; Howard, "Sex" 178–79, 186; Leinwand 75). Were Moll present, she might admonish Master Gallipot as she had earlier admonished Master Openwork: "Prithee tend thy shop and prevent bastards!" (2.1.390).

Through a focus on the sexual opportunities afforded to citizen wives during their leisure time, good husbandry is also at stake in the resolution of the conflict between Master Openwork and Goshawk. Scheming to punish Goshawk for having accused Master Openwork of infidelity, Mistress Openwork and Mistress Gallipot express a new appreciation for their husbands: "'Las, what are your whisking gallants to our husbands, weigh 'em rightly, man for man?" (4.2.51–2). Yet the wives' plot exposes them to a further assault on their reputations. Upon learning that both women desire to accompany him to the

Thames village of Brentford (or Brainford), where he intends to seduce Mistress Openwork, Goshawk revises his plan:

> [*Aside*] Foot, how shall I find water to keep these two mills going?—
> [*To them*] Well, since you'll needs be clapped under hatches, if I sail
> not with you both till all split, hang me up at the main-yard and
> duck me.—[*Aside*] It's but liquoring them both soundly, and then
> you shall see their cork-heels fly up high, like two swans, when their
> tails are above water and their long necks under water, diving to
> catch gudgeons.—[*To them*] Come, come! Oars stand ready; the tide's
> with us. On with those false faces. Blow winds, and thou shalt take
> thy husband casting out his net to catch fresh salmon at Brentford.
> (4.2.78–88)

Although Middleton and Dekker have established that the wives intend to punish Goshawk for his sexual treachery, they nonetheless invite the audience to enjoy Goshawk's satiric portrait of sexually insatiable citizen wives indulging in a comically gymnastic, drunken ménage-a-trois. Playgoers would have been familiar with Brentford's reputation as a site of illicit female sexuality; during this scene, the wives even allude to Dekker and Webster's city comedy *Westward Ho* (1604), in which Brentford plays a prominent role in the sexual intrigue. Jean Howard describes Brentford's fame in city comedies as a "rendezvous for lovers and pleasure seekers"; even more to the point, it is "the conventional place beyond the immediate London suburbs where gallants and city wives go to outwit jealous husbands" ("Women" 158, 161). Given Brentford's reputation as a destination for adulterous city wives, Goshawk seems justified in assuming that Mistresses Openwork and Gallipot desire to be "clapped under hatches." Moreover, in planning "to hoise up sail" with a gallant (4.2.33), Mistress Openwork recalls the unfaithful wife chastised for "hois[ing] up sails" with a sailor in Moll's song of the previous scene (4.1.120).

Intercepting the trio on their way to Brentford, Master Openwork plays the part of the jealous citizen husband eager to protect not only his wife's reputation for honesty (chastity) but also his own reputation for honesty (truthful business dealing). Tellingly, he chastises Mistresses Openwork and Gallipot for wearing "false faces" or masks in terms that associate female duplicity with illegitimate financial dealings. Women who mask, he first observes, resemble wicked usurers or hoarders who remove their wealth from proper circulation: "as caves / Damn misers' gold, so masks are beauties' graves" (4.2.122–23). He goes on to develop a more elaborate metaphor in which beautiful faces are compared to the "fine wares" sold by industrious merchants:

> Good faces, masked, are jewels kept by sprites.
> Hide none but bad ones, for they poison men's sights;
> Show them as shopkeepers do their broidered stuff:
> By owl-light; fine wares cannot be open enough.
> Prithee, sweet Rose, come strike this sail. (4.2.128–32)

If "bad," women's faces should be concealed behind masks like inferior wares that are disguised by dim lighting; if "good," women's faces should be uncovered like valuable jewels or textiles that are prominently displayed to allure customers. Perhaps identifying his wife's mask with the "sail" that carries unfaithful spouses to Brentford, Master Openwork enjoins her to emulate the good shopkeeper by openly displaying her beauty. The problem with this request, however, is that it returns Mistress Openwork to the ideological dilemma introduced in the first market scene of the play, in which the sexual connotations of a shopwife's openly displaying her wares for public purchase enable Moll to defame Mistress Openwork for "prick[ing] out a poor living" (2.1.237).

Through her entrapment of Goshawk, Mistress Openwork ironically comes to resemble Moll, against whose scandalous example she had initially defined her own chastity and industriousness. Earlier in the play, Moll had promised to meet Laxton in a disreputable locale, Gray's Inn Fields, for what he believed would be a sexual encounter; instead, Moll disguises herself in male apparel and punishes his lechery. Likewise, Mistress Openwork promises to accompany Goshawk to a disreputable locale for what he believes will be a sexual encounter; instead, she arrives in a mask and punishes his lechery. Mistress Openwork even appears to fulfill the role of whore in which Laxton had earlier cast Moll: "Thou'rt admirably suited for the Three Pigeons at Brentford" (3.1.56–57). Adopting the deceptive behavior and presumed sexual availability that motivate her own slander of Moll, Mistress Openwork blurs the line between the "chaste wife" and the "whore."

Master Openwork ultimately forgives Goshawk and welcomes him as a guest to his home. No longer concerned that Goshawk will seduce his wife, Master Openwork identifies her chastity with the fortress-like durability of his house: "Seeing, thus besieged, it holds out, 'twill never fall!" (4.2.234). The suggestion of overconfidence in Master Openwork's declaration is confirmed when the image of a besieged household returns in a significantly compromised form slightly later in the scene, during Laxton's fabricated account of how he "laid siege" to Mistress Gallipot (4.2.318). Like Mistress Openwork, Mistress Gallipot "holds out" against sexual occupation, but only because of Laxton's "want of doing ill," as Master Gallipot wryly notes (4.2.338). Symptomatic of a lingering anxiety about the citizen wife's agency, the last words spoken by a citizen in *The Roaring Girl*—"Wife, brag no more / Of holding out: who brags most is most whore" (4.2.342–43)—bypass any thoughtful reconsideration or renegotiation of the contradictory status of the wife as producer in the urban marketplace. Rather, these words simply reinscribe, through the ever-present threat of sexual defamation, the porous ideological boundary between working women and whores.

The conclusion of *The Roaring Girl* imposes upon all the citizens the silence that Master Gallipot enjoins upon his wife. Returning on stage to celebrate the marriage of Sebastian and Mary, the citizens say nothing. Their dramatic purpose as emblems of conjugal harmony becomes evident only in the closing speech of the play, in which Sir Alexander praises the wives: "And you, kind gentlewomen, whose sparkling presence / Are glories set in marriage, beams of society, / For all your loves give lustre to my joys" (5.2.259–61). Notably, Sir Alexander elevates the citizen wives to the status of gentlewomen, a gesture that contrasts sharply with Laxton's scornful labeling of Mistress Gallipot as a "she-citizen" in the previous act (4.2.317). Sir Alexander apparently perceives Mistresses Gallipot and Openwork as models of the kind of virtuous wife his daughter-in-law Mary will become. His casting of the citizen wives as emblems of companionate marriage and communal harmony ("beams of society"), however, erases the economic discrepancy between citizen wives and gentry wives—the very source of the resentment that motivated the citizen wives to seek gallant lovers. Mary plays the role of a seamstress to facilitate her marriage to Sebastian; as a gentleman's wife her labor will likely consist of managing the household and doing needlework during leisure time. Unlike the citizen wives, Mary will not work in the public market as a producer and seller of goods.

As I have argued, it is precisely the threat represented by the sexual and economic agency of urban working women that has prevented the citizen wives from achieving in their own husbands' eyes Sir Alexander's sparkling vision of them as "glories set in marriage, beams of society." In the final moments

of the play, Sir Alexander's idealism serves the ends of comic resolution. Nonetheless, through the play's representation of the sexual type of the citizen wife,
playgoers might have been better able to appreciate the dilemma faced by
women whose market activities made them vulnerable to sexual defamation.
If Sir Alexander's dazzling vision of companionate marriage temporarily dis-
tracted playgoers from acknowledging the association between urban women's
sexual and economic agency, all they had to do was look at all the "city-roaring
girl[s]" in their midst (Prologue 22).

Part 3

Sexual Types and Intermediary Functions

Chapter 5

Making Common

Familiar Knowledge and the Bawd's Seduction

> Her envy is like that of the Devill, to have all faire women like her;
> and because it is impossible they should catch it being so young,
> she hurries them to it by diseases. Her *Parke* is a villanous barren
> ground; and all the Deere in it are Rascall: yet poore Cottagers in
> the Countrey (that know her but by heare-say) thinke well of her;
> for what she encloses today, she makes *Common* tomorrow.
> —Sir Thomas Overbury, *Characters* (1616)

Female bawds are a common type on the early modern English stage, in part because a "bawd" might be considered any woman who facilitates another woman's entry into an illicit sexual relationship. Whether she is a professional brothel-keeper who actively recruits women into her trade, or simply a nurse, servant, relative, or neighbor who takes advantage of her intimacy with a female companion, the figure of the bawd, I will argue, represents the dangerous sexual potential of the common. I intend "common" to convey three interrelated meanings. Most broadly, the common refers to what is "usual" or "ordinary."[1] To situate the bawd as a sexual type, I will explore how the common, unremarkable intimacies of women in domestic or communal settings give occasion to illicit social and sexual practices. Illicit sexual practices often shade into the second sense of "common" as "possessed or shared by all," as in the familiar early modern locution "common woman."[2] Finally, I analyze the skillful deployment of rhetorical commonplaces or proverbs by which the bawd actively ushers another woman into "common" sexuality.[3] As William Camden explains in *Remaines concerning Britaine* (1614), proverbs are "concise, witty, and wise Speeches grounded upon long experience, conteining for the most part good caveats, and therefore both profitable and delightfull" (sig. Pp3r). The bawd's use of proverbial wisdom as an instrument of sexual corruption shows how the familiar or commonplace—the consensus of long and general experience—can be deployed to undo orderly familial and social relations. In this regard, the mostly aptly named bawd in early modern English drama must be Marre-Maide from S. S.'s *The Honest Lawyer*: a woman who uses the enchanting voice of the *mermaid* (or siren) to *mar maids*, or ruin virgins.

If it also made for good theater, the premise that common intimacy and common speech among women could promote unchaste sexuality understandably generated patriarchal anxiety. The patriarchal concern over women's familiar intimacies is given overt expression in Giovanni Michele Bruto's conduct book the *Education of a yong Gentlewoman*, translated from Italian into English in 1598.[4] The *Education* addresses itself to gentlemen who wish to inculcate proper manners in their daughters. To this end, Bruto carefully delimits the female companions appropriate for an impressionable young gentlewoman. For the young woman's governor he recommends "some Gentlewoman full of gravitie and wisedome, of good conscience and behaviour" (sig. C4r). Keeping "continuall familiaritie" with her charge, this grave matron must persuade her to despise vicious inclinations and to avoid lascivious books and wicked companions (sig. D8v):

> Among the which (it is hardly to beleved [*sic*]) what mischiefe is bred by the familiaritie of those dames that under pretence of gentilitie, giving of apparell, jewels, gold, and precious stones: or (which is much more dangerous) under shew of religion and honestie, use most corrupt & most beastly enticings and allurements. (sig. D6r)

The impressionable gentlewoman must shun not only such lascivious dames but also the "maides, servants, and other prating women, that most commonly haunt the houses of gentlewomen of account, & many times are causes of great mischiefes" (sig. D8r). In this paranoid formulation, the common (that is, non-gentle) women who circulate through gentle households are blamed for spreading the common language—immodest "tales & prating speeches"—that "yong girls do much delight in at night when they sit by the fire" (sig. D8r). Bruto reiterates that the gentlewoman should "shunne too much familiaritie of her equals, but much more of her servants and maides, and such light women . . . who for the most part are wicked, and many of them readier to speake that which becommeth them not, than to heare that they ought to heare" (sig. K4r). Although the tract's capacious language of corruption, mischief, and wickedness encompasses many vices that might lure a young gentlewoman away from virtue, the "filthy abomination" of sexual vice is an ever-present threat (sig. D4v).

Whereas the *Education of a yong Gentlewoman* recommends a grave matron as the preserver of youthful virtue, in the dramatic representation of bawdry an older woman is much more likely to be the agent of a younger woman's sexual corruption. The figure of the experienced bawd embodies the paradoxical situation of elderly women in early modern culture.[5] On the one hand, as Laura Gowing remarks, the authority that generally came with old age in early modern society manifested for older women "in roles of caretaking, supervising, and nursing the community's bodies" (*Common* 76). On the other hand, older women were sometimes scorned as ridiculous or dangerous figures, as in stereotypical representations of the old crone, widow, or witch.[6] Cultural stereotype held that bawds were former prostitutes who were no longer young enough, attractive enough, or energetic enough to sell their own bodies; hence they sought out fresh women to take up the trade.[7] In the drama, the old bawd's agency in bringing innocent women to spiritual and physical ruin sometimes elicits fulminations against her rotten and decrepit body. At these moments, the aged female body, portrayed as grotesquely dried up and worn out, signifies the loathsomeness of sexual commerce and the betrayal of the ideal of female chastity. Ostensibly, the ideological lesson to be learned from the decrepit body of the bawd is that physical degeneration constitutes the "natural" punishment for sexual degeneracy.[8]

When a young, able-bodied, male actor performed the role of bawd on the London stage, however, the ideological association between habitual sin and physical decrepitude would have been open to demystification. Moreover, the persuasive speech of a stage bawd potentially conveys an intellectual agency and social authority that countered the typically satirical emphasis on her grotesque, debilitated body. Whereas Jeanne Addison Roberts argues that in early modern texts the threat represented by the old bawd is effectively "dealt with by law and authority" (122), I argue that the bawd's appropriation of familiar wisdom to defend her profession could expose the rhetorical foundations on which "law and authority" rested.[9] That the proverb-spouting bawd could be understood to seize moral and intellectual authority for illicit ends becomes even more evident when we consider that the names attached to collections of proverbs in the period include those of Camden, Erasmus, and King James.[10] Finally, I suggest that the rhetorical power of vitriolic anti-bawd tirades is diminished to the degree that these tirades themselves routinely deploy rhetorical commonplaces.[11] Ironically, the anti-bawd tirade becomes just as "stale" and "toothless" as the stereotypical old bawd it reviles. John Marston doubtless expected audiences of *The Dutch Courtesan* to recognize how Cocledemoy's long "oration" in praise of the bawd Mary Faugh humorously inverts the hoary anti-bawd tirade (1.2.26–56).

In this chapter, I have organized my analysis of dramatic texts in terms of the increasing agency of the bawd, an agency I measure in terms of the bawd's successful manipulation of common knowledge and the common spaces of same-sex intimacy. I begin with John Fletcher's *A Wife for a Month*, in which the anti-bawd rhetoric is greatly out of proportion to the bawd's agency; I also explore similar rhetoric in other plays and prose texts. Next, turning to Thomas Dekker and John Webster's *Westward Ho*, I consider how a bawd manages to seduce a married woman through the use of rhetorical commonplaces and homoerotic insinuation. The bulk of the chapter is devoted to a major Jacobean tragedy, Thomas Middleton's *Women Beware Women*. Betrayed into adultery by Livia's schemes, Bianca might well consider her a "damned bawd" (2.2.464), but with her considerable wealth and intelligence Livia is far from the decrepit old bawd of satiric stereotype. One of the great schemers of early modern tragedy, Livia exerts her social, economic, and rhetorical powers to maneuver other women into sexual relationships that serve her own ambitions and pleasures. Concluding with the Bawd in *Pericles*, I consider what Shakespeare does with this set of cultural materials in his only extended treatment of a professional female bawd.[12]

*   *   *

Before considering dramatic representations of bawds, it is important to observe that although the preponderance of professional female bawds on the stage corresponds to social historians' findings regarding the structure of prostitution in early modern England, the relative absence of nonprofessional male bawds in the drama has significant ideological implications. A valuable, though problematic, source of information about professional prostitution in early modern England is the court of the London Bridewell, one of four London hospitals founded in the mid-sixteenth century "to cope with the problems raised by poverty, vagrancy and ill health" (P. Griffiths 42).[13] Many records survive from the later 1570s, when the Bridewell governors launched a campaign against organized prostitution centered in the brothels (P. Griffiths 43). Paul Griffiths's examination of these records indicates that the majority of professional bawds were women:

> Of the 104 keepers who can be linked with particular "bawdys"—and some of course kept more than one house—74 were women (71.2 per cent) and 15 men (14.4 per cent). Fifteen other brothels were kept by a joint husband/wife team. . . . Of the 35 procurers 27 were women (77 per cent) and 5 were male (14.3 per cent), while there are 3 examples of a husband/wife team procuring their daughter in one case and their maid in the other two. (46)

Laura Gowing's analysis of London consistory court deposition books supports Griffiths's findings in that women significantly outnumbered men as plaintiffs in sexual defamation suits. Between 1572 and 1640, records survive of 139 women and 43 men who litigated against those who slandered them as "bawd" (*Domestic* 64).[14] Griffiths's and Gowing's evidence for London suggests that bawds—both in practice and in perception—were primarily women. From a purely statistical perspective, the drama reinforces this gender slant. In an examination of 77 plays identified by the *Index of Characters in Early Modern English Drama* as containing "Bawds" and "Panders," I counted female procurers in 50 plays, and male procurers in 35.[15]

Significantly, however, it is difficult to find dramatic representations of those forms of nonprofessional bawdry commonly practiced by men in early modern England.[16] Given the drama's interest in all manner of illicit sex—including fornication, adultery, bigamy, incest, group rape, and necrophilia—it is surprising how rarely playwrights drew upon the richly varied misconduct of nonprofessional male bawds. According to Martin Ingram, one "serious form of bawdry which occasionally came before the courts was when a man was bribed to marry a woman who was with child by a third party" (282). I can identify only a single comparable dramatic scenario, from Dekker, Ford, and Rowley's *The Witch of Edmonton*, in which Sir Arthur Clarington offers Frank Thorney a £200 portion to marry Winnifride, Sir Arthur's secret mistress. Another kind of bawdry was "when a husband agreed to tolerate and conceal his wife's adultery" (Ingram 283). Cuckoldry is ubiquitous in early modern drama, but wittols (knowing, complaisant cuckolds) show up in relatively few plays, most memorably in Middleton's *A Chaste Maid in Cheapside* and

Shakespeare's *A Midsummer Night's Dream*, if we consider it "self-cuckoldry" for Oberon to encourage Titania's passion for Bottom (Bruster, *Drama* 52). The husbands in Jonson's *Volpone* and Dekker's *The Honest Whore, Part Two* attempt to prostitute their wives, but the women refuse to comply.[17] In *All's Well That Ends Well*, Lavatch quips that whoever cuckolds him does him the friendly service of performing his conjugal labor, but there is no indication that Lavatch actually intends to cuckold himself.

Perhaps even more surprising than spousal bawdry is parental bawdry. Parents were occasionally "prosecuted for acting as bawds to their own children, by deliberately allowing them to fornicate under the parental roof" (Ingram 284).[18] Shakespeare depicts parental bawdry in two plays based on classical mythology: in *Troilus and Cressida*, Calchas allows Diomedes into his tent to visit his daughter Cressida, and in *The Two Noble Kinsmen*, the Jailer reluctantly allows the Wooer to have sex with his daughter as a cure for her madness. *Troilus and Cressida* also features the mythical "father" of all panders, Pandarus, who is Cressida's uncle. More sensationalistic instances of familial bawdry include Tamora in *Titus Andronicus*, who encourages her sons to rape Lavinia (albeit in the forest, not "under the parental roof"); and the Duke and Duchess in *The Revenger's Tragedy*, who authorize their sons' sexual rapacity. Edward Sharpham depicts a farfetched scenario of parental bawdry in *The Fleire*, in which two Italian sisters become courtesans in London. Disguised as a servant, their father infiltrates their household but does not interfere in their business. Instead, he schemes to marry his older daughter to the son of his political enemy, and his younger daughter to an English knight.[19]

Ingram concludes that "What aroused most parochial concern, and accounted for the great majority of prosecutions" for bawdry "was 'harbouring' pregnant women, especially females from other parishes" whose bastards would financially burden the community (286). Again, London playwrights did not exploit the dramatic potential of plots involving the harboring of pregnant women, even in domestic tragedies or city comedies, where sexual and economic concerns are paramount.[20] The title character of Heywood's *Wise-woman of Hogsdon* boasts of harboring pregnant women, although we never see her do so in the course of the play. There is something appealing about Heywood's depiction of an older, independent woman who assists vulnerable single women. Nonetheless, in the instances Ingram cites from court records, four times as many men as women were prosecuted for harboring pregnant women, and in cases involving kindred most often the harborer was the pregnant woman's father (289).[21]

In sum, while the preponderance of female bawds in the drama does appear to reflect the predominance of professional female bawds in London, the drama's relative neglect of equally stage-worthy kinds of informal bawdry perpetrated by men—particularly fathers and husbands—reveals an ideological tendency to associate sexual criminality with women.[22] This bias becomes even more evident in that a significant number of the bawds who populate sixteenth- and seventeenth-century drama conform to a specific character type. Usually, the bawd is an older, unmarried woman who enjoys an intimate relationship with one or more younger women. Sometimes bawds are the keepers of urban or suburban brothels: examples include the Bawd in Heywood's *The Royall King, and The Loyall Subject*; Mistress Overdone in Shakespeare's *Measure for Measure*; Mistress Fingerlock in Dekker and Middleton's *The Honest Whore, Part One*; Mistress Sweatman in Cooke's *Greenes Tu quoque*; and the Bawd in Massinger's *The Unnaturall Combat*. At the upper end of the social scale, the bawd might be a court lady, such as Maquerelle in Marston's *The Malcontent*; Lady Dildoman in Dekker's *Match Me in London*; the Bawd in Fletcher's *The Loyal Subject*; or Cardente in Nabbes's *The Unfortunate Mother*. In certain circumstances, a nurse, servant, or neighbor might function as a bawd. Examples include Juliet's Nurse in *Romeo and Juliet* (notably called a "bawd" by Mercutio [2.3.116]); Anne Drury, the widowed neighbor of Anne Sanders in *A Warning for Fair Women*; the waiting woman Temperance in Chapman's *May-Day*; Puttana, Annabella's nurse, in Ford's *'Tis Pity She's a Whore*; Calypso, a "confidante" and neighbor of Jolante, in Massinger's *The Guardian*; and Cibile, a "chambermaid, nurse, and bawd," in Gough's *The Strange Discovery*. Finally, there are women who entice their daughters or nieces into illicit sexual relationships. Such familial pairings include Gratiana and her daughter Castiza in *The Revenger's Tragedy*; the Mother, a bawd, and her daughter Frank, a courtesan, in Middleton's *A Mad World, My Masters*; Mistress Gullman, a bawd, and her daughter Flavia, a whore, in Daborne's *The Poor-Mans Comfort*; and Livia and her niece Isabella in Middleton's *Women Beware Women*.[23]

Across such a wide range of plays, bawds are treated with varying degrees of indulgence and contempt, but it is useful to consider the extremity of disgust that the type of the old bawd could provoke. In John Fletcher's *A Wife for a Month*, anti-bawd rhetoric reaches a particularly shrill pitch.[24] At the beginning of the play, King Frederick adulterously pursues Evanthe, a lady in waiting to his Queen. On behalf of the king, Evanthe's brother requires her waiting-woman Cassandra to send the cabinet in which Evanthe

keeps her letters, among which are verses from her lover. At this point in the
play, and despite her description in the Dramatis Personae as "an old Bawd,
Waiting-woman to Evanthe," Cassandra appears simply to be following what
she believes to be her mistress's orders to send the cabinet. Nonetheless, when
Evanthe discovers that Cassandra's compliance has revealed the existence of
her lover to the king, she rages:

> I could curse thee wickedly,
> And wish thee more deformed then age can make thee;
> Perpetuall hunger, and no teeth to satisfie it,
> Waight on thee still, nor sleep be found to ease it:
> Those hands that gave the Casket, may the Palsie
> For ever make unusefull, even to feed thee;
> Long winters, that thy bones may turne to Isicles
> No Hell can thaw againe, inhabit by thee.
> Is thy care like thy body, all on crookednesse?
> How scurvily thou criest now, like a drunkard!
> Ile have as pure teares from a durty spout:
> Do, sweare thou didst this ignorantly, sweare it,
> Sweare and be damn'd, thou halfe witch. (1.2.122–34)

Perhaps understandably, Evanthe wishes palsy upon the hands that have betrayed her trust by sending the cabinet, but she goes much further in curs-
ing her servant with toothlessness, hunger, sleeplessness, coldness, and brittle
bones. When Cassandra complains about having been tricked into relinquishing the cabinet, King Frederick abuses her as an old bawd:

> Peace, good antiquity, Ile have your bones else
> Ground into Gunpowder to shoot at Cats with,
> One word more, and Ile blanch thee like an Almond;
> There's no such cure for the she-falling-sicknesse,
> As the powder of a dried bawds skin, be silent.— (1.2.165–69)

In the king's conceit, a powdered bawd's skin cures the "she-falling-sicknesse"
because dried up old bawds provide relief for the sexual yearnings of younger
women. Even when the king hires Cassandra as his own bawd, he cannot restrain himself, in an aside, from expressing disgust at her body: "Her
breath stinks like a Fox, her teeth are contagious, / These old women are all

Elder-pipes" (4.2.16–17). Whatever pleasure Cassandra might take from her newfound intimacy with the king is short-lived. Reviling Cassandra as a "rude bawde" and "studied old corruptnesse," Evanthe dismisses her from service and wishes her a horrible death (4.3.68–69).

As harsh as the anti-bawd rhetoric may be in *A Wife for a Month*, it receives even fuller elaboration in moral treatises and character books that anatomize the bawd's body and vices without giving her any voice in return.[25] Sir Thomas Overbury's portrait of the "Maquerela" in his popular *Characters* (1616) rehearses the stereotypical traits cited again and again in contemporary accounts of the bawd: she began as a prostitute; she is old, ugly, and diseased; she drinks aqua vitae; she cheats when measuring wine; she fears whipping and carting; she bribes constables.[26] According to Overbury, the decaying of the bawd's body intensifies her malice against the fair women she seeks to corrupt:

> Her teeth are falne out, marry her nose, and chin, intend very shortly to bee friends, and meet about it. Her yeeres are sixty and odde: that shee accounts her best time of trading; for a *Bawde* is like a Medlar, shee's not ripe, till shee bee rotten. Her envy is like that of the Devill, to have all faire women like her; and because it is impossible they should catch it being so young, she hurries them to it by diseases. Her *Parke* is a villanous barren ground; and all the Deere in it are Rascall: yet poore Cottagers in the Countrey (that know her but by heare-say) thinke well of her; for what she encloses today, she makes *Common* tomorrow. (sigs. K1r–v)

The "barren ground" of the brothel serves as macrocosm to the microcosm of the bawd's barren body, crooked and stooped, nose and chin grotesquely collapsing in on each other in a parody of friendly intimacy. Although she is accused of enclosing—the conversion of common land into private sheep pasture, a practice widely excoriated during the sixteenth century for displacing and dispossessing of poor cottagers—the bawd ironically profits by making her private property common once again.

The belief that the bawd acts maliciously in bringing young women to her own state of physical deterioration informs other contemporary texts, such as *The Araignement & burning of Margaret Ferne-seede* (1608), a moralizing account of the execution for murder of an actual London bawd. According to the anonymous author, Margaret worked as a prostitute until age, disease, and staleness necessitated a change of career:

in this more then beastiall lasciviousnes, having consumed the first
part of her youth, finding both the corruption of her blood to check
the former heate of her lust, and the too generall uglinesse of her
prostitution, to breed a loath in her ordinarie customers, being then
confirmed in some more strength of yeares, [she] tooke a house neare
unto the Iron-gate of the Tower, where she kept a moste abhominable
and vilde brothell house, poysoning many young women with that sinne
wherewith her owne body long before was filthilie bebotched. (sig. A3v)

The metaphor of poisoning with sin carries an almost literal force in suggesting that the bawd's filthy body infects the bodies of the young women
whom she keeps. The word "bebotched" is particularly compelling: seemingly
an error (or possibly an alternate spelling) for "debauched," it conveys the
scabrous loathsomeness of "botch": a "boil, ulcer, or pimple," or "an eruptive
disease."[27] Nicholas Breton's character book *The Good and The Badde* (1616)
expresses similar concern about the bawd's infectiousness: she "is dangerous
among young people, for feare of the infection of the falling sicknesse, and not
to teach children to spel, lest she learne them too soone to put together" (sig.
E4v). For Breton, the Bawd threatens both in her passive ability to commu-
nicate disease to young bodies and through her active instruction in teaching
young minds too much too soon.

These moralizing portraits of the bawd's vicious agency are remarkably
consistent with the testimony found in the Bridewell Court Books. According
to Cristine Varholy, the Bridewell records include "many accounts of young
women lured out of service by a seducer or a bawd and then abandoned"
(113).[28] For instance, Fathrell Smyth deposed that she was "procured and en-
tysed thereunto [to this lewdness of lyfe] first by one Warde's wyfe a widowe
dwellinge in St. James Strete whome as she saieth is comonly knowen or re-
puted to be a comon Bawde" (qtd. Varholy 113, n. 14). Laura Gowing draws
attention to a "puzzling" entry in the Bridewell Court Book that records the
presentation of Anne Bowell for "keeping company with another mans wief"
("Politics" 137). Gowing speculates that the locution "keeping company"
probably denotes the Bridewell authorities' belief that women seduced other
women into prostitution:

Bridewell's governors were much concerned with the origins and
structure of prostitution in the city; they often questioned women about
how they fell into whoredom, and who had corrupted them. Obligingly,

Figure 24. An emblem of lechery, from Stephen Batman, *A christall glasse of christian reformation* (1569). By permission of the Folger Shakespeare Library.

women responded with details of other women: their mistresses, or their friends, they said, had persuaded them to meet a man in an alehouse, or go to strange houses, or serve drinks to "gentleman" [*sic*] and sit about with them afterwards. ("Politics" 137)

Citing two further instances from the Bridewell Court Book in which a woman complained that another woman "enticed" or "envegled" her to sexual relations with a man or men, Gowing concludes that such incidents seemed to demonstrate that "Unchastity could infect women, spreading from mistresses to servants, between neighbours and friends" ("Politics" 137).

The bawd's malicious double agency as infector and seducer is neatly illustrated in an emblem on Lechery from Stephen Batman's *A christall glasse of christian reformation* (1569). Representing "*meretrix,* the baude," who "procure[s]" youth to lechery, the emblem shows an old woman leading a goat upon which an elaborately dressed younger woman rides (see Figure 24). Old age is signified by the bawd's wrinkled face, cane, and modest apparel, as well as by the suggestion of a stooped or limping gait. The fashionably appareled younger woman represents what the verse calls the "alure" of lechery: her hands are confidently placed, one stroking the goat's phallic horn, and the other, fingers chinked into a "V," accentuating the "V" of her skirts. Despite her brash pose, the whore does not really control her own sexuality. As the embodiment or agent of the devilish "guide" that glides above, the old bawd guides the goat of lust.

A final example from the character genre, Francis Lenton's *Characterismi* (1631), focuses with remarkable bitterness on the bawd's hideous physiognomy. Inherently filthy, the "old Bawd" infects through her very presence:

> [She] Is a menstruous beast, engendred of divers most filthy excrements, by the stench of whose breath the Ayre is so infected, that her presence is an inevitable contagion, her eyes more poysonous than the Basilisk; her nose (if any) most pestilently pocky, her tongue more subtile than the Hyena, who stil howles in some fained voyce for the devouring of innocents, one who hath damnably destroyed her own soule, and is divellishly devising the destruction of others. Shee is the mother of impudency, the Dungeon of diseases, the daughter of lust, and the most obscene sister of scurrilous and lascivious delights. . . . All the credite shee hath got by her abomination, is carting without commiseration & casting of loathsome things at her defiled Carkasse. Diseases at last dry up her marrow, and rottennesse so shivers her, that shee drops asunder on a sudden, and wretchedly dyes without pitty; for whom, a Christian buriall is too courteous. (sigs. C3r–4v)

Seeking to draw younger women to her own state of damnation, the bawd operates through passive "contagion" as well as active manipulation. Lenton's striking use of the term "menstruous" puns on the bawd's "monstrous" physical and moral deformity, but also alludes to popular scientific belief that "menstrual blood, always polluted and destructive," becomes even more dangerous after menopause, because it "festers so that women's bodies became defiled in their very composition" (Taunton 102). As Lenton's Old Bawd ages, this defilement manifests as a spectacular disintegration from within, as she dries up, breaks apart, and suddenly "drops asunder."

Although Lenton attributes to the Bawd the subtlety of a hyena's tongue, it takes the drama to give that tongue agency. Free from the constraints of plot and dialogue, character books can sweepingly range across the bawd's grotesque body or narrate her devolution from alluring prostitute to repulsive carcass. The familiar claim that the bawd physically and spiritually infects other women by her very presence is easily asserted in a character sketch—"her eyes more poysonous than the Basilisk"—but fails as a compelling premise for dramatic conflict. In the drama, even when the bawd is subjected to withering invective, her persuasive charms can give the lie to the simple metaphor of infection. Compelling stage bawds do not passively infect other women with sexual desire or sexual disease. They seduce women by evoking moral commonplaces that make illicit relations appear both attractive and familiar.

Dekker and Webster's *Westward Ho* shows how homoerotic intimacy can function as a persuasive form of familiar knowledge linking women of different social and economic statuses.[29] In the first scene of the play, Mistress Birdlime, an "olde Gentlewoman" (1.1.49), tempts Mistress Justiniano, a merchant's wife, into committing adultery with an Earl. Offering Mistress Justiniano a velvet gown sent by the Earl, Mistress Birdlime does not tout the Earl's desirability, but rather flatters Mistress Justiniano:

> **Bird[lime]:** I dreamt last night, you lookt so prettily, so sweetly, me thought so like the wisest Lady of them al, in a velvet gowne.

> **Mist[ress] Just[iniano]:** Whats the forepart?

> **Bird[lime]:** A very pretty stuffe, I know not the name of your forepart, but tis of a haire colour. (1.1.65–70)

The "forepart" of a dress is the stomacher, but Birdlime's admiration of the "haire colour" of "your forepart" seems to evince a sexual interest in Mistress

Justiniano's own "pretty stuffe."[30] Arguing for a woman's right to maintain her beauty, Birdlime soothes and strokes Mistress Justiniano:

> beauty covets rich apparell, choyce dyet, excellent Physicke, no German Clock nor Mathematicall Ingin whatsoever requires so much reparation as a womans face, and what means hath your Husband to allow sweet Docter *Glister-pipe*, his pention. . . . I have heard he loved you before you were married intyrely, what of that? I have ever found it most true in myne owne experyence, that they which are most violent dotards before their marryage are most voluntary Coucouldes after. Many are honest, either because they have not wit, or because they have not opportunity to be dishonest, and this Italian your Husbands Countryman, holdes it impossible any of their Ladies should be excellent witty, and not make the uttermost use of their beauty, will you be a foole then? (1.1.77–80, 86–94).

Birdlime grounds her argument in a series of conventional comic platitudes: received wisdom about the demanding upkeep of female beauty, the difference between an ardent wooer and a neglectful husband, and the wit of a wife who can cuckold her husband.[31] Even the striking comparison between a woman's face and a German clock is proverbial in the drama of the period, first appearing in Shakespeare's *Love's Labor's Lost*— "A woman, that is like a German clock, / Still a-repairing, ever out of frame, / And never going aright" (3.1.175–77)—and resurfacing in plays by Jonson, Dekker, Middleton, and Fletcher.[32] Convinced by the bawd's rehearsal of gender commonplaces, Mistress Justiniano accepts the Earl's velvet gown.[33]

When she comes to regret her decision, Mistress Justiniano blames the bawd's seductive charms, but her account of that seduction does not exactly correspond to what Dekker and Webster have presented in the earlier scene. Whereas Mistress Birdlime, as we have seen, ushers Mistress Justiniano into adultery by openly engaging in a same-sex courtship, Mistress Justiniano accuses the bawd of using a subtle form of witchcraft, a homoerotic deception associated with the cross-dressing practices of the London theater. Mistress Justiniano complains to the Earl:

> you sent a Sorceres
> So perfect in her trade, that did so lively

Breath forth your passionate Accents, and could drawe
A Lover languishing so piercingly,
That her charmes wrought uppon me, and in pitty
Of your sick hart which she did Countefet,
(Oh shees a subtle Beldam!) see I cloth'd
My limbes (thus Player-like) in Rich Attyres,
Not fitting mine estate, and am come forth,
But why I know not? (2.2.102–11)

In other words, Mistress Justiniano claims to have been seduced by Mistress
Birdlime's moving impersonation of a heartsick lover. Evoking the anxious hy-
potheses of English anti-theatrical writers, Mistress Justiniano complains that
her subjection to this cross-gendered performance has moved her to vicious
emulation: player-like, she has dressed above her rank and adopted the role of
a "common Venturer" (2.2.160). Mistress Justiniano acknowledges her susceptibility to the bawd's homoerotic charms; she distances the intimacy of that
seduction, however, by portraying the bawd as a counterfeit substitute for the
male client she represents, in both the business and theatrical senses of that term.

Even more than the comedic *Westward Ho*, satiric and tragic plays tend
to emphasize the sexual aggression motivating the bawd's manipulation of
same-sex intimacies.[34] In John Marston's bitter satire *The Malcontent*, for instance, Malevole taunts the court bawd Maquerelle for abusing her intimacy
with young women: "methinks thou liest like a brand under billets of green
wood. He that will inflame a young wench's heart, let him lay close to her an
old coal that hath first been fired, a pandress, my half-burnt lint, who though
thou canst not flame thyself, yet art able to set a thousand virgins' tapers afire"
(2.2.4–9). Typically, the old bawd is too spent to have sex with a man, yet
Malevole claims that she retains enough heat from her former life to warm
up a cold virgin. That the smoldering bawd must "lay close" to those women
she wishes to initiate into sexual knowledge suggests an intimacy that is itself
homoerotic, even if ultimately in the service of male sexual desire.

William Rowley's tragedy *All's lost by Lust* (1633) depicts a bawd's seductive
powers in unabashedly corporeal, and homoerotic, terms. Having failed to seduce the lady Jacinta on behalf of King Roderigo, Lothario, the king's favorite,
turns to the bawd Malena for assistance:

Come old reverence, if ever thou hadst musique in thee,
To inchant a maydenhead, now strike up.

> **Mal[ena]:** You play well
> On the Pandora, Sir I wonder your skill
> Failes to make her dance after it.
>
> **Lo[thario]:** Tush, I give thee
> The precedence, wire strings will not doote, it must be
> A winde instrument thats govern'd with stopping of holes,
> Which thou playest well on, my old Violl de gamb,
> Come, thou shalt have reward. (sig. C2v)

In an extended conceit comparing sexual enticement to the playing of musical instruments, Malena expresses surprise that Lothario's fingering of the pandora, a stringed instrument, fails to excite Jacinta. Implying that a woman can best stimulate another woman, Lothario commends Malena's skill with wind instruments, in which one produces sound by "stopping of holes." Somewhat confusingly, Lothario refers to Malena herself as a viola da gamba, presumably because this stringed instrument is played between the legs, an allusion to Malena's prior experience as a prostitute. But his point is that Malena's sexual experience with her own "holes" qualifies her to enchant a younger woman into taking pleasure in her holes.

When recommending Malena's services to King Roderigo, Lothario represents the bawd's seductive powers in terms of physical conquest more than erotic enchantment. Malena, he boasts, "shall wrastle a fall / With the strongest Virgin in *Spaine,* & throw her down too" (sig. B2r). In the ensuing conversation, Malena's faulty understanding of Latin aptly turns "*foeminae vincunt*" (women surpass or conquer) into an allusion to the female body part she intends to conquer:

> **Rod[erigo]:** Come, come, you must not plead an insufficiency.
>
> **Mal[ena]:** I'le doe my best my Lord.
>
> **Lo[thario]:** Tush, *in malo consilio foeminae vincunt viros.*[35]
>
> **Mal[ena]:** Does he not abuse me my Liege?
>
> **Rod[erigo]:** Not at all, he sayes women overcome men in
> Giving counsell.

Mal[ena]: Is there not a faulty word amongst them?

Lo[thario]. Thou art able to corrupt any good sense, with bad
construction:
I say *foeminae vincunt,* that is, *quasi vincere cunctos,*
Overcomes all men.

Mal[ena]: Go to, go to, there is a broad word amongst'm, *vincunt*
Quotha, is it spoke with a K, or a C? But in plaine
Language I will doe my best, if she be of my sexe, *I*
Will shew her the end of her function, men follow
The traditions of their forefathers, so should
Women follow the trades of their fore-mothers.

Rod[erigo]: I see thou hast perswasive oratory.
Here's juyce of liquorish, good for thy voice,
Speake freely, and effectually.

Mal[ena]: I will speake the words that have o'rethrowne a
Hundred in my time.

Lo[thario]: I was within compass then.

Mal[ena]: Let me have accesse to her, if she be flesh & bloud,
I'le move her, I will not leave her till I turne her to a stone. (sig. B2v)

Like Lothario in the earlier passage, Malena implies that a woman is best
equipped to show another woman "the end of her function." She grounds
her persuasive oratory in the traditional wisdom that men should follow the
trades of their fathers, and women of their mothers. Malena's oddly inapposite
metaphor for a successful seduction—"turn[ing] her to a stone"—seems to invert the proverbial notion of successful persuasion as the ability to move or to
soften even a stone.[36] Aside from taking a swipe at Malena's ignorance, Rowley
may well be punning on "stone" as testicle, in that the bawd's homoerotic
manipulation of Jacinta's "flesh & bloud" aims to "turne" the young woman
toward a sexual encounter with a man.

Having examined the language of homoerotic seduction as physical
conquest in *All's lost by Lust*, we can return to *Westward Ho* with a better

appreciation of the light touch Mistress Birdlime uses to establish intimacy with Mistress Justiniano. When it comes to rhetorical persuasion, however, Mistress Birdlime unleashes her formidable powers. To justify the wisdom of having a sexual relationship with the Earl, the bawd reels off a series of homely proverbs: "Is not old wine wholesommest, olde Pippines toothsommest, old wood burne brightest, old Linnen wash whitest, old souldiors Sweet-hart are surest, and olde Lovers are soundest" (2.2.165–68). In an even more remarkable passage, Mistress Birdlime draws upon an eclectic rhetorical arsenal comprised of common knowledge, Petrarchan cliché (cherry lips and ivory teeth), theatrical catchphrases ("*Jeronimo*: goe by"), and proverbial wisdom:

> your husbands down the wind, and wil you like a haglers Arrow, be
> down the weather, Strike whilst the iron is hot. A woman when there
> be roses in her cheekes, Cherries on her lippes, Civet in her breath,
> Ivory in her teeth, Lyllyes in her hand, and Lickorish in her heart, why
> shees like a play. If new, very good company, very good company, but if
> stale, like old *Jeronimo*: goe by, go by. Therefore as I said before, strike.
> Besides: you must think that the commodity of beauty was not made
> to lye dead upon any young womans hands: if your husband have given
> up his Cloake, let another take measure of you in his Jerkin: for as the
> Cobler, in the night time walks with his Lanthorne, the Merchant, and
> the Lawyer with his Link, and the Courtier with his Torch: So every lip
> has his Lettice to himself: the Lob his Lasse, the Collier his Dowdy, the
> Westerne-man his Pug, the Serving-man his Punke, the student his Nun
> in white Fryers, the Puritan his Sister, and the Lord his Lady: which
> worshipfull vocation may fall upon you, if youle but strike whilest the
> Iron is hot.[37] (2.2.179–96)

At least five proverbs are embedded in this short speech: "to go down the wind"; "to go down the weather," meaning to go bankrupt (*OED*); "an old cloak makes a new jerkin"; "such lips such lettice" (included by Camden in his collection of English proverbs, sig. Qq4v); and "strike while the iron is hot" (also in Camden, sig. Qq3r).[38] Rejecting the proverbial advice to strike while the iron is hot, Mistress Justiniano skeptically "breake[s]" the bawd's rhetorical "Spels" (2.2.197). Birdlime's failure to complete Mistress Justiniano's transformation from faithful wife to "common Venturer" might be attributed, in part, to the nakedness of her seductive tactics (2.2.160). That these proliferating commonplaces are insufficiently digested into the bawd's discourse only calls attention to her self-interested deployment of rhetorical artifice.

A more successful seducer of women than Mistress Birdlime, Livia from Middleton's *Women Beware Women* represents a significant departure from the outlines of the typical bawd reproduced by character books, satires, and plays.[39] Such texts commonly suggest that the old bawd suffers corporeal and social degeneration as a consequence of her sexual transgressions. Livia, however, is a wealthy, attractive, aristocratic widow, and her sexual manipulation of other women has nothing to do with financial need or subjection to the will of a more powerful man. Like the typical bawd, Livia manipulates common knowledge and same-sex intimacy for illicit ends. Unlike the typical bawd, she derives erotic and intellectual satisfaction from her successful management of other women's bodies and pleasures. Enjoying and exploiting her considerable social, economic, and sexual agency, Livia cannot be adequately contained by the disciplinary parameters of her sexual type.

In the opening scene of *Women Beware Women*, Middleton establishes his characters' awareness of the benefits to be derived from managing conventional wisdom about women. Leantio and his mother are discussing his new wife, Bianca, a wealthy Venetian gentlewoman with whom he has eloped to Florence. Worried that Bianca will have difficulty adjusting to her impoverished circumstances, Leantio's mother cites her own experience to conclude that "ev'ry woman of necessity" seeks to be maintained at or above the level of her birth (1.1.67). Leantio protests that Bianca remains innocent of the doctrine that teaches other wives "To rise . . . in commotion / Against their husbands, for six gowns a year" (1.1.76–77); rather than follow "the licentious swinge of her own will, / Like some of her old school-fellows," Bianca, he insists, will conform her desires to his means (1.1.92–93). Despite his confidence in Bianca's self-restraint, however, Leantio expresses relief that during his absences from home his mother will remain to keep watch over his wife: "Old mothers know the world, and such as these / When sons lock chests, are good to look to keys" (1.1.175–76). Through a neat couplet, Leantio attempts to manage the anxiety produced by the conventional wisdom about women's appetites by citing equally conventional wisdom about maternal prudence.

If Leantio aspires to contain his wife in a locked chest, Livia's nuanced defense of wives' domestic agency undermines the very premise that a woman's desires can be deciphered and controlled. To defend her niece's right to marry the man she loves, Livia draws upon a hard-won wisdom that belies her thirty-nine years of age (2.2.157). Unlike Leantio and his mother, Livia avoids simple aphorisms and metaphors when speaking on the subject of wifely obedience. Instead, she develops a complex analogy between marriage and cooking. The husband, Livia argues, has the advantage in marriage, because

> he tastes of many sundry dishes
> That we poor wretches never lay our lips to:
> As obedience forsooth, subjection, duty, and such kickshaws,
> All of our making, but served in to them.
> And if we lick a finger then sometimes,
> We are not to blame; your best cooks use it. (1.2.40–45)

Livia's conclusion is rather puzzling. She cites a common practice—the "best cooks use" to taste their own dishes—behind which lies a proverb: "An ill cooke cannot licke his owne fingers" (Camden, sig. Pp4r). However, the implications of her comparison between wives and cooks remain obscure. If the "dishes" wives serve to their husbands are obedience and duty, then the freedom to "lick a finger" of these dishes suggests that wives might sometimes enjoy a bit of the authority usually reserved for men. But in what circumstances might a wife exert such authority, and with whom? Does Livia mean that wives can occasionally invert domestic hierarchy by controlling their husbands, or that wives can occasionally exploit domestic hierarchy by misusing servants? Does the sensual image of "lick[ing] a finger" imply that the wife seeks domestic power through sexual pleasure, or does the sensual pleasure of taste merely convey the thrill of achieving domestic power? What kind of knowledge does Livia possess of household power relations? Livia's very language seems to maintain the secrecy that she attributes to strong-willed wives.

Livia's admiration of those wives who "lick a finger" for their own pleasure hints at the erotic pleasure she will take throughout the play in manipulating female intimacies. In her function as bawd, Livia orchestrates heteroerotic relationships between Isabella and Hippolito and then between Bianca and the Duke; thus Douglas Bruster argues that Middleton "eroticizes female-female contact while having it function 'for' adulterous heterosexuality" (*Shakespeare* 139). Moreover, Bruster posits that Livia's prior experience with two husbands "enables her to seduce both Isabella and Bianca—it takes one dead husband for each woman Livia helps seduce, seduction predicated on a sexual displacement or equivalency" (139). Livia's same-sex seductions, however, are not simply displacements of, metaphors for, or instruments of heteroerotic seduction. Rather, the play suggests that Livia gets erotic satisfaction from subjecting other women to her sexual and social authority, thus placing them in the same kind of subordinated position that she avoids by refusing to remarry.[40]

Livia's orchestration of an incestuous relationship between her brother Hippolito and their niece Isabella is a daring accomplishment that both manifests her sisterly affection and gratifies her ego. Editor J. R. Mulryne argues that Livia here evinces "moral blindness or lack of scruple" (*Women* lv)—that is, a spiritual or ethical deprivation—but it would be more accurate to say that Livia is driven by an *excess* of feeling. Lavishly praising her brother as "all a feast," Livia regards as "a most happy guest" the woman who will sexually enjoy him (1.2.149–50). She blames her excessive affection for her decision to put Hippolito's pleasure before family honor: "Beshrew you, would I loved you not so well. . . . / I am the fondest where I once affect" (2.1.63, 65); and she admits that there are "few sisters / That love their brothers' ease 'bove their own honesties" (2.1.70–71). Corroborating the claims of earlier critics such as Roma Gill and Daniel Dodson, Stephen Wigler states categorically that Livia "has incestuous feelings" for Hippolito (196). Whether or not we regard Livia's feelings for her brother as sexual, her eagerness to fulfill his illicit desires reveals an intense affection for him, as well as a desire to achieve "glory" for her powers of persuasion (2.1.56).

Significantly, Livia decides to help Hippolito only after having articulated the conventional arguments against incest. What this seeming contradiction suggests is not that Livia's passion finally overtakes her reason or moral scruples, but that she is able to weigh opposing sides of an argument and to determine which course of action will give her the greater satisfaction. When Hippolito first confesses his incestuous desire, Livia responds with requisite wonder at the "strange affection" that jeopardizes the family's ability to extend its power through marital alliance—the kind of alliance sought in the arranged marriage between Isabella and the foolish but wealthy Ward (2.1.1). Lecturing Hippolito on good husbandry, she concludes with a platitudinous rhyming couplet: "So he heaven's bounty seems to scorn and mock / That spares free means, and spends of his own stock" (2.1.15–16). According to the conventional patriarchal wisdom articulated here, Hippolito's duty is to preserve the family's stock of cultural and financial capital against "unkindly" and self-destructive desire (2.1.8).

Once Livia decides to sacrifice family honor for her brother's happiness, however, she cites conventional wisdom about human frailty to justify the alternative course of action: "This is the comfort, / You are not the first, brother, has attempted / Things more forbidden than this seems to be" (45–47). As in her elaborate analogy between marriage and cooking, Livia's citation of common practice actually obscures what it promises to illuminate. Initially, Livia seems ready to offer her brother the unambiguous comfort of the universal: you are not the first to sin; we are all sinners. But she undermines the simplicity of this truism by introducing a comparative: others have sinned even more gravely than you by pursuing "things more forbidden than this seems to be." Livia implies that there are "things more forbidden" than incest between an uncle and a niece. What, exactly, might those things be, and how, in any case, might one measure degrees of forbiddenness? Is Livia referring to degrees of consanguinity, with the implication that incest between uncle and niece is less serious than incest between brother and sister, or parent and child? Livia further muddies the moral terrain by claiming that incest only "seems to be" forbidden. Although Hippolito has flatly admitted that incest is "not a thing ordained, Heaven has forbid it" (1.2.153), he puts up no resistance to Livia's relaxation of moral standards. Crucially, Middleton does not develop the kind of ideological debate about incest that John Ford, in *'Tis Pity She's a Whore*, stages between the Friar, the spokesperson for the church, and Giovanni, the advocate of transgressive love. Whereas Giovanni presents passionate (if flawed) arguments on behalf on his love for his sister, Livia simply sweeps argument aside. Livia gratifies her deep affection for her brother by fulfilling his sexual longing for Isabella.

If Livia takes any erotic pleasure from this scheme, however, it would seem to derive not from her affection for Hippolito but from the manipulation of her intimacy with Isabella. Livia boasts in richly corporeal terms of her ability to enflame her niece's desires:

> Sir, I could give as shrewd a lift to chastity
> As any she that wears a tongue in Florence:
> Sh'had need be a good horsewoman, and sit fast,
> Whom my strong argument could not fling at last. (2.1.36–39)

The metaphor of tilting at the lists turns Livia's tongue into a weapon, a phallic lance.[41] But "horsewoman," as Douglas Bruster observes, might refer not only to a woman on horseback but also to a horse-woman, a monstrous centaur, and as such might evoke the figure of the tribade with her "unnaturally" enlarged clitoris (*Shakespeare* 140, 133). Livia certainly implies that she has taken Isabella's virginity when she crows, "Who shows more craft t'undo

a maidenhead, / I'll resign my part to her" (2.1.178–79). In drawing attention
to Livia's "part," Middleton alludes to her performance as bawd, to her persuasive tongue (Bruster, *Shakespeare* 140), and to her tongue as a synecdoche
for "the woman's part."[42] Likewise, when Livia jokes about running a "shop in
cunning" (2.2.27), we can hear a pun on her ability to manipulate the "cunny"
of other women.[43] Hippolito, too, marvels at the mysterious craft Livia has
employed against Isabella:

> What has she done to her, can any tell?
> 'Tis beyond sorcery this, drugs, or love-powders.
> Some art that has no name sure, strange to me
> Of all the wonders I e'er met withal
> Throughout my ten years' travels; (2.1.231–35)

Hippolito wonders not what Livia has *said* to Isabella but what she has *done*
to her. His emphasis on Livia's nameless "art," a wonder stranger than anything he has encountered on his travels, recalls the common belief that Africans and Easterners used illicit means, such as sorcery, drugs, or love-powders,
to induce desire. In *Othello*, for instance, Brabrantio accuses Othello of seducing Desdemona through witchcraft, and Leo Africanus's account of African
witches connects the dark arts with female homoerotic seduction (see Chapter
2). Astonished by this strange manifestation of female intimacy, Hippolito is
unable to name the kind of pleasure his sister takes from the young woman
who will finally gratify his own sexual longings.

Homoerotic seduction is also central to the famous scene in which Livia
plays chess with Leantio's mother while the Duke ambushes Bianca in the
gallery above. The chess game is often understood simply as a metaphor for
the Duke's manipulation and sexual conquest of Bianca. It is important to
recognize, however, that Livia's victory over the Mother in chess represents
the climax of an aggressive sexual seduction that originates with Livia's desire to lure Bianca to her home. As Livia's poorer neighbor, the Mother is
described as the "Sunday-dinner woman" and "Thursday-supper woman"
regularly invited over for friendly meals (2.2.3–4). Exploiting this social
familiarity, Livia complains that the Mother has violated true neighborli-
ness by limiting her visits to these formal occasions: "You make yourself so
strange, never come at us, / And yet so near a neighbour, and so unkind"
(2.2.140–41). Livia shrewdly elaborates her supposed longing for intimate
companionship:

> I sit here
> Sometime whole days together without company,
> When business draws this gentleman from home;
> And should be happy in society,
> Which I so well affect as that of yours.
> I know y'are alone too; why should not we
> Like two kind neighbours then supply the wants
> Of one another, having tongue-discourse,
> Experience in the world, and such kind helps
> To laugh down time, and meet age merrily? (2.2.145–54)

Erasing her social superiority, Livia identifies herself and the Mother simply as "two kind neighbours" who enjoy "tongue-discourse." When the Mother reasserts social distinction by remarking the difference in their ages, Livia insists that they are both old, because equally undesirable to young men. Livia finally insists on her right to greater intimacy:

> One afternoon
> So much to spend here! Say I should entreat you now
> To lie a night or two, or a week with me,
> Or leave your own house for a month together—
> It were a kindness that long neighbourhood
> And friendship might well hope to prevail in. (2.2.195–200)

Although it was not uncommon in this period for women of different status (such as mistresses and servants) to lie with each other, Livia minimizes status differences by suggesting that such physical intimacy would take place under the aegis of "friendship." Significantly, Livia first mentions chess as a neighborly pastime and occasion for mirthful same-sex intimacy: "Go to then, set your men; we'll have whole nights / Of mirth together, ere we be much older, wench" (2.2.203–4).

Previous criticism of the chess scene has failed to recognize the pervasive homoerotic innuendo that reveals the pleasure Livia takes from having seduced and conquered the Mother.[44] In "Middleton's Chess Strategies," Neil Taylor and Bryan Loughrey argue that Middleton represents "the relationship between these players and their chess pieces as a heterosexual one" (346), because Bianca, speaking of the chess pieces, quips that "there's men enough to part" Livia and the Mother (2.2.265). In Livia's response, "Ho! but they set us on, let us come off / As well we can, poor souls, men care no farther" (2.2.266–67), Taylor and Loughrey find further evidence of a heterosexual analogy: "The male, she says as she fingers the phallic chess pieces, has no care for the female orgasm" (346). If Livia's fingering of the chess pieces can be interpreted as a sexual act, however, it would make more sense to claim that she is fingering her own "piece," perhaps hinting to the Mother that women do not need men to give themselves and each other pleasure. In this reading, Livia, a sexually experienced widow, counters Bianca's naïve view of sex (and chess) as simply an affair between men and women. Moreover, the dialogue during the chess game frequently alludes to Livia's "cunning" domination of the Mother:

> **Livia:** Alas, poor widow, I shall be too hard for thee.

> **Mother:** Y'are cunning at the game, I'll be sworn, madam.

> **Livia:** It will be found so, ere I give you over.
> She that can place her man well—

> **Mother:** As you do, madam.

> **Livia:** As I shall, wench, can never lose her game. (2.2.294–98)

Toward the end of the game, Livia taunts, "Has not my duke bestirred himself?" (415). Although this question directs our attention offstage, where the Duke has "bestirred himself" sexually with Bianca, it simultaneously points back to Livia's earlier plan to "bestir [her] wits" in seducing Isabella (2.1.62). Middleton requires us to maintain a double perspective throughout the chess match, which at once refers to an off-stage (heteroerotic) seduction and constitutes an on-stage (homoerotic) seduction.

Nonetheless, critics often reduce the complexity of this scene by regarding the chess game not as a sexual seduction in itself, but as a symbolic or allegorical version of the heteroerotic seduction that constitutes the scene's "real" purpose. For instance, Christopher Ricks argues that when Livia speaks of chess, she generates sexual double entendres through words such as "business" and "employed"; he concludes that "Livia enjoys comparing the game of chess (with which she will occupy the Mother) with the seduction that awaits Bianca" (240). Ricks does not regard the chess game itself as a seduction, even though he recognizes that Livia's use of "business" to describe her manipulation of the Mother anticipates the Duke's use of "business" to describe his sexual manipulation of Bianca (2.2.262, 365). In fact, Ricks seems to miss the (homo)sexual connotations of his own language when he writes that Livia "occupies" the Mother with chess. Whereas Ricks regards the chess game as a distraction that facilitates the Duke's seduction of Bianca, Anthony Dawson posits a functional equivalence between the two events, in that "the elaborate charade of the chess match . . . acts out in comic ritual the deadlier game being played on the upper stage and behind the scenes" (313). Dawson argues that both Livia and the Duke enjoy exerting power over others, but he does not admit the parallels in their sexual manipulations of the Mother and Bianca. As a final example, Celia Daileader writes that when the Duke and Bianca leave the stage, Livia's "*double entendres* throughout the game keep the audience alert to the unseen act" of sex taking place offstage (26). I would argue instead that, along with her sexual double entendres, Livia's sexually charged encounter with the Mother during the chess match keeps the audience aware of the offstage sexual encounter between the Duke and Bianca.

As I hope to have demonstrated, in her manipulation of same-sex intimacy and deployment of the common(place) as an instrument of seduction, Livia embodies the typical traits of the dramatic bawd. Livia does not, of course, resemble the decrepit, diseased old bawd typically found in satire and character books. Nonetheless, through Livia's participation in the play's concluding wedding masque Middleton complexly, if obliquely, evokes the figure of the old bawd who seduces and corrupts a younger woman. During the planning of the wedding masque, Livia agrees to play the role of "Juno Pronuba, the marriage-goddess" (4.2.217). During the performance of the masque, however, it becomes apparent that Livia has secretly altered the script so as to visit upon Isabella the combined fates of two mythological figures: Semele, who dies from Jove's fiery embrace, and Danaë, who is impregnated by Jove in a shower of gold. Casting Isabella as Semele/Danaë, Livia implicitly casts herself as one of the potent, dangerous figures who appear in each of those myths: the vengeful Juno who, disguised as an old nurse, betrays Semele to her death; and the sexually aggressive, inexorable Jove who penetrates Danaë in the presence of her old nurse.

Like Juno in the myth of Semele, Livia dissembles her desire to take revenge against a woman who has wronged her. In Arthur Golding's translation of Ovid, Juno, incensed by Semele's adultery with Jove, secures the mortal woman's trust by presenting herself in the likeness of her old nurse:

>   she takes an olde wyves shape
> With hoarie haire and riveled skinne, with slow and crooked gate.
> As though she had the Palsey had, hir feeble limmes did shake,
> And eke she foltred in the mouth as often as she spake.
> She seemde olde Beldame Beroe of Epidaure to bee,
> This Ladie Semelles Nourse as right as though it had
>   beene shee. (3.337–42)

Posing as a trusted counselor, Juno advises Semele to encounter Jove in his full glory, as proof that he is really Jove and not some varlet pretending to be a god.[45] Semele takes Juno's advice, and Jove, compelled by an earlier vow to grant Semele's wishes, visits her in his divine form as god of thunder, thereby consuming her with firebolts. Playing Juno in the masque, Livia throws "flaming gold" upon Isabella while announcing that "Our brother Jove / Never denies us of his burning treasure, / T'express bounty" (5.2.117–19). According to mythographer George Sandys, the moral of the Semele story is that "unlawfull requests were punished by the Gods in consenting" (101). Presenting herself as Jove's sister, Livia hypocritically punishes Isabella for having agreed to an "unlawful" sexual relationship with her uncle as a result of Livia's untruthful persuasions. Despite her inflated self-representation as a divine authority, then, Livia resembles the type of the infectious old bawd, a betrayer and destroyer of young women.

Livia's appropriation of the Semele myth provides her with a high-culture template for unleashing her perverse justice against Isabella, but fails to explain why that justice should manifest as a shower of flaming gold, an unmistakable allusion to the myth of Danaë. To preserve her virginity, Danaë's father locks her in a tower (or, alternatively, in a brass cell), but to no avail, as Jove enters in the form of golden rain and falls into Danaë's lap, impregnating her.[46] A. A. Bromham discusses the significance of the old nurse who commonly appears as Danaë's companion in Renaissance illustrations of the myth. Sometimes interpreted as a figure of avarice, the nurse "is often shown with a sack, apron, or basin to catch some of the gold showering down on her mistress, often in the form of coins" (Bromham 75). As the examples below indicate, Renaissance painters imagined the old nurse in various relations of physical intimacy to Danaë's naked, ecstatic body. The closer she gets to Danaë, the more plausible it becomes to interpret the nurse as a bawd who mediates between a powerful male visitor and her vulnerable female charge (see Figures 25, 26, and 27).

Figure 25. Artemisia Gentileschi, *Danaë* (ca. 1612). Reproduced by permission of the St. Louis Art Museum.

Bromham argues that Bianca is the play's Danaë figure. Like Danaë, he observes, Bianca is guarded by an older woman, Leantio's Mother, and she receives financial reward from the Duke in exchange for sex (74). Yet it is Isabella, not Bianca, who suffers the shower of flaming gold in the masque. Furthermore, Bromham's reading problematically casts the relatively innocent Mother, instead of the calculating Livia, as the figure of the old nurse/bawd who controls access to a younger woman's sexuality. By showering gold into Isabella's lap, Livia associates herself with Jove, legitimate dispenser of bounty and punishment, thus forestalling an interpretation of the masque that might connect her instead with Danaë's greedy and bawdy old nurse. Arguably, Livia uses the elite form of the court masque publicly to repair the damage she has done to her aristocratic reputation both as bawd to Isabella and Bianca, and as sexual patron of Leantio, a mere merchant.

If Livia intends to glorify herself as Jove, however, it is ironic that she chooses the Danaë myth to do so. In sixteenth- and seventeenth-century interpretations of the Danaë myth, Jove often signifies a type of the wealthy

Figure 26. Titian, *Danae* (ca. 1544). Museo del Prado, Madrid, Spain. Erich Lessing/ Art Resource NY.

man who purchases sexual favors.[47] According to Thomas Cooper's *Thesaurus linguæ Romanæ & Britannicæ* (1565),

> By this fable is signified, that Jupiter sent treasure pryvilye unto Danae, and also to them that had the kepynge of hir, wherewith they being corrupted, suffered Jupiter to enter into the towre, and accomplyshe his pleasure. The fable declareth the force of money and giftes in assauting of chastitie. (sig. G4v)

Another mythographer, George Sandys, explains that Jupiter, "endeavoring to violate *Danaë*, with store of gold corrupted her chastity" (166). The Danaë myth also informs more colloquial references to prostitution. In Thomas Dekker's play *Match Me in London* (1631), a bawd instructs the king on seducing a citizen's wife: "I would have you first disguis'd goe along with mee, and buy some toy in her shop, and then if you like *Danae* fall into her lap like *Jove*, a net of Goldsmiths worke will plucke up more women at one draught, then a Fisherman does Salmons at fifteene" (1.4.134–37). Shackerley

Figure 27. Hendrick Goltzius, *The Sleeping Danae Being Prepared to Receive Jupiter* (1603). Los Angeles County Museum of Art, Los Angeles, California. Digital Image © 2009 Museum Associates/LACMA/Art Resource NY.

Marmion's *Hollands leaguer* (1632), a play about the famous London bawd Britanica Hollandia, features a pander who asks potential customers, "Have you any gold? / Tis that must breake our gates ope: there are lockt, / A score of *Danaes* wenches of delight, / Within this Castle" (sig. H1v). For all Livia's social and intellectual agency, then, she is ultimately constrained by the shared cultural meanings of the texts that she seeks to turn to her own ends. To the degree that the Danaë myth signifies, in elite and popular contexts alike, a tale of bawdry, Livia cannot, as it were, escape the brothel, cannot fully dissociate herself from the stigma of having played the "sinful bawd" (*Women* 4.2.225). Middleton reveals Livia's courtly manipulation of mythological material to be simply a more literate version of the typical bawd's manipulation of proverbs and commonplaces.

With the aristocratic, wealthy, and attractive Livia, Middleton works significant variations on the conventional appearance and status of the bawd, while retaining the bawd's typical strategies of homoerotic seduction and rhetorical manipulation. In *Pericles*, Shakespeare departs from the satiric type of the bawd in different ways and with different consequences than Middleton. The brothel episode in *Pericles* functions as a test of Marina's chastity, and her successful endurance of this trial is the precondition for the play's comic conclusion, in which Marina redeems her broken father, is reunited with her mother (a votaress of Diana), and secures an aristocratic husband. Marina must not only preserve her physical virginity in order to carry on Pericles's royal bloodline, she also must maintain the spiritual and moral chastity that endue her with the "sacred physic" that cures Pericles's despair (21.63). Despite her presence in the physically and morally corrupt environment of the brothel, Marina remains chaste, and Shakespeare's alterations to the bawd type contribute to that comic desideratum.[48]

Although she carries the generic name of "Bawd," the procuress in *Pericles* is not the typically decrepit, unmarried bawd of contemporary drama, satire, and character writing. As if to suggest a kind of archetypal brothel family, the Bawd is married to the generically named Pander and retains a household servant, Boult. The Bawd also raises the female children of her prostitutes and, if Boult is to be believed, impresses them into prostitution when they turn eleven. The Bawd's domestic unit thus constitutes one of several disorderly, broken, or incomplete families that fill the play, including King Antiochus and his unnamed daughter/wife; Cleon and his wicked wife Dionyza, parents to Philoten and foster parents to Marina; and Pericles, Thaisa, and Marina, who come together as a family only in the last scene of the play. *Pericles* places particular emphasis on the family as an agent of destruction as well as redemption. Like Dionyza, who attempts to murder Marina, the Bawd serves as a nightmare stepmother for Marina before she completes her arduous romance journey and rejoins her true parents.

Because the generic imperative of the play requires Marina to remain chaste despite the degradations of the brothel, Shakespeare does not portray the Bawd as the typical figure of contamination whose very presence infects young women with sickness and sin. Venereal disease in the Mytilene brothel is restricted to the bodies of "rotten" prostitutes and syphilitic customers, who remain safely offstage (16.7). Never is the Bawd accused of carrying venereal disease, not even by the irreverent Boult or the converted Lysimachus, who describes the brothel itself as a sin-riddled structure on the brink of collapse

(19.138–39). Although Marina fails to convert the Bawd to virtue, her virginal presence comically purifies the Bawd's household, converting it into a school and a chapel.

Perhaps most important, the Bawd does not possess the seductive rhetorical skills of the typical dramatic bawd. It is not that the typical bawd's homoerotic strategies of seduction are entirely missing in *Pericles*. Douglas Bruster argues that the Bawd is a predatory figure who sexually objectifies Marina, threatening to "whip" and "bow" her into the kind of woman that her male customers—and she herself—find desirable (*Shakespeare* 138–39). A footnote in the Norton edition of *Pericles* glosses the homoerotic connotation of the Bawd's complaint that Marina refuses to do her "the kindness of our profession" (19.15). The Bawd's attempts to bend Marina to her will, however, are comically ineffective against Marina's fierce piety. Marina's copious rhetorical skills—"her quirks, her reasons, her master reasons, [and] her prayers"—could "make a puritan of the devil," the Bawd grouses (19.15–17). For once, the common proverbial knowledge of the bawdy house is found in the mouth of the chaste.

What Shakespeare does in the brothel scenes of *Pericles*, then, is to stage a contest between two antithetical sexual types, the bawd and the virgin. When Marina is brought to Mytilene, it is her virginity that defines her and establishes her value for the Bawd. Prizing Marina for the profit her maidenhead will generate, the Bawd perverts the traditional valuation of virginity as a sign of feminine perfection.[49] Although the notion of virginity as the highest state of perfection is a Catholic tenet displaced by the Protestant valuation of chaste marriage, early modern English writers still expressed admiration for virginal purity. In his character of "A Virgin," for instance, Nicholas Breton writes, "Shee is of creatures the Rarest, of Women the Chiefest, of nature the Purest, and of Wisedome the Choysest" (*Good* sig. E2r). For the Bawd, Marina is indeed a rare "paragon," but only because her exceptional beauty will draw more paying customers (16.123). What finally saves Marina from the sexual economy of the brothel, however, are precisely her "absolute" and rare accomplishments (15.31). Her holy eloquence converts the brothel customers, including Lysimachus, who rewards her with gold. Marina gives this gold to Boult as evidence of the money she can earn by teaching her "virtues" to "honest women" (19.196, 206). According to Gower's Prologue, Marina "sings like one immortal, and she dances / As goddess-like to her admirèd lays"; moreover, she baffles scholars with her wisdom and she vies with nature in her needlework (20.3–4). Virginity is the source and sign of the "magical power" that gives Marina remarkable agency, despite her subjection to the Bawd (Jankowski, *Pure* 134).[50]

By staging this contest between the bawd and the virgin, Shakespeare effectively denies the Bawd access to the seductive resources of the "common." Whereas the typical bawd seduces her target into prostitution or adultery by deftly manipulating familiar same-sex intimacies, Shakespeare's Bawd purchases Marina outright from the pirates who seized her. From the start, the brute physical and economic coercion that brings Marina to the Bawd renders impossible the kind of scenario in which a bawd employs flattering, insinuating seduction tactics against a woman who is inclined to trust her.[51] Secondly, the Bawd's efforts to turn Marina into a "common" woman meet the insuperable resistance of Marina's innate royal identity. Whatever her current circumstances, Marina is a noblewoman, and her "virginity will certainly be required" to fulfill the social and generic expectations of a "propertied or dynastic marriage" (Jankowski, *Pure* 133). Finally, the typical bawd's strategy of deploying rhetorical commonplaces to make the illicit seem familiar—as when the Bawd opines that "your bride goes to that with shame which is her way to go with warrant" (16.111–12)—utterly fails with Marina, whose inflexible chastity makes her incapable of understanding any subject position the Bawd offers that exceeds the narrowest definition of what it means to be an "honest woman" (16.74).

Shakespeare does not, of course, stage a fair fight between the virgin and the bawd: since Marina must remain chaste for *Pericles* to end on a comic note, the Bawd never has a chance of convincing Marina to prostitute herself. Quite understandably, in her exasperation the Bawd denounces Marina's virginal powers as prodigiously unnatural: "she's able to freeze the god Priapus and undo the whole of generation" (19.12–13). From a metadramatic perspective, Marina's exceptional resistance to the Bawd's seduction can be attributed to her dramatic status as a virginal archetype, a fabulous romance princess. The Bawd is right: there is something unsettling about Marina, a type of absolute virginity in a debased world where even the bawds cannot live up to type.

Chapter 6

Making Monsters

The Caroline Favorite and the Erotics of Royal Will

> This Error did my government disfashion
> That *Gaveston* unworthily was grac'd
> And made too great a monster, huge and vast;
> —Sir Francis Hubert, *The Historie of Edward the Second* (1629)

Most readers of early modern drama owe their familiarity with the figure of the favorite to Marlowe's *Edward II* (ca. 1592), which represents with startling frankness the passionate relationship between King Edward and his minion, Gaveston. As I argue in *The Homoerotics of Early Modern Drama*, Gaveston represents the type of favorite that predominated in Elizabethan and Jacobean texts: the Ganymede, an attractive young man who is blamed for weakening the monarch's judgment and sapping his political strength (100–133). Much less familiar to us than the Ganymedean favorite are the many favorites who appear in later Jacobean and Caroline plays, poems, and political tracts. During the Caroline period, as I will argue in this chapter, the Ganymedean favorite was displaced by the more sinister type of the "monstrous favorite": an ambitious politician imagined in terms of grotesquely excessive influence, treachery, and violence. Curtis Perry shows that the monstrous favorite, a figure of "impossibly total malevolence," was not, in fact, a Caroline invention, but first appeared during the late sixteenth century in attacks against Queen Elizabeth's powerful favorite, the Earl of Leicester (*Favoritism* 14). This Elizabethan "set of stereotypes concerning the domineering favorite," Perry explains, continued "to shape perceptions and responses to court corruption for the next sixty years" (*Favoritism* 24). Despite this continuity, I intend to demonstrate that during the seventeenth century a shift occurs, at least in same-sex contexts, from the type of the Ganymedean favorite to the type of the monstrous favorite.[1]

The dominance of the monstrous favorite in Caroline texts certainly reflects resentment over King Charles's patronage of the vastly influential Buckingham.[2] Nonetheless, the monstrous favorite continues to appear in dramatic texts written, performed, and published after Buckingham's death in 1628. Although Buckingham's career might have given impetus and shape to such representations, the social and political problems posed by favoritism, as Perry has compellingly shown, were located in a structure, not in an individual (*Favoritism* 11–13). Perry provides the most comprehensive account of early modern favoritism, and his argument that the period's "fascination with the figure of the corrupt royal favorite . . . reflects a profound ambivalence about the legitimacy of personal intimacy as a political mechanism" (*Favoritism* 3) accords with my own analysis of Caroline drama. Having analyzed the careers of powerful favorites under Elizabeth, James, and Charles, Perry concludes that "the kinds of invective leveled against successive favorites are so consistent as to hint at habits of political imagination that extend beyond the context of any single career" (*Favoritism* 2). I concur with Perry that invective against favorites indicates pervasive "habits of political imagination" that extend beyond resentment at a particular individual; even so, I demonstrate that the dramatic type of the monstrous favorite serves to embody political anxieties in a hyperbolically evil individual who attempts to enlarge his power through illicit sexual alliances. Caroline playwrights represent the favorite's erotic access to the prince, along with the favorite's mediation of sexual relations between the prince and female subjects, as symptomatic of the dangers of personal rule. The type of the monstrous favorite thus generates critical reflection on the institution of personal monarchy itself, regarding the capacity of the king to ensure the well-being of the state he is charged with protecting and preserving.

It is surprising that so little work has been done on the extensive depiction of favoritism in Caroline drama.[3] In fact, a comprehensive analysis of favoritism in Caroline drama has never to my knowledge been undertaken, despite the appearance of favorites, often as central characters, in no fewer than 30 plays written between 1625 and 1640.[4] The *Index of Characters in Early Modern English Drama* (ed. Berger, Bradford, and Sondergard) identifies "Favourite(s)" in 45 printed plays from the sixteenth and seventeenth centuries (45): of these, two are Elizabethan plays, Marlowe's *Edward II* (1592) and

Shakespeare's *Richard II* (1595); four are Jacobean plays composed between 1617 and 1621; and three are plays from the 1650s. According to the *Index*, then, the great majority of plays containing a favorite fall in the Caroline period.[5]

Mercifully, I do not attempt to survey all of these plays. Instead, after a short account of the discourse of monstrous favoritism surrounding the Duke of Buckingham, I will focus on a set of tragicomedies and tragedies by Philip Massinger, Thomas Killigrew, and James Shirley in which the monstrous favorite uses the power derived from his intimacy with the prince to manipulate heteroerotic alliances for his own advancement. My approach thus differs from Perry's compelling analysis of the favorite in early modern English culture. According to Perry, "the cultural fantasy of the corrupt royal favorite" imagines him as a "radically disaffiliated figure," a "monstrous progeny of royal affection" who appears to operate free of "the kinds of alliances and loyalties that might otherwise involve ethical constraint" (*Favoritism* 9). Although the corrupt favorite might have generally been portrayed as free from ethically constraining alliances to kin, local community, or the status community of aristocrats, the plays I discuss develop a different cultural fantasy in which the ambitious favorite actively manipulates sexual and marital alliances.[6] This focus on how the favorite's intimate access to the monarch works, in the words of my epigraph, to "disfashion" the authorized political aims of aristocratic alliance provides insight into the ideological conflicts being waged in Caroline England over the exercise and extent of royal authority.

Of the six sexual types in my study, the monstrous favorite possesses by far the most authorized kind of agency: he exists as a manifestation of the prince's will. That the favorite is depicted as a monstrous beast, "huge and vast," suggests the anxiety evoked by his political influence, even as such representations exaggerate the power that any single man could possess. As a sexual type, the monstrous favorite is an easy target of hatred and paranoia. Nonetheless, the Caroline plays that I discuss suggest that the political disruptions for which he is blamed have more systemic causes, such as the prince's absolutist reliance on royal prerogative, indulgence of personal affections, and employment of unjust ministers as agents of rule.

*   *   *

Although some hostile seventeenth-century commentators alleged that Buckingham erotically enchanted Charles, most contemporary scholars maintain that after his favorite's assassination in 1628 Charles successfully distanced himself from his father's legacy of sexual scandal.[7] For corroboration, they cite the blossoming of romantic love between Charles and Henrietta Maria after 1628 (Sharpe, *Personal* 170–72; Patterson 175); the crown's vigorous prosecution and conviction of the Earl of Castlehaven for sodomy in 1631 (Marotti 111–12; Bellany, *Politics* 261–62); or the celebration of the court's moral reformation in masques such as Thomas Carew's 1634 *Coelum Brittanicum* (P. Hammond 147; Perry, "Access" 1078).[8] Through the thin veil of classical mythology, Carew overtly alludes to the banishment of homoerotically alluring young pages from the Caroline court: "*Ganimede* is forbidden the Bedchamber, and must only minister in publique. The Gods must keepe no Pages, nor Groomes of their Chamber under the age of 25, and those provided of a competent stocke of beard" (qtd. Young 110). Michael Young cites this passage as evidence that Charles, having purged "[h]omosexuality" from his court, "became conspicuously heterosexual and uxorious," actively promoting his marriage as a model of domestic love (108).

Although it is fair to draw distinctions between the sexual mores of the Jacobean and Caroline courts, it is misleading simply to attach homosexuality to James and heterosexuality to Charles. Carew might have symbolically forbidden Ganymede the bedchamber, but patronage relations at court continued to be structured by homosocial and homoerotic bonds. Likewise, despite Young's confidence that Charles successfully purged "homosexuality" from his court, it is difficult in early seventeenth-century terms to understand the claim that Charles became "conspicuously heterosexual," whatever the sincerity of his affection for Henrietta Maria. Given the common early modern typology of passionate men as effeminate, Charles's "uxorious" behavior might instead have served to confirm rather than refute suspicions that he was dangerously susceptible to the erotic charms of an intimate partner, whether favorite or wife.[9] In fact, Privy Councilors complained that Charles spent too much time alone with Henrietta Maria "as their new-found passion settled into a loving partnership" (Sharpe, *Personal* 171). Ganymede's banishment from court after Buckingham's death might therefore be understood to reflect not an eradication of the symbolic legacy of favoritism altogether, but the growing obsolescence of a distinctly homoerotic figuration of favoritism associated with King James.[10] Caroline writers continued to grapple with the residual Ganymede type even as they used the more sinister type of the monstrous favorite to suggest the dangers of ungoverned royal will.

William Davenant includes a Ganymedean favorite in his tragedy

Albovine (1629), yet the play locates the source of political disorder not in the Ganymede's manipulation of the monarch's affections, but in a monstrous favorite's manipulation of political and marital alliances.[11] At the beginning of the play, King Albovine adopts the captive soldier Paradine as his "Minion" (sig. B2r). The king's exaggerated affection for his minion evokes the dangerous physical allure of the Ganymede. Court observers marvel at the king's passion in bestowing on Paradine such "Ravenous kisses, that you would thinke, he meant / To eate his lips"; through his erotic allure, the "Captive captivates the Conquerour" (sig. B2r). Albovine himself confesses to Paradine, "Thou doest delight me more then victory. / Retire. I am in love too violent. / My embraces crush thee, thou art but yet / Of tender growth" (sig. B3r). For all the king's dotage on Paradine, tragedy springs from his dotage on Rhodolinda, a female captive. By marrying Rhodolinda, Albovine arouses the jealousy of her own favorite, Hermegild, who hatches a complex revenge scheme in which Paradine is tricked into a sexual encounter with Rhodolinda and then reluctantly enlisted in their conspiracy to kill the king. To convince Paradine that the king has rescinded his favors, Hermegild claims to be the new object of royal desire:

> He hath of late, hung thus—
> Upon my neck; untill his amorous weight
> Became my burden: and then lay slabbering o're
> My lips; like some rhumatick Babe. This sport
> My serious braine abhor'd. 'Twas my wonder
> (Since you are cal'd his Minion) he could ere
> Affect my looke.   (sig. K4r)

Exploiting his intimacy with the queen to undermine the homoerotic bond between king and favorite, Hermegild aims to achieve political supremacy. Paradine, however, ultimately remains loyal to the king, with whom he reconciles before the unavoidable tragic conclusion. The monstrous favorite in *Albovine*, then, is not the king's minion, who represents the residual type of the Ganymede, but the queen's minion, who violently dislocates political and sexual alliances in his bid for power.

Whereas Davenant distinguishes the Ganymedean favorite from the monstrous favorite, Caroline manuscript libels against Buckingham attack the excessive influence of the monstrous favorite by representing him as a demonized version of the Ganymede. Attributing terrible powers to Ganymede's archetypal beauty, a "Satyre on the D.[uke] of B.[uckingham]" complains that the "Brittaine crownetts and the clergie's bookes, / Were vail'd or burnt at's Ganimedian lookes" (Fairholt 49).[12] Perhaps recalling the Ovidian myth of Ganymede's flight from earth to heaven, the poem suggests that through his privileged intimacy with the monarch Buckingham does not transcend the sublunary world so much as he engrosses it, being "A little world, that deem'd to sore more high / Then his horizon, or the fleeting skie." Another manuscript libel, an "Epitaph" sonnet on Buckingham's death, evokes the Ganymede by introducing its subject as a cherished minion: "Fortune's darling, king's content." After no fewer than 14 epithets cataloguing the Duke's notorious crimes, the poem concludes with a biting couplet: "All this lies underneath this stone, / And yet, alas! heere lies but one" (Fairholt 65). Despite its opening image of a Ganymedean "darling," then, the poem achieves its satirical bite not by condemning the favorite's manipulation of the king's desire but by facetiously marveling that a single man could embody so many political vices.

In other Caroline representations of Buckingham, the Ganymede figure disappears altogether. Such texts make recourse to the paradoxical language of "greatness" to suggest that the duke uses his access to the king's body to achieve enormous political power. "Upon the D.[uke] of B.[uckingham]," a manuscript poem, depicts the beloved favorite as a "great" beast who imposes his tyrannical will on "lesser" subjects:

> Of Brittish beasts the Buck is king,
> His game and fame through Europe ringe,
> His horne exalted, keepes in awe
> The lesser flocks; his will's a lawe.
> Our Charlemaine takes much delight
> In this great beast soe faire in sight
> With his whole heart affects the same
> And loves too well *Buck-King* of *Game*. (Fairholt 5)

In another manuscript poem, "Upon the Dukes Goeing into Fraunce," the ambiguity of "great" signifies the favorite's ability to collapse sexual and political boundaries:

> And wilt thou goe, great duke, and leave us heere
> Lamenting thee, and eke thy pupill deere,
> Great Charles: O who shall then the scepter sway
> And kingdomes rule, when thou art gone away? (Fairholt 9)

Swaying the scepter of "Great Charles," the "great duke" reduces the king to a mere pupil. Unnaturally, the bodily presence of the duke has become essential to the rule not only of the king and kingdom, but also of unspecified "king-domes." In Sir Francis Hubert's narrative poem *The Historie of Edward the Second*, the king describes in similarly hyperbolic terms the danger of countenancing a great favorite:

> This Error did my government disfashion
> That *Gaveston* unworthily was grac'd
> And made too great a monster, huge and vast;
> Who in his growth being unproportionall
> Became offensive to himselfe and all. (47)[13]

This passage nicely illustrates the "correlation between government and self-government" that is "an absolute commonplace of early modern political theory" (Perry, *Favoritism* 7). His affection for Gaveston "disfashion[s]" or warps Edward's ability to govern his passions as well as his realm. Nourished by royal affection, the favorite swells into a monster who offends "himself and all."

The discourse of offensively great favoritism comes to fruition in Sir Edward Peyton's antiroyalist tract *The divine catastrophe of the kingly family of the house of Stuarts* (1652). According to Peyton, boundless self-conceit "made the duke swell like a toad to such a monstrous proportion of greatness in vast thoughts, as multiplying to an ocean from the rivers of pride, power, and ambition, he sate as a gyant on the shoulders of King James" (360). Peyton suggests that the monstrously reproductive power of the "swell[ing]" and "multiplying" duke poisoned both same-sex and heteroerotic relations at court, for James authorized Buckingham to seduce "many gentile and noble virgins" (353). Buckingham's sexual predations also tainted Charles's court, where "sin was hatched from an egg to a dragon, to devour holiness of life; insomuch, that the masks and plays at Whitehal were used onley for incentives of lust: therefore the courtiers invited the citizens wives to those shews, on purpose to defile them in such sort" (369). However exaggerated or fabricated Peyton's account of royal debauchery might be, it articulates a culturally resonant connection between the same-sex intimacy of favoritism and the monstrous violation of heteroerotic alliance imagined as favoritism's consequence and sign.

Perhaps the most striking attributions of monstrosity to Buckingham appear in a remarkable speech Sir John Eliot delivered to Parliament on May 10, 1626, to conclude a series of charges brought against the favorite by the House of Commons. To indict Buckingham's monstrous political transgressions, Eliot hints at his sodomitical practices. Evoking the stellion—a strangely "discolored beast"—as a symbol of Buckingham's "odious and uncertain" crimes (see Figure 28), Eliot charges that the favorite has committed offenses full of

> collusion and deceit, crimes in themselves so odious and uncertain
> as the ancients knew not by what name to term them and therefore
> they expressed them in a metaphor, calling them *stellionatus* from a
> discolored beast so doubtful in appearance as they knew not what to
> make it. (*Proceedings*, vol. 1, 220)[14]

With similar indirection, Eliot adduces parallels between Buckingham and Sejanus, the favorite of the emperor Tiberius, but coyly insists that he will refrain from mentioning Sejanus's "veneries" and "venefices" (223). According to the transcription of a parliamentary diarist, in a subsequent attempt to justify these accusations Eliot explained that by veneries and venefices he meant Sejanus's "lechery with Livia and his poisoning of Drusus," but did not mean to imply that Buckingham was guilty of comparable crimes (*Proceedings*, vol. 3, 295). Finally, in his original speech Eliot's strategies of obfuscation approach sublimity when he charges that Buckingham's

> attempts go higher to the person of his sovereign, making in that his
> practice in such a manner and with such effects as I fear to speak it, nay,
> I doubt to think it, in which respect I'll leave. Cicero did the like, *Ne
> gravioribus utar verbis quam [rei] natura fert aut levioribus quam causae
> postulat.*[15] The examination with your Lordships will show you what it is.
> I need not name it. (*Proceedings*, vol. 1, 222)

Along with his vague references to Buckingham's "attempts" and practices against "the person" of the king, Eliot's avoidance of "harsher words than nature has made" raises the specter of unnatural sodomy, which, at least in this political arena, remains literally unnamable.[16] In Eliot's intimations of sodomy, the favorite's dangerous intimacy with the king manifests not as a particular sexual practice but rather as a violation of sexual, social, economic, and political order itself. As the parliamentary diarist Sir Richard Grosvenor recognized, Eliot strategically implies that the Duke's crimes were so monstrous that even Cicero, "an excellent orator, had not words to explain so much. This was delivered as though something more in that not yet discovered" (*Proceedings*, vol. 3, 294).

OF THE STELLION.

Figure 28. The stellion, from Edward Topsell, *The historie of serpents* (1608). By permission of the Folger Shakespeare Library.

Renaissance beast lore can help to discover Eliot's evocation of the stellion to indict Buckingham's monstrous crimes. In his *Historie of serpents* (1608), Edward Topsell describes the stellion as an "envious and subtile" lizard that will devour its own shed skin in order to prevent human beings from enjoying its medicinal properties (277). Topsell provides an English translation of Andrea Alciati's emblem "In fraudulentos," which represents the stellion as a symbol of vengeful deceit:

> The little Lyzard, or Stellion starred in body graine
> In secrete holes, and graves of dead which doth remaine,
> When painted you it see, or drawne before the eye,
> A symbole then you view of deepe deceit and cursed envy:
> Alas, this is a thing to jealous wives knowne too well,
> For whosoever of that Wine doth drinke his fill
> Wherein a Stellion hath been drencht to death,
> His face with filthy lentile spots all ugly it appeareth,
> Here-with a Lover oft requites the fraude of concubine,
> Depriving her of beauties hiew by draught of this same wine. (278)

The smallness of this furtive monster belies the potency of its venom.[17] In Alciati's emblem, the stellion's "deepe deceit and cursed envy" describe both the sexual treachery of the adulterous husband and the vengeful treachery of the jealous wife. When Eliot described Buckingham's crimes as *stellionatus*, then, his interlocutors might well have recognized in the stellion a figure for the monstrous favorite, characterized by crimes of betrayal and deceit as well as "veneries and venefices," Eliot's protests to the contrary notwithstanding.

Eliot, of course, was careful to portray King Charles as the victim, not the authorizer, of Buckingham's crimes. Late Jacobean and Caroline playwrights go further in suggesting the culpability of princes who empower and advance monstrous favorites. Yet unlike those Elizabethan and Jacobean playwrights who focus dramatic conflict on a prince's or nobleman's intense desire for a favorite (DiGangi, *Homoerotics* 100–133), Caroline playwrights emphasize how the favorite strategically uses his position to fashion or to disrupt sexual and marital alliances. Favoritism is thus understood not as a homoerotic relationship in competition with heteroerotic relationships, but as a public and affective relationship between men that provides privileged access to women's sexuality and to their disposal in marriage. Favoritism, in short, is represented as a practice that destabilizes and dislocates the foundational institutions of early modern social order.

Through the type of the monstrous favorite, Caroline playwrights communicated in terms of sexuality what Martin Butler refers to as "the Caroline dilemma." According to Butler, English subjects were caught between a "reverence for kingly authority" and a "perception that Charles was not conforming to type" in allowing himself to be abused by wicked servants or misled by his personal affections (90).[18] In the words of the manuscript libel cited above, the king's devotion of "his whole heart" to Buckingham endows the "will" of a rapacious courtier with the agency of a "lawe." But even after Buckingham's death, the type of the favorite could be deployed to critique the abuses of a system of rule in which the personal will of a single man might have the power of law. Through the monstrous favorite, Caroline playwrights draw critical attention to the royalist ideologies that justified favoritism's existence and shaped its practices.

I begin with four tragicomedies—Philip Massinger's *The Maid of Honor* and *The Great Duke of Florence*, Thomas Killigrew's *Claricilla*, and James Shirley's *The Royal Master*—in which a favorite betrays his patron's trust by attempting to marry into a noble or royal family. Whether motivated by lust, greed, or political ambition, the favorite violates the authority of his position to achieve his illicit desires. Although the favorites are clearly the villains of these plays, the princes are guilty of making shortsighted and preemptory assertions of royal prerogative that oppress loyal subjects and fuel the ambitions of their grasping ministers. Often, the favorite's abuse of authority exposes the prince to a critical assessment of his rule. How should the prince weigh the claims of the favorite's victims against his own investment in royal prerogative? Should he punish or forgive the treacherous favorite? What lessons, finally, will the prince learn about his own authority from the failures of his closest friend, minister, and representative? I conclude by examining two plays by Shirley—*The Duke's Mistress*, a tragicomedy, and *The Traitor*, a tragedy—in which a favorite attempts to seize power by exploiting the political disorder surrounding a licentious prince. In these plays, the prince's errant affections, both for a male favorite and for a female subject, are symptomatic of a mode of rule based on willful assertions of power.

Written between 1621 and 1627, the two Massinger plays under consideration introduce characteristics of the favorite that will develop into the monstrous figure of later Caroline tragedy, particularly after Buckingham's death.[19] By focusing on a favorite's disruptive, yet ultimately frustrated, attempt to possess an aristocratic woman, both *The Maid of Honor* and *The Great Duke of Florence* allow political problems to be articulated in terms of, and symbolically resolved through, the conflict between immoderate desire and self-possessing chastity. *The Maid of Honor* provides a particularly clear illustration of how the abusive sexual mediation of a favorite could be rendered as a symptom of misgoverned royal will. Through her inviolable chastity, the eponymous maid, Camiola, achieves the moral authority to thwart an ambitious favorite and instruct her king in just government.

From the very start of the play, King Roberto's favorite, Fulgentio, is defined in terms drawn from the conventional Jacobean discourse of the favorite as Ganymede or parasite (DiGangi, *Homoerotics* 112–24). Labeled in the dramatis personae as a "mignion," Fulgentio is derided by other courtiers as a "state Catamite" and "caterpiller in the state" (1.1.272, 2.2.94). These conventional epithets serve unambiguously to establish the king's folly in bestowing such great authority on a man whose wickedness seems transparent to all but himself. Like the king, Fulgentio believes that as the recipient of royal favor he acquires an unimpeachable honor; as "a man in grace," he expects to "challenge awe, and priviledge by his place" (2.1.57–58). Traveling from the court to the country, Fulgentio functions as a mediating figure between the prince and his subjects. His attempt to use his status as favorite to coerce a marriage vow from the beautiful and wealthy Camiola, however, earns only her scornful appraisal of his manhood: "I am doubtfull whether you are a man, / Since for your shape trimmd up in a Ladies dressing / You might passe for a woman" (2.2.137–39). More than a dig against courtly finery, Camiola's mockery of Fulgentio's inappropriate "shape" interprets the outward signs of royal favor in terms of a typically feminine bodily excess that she herself has eschewed. Deflating the favorite's masculine posturing, she reduces his elevated political "place" to the purely ornamental role of a court lady trimmed up for display.

When King Roberto reprimands Camiola for rejecting his favorite, she explains, in pointedly political terms, why the king should regard Fulgentio as nothing more than an object of personal pleasure. Camiola distinguishes between the lawfulness of Roberto's personal or "natural" desires and the tyrannical imposition of those desires upon his subjects through the authorization of his favorite's ambitions:

> Say you should love wine,
> You being the king, and cause I am your subject,
> Must I be ever drunke? Tyrants, not Kings,
> By violence, from humble vassals force
> The liberty of their soules. I could not love him,
> And to compell affection, as I take it,
> Is not found in your prerogative. (4.5.61–67)

As the distinction between "lov[ing] wine" and being "ever drunke" suggests, the king cannot force his subjects to love what he loves without transforming the healthy affection that should obtain between subject and king into a destructive and deforming force. By negating the favorite's sexual privilege over female subjects, Camiola thus articulates the need to limit royal prerogative.[20] She caps her lesson about royal prerogative with a neat aphorism: "Happy are subjects! when the prince is still / Guided by justice, not his passionate will" (4.5.92–93).

In the play's conclusion, Camiola's commitment to chastity blocks the formation of marital alliances even as it reconciles Roberto and Fulgentio. Instructing her former suitor, a Knight of Malta, to remain faithful to his vow of chastity, Camiola reveals her intention to enter a convent. She also urges the king to pardon his favorite and to love him according "to his merits . . . and no further" (5.2.284). Although the abuses of favoritism are finally reformed in *The Maid of Honor*, Massinger's emphasis on Fulgentio's corrupt mediation of the "love" between king and subject largely defines the institution of favoritism itself as a means by which the king might impose his "passionate will" upon his subjects' liberties (4.5.93). Since the comic dispensation allows the monarch to determine for himself the righteousness of his love for his favorite and the difference between prerogative and tyranny, the political structures that license a monarch's willful misrule have not been reformed.

Whereas in *The Maid of Honor* a chaste heroine effectively disciplines an ambitious favorite, in *The Great Duke of Florence* an absolutist prince's self-imposed chastity enables him to maintain political stability despite his favorite's attempt to take control of the exchange of aristocratic women. As a prince with absolute power, Duke Cozimo de Medici is free to exert precisely the kind of sexual authority over his female subjects that Camiola denounces in *The Maid of Honor*. Cozimo's favorite, Sanazarro, and nephew, Giovanni, anticipate that the Duke will claim the right to possess a beautiful young noblewoman named Lidia whom both men desire, and it is this structural imbalance in their sexual access to Lidia that provokes Sanazarro to betray his master's trust. Even though Cozimo has no intention of breaking his widower's vow, Sanazarro's perception of sexual disenfranchisement reveals a faultline in the ideology of absolutism with regard to the favorite's affective loyalties: for all his power, the prince ultimately cannot command his favorite's heart. The favorite's hyperbolic transformation from virtuous counselor to wicked traitor suggests that in wresting control over the power of marital exchange Sanazarro has appropriated the prince's reliance on personal will as a mechanism of absolutist government. The comic resolution of *The Great Duke of Florence* depends not on any limitation of the prince's absolute power, however, but on the happy circumstance of the duke's voluntary commitment to chastity and moderation.

Cozimo's power to organize sexual and marital alliances among the Florentine aristocracy is connected to the secrecy of purpose he cherishes as an absolutist ruler. Despite his counselors' concern about his lack of an heir, Cozimo remains devoted to the memory of his wife. Moreover, he refuses to comfort his counselors with the knowledge that he has provided for the succession in his nephew Giovanni, whom he intends to marry to his ward, Fiorinda, daughter of the late Duke of Urbino. Giovanni, however, has a secret of his own: he has fallen in love with Lidia, the daughter of his tutor, Carolo

Charomonte. Accustomed to complete control over his dominions, Cozimo is clearly vexed to learn of Lidia's existence: "A Diamond so long conceal'd, / And never worne in Court! of such sweet feature?" (1.2.147–48). Suspecting that Giovanni seeks to marry this concealed beauty, Cozimo sends Sanazarro to Charomonte's country house to assess her virtues and her intentions. Keeping his purposes to himself, Cozimo only warns Sanazarro not to tempt Lidia into falling in love with him. Although Sanazarro wonders about the purpose of his mission, he reminds himself that "th'intents / And secrets of [his] Princes heart must be / Serv'd and not search'd into" (2.3.13–15). A sign of his commitment to absolutism, the favorite's refusal to plumb the secrets of his prince's heart will ironically precipitate his betrayal of the absolutist prince. Plotting his own secret designs, the virtuous favorite is hyperbolically transformed into the monstrous favorite who appropriates from his master the right over sexual exchange.

Irresistibly attracted to Lidia, Sanazarro finds himself both sexually and politically reoriented. A warrior generally averse to women, Sanazarro suspects that his desire for Lidia must have been anticipated by Cozimo as a cruel test of virtue: "If the great Duke / Made this his end to try my constant temper, / Though I am vanquish'd, 'tis his fault, not mine. / For I am flesh and blood, and have affections / Like other men" (2.3.109–13). Whereas in *The Maid of Honor* Camiola complains of a tyrannous prince who attempts to compel a subject's affection, Sanazarro regards as tyrannical a prince who tries to compel a subject's chastity in the face of natural affections. Worse, the Duke might have sent his favorite to woo Lidia on his behalf, an even more flagrant abuse of his power, for it is "tyrannie / To call one pinch'd with hunger to a feast, / And at that instant cruelly deny him / To taste of what he sees" (2.3.126–29). Although Sanazarro misreads his master's intentions, he is not entirely wrong to suspect that he is being employed without his knowledge or consent as a kind of bawd. In this way Massinger pointedly represents the favorite's role as intermediary between prince and subjects as a form of sexual labor. Having decided to deceive the deceiver, Sanazarro enlists Giovanni's aid in thwarting Cozimo's apparent pursuit of Lidia, and they misrepresent her to Cozimo as homely and ill-mannered. This slandering of a noblewoman, and, by implication, of her father, might be justified as a ruse to protect Lidia from Cozimo's predations; nonetheless, it suggests the price that subjects pay in struggles for power between princes and favorites.

In Massinger's dramatic representation of a favorite's fall from grace, Sanazarro's response to the new political insight precipitated by his sexual awakening quickly transforms him from ideal favorite to disobedient traitor. Massinger conveys Sanazarro's wrenching political alteration by modifying an earlier image of political favor as an impress of honor upon the body into an image of sexual desire as a deforming bodily impress. In the first scene of the play, Charomonte sets off Sanazarro's virtues as loyal favorite through a contrasting portrait of the monstrous favorite. Charomonte speaks of the damage caused when capricious princes advance

> (Not out of judgement, but deceiving fancie)
> An undeserving man, how ere set of
> With all the trim of greatnesse, state, and power,
> And of a creature ev'n growne terrible
> To him from whom he took his Gyant forme,
> This thing is still a Comet, no true starre;
> And when the bounties feeding his false fire
> Begin to faile, will of it selfe goe out,
> And what was dreadfull, prooves ridiculous.
> But in our *Sanazarro* 'tis not so,
> He being pure and tride gold; and any stamp
> Of grace to make him currant to the world
> The Duke is pleas'd to give him, will adde honor
> To the great bestower, for he though allow'd
> Companion to his Master, still preserves
> His Majestie in full lustre. (1.1.76–91)

According to Charomonte, a monstrous favorite grows "terrible" from the foundation of royal power, yet soon devolves from his master's "dreadfull" majesty into something "ridiculous." The good favorite, instead, is the raw metal transformed into valuable currency when stamped with the prince's image. A similar representation of the faithful favorite as raw material fashioned by the royal hand informs Henry Wotton's account of Buckingham's political career:

> he sprung without any help, by a kind of congenial composure
> (as we may term it) to the likeness of our late Sovereign and
> Master of ever blessed memory; who taking him into his regard,
> taught him more and more to please himself, and molded him,
> (as it were) Platonically, to his own idea; delighting first in the
> choice of the materials, because he found him susceptible of good

form; and afterward, by degrees, as great architects use to do, in the workmanship of his regal hand: nor staying here, after he had hardened and polished him about ten years in the school of observance, (for so a Court is,) and in the furnace of trial about himself, (for he was a king could peruse men as well as books,) he made him the associate of his Heir Apparent. (5–6)

According to Wotton's Platonic fantasy, the monarch enjoys complete agency in molding the favorite to his own image. James's hand carefully shaped Buckingham, "harden[ing] and polish[ing]" him into a loyal servant of the court. For Wotton, the monarch's "furnace of trial" perfects the favorite and strengthens his link to the royal family. For Massinger's Sanazarro, as we have seen, resentment at having his loyalty tried in an apparent test of sexual temperance violently shatters his link to his patron:

> I may as well
> Walke over burning iron with bare feet
> And be unscorch'd, as looke upon this beauty
> Without desire, and that desire pursu'd to,
> Till it be quench'd with the enjoying those
> Delights, which to atchieve danger is nothing,
> And loyalty but a word. (2.3.115–21)

Inverting the image of the good favorite as pure gold converted into legal coinage through a stamped figure of the Duke's head, Sanazarro imagines his subjection to immoderate erotic desire as the impress of burning iron upon naked feet.[21]

Massinger thus represents as an emasculating sexual rivalry the political strain produced by the favorite's utter dependency on an absolutist prince. Although Sanazarro's deception in hiding Lidia's value from Cozimo might seem a relatively minor offense, both favorite and prince concur in regarding it as a monstrous betrayal of their relationship. Sanazarro recognizes that without the Duke's patronage his own virtue amounts to nothing:

> Power that stands not on
> Its proper base, which is peculiar onely
> To absolute Princes, falls, or rises, with
> Their frowne, or favour. (5.1.15–18)

Sanazarro's ability to "stand" thus depends not on Lidia's sexual favor but on the Duke's political favor. Vowing to punish Sanazarro, Cozimo articulates a similar understanding of the delicacy of the bond between prince and favorite: the "Prince that pardons / The first affront offer'd to majestie, / Invites a second, rend'ring that power / Subjects should tremble at, contemptible" (5.1.68–71). Justifying his anger at Sanazarro, Cozimo presents the tyrannical argument that only he is worthy of enjoying Lidia's extraordinary beauty. Although Massinger appears to invite critical scrutiny of the sexual rapaciousness that absolutism here would authorize, none of the Duke's subjects voice that critique. Far from challenging the Duke's self-evident right to possess his female subjects, Giovanni implicitly supports that right when he laments that he might as well persuade Cozimo to give up his crown as to give up Lidia.

Though Giovanni might demonstrate an accurate understanding of the Duke's absolutism, he underestimates Cozimo's commitment to chastity and to the political stability that, under these circumstances, chastity ensures. In order to assure Giovanni's uncontested inheritance of the dukedom, Cozimo has sacrificed the right to sexual pleasure granted by his supreme position and his potent manhood: he has kept constant to a "widdowed bed, / And did deny our selfe those lawfull pleasures, / Our absolute power and height of blood allow'd us" (5.2.136–38). Ultimately, Cozimo's remarkable sexual temperance preserves political order and ushers in a comic ending for his heir and his favorite. Forgiving Giovanni and Sanazarro on the grounds that his vow to chastity renders moot his right to possess Lidia, Cozimo approves his nephew's marriage into Charomonte's noble family. His pardon releases his favorite to fulfill his promise to marry Fiorinda, who has actively courted Sanazarro and intervened on his behalf with the Duke. Sanazarro will no longer be the Duke of Florence's favorite, as his marriage to Fiorinda will make him Duke of Urbino. In this comic resolution, the structures of absolute power, including the dangers of favoritism as an expression and extension of royal will, remain untouched.

Less perceptive than Massinger's Duke of Florence, the kings in Killigrew's *Claricilla* and Shirley's *The Royal Master* inadvertently provoke disorder by obstructing the marital (and hence political) ambitions of the favorites they nonetheless immoderately love and reward.[22] To the degree that each play explores the political crisis precipitated by a sovereign's mismanagement of patronage relationships and marital alliances, it is important to note that neither Killigrew nor Shirley, despite their associations with the court, blindly endorsed its policies or moral postures. For instance, in *The Parson's Wedding*

Killigrew treats the fashionable cult of Platonic love "as the subject of bawdy humour and derision" (Sharpe, *Criticism* 24); and even in an overtly celebratory masque, *The Triumph of Peace*, Shirley "registers a potential criticism of the royal government," however muted or disguised that criticism might be (Venuti 197).[23]

Through a critical focus on the monstrous favorite, *Claricilla* and *The Royal Master* expose a central contradiction of early modern kingship as a form of rule based at once on traditional, ostensibly fixed standards of value such as bloodline and hereditary succession, as well as on the sovereign's wavering affections and subjective measurements of desert. In these plays, the contradiction becomes evident when a sovereign cherishes and indulges his favorite, yet refuses to authorize his marriage into the royal family. Thus opens a rift in the bonds of affection and loyalty between prince and favorite. Forced to acknowledge that their power rests upon the shifting ground of royal affection, these favorites seek at great cost the security and permanence that seem to be promised by a connection to the royal blood.[24] In his tragedy *Sicily and Naples* (1640), Samuel Harding effectively captures a favorite's resentment at his dependence on royal caprice:

> it is
> The pride of Princes, to be thought Gods here
> On earth, daring to mocke omnipotence,
> To create them favourites, set them aloft
> In their owne spheare, till remote Kingdomes gaze
> At their prodigious height, then in an instant
> Shoote them from thence, like falling meteors: (1.4, p. 12)

Given this perspective, it is easy to understand why Henry Wotton measured the Duke of Buckingham's success as favorite by his ability to thrive in that precarious position under two successive monarchs. After King James died, Wotton explains, Buckingham was "secondly seized of favour, as it were by descent (though the condition of that estate be commonly no more than a tenancy at will, or at most for the life of the first lord) and rarely transmitted" (7). The favorites in *Claricilla* and *The Royal Master* attempt to seize through unauthorized marital alliances the security of power that Buckingham uniquely achieved through the "descent" of royal favor.

In *Claricilla*, a shortsighted monarch fails to appreciate the precariousness of his situation as the patron of favorites who are determined to escape the uncertainty of what Wotton calls a "tenancy at will." At the beginning of the play, the paradoxical insecurity of the favorite's otherwise supremely privileged position is suggested by the treachery of Silvander, who has exploited his intimacy with the King to usurp his throne and abduct his daughter Claricilla. The King describes Silvander as one who "having by my love gain'd an interest, and by my smiles climb'd o're the Heads of all his Fellows in the strength of that trust grew too powerfull for me" (1.1.22–25). Silvander justifies his treason on the grounds that his love for Claricilla was so great that he could not consent "to have worn such a Jewel in less than a Crown, or been satisfied to have seen her . . . stand second to any" (1.3.35–37). Even as Silvander explains his desire for the crown as a consequence of his desire to make Claricilla a queen, he simultaneously objectifies Claricilla as a jewel in the crown he desires to possess.

Although the King's forces prevail against Silvander, the new favorite, Seleucus, threatens to repeat his predecessor's treachery. Like Silvander, Seleucus cannot separate his love for Claricilla from his hopes of political advancement. Seleucus remarks on his sluggishness to join the battle against Silvander, toward whom Appius, the Prince of Calabria and the King's choice for his daughter's hand, has already made his way: "O Love, thy power hath disarm'd me, or rather Envy hath disarm'd my Love; could it be else that I should stand thus unspirited in Claricilla's cause, while others gild their Swords in her revenge?" (1.1.55–58). Tellingly, in speculating that his envy of a male rival has weakened his resolve, Seleucus modifies the commonplace notion that love for a woman emasculates a man. His jealousy is both sexual and political, in that the proposed dynastic marriage of Appius and Claricilla stands in the way of his own advancement. In the event, the soldier Melintus (actually the King's nephew in disguise) kills Silvander, thus achieving military honor as well as Claricilla's favors. Defeated by a rival, Seleucus makes a preemptory decision to abandon his scruples in pursuit of the princess: "Love and Honour, farewell to both; my ends are the gods I'll worship now; and my Net once thrown, I'll catch 'em though they swim in blood" (1.4.141–43).

Seleucus's courtship of Claricilla reveals a crucial tension over the favorite's status and worth relative to those of royal blood. Responding to Seleucus's complaint that she has not adequately rewarded his services by offering her favor, Claricilla draws a sharp line between her status as princess and the favorite's status as subject: "The love of Subjects to their Prince is duty; and those whom we pay we do not thank; the Hireling ought to serve" (2.3.74–75). Seleucus boldly observes that his status as subject derives not from any inherent deficiency, but only from divine will in appointing certain men as kings; he closes the distance between himself and Claricilla by pointing out that she no less than himself is a subject to the king. Melintus, who has also been courting Claricilla, intervenes to denounce the favorite as a base and treacherous servant: "Know in the best of all thy ills, thy love, thou art a Traitor; else thou durst not hope this Princess would be food for servants" (2.3.86–88). Remarkably, Melintus accounts as a form of treason the favorite's presumption in even daring to love the princess and hoping that she might reciprocate his affections. Later, Melintus reports Seleucus's "treason" to Appius, urging him to complain to the King: "'tis the first step to a Favourit's fall when the Prince will hear complaints of him" (3.2.72–74). Encountering Seleucus on his way to the King, Appius echoes Melintus's damning account of the favorite's treacherous courtship of the princess, the "saucy flames" of desire and ambition that have "aim'd at the top of thy Masters house" (3.2.86–88). Fearing his imminent ruin, Seleucus rushes to inform the king of Melintus's equally treacherous courtship of Claricilla.

The central scene of the play offers a test of the King's perspicacity as a ruler. Will the King be willing to hear complaints about his own favorite? Will he rein in the ambition of the very man he has promoted to greatness? In the event, the King, responding with immoderate passion to the news of Seleucus's unauthorized courtship, fails to regain his favorite's loyalty either by threatening punishment or promising reward. Evoking the type of the monstrous favorite, the King denounces Seleucus for the "poysonous ingratitude that swells him thus ambitiously" (3.3.8–9) and marvels that his favorite would dare pursue the same course that "threatn'd [his] ruine in *Silvander*" (3.3.57). Killigrew remains consistent in representing the aristocrats of the play as deeply scandalized by the favorite's treasonous presumption in wooing the princess. However, the King's heated reprimand of Seleucus gives the favorite the opportunity to protest that he is being treated unjustly, not even "heard ere condemn'd"; in a melodramatic turn, Seleucus even offers to commit suicide as proof of his "faith and readiness to serve" (3.3.39, 41–42). Seleucus craftily conveys his submission to royal authority through an allusion to the myth of Semele, who was destroyed by thunderbolts when she asked Jove to visit her bed in his divine form. Seleucus's allusion to Semele not only reminds the King of his privileged physical intimacy as favorite, it also connects the eroticism of this intimacy with the favorite's "longing" to perform for his master "the greatest service that ever yet [his] faith pleaded reward for" (3.3.34–36). Killigrew reinforces this suggestion of intimacy by having Seleucus whisper to the King his news of Melintus's courtship. After Seleucus has twice whispered in the King's ear, the King declares his restored faith in his favorite's loyalty and graces him with the elevated title of "friend" (3.3.79). Nonetheless, Seleucus has discovered how quickly he can fall from the King's favor, how dependent his power on the King's will. Alone on stage, Seleucus thus determines to achieve the crown for himself.

Claricilla's role in Seleucus's plan to seize the crown is not immediately apparent. In that Seleucus continues to speak of his sexual desire for Claricilla, it seems that he is planning to rape her in revenge of the contempt she has shown him. Admitting that Claricilla hates him, Seleucus determines that only "policy or force" can "gain the pleasure" he seeks from her (5.4.12). His fantasy is to "possess" Claricilla, "whose beauties increas'd by the sweetness of force will make me more a King than all the power that a Crown can give" (5.7.13–15). Here, the favorite's longing for the crown is subordinated to his desire to control and defile the princess who scorned him as a hireling. Yet as soon as he has succeeded in deposing the King, Seleucus gloats about his intention not to rape but to marry the princess. The motive of sexual revenge is still present, as Seleucus threatens to force Claricilla's "Sweets" in the presence of Appius (5.8.101); at the same time, he tauntingly reminds Appius that the failure of Appius's dynastic marriage to Claricilla means the loss of any political claim to Sicily: "Do you perceive how small a share you are like to have in this Kingdom?" (5.8.104–5). Clearly, this favorite turned "Monster" intends to strengthen his spurious claim to the throne through a forced marriage into the royal family (5.8.108).

Like Silvander, Seleucus is finally defeated by subjects loyal to the King, but his nearly successful attempt to secure power through an unauthorized marriage into the royal family exposes a troubling contradiction in the practice of favoritism, and by extension, in the principles of personal monarchy. As political theorist Edward Forset explains in *A comparative discourse of the bodies natural and politique* (1606), the "favorites of a Prince may be resembled to the fantasies of the Soule, wherewith he sporteth and delighteth himselfe." To achieve contentment, the king must be allowed to "follow and feed his fantasies, give scope unto them, suffer them to prevaile with him" (15). By giving scope to his fantasies, however, the sovereign might encourage the courtly aspirants empowered by his love to "follow and feed" fantasies of their own. In *Claricilla*, Melintus articulates this danger, berating Seleucus as a hungry dog who will not be satisfied with scraps when a more tempting dish is in view: "thy fawning on thy Masters feet hath been cherish'd so that thou hast left the Crums there, and are now set by him, snatching at his own dish" (2.3.88–90).

The king might set his favorite by his side and address him in the equalizing language of affectionate friendship, yet he thereby erases neither the favorite's awareness of his dependent status nor his craving for the royal alliance that promises to repair that status.[25]

At the play's conclusion, Seleucus commits suicide in a fit of remorse, a somber moment quickly brushed aside by the King's consent to the marriage between Claricilla and Melintus. In allowing his nephew to marry the princess, the King resolves the political instability produced by the rivalry among the several aspirants to his daughter's hand. By representing the monstrous favorite's skillful manipulations both of this homosocial rivalry and of his privileged intimacy with the monarch, however, the play points to the danger of political rule grounded in bonds of affection. That Seleucus essentially re-enacts Silvander's sexual and political treachery suggests that the problem lies not in a particular favorite, but in the very structure of favoritism.

In Shirley's *The Royal Master*, a king's overconfidence in the effectiveness of favoritism as a means of sustaining and rewarding loyalty blinds him to his discontented favorite's designs to marry into the royal family. Although the King of Naples believes himself to be in possession of the love and gratitude of his favorite, Montalto, observant courtiers marvel at the "witchcraft" that seems to cloud the King's senses and to keep him "so strangely" enamored of such a monstrous "colossus" and "Protean favourite" (1.1, pp. 107, 110). As the courtiers recognize and as his name suggests, Montalto aspires to mount high, to transform himself into something greater than a favorite, and his aspirations are fueled by resentment that the King should have overlooked him in promising his sister Theodosia to the Duke of Florence. To obtain Theodosia for himself, Montalto proceeds to shatter this dynastic alliance between Naples and Florence by convincing the King that the Duke and Theodosia have betrayed his trust. Shrewdly masking his true intentions, Montalto feigns gratitude when, as a reward for his services, the King offers him the noblewoman Domitilla for his bride:

> you are too bountiful.
> In you I kneel both to my king and father:
> But my aspiring will be satisfied
> To be your servant still; in your grace I
> Enjoy the bride my heart affects. Let me
> Grow old with duties here, and not translate
> My affection, till my weary soul throw off
> The burden of my dust. (4.1, p. 159)

Montalto voices the traditional rhetoric of loyal service, at the same time affirming his personal devotion by addressing his master as a father and by evoking imagery of conjugal bliss and erotic satisfaction to convey the joy of receiving the King's grace. This language disarms the King, encouraging him to believe that the favorite's "aspiring will be satisfied" by occupying the *symbolic* roles of son and spouse to the monarch, when what Montalto actually seeks is a direct connection with the royal blood through marriage. Despite his protests to the contrary, Montalto desires precisely to "translate [his] affection": to use the power derived from the King's love to escape the dependence on that love that defines—and delimits—the favorite's power. Although Montalto is ultimately exposed and banished, his skillful manipulation of the King's affections exposes the danger of a prince's inability to see that, from the favorite's perspective, the bonds of favoritism might seem to operate as constraints.

So far, I have examined plays in which favorites attempt to manipulate the access and privilege that derives from royal affection to secure even greater power through advantageous marriages. In *The Maid of Honor*, *The Great Duke of Florence*, *Claricilla*, and *The Royal Master*, the princes themselves are devoted entirely to their favorites; unmarried and sexually uninvolved with women, they are, as Camiola says of King Roberto, "Abstemious from base and goatish loosenesse" (*The Maid of Honor*, 2.2.172). By contrast, the princes in Shirley's *The Duke's Mistress* and *The Traitor* indulge their passions for women, thus making themselves vulnerable to their favorites' treacherous manipulations of sexual and political alliances. *The Duke's Mistress*, a tragicomedy presented at court in 1636, "carefully rehabilitates faith in the integrity of the royal will" by allowing the duke to repent his erotic lapses and to retain his power (M. Butler 42). A tragedy, *The Traitor* depicts the fall of a sexually predatory duke at the hands of a disloyal favorite who seeks his throne and a discontented gentleman who resists his tyrannical will.[26] Shirley's sexually errant dukes might seem quite remote from King Charles, who conspicuously displayed a "preoccupation with ordered self-control" (Sharpe, *Personal* 191). Nonetheless, the presence in these plays of the mediating figure of the favorite prompts us to understand the prince's indulgence of heteroerotic passion as a manifestation of misgoverned royal will responsible for social and political disorder.[27]

In *The Duke's Mistress*, the Duke of Parma asserts his political prerogative through the maintenance of an adulterous relationship, the disorderly consequences of which provide his favorite and kinsman Leontio with a method and a motive for seeking his demise. Leontio secretly loves the neglected Duchess, Euphemia, and consoles her with the hope that the Duke will renounce his lustful ways. News of Leontio's rebuke, however, only incenses the Duke to assert his absolutist right to gratify his desires: "Presumes he on his blood, above our favour? / Dares he but in a thought control our pleasure?" (1.1, p. 204). The Duke retaliates against his favorite's insolent wish to "control [his] pleasure" by treating Euphemia even more cruelly, provoking Leontio openly to declare his love to her. Euphemia remains loyal to her husband, but her virtuous example aggravates the discontented favorite's resentment and seals his determination to procure the Duke's downfall. Although unrequited desire for Euphemia might motivate Leontio's treachery, the Duke's vicious behavior provides him with a plausible pretext for usurping the throne: the restoration of justice to the state. Persuading a captain to assassinate the Duke, Leontio evokes sympathy for his cause by comparing himself to a galley slave desperately trying to unchain himself from an oar.

Despite his disastrous misgovernment of marital and political affairs, the Duke is spared a tragic fall because Euphemia and the captain undermine Leontio's schemes and ultimately inspire the Duke to reform his ways. Destroyed by his own plot, Leontio confesses that "[l]ust and ambition" led him astray; however, he also blames his "misfortunes" on the "license" he took from the example of the Duke's indulgence of "wanton blood"—his neglect of princely and conjugal duties (5.4, p. 271). *The Duke's Mistress* ultimately upholds the sanctity of the Duke's status as husband and prince by celebrating the unwavering devotion of a chaste wife and loyal subject and by implying the rightness of the royalist axiom that "Subjects must know their place, and trust the duke (or king) to know his" (M. Butler 44). Nonetheless, through its depiction of the disorderly consequences of the Duke's errant sexuality, the play also reveals the dilemma of subjects who are simply required to trust, by an act of faith or will, in the moral and political probity of their prince's affections.

Another sexually errant prince, the Duke of Florence in *The Traitor* meets the bloody death spared his counterpart in *The Duke's Mistress* because his inability to control the urgings of his "youthful blood" fatally betrays him to the machinations of his cousin and favorite Lorenzo (3.2.79). Plotting the Duke's demise, Lorenzo fans his lust for a young noblewoman, Amidea, and then allies himself with her proud and ill-tempered brother, Sciarrha, who vows to kill the Duke for dishonoring his family. Lorenzo cleverly uses his privileged position as the Duke's favorite and cousin to denounce the abuses of absolutist government and to encourage Sciarrha's hopes of restoring Florence to a commonwealth. Nostalgically recalling the "religious days / Of commonwealths," Lorenzo claims that he himself is a victim of the Duke's misgovernment: "'Tis policy in princes to create / A favorite who must bear all the guilt / Of things ill manag'd in the state" (2.1.87–89). When Sciarrha responds by vowing to rid Florence of the "tyrant" (2.1.99), Lorenzo promises that in the event of the Duke's death, he would restore Florence to a commonwealth:

> Heaven knows I've no particular design
> To leap unto a throne. I will disclaim
> The privilege of blood. Let me advance
> Our liberty, restore the ancient laws
> Of the republic, rescue from the jaws
> Of lust your mothers, wives, your daughters, sisters— (2.1.139–44)

Significantly, Lorenzo cites the Duke's sexual rapacity as the sign of the absolutist ruler's abuse of his "privilege of blood." Lorenzo's success in tarnishing the Duke with the traditional association between lust and tyranny is indicated by Sciarrha's subsequent description of the Duke as a "Tarquin" who comes to "revel at our house" (2.1.264–265).

Just as Lorenzo cynically advocates republicanism to incite Sciarrha's violence against the Duke, so he elicits the Duke's worst absolutist tendencies by fueling his desire for Amidea. When the Duke first solicits Amidea, she cuts her arm to prove that she would commit suicide rather than be ravished. Reminding the Duke that he cannot compel a subject to commit an irreligious act, Amidea calmly insists, "I must not obey / To be your strumpet" (3.3.92–93). The chaste subject thus shames the licentious prince into renouncing his lust. Yet Amidea lacks the favorite's free access to the prince, and Lorenzo quickly undoes her salutary influence. Lorenzo hints to the Duke that Amidea's "Pretty dexterity at the poniard" should not be regarded as a sign of her absolute dedication to chastity, for other women have gone farther in actually killing themselves in order to "save their sullen chastities" (4.1.328, 334). "Chastity's great example" (4.1.342), Lucrece, famously stabbed herself after Tarquin raped her, but, Lorenzo proposes, her suicide was actually a sign of lust, not purity:

> She knew of Tarquin first,
> And then suspecting she should never meet
> Again the active gentleman, having
> Determin'd of his death, with well-dissembled

Sorrow did stab herself in hope to meet
The gamester in Elysium. Amidea,
You will allow beneath this Roman dame. (4.1.343–49)

Lorenzo implies that the lusty Amidea, who is "beneath" Lucrece in her dedication to chastity, will freely give herself to the Duke. Nonetheless, in an
echo of Angelo from Shakespeare's *Measure for Measure*, Lorenzo ultimately
argues that the Duke should demand Amidea's chastity in exchange for her
brother's life:

> Sciarrha's life
> And fortunes are already growing forfeit.
> These brains have plotted so. Your mercy shall
> Purchase what you can wish for in his sister,
> And he acknowledge rifling of her honor
> A fair and cheap redemption.
> **Duke:** Do this
> And I'll repent the folly of my penitence,
> And take thee to my soul, a nearer pledge
> Than blood or nature gave me. (4.1.371–79)

The Duke seems to expresses more delight at Lorenzo's tyrannical proposal
to pardon Sciarrha in exchange for his sister's chastity than he does at the
prospect of consummating his desire for Amidea. "Prepare your blood / For
amorous game," Lorenzo goads the Duke as he leads him into Sciarrha's trap
(4.1.383–84). "Thou mak'st my spirit caper in my veins," the duke giddily replies, displacing his sexual excitement about Amidea onto the favorite who has
orchestrated his assassination (4.1.387).

The Duke's inability to pause to consider the political and ethical implications of Lorenzo's bargain is of a piece with his promise to take the treacherous
favorite to his soul. The closer the Duke draws his favorite, the more control
he relinquishes over his passions and over his state. Shortly before Lorenzo
murders the Duke, Shirley conveys the danger of the favorite's privileged access
to the prince's body through a grimly humorous monologue in which Lorenzo
confesses to a bizarre, sexually evocative, ritual. Every day, he "kill[s] a prince"
by stabbing a portrait of the Duke, "Which though it bleed not, [he] may
boast a murder" (5.2.22–23). Repeatedly knifing the portrait is an ingenious
method for inuring himself to any scruples that might arise when the time

Figure 29. An assassin stabbing a portrait, from Claude Paradin, *The heroicall devises* (1591). By permission of the Folger Shakespeare Library.

comes actually to shed his prince's blood. Shirley bases this episode on an incident recounted in Claude Paradin's *Heroicall devises* (1591), which relates how the Milanese nobleman Giovanni Andrea Lampugnani stabbed a portrait of the Duke of Milan in preparation for his assassination (see Figure 29).

Acknowledging that the powerful appeal of the Duke's "youth," "beauty," and "charms" might otherwise dampen his resolution to murder him, Lorenzo conflates the pleasure of erotic intimacy with the pleasure of sadistic violence when, in the act of stabbing the painting, he muses that "the duke should feel me now" (5.2.28, 35, 37). "Is not / His soul acquainted?" he wonders, ironically recalling the earlier scene in which the Duke had offered his soul as a "nearer pledge" of his love than "blood or nature" (5.2.37–38; 4.1.378–79). Smiling, a sign of affection and grace that any favorite might desire from his prince—"He smiles, he smiles upon me"—Lorenzo twists into a grotesque fantasy of physical violation: "I will dig / Thy wanton eyes out, and supply the dark / And hollow cells with two pitch-burning tapers" (5.2.45–47).

Thanks to the countless imaginary performances of this violent consummation of his bond with the Duke, Lorenzo does not hesitate to strike in earnest when the opportunity arrives. Significantly, Lorenzo arranges for the assassination to take place at Sciarrha's home, to which he has lured the Duke with the promise of consummating his desire for Amidea. To preserve his sister's chastity and punish the Duke's lust, however, Sciarrha has already killed Amidea and placed her body in a dark room where the Duke, as the final act of his life, will unknowingly undertake a grotesque seduction. Before he discovers the horrible truth, the Duke kisses Amidea's corpse, a gesture that symbolizes his fatal affection for a duplicitous, degenerate favorite as well as the collapse of the bonds of chaste love and mutual obligation that should bind prince and subject. In a wonderful irony, Lorenzo takes the Duke at his word when, expressing his amazement at Amidea's death, he blurts out, "I prithee kill me." Stabbing him, Lorenzo mockingly explains to his absolutist master, "It was my duty to obey you, sir" (5.3.52, 57). As the agent of such poisoned intercourse between prince and subject, Lorenzo finally meets his death at Sciarrha's hands. Tragically, it is only by destroying his own family, particularly by negating any chance of forming an advantageous marital alliance through his chaste sister, that Sciarrha manages to rescue the state from the violence of rapacious royal will.

As I hope to have shown, these tragicomedies and tragedies of the 1620s and 1630s reveal the persistence of an association between favoritism and sexual transgression, even during the years in which Charles ruled without a favorite. Rather than use favoritism to construct James as homosexual and Charles as heterosexual, I have aimed to show that late Jacobean and Caroline playwrights used the type of the monstrous favorite in the service of a political critique. In these plays, the representation of the monstrous favorite allows for a different perspective on the problems of monarchical government than in the Elizabethan and Jacobean representation of the favorite as a Ganymede. In Marlowe's *Edward II*, for instance, the aristocratic opposition readily identify the seductive favorite as the source of the king's weakness: they correctly predict the disastrous consequences of government based on the indulgence of passion and the counsel of parasites, and they use persuasion and coercion to oppose these destructive influences.

Caroline tragedies and tragicomedies instead emphasize the opacity of the prince's desires. The prince's love for the favorite is simply a given, sometimes wondered at but rarely challenged or made accountable to justification. As a result of the prince's willful affection for and empowerment of an undeserving favorite, subjects often find themselves unable to intervene effectively in a political process based on what Henry Wotton, referring to Charles's affection for Buckingham, called the "secret of high inclinations" (7). By focusing on the monstrous favorite's self-serving manipulation of the heteroerotic alliances that undergird social and political order, Caroline playwrights generate critical reflection on the problem of royal will: namely, the king's reliance on inscrutable affections or "high inclinations" to govern the baffling network of alliances and affiliations that comprise the political nation. The lack of a distinction between heterosexual and homosexual identities in the period only contributes to the perception of the favorite's monstrously elastic agency, in that he could embody fears of any kind of alliance, no matter the precise sexual configuration. Through his attempts to "disfashion" the royal family in his own image, the type of the monstrous favorite provided Caroline subjects with compelling, if terrifying, imaginative access to the occluded operations of royal will.

Epilogue

When I began this project, I imagined it not as an intervention into character studies, but as an exploration of how the representation of sexual transgression on the London stage might have served to articulate tensions over social, economic, and political change in early modern culture. As the book took shape, however, sexual types emerged as the organizing principle, and my focus shifted to understanding the typical character as the field on which struggles over the imposition and resistance of social norms were waged. In the event, this volume fortuitously appears at a time when scholarship on early modern dramatic character has been in the ascendant.[1] I herein offer some concluding thoughts about how my project speaks to the larger methodological issues raised by this recent work.

A sign of the renewed interest in character studies is the anthology *Shakespeare and Character* (2009), edited by Paul Yachnin and Jessica Slights. In their introduction, the editors observe that, after the neglect of character in New Criticism, post-structuralism, and cultural materialism, "the idea of character has now begun to reemerge as an important—perhaps even as an essential—way of thinking about the political, ethical, historical, literary, and performative aspects of early modern theater" (1).[2] Although Yachnin and Slights refer to "early modern theater," it is no accident that their anthology centers on Shakespeare. In terms of the reception history of Shakespeare, they observe, a focus on character is unavoidable because character "has stood at the center of the literary and theatrical engagement with Shakespeare for at least the past 350 years" (5).[3] Moreover, Yachnin and Slights affirm that "character is the organizing principle of Shakespeare's plays": first, because the meaning of plot events is conveyed through characters' experiences of and reflections on those events (6); second, because "characters gather into themselves the competing ideological positions that circulate in the play worlds" (8). Despite the case Yachnin and Slights make for a renewed critical focus on

Shakespearean character, their claim about character as an "organizing princi-ple" of drama does not necessarily hold true for early modern playwrights who do not rely on character psychology as the refracting lens of plot developments and ideological positions. Hence, a renewed critical and theoretical focus on Shakespearean characters might actually contribute to the long-standing mar-ginalization of the different modes of characterization employed by Shake-speare's contemporaries.

In fact, two contributors to *Shakespeare and Character*, Michael Bristol and William Dodd, unfavorably contrast the emotional complexity and in-dividualized identities of Shakespeare's characters with the flatter outlines of generic and historical character types. Bristol argues that Shakespeare's charac-ters engage us through a shared "human vulnerability to loss and grief" (Bris-tol 38). Because of our ability to connect emotionally and ethically with the suffering of others, "We don't need any specialized historical knowledge to un-derstand Constance or Shylock or Lady Macduff" (38). One might fairly ask whether the "specialized historical knowledge" of the professional Shakespeare critic inevitably colors—and possibly distances—his or her "emotional" con-nection to a character such as Shylock or Lady Macduff. Nonetheless, Bristol holds that to attend to the passionate language of a Shylock or Lady Macduff is to regard that character as if he or she were a person like us and not merely "the expression of a generic or historical type" (25).

Whereas Bristol emphasizes the way Shakespeare's characters express fa-miliar desires and fears, William Dodd describes how Shakespeare creates the effect of unique personhood through a "discourse biography": the "unique history of interactions that accrues to [a] character and is more than the sum of its social determinations" (63). According to Dodd, "Verbal interactions ad-here" to dramatic characters and "define their relation, moment by moment, to semantic identities" (63). Dodd argues, for instance, that Othello uses dig-nified rhetoric to contest cultural stereotypes of the Moor and to cultivate the elevated image of a suffering hero. Othello's projection of a "rather obsolete, narcissistic" persona for himself, however, is thwarted by Iago's reductive and stereotypical characterizations of his general as a cuckold and a wandering stranger (66). Dodd describes this conflict as a dialectic between the "indi-vidualizing process inscribed in Othello's scripted discourse biography" and the "distancing, typifying process to which he is subjected" by Iago's mastery of theatrical improvisation and linguistic manipulation (75).

A renewed focus on the "personhood" of Shakespearean characters does not, however, mean that we need devalue either the "generic or historical type" of character (Bristol) or the "typifying process" that erodes the unique contours of a character's individual discourse biography (Dodd). In her analysis of Shakespeare's different strategies of characterization in *The Comedy of Errors* and *Hamlet*, Dympna Callaghan insists that Hamlet is not a "better" character than those in the earlier play. Rather, Hamlet represents a different conception of character, grounded on the premise that "unlike the Antipholi and the Dromios, he and his experience cannot be duplicated" ("Characters" 43). Callaghan goes on to explain that the "difference between an Antipholus and a Hamlet alerts us to distinct methods of characterization appropriate to different genres and productive of different theatrical effects as well as different emotional *affects*" (45). Similarly, Jonathan Crewe observes that, despite the enduring popular appeal of Shakespeare's characters, "Shakespeare questions character as much as he produces it" through theatrical practices such as mistaken identity and cross-dressing (35). Moreover, "Characters in Shakespeare may also be deindividualized by their typicality, by their substitutability, or by their specular or anagrammatic relation to each other" (36).[4] As Callaghan and Crewe recognize, strategies of characterization that tend toward the typical—duplication, substitution, specularity—are as valid a part of Shakespearean dramaturgy as his celebrated ability to produce "virtual personhood" (Crewe 36).

Precisely because playwrights such as Jonson, Middleton, Fletcher, and Shirley are less likely than Shakespeare to be credited with creating virtual persons, it is crucial that we continue to study those typifying strategies of characterization that inform their plays. A focus on sexual types in Shakespearean and non-Shakespearean plays represents just one approach for exploring what the shared traits of generic characters might reveal about the drama as a site of collective social meaning. To adopt a formulation from Judith Butler, sexual types starkly reveal how the terms of gender and sexuality are, "from the start, outside oneself, beyond oneself in a sociality that has no single author" (1). By referring to a "sociality that has no single author," Butler points to the collective regulatory forces that shape what gender and sexuality can mean within a given historical and cultural formation. In this regard, all the characters I have examined enter their plays stamped with gender and sexual histories that have no single, identifiable origin or source.

At the same time, a type exists only through the individual instantiations that continue to make the category intelligible.[5] Hence a particularly dissident instantiation of a type can open up a space of indeterminacy and improvisation that allows for the critical scrutiny of the category's authority to restrict the possible meanings attached to a certain set of behaviors.[6] Even with a character such as Ben Jonson's Amorphus, I have argued, this critical space becomes available despite what I take to be Jonson's purpose in imposing norms of civility through the ridicule of male effeminacy. By exploiting the typically effeminate traits of the narcissistic courtier and by contrasting the courtier's excesses to the ascetic discipline of the scholar Crites, Jonson suggests that courtly deformity is easy to detect, expose, and expunge. In elaborating the type of the narcissistic courtier, however, *Cynthia's Revels* reveals that the implied norm of the legitimate courtier is far from self-evident. How is one to identify "effeminate" sartorial or verbal affectation in a milieu defined by conspicuous display and artifice? Without the powers of discernment possessed by the divine Cynthia, how does one assess a courtier's fidelity to the norm of civilized behavior? Might not the play's very celebration of this norm expose it as a residual formation no longer suited to an era of rapid social and economic change, an era in which the unauthorized self-display that has previously gone under the name of "effeminacy" might well be regarded as the prerogative of wealthy and ambitious young men?

If Amorphus is capable of generating such reflection despite the play's apparently conservative designs, a more individuated character such as Livia in Middleton's *Women Beware Women* seems designed to provoke scrutiny of the type from which she emerges. To the degree that the characters in the plays I discuss evince the kind of "individualizing process" Dodd finds in *Othello*, I have regarded those signs of individualization as opportunities for playwrights to interrogate the dominant social, economic, or political assumptions conveyed by the features of a particular type. When a playwright develops a sexual type beyond the expectations generated by its multiple cultural and literary iterations, as Middleton does by fashioning Livia through and against the type of the common bawd, the type itself is more likely to be revealed as the product of a disciplinary norm (cf. J. Butler 41–43). Livia's difference from the type of the decrepit, diseased bawd disjoins and exposes the ideological link between female sexual agency and physical degeneration that informs the type. Livia is a threatening figure because she manipulates common knowledge with the zeal and savvy of the typical bawd, but from a position of uncommon social, economic, and intellectual authority.

It might well be that the kind of individualizing process we find in the characters of a Middleton, Massinger, or Shirley does not produce the same density of dramatic personhood to which we are accustomed in (some of) Shakespeare's characters. For instance, Shirley does not weave a "discourse biography" throughout *The Traitor* to individuate Lorenzo from the generic type of the traitor. Early in the play, Lorenzo reveals information about his past in the course of recounting his loyal services to the Duke. Nonetheless, Lorenzo reveals little about how these political accomplishments have impacted his ethical or emotional subjectivity; instead, he limns his identity via a generic portrait of the envied favorite: "But what story / Mentioned his name that had his prince's bosom / Without the people's hate? 'Tis sin enough / In some men to be great" (1.2.59–62). In a mid-play soliloquy, Lorenzo vents his frustration at the stalling of his plots in language entirely conventional for an ambitious aristocrat (4.1.1–25); personal revelation goes no further than a confession that he lacks the patience to wait for the dukedom to devolve to him. Instead of fleshing out biographical cues, Shirley gives Lorenzo a sensationalistic Act Five soliloquy in which he graphically describes and enacts his daily ritual stabbing of the Duke's portrait. This late revelation makes Lorenzo a memorable, if not grotesque, character, and the soliloquy's vivid sexual imagery is certainly ripe for a psychoanalytic reading; still, this lone passage might not make Lorenzo an empathetic or even theatrically satisfying character.[7]

Nevertheless, the individuating detail of Lorenzo's soliloquy—the cloistered, ardent rage he directs against the Duke's image—draws our attention to the ideological work performed by the type of the monstrous favorite in associating misgoverned royal will with ungoverned sexual will. If we seek to understand dramatic character as a rich source of insight into the theater's role in social conflict and social change, then we need to look outside Shakespeare, and the ideal of virtual personhood that has become synonymous with his aesthetic achievements. Looking beyond the Shakespearean norm is especially crucial for those of us who strive to understand the modes of queer embodiment and dissidence that were thinkable in early modern culture.

Notes

INTRODUCTION

Epigraphs: Hannah Arendt, "Introduction," *Illuminations* (3). For an attempt "to recuperate Hannah Arendt's vision of democratic politics" for lesbian and gay rights, see Morris Kaplan (151). According to Kaplan, Arendt is "pre-eminently the philosopher of plurality: for her, to be human simply *is* to be in the world with others" (154). Edward Albee, *The American Dream* (113).

1. William Shakespeare, *1 Henry IV*, in *The Norton Shakespeare*, ed. Greenblatt. Unless otherwise indicated, all citations from Shakespeare plays will come from this edition and will be cited parenthetically in the text.

2. In this context, "fresh" might mean "blooming, looking healthy or youthful"; "gaily attired, finely dressed"; "brisk, vigorous, active"; or "ready, eager" (*OED*, fresh *adj.* A.II. 9.b, 9.c, 10.a, 11.a).

3. On the association of beards with masculine sexual potency, see Fisher's chapter on beards in *Materializing Gender*.

4. The narcissistic courtier, citizen wife, bawd, and monstrous favorite appear in character books such as Thomas Gainsford's *Rich Cabinet* (1616), Nicholas Breton's *The Good and The Badde* (1616), Sir Thomas Overbury's *Characters* (1616), John Earle's *Microcosmography* (1628), and Francis Lenton's *Characterismi* (1631). The narcissistic courtier can be gleaned in Lenton's "Gallant Courtier," Overbury's "Affected Traveller" and "Courtier," and Gainsford's "Courtier." Although the citizen wife is more elusive than the courtier, she is featured in Lenton's "Sempster Shopkeeper" and makes a brief appearance in Gainsford's account of the "Citizen." Bawds are popular, as attested by Lenton's "Bawd," Overbury's "Maquerela, in Plain English, a Bawd," and Earle's "Handsome Hostess" of an inn, who "do[e]s not startle at bawdry" and "may be an honest woman, but is not beleev'd so in her parish" (sigs. N4r–v). Finally, the "Unworthy Counsellor" in Breton's *The Good and The Badde* approximates the monstrous favorite.

5. The concepts of sexual identity and sexual subjectivity are not germane to my

project, which primarily treats figures defined according to a particular social function or role (the courtier, citizen wife, bawd, and favorite). To be sure, the sodomite and tribade are defined by a sexual trait; nonetheless, in the texts I examine they are not represented as possessing a distinct sense of selfhood based on sexual object choice, which I understand as fundamental to the concepts of homosexual identity and homosexual subjectivity. An additional reason to avoid the concept of identity is cogently spelled out by Valerie Traub in "The Present Future of Lesbian Historiography." Traub observes that "too often the concept of identity remains undertheorized and hazily defined, associated with such different concepts as sexual inclination, tendency, preference, predisposition, orientation, consciousness, subjectivity, self-perception, and subculture—listed here according to a spectrum from 'soft' to 'hard' identity claims" (140 n. 12). However, see Knowles, "Sexuality: A Renaissance Category?" for a thoughtful consideration of the possibility of an early modern "sense of sexual consciousness" (685) or identity that rejects the rigid acts/identity binary. In the same volume, A. J. Piesse's investigation of early modern "identity" is also informative.

6. In an analysis of the prose "Character" genre, Christy Desmet observes how the character portrait is subject to deconstruction, "for the dramatic scene around which the Characters take shape and the nature of the persons under observation work against the portrait's implicit claims to objectivity and truth" (51). I am making a similar claim about the dramatic representation of sexual types.

7. As André Bourassa writes, "the actor who gives an innovative face to his *personnage* is also a creator of meaning: he must take the *personnage* where the author placed him and make him move" (95). Leanore Lieblein similarly observes that "it is only when personated or filtered through the body of the performing actor who is himself transformed by it" that a dramatic character "can be thought of as a character" (123). Lieblein's larger project is to use phenomenological theory to "propose a notion of early modern character as the product of a physically informed communication that results from the actor's embodiment and the spectator's experience of the person personated" (118). Lieblein reminds us of the Renaissance meaning of "character" as a form of writing: "a crafted artefact, not a representation of a person who exists in the world" (121).

8. My aims are consistent with those of materialist critics, who "analyze the moments at which character effects break down, disclosing the ideological project of the play" (Sinfield, "From Bradley" 33).

9. Lisa Jardine's *Still Harping on Daughters* (1983) and Linda Woodbridge's *Women and the English Renaissance* (1984) exemplify groundbreaking feminist criticism on female types. More recent work by Jyotsna Singh on prostitutes, Jennifer Panek on widows (*Widows*), and Pamela Brown on shrews and patient wives follows in this tradition. Though not explicitly feminist in purpose, Michael Shapiro's *Gender in Play on the Shakespearean Stage* draws upon feminist criticism in its analysis of the cross-dressing female page in early modern drama. Shapiro's aim is to explore the theatrical effects of the multiple layerings of gender and sexual identity produced by typical cross-dressing characters such as the "saucy wag" and "frail waif."

10. See, for instance, Bartels, Callaghan (*Shakespeare*), Sandra Clark, D'Amico, Hoenselaars, Jones ("Italians"), Loomba (*Shakespeare*), and Vitkus.

11. Female same-sex types such as the virgin, tribade, Amazon, and friend are discussed by Andreadis, Jankowski, Schwarz, Shannon, Traub, and Walen; male same-sex types such as the sodomite, favorite, ganymede, and friend are discussed by Bray (*The Friend*), Di-Gangi, Masten, Perry, Shannon, Shepherd, and Smith (*Homosexual*). Some of this work is not strictly limited to same-sex scenarios. For instance, Jankowski defines virgins as "queer" to the degree that they resist the expectation of marriage and reproduction, while Schwarz addresses the representation of Amazons in both same-sex and heteroerotic contexts.

12. In "The Present Future of Lesbian Historiography," Traub addresses the "typological impulse" of lesbian history, including her own work on the tribade and friend. She describes her current interest as "investigating the cultural conditions that render such types culturally salient at particular moments" (127).

13. To a surprising degree, most single-authored studies of early modern homoeroticism are sharply divided by gender, concentrating primarily either on male-male or female-female relations.

14. See Douglas Bruster's eloquent defense of source study as "a powerful tool with which to examine the materials—cultural and otherwise—that make up every text" (*Shakespeare*, 189).

15. Although I occasionally use the language of "norms" to describe implicit or explicit prescriptions on sexual, gender, and social comportment, I do not mean to suggest that there was a "normative" sexuality in the early modern period, let alone that "heterosexuality" was normative. I understand a norm simply as a "standard or pattern of social behaviour that is accepted in or expected of a group" (*OED*, norm, *n.* 1.b). For an incisive critique of the anachronistic projection of the statistical concept of the normative onto premodern culture, see Lochrie, *Heterosyncrasies* (1–25).

16. See Harold Bloom's *Shakespeare: The Invention of the Human* and the responses to it in Desmet and Sawyer, eds., *Harold Bloom's Shakespeare*, especially the cluster of essays on "Reading and Writing Shakespearean Character." Margreta de Grazia's Hamlet *Without Hamlet* argues that overemphasis on the character of Hamlet has prevented us from appreciating the degree to which larger social, economic, and political structures drive the action and significance of *Hamlet*.

17. Elizabeth Fowler similarly observes that, after the crucial interventions of theory, "we are now in a position (as we have been with the 'author' for some time) to allow character—surely among the richest resources of language and fiction—to reappear to us, ready for a reassessment of its historical nature, formal effects, and social consequences" ("Shylock's Virtual Injuries," 56).

Chapter 1. Keeping Company: The Sodomite's Familiar Vices

1. According to Bruce Smith, the revisions of Henry VIII's sodomy law under Edward VI (in 1548) added five provisos that personalized what had been a political crime designed to eliminate priests loyal to Rome by making clergy subject to secular law. The Edwardian

revision "reifies the criminal act itself. It could no longer, as under Henry VIII, be a vague accusation that masked some other grievance against the accused (the fact that he was a Catholic friar whose highest loyalty lay to the pope) but was now given specificity in time (accusation had to be made within six months of the alleged act) and in social context (since witnesses were not supposed to gain from a conviction, their interest in the crime was presumed to be moral, not political or economic). The law was becoming ever more exact in putting homosexuality into discourse" (Smith, *Homosexual* 46). Elizabeth's first Parliament (1559), reacting dogmatically to the prior reign of Mary I, "had lumped sodomy with conjurations, sorcery, and witchcraft in an omnibus bill to reinstate the felonies that the Catholic queen had abolished" (47). This bill, however, did not pass. Elizabeth's second Parliament (1562) passed a reformulated sodomy statute that "detached conjurations, sorceries, and witchcraft" from sodomy, a bill that Smith describes as "an attempt to regulate the sex lives of a sovereign's subjects" (47). Although Smith points to significant changes in the language of the secular sodomy laws, he also notes that the medieval religious rhetoric of sodomy cast a long shadow. In his *Institutes* of 1644, Sir Edward Coke summarizes three hundred years of British legal history on sodomy, amplifying the "religious rhetoric" of the thirteenth-century law that described sodomy as "a detestable and abominable sin, amongst Christians not to be named, committed by carnal knowledge against the ordinance of the Creator and order of nature" (qtd. Smith, *Homosexual* 50).

2. Correcting Smith's account of the aim and subsequent influence of Henry's sodomy law, Kenneth Borris argues that "its motivations were not just politically circumstantial" and that it "did not specifically target ecclesiastics" (87). Borris reproduces the texts of the Henrican, Edwardian, and Elizabethan sodomy statutes, as well as that of the Marian act repealing the earlier sodomy statutes (87–90).

3. My claim that the same activities might be regarded as sodomitical or as authorized appears to resemble Alan Bray's argument in "Homosexuality and the Signs of Male Friendship in Elizabethan England" (first published in 1990, reprinted in *Queering the Renaissance*, 1994, and incorporated into a chapter on "Friends and Enemies" in *The Friend*). Bray demonstrates that the same-sex intimacies that were signs of traditional friendship could also be perceived as signs of sodomy under certain socially or politically charged circumstances. However, Bray narrowly regards "sodomy" as essentially synonymous with homosexual sex. I argue that definitions of the sodomite that exclude him from the boundaries of normative community could end up revealing the familiarity of both the sexual and the non-sexual transgressions associated with the category of "sodomy."

4. In his reading of William Bradford's *Of Plymouth Plantation*, Jonathan Goldberg elucidates a dynamic in which the "sexuality that flows at such moments in the representation of the ideal male community suggests how close sodomy is to this discourse and why, when sodomy 'broke forth,' as Bradford puts it (351)—when it became visible—it was violently repudiated" (237). In short, Bradford's text reveals "the proximity of the ties that bind these men together and the possibility of literally enacting them," and thus the sodomite "represents at once the negation of the ideal and its literalization" (237–38). As I read him, Goldberg argues here that the textual representation of the literal sodomite (a man

who commits anal intercourse or bestiality) undoes the text's idealizing strategies by reveal-ing the logic of sodomy (intimate male-male relations) at the heart those very ideals. My argument works with a different logic: I suggest not that the sodomite repudiates an ideal of nonsexual male-male love by "literalizing" its bonds as sexual, but that the sodomite embodies a range of sexual and *nonsexual* practices that could be recognized as constitutive of the "normative" communities from which he is to be excluded.

5. Richard Halpern captures a sense of the transcendent opacity and otherness that Bray associates with sodomy when he observes that sodomy "constitutes a kind of empty hole in discourse, about which nothing directly can be said. This is one of its points of contact with the sublime" (9).

6. Earlier forays into the debate about homosexual subjectivity in early modern Eng-land include Bredbeck (143–48, 184–85); Smith, *Homosexual* (221–23, 232–34); and Cady (18–21).

7. However, in a reading of Shakespeare's *Titus Andronicus*, Christina Mohler argues that the role of sodomite offered a site of possible identification for those seeking transgres-sive agency against social authority.

8. In his final chapters on the persecution of sodomites in the New World, Goldberg turns more directly to "the worldly consequences of literature" (24).

9. Smith also discusses political satires against King James and his favorites, material that I address in Chapter 6. Smith's reading of *Edward II* posits that Marlowe transposes "satirical stereotypes of sodomy and sodomites . . . into dramatic situations in which they do not quite fit" (*Homosexual Desire* 209–10). Consequently, Marlowe goes beyond the limitations of the satirists' portrait of the sodomitical type in presenting his protagonist as "both a sodomite and a man who feels homosexual desire" (222). The possibility of a *non-sodomitical* "homo-sexual subjectivity," Smith claims, is thus introduced by Marlowe and further developed by Shakespeare in the *Sonnets*, although Shakespeare's "subver[sion]" of the "sexual rules of early modern English society" was historically anomalous and fleeting (223, 268).

10. In his *Defence of Poesy* (1595), Philip Sidney defines comedy in terms of the effect of disidentification it produces in male audience members. Sidney argues that comedy repre-sents the "common errors" of negative social types (the niggard, flatterer, or braggart), "So as it is impossible, that any beholder can be content to be such a one" (sig. F3r).

11. Assize and Quarter Session records from approximately 1560 to 1680 reveal only three cases involving same-sex behavior; records of the Home County Assizes, which are largely complete for the period between 1559 and 1625, show only four indictments for sodomy (Bray, *Homosexuality* 71).

12. Alan Stewart observes, however, that in seventeenth-century legal texts there is some confusion about whether penetration or simply emission of semen was enough to constitute "buggery" or sodomy ("Bribery" 126).

13. According to Randolph Trumbach, we first see men defaming other men as sod-omites in the mid-eighteenth century: "the few cases brought by men in the consistory court in the early eighteenth century in which men complained of being called whoremon-gers disappeared by midcentury and were replaced by actions at quarter sessions in which

men and boys brought charges of sodomitical assault and blackmail" (*Sex* 24). Trumbach connects this development to the early eighteenth-century emergence of sodomites as a "third gender" or distinct social minority of effeminate men, as indicated by the presence of "a protective subculture of meeting places and ritual behavior," as well as attacks against them by the Societies for the Reformation of Manners (6).

14. Like Gowing, Alan Stewart notes that "the courts to which people were accustomed to turn for slanders of their personal morality or sexuality"—the ecclesiastical courts—"had no jurisdiction" over sodomy ("Bribery" 137). Stewart also argues that because sodomy was essentially "a household crime, taking place between the walls" of a single house, "insult about sodomy is by its very nature a domestic matter, and thus not amenable either to prosecution or to defense by prosecution of the slanderer" (138). Stewart's logic is problematic, first in so narrowly defining sodomy as a "household crime" usually between a master and his servants, and secondly in omitting consideration of male same-sex relations that might cross household boundaries—such as sexual acts between neighbors. In the sodomy case I describe below, Edward Coke reports that Humfrey Stafford had sex with a boy at another man's home.

15. Ben Saunders provides a similar analysis of this passage from Bodley (220–21 n.27). Noting Bodley's "lack of outrage" toward the male-male anal intercourse he witnesses, Saunders suggests that Bodley operates according to the same interpretive principle we find in the writing of John Donne: "between friends, there can be no such thing as sodomy" (80).

16. Martin Ingram similarly observes that church courts "made virtually no effort to punish autoerotic activities and sexual irregularities which took place between husband and wife" or "extramarital sexual activities which fell short of full intercourse" (239–40). The church courts were most vigilant in prosecuting cases involving bastardy because it posed the most serious social and economic threats to the local community (261). Regarding the church courts' limited surveillance over many forms of male-female sexual activity, Ingram concludes that "Local communities did not normally intrude themselves into people's lives to seek out cases of immorality: they usually waited until the circumstances became blatant or a matter of common knowledge and insistent gossip" (245). It makes sense that a similar reticence would characterize community interference into male same-sex activities as well.

17. In *Controlling Misbehavior in Early Modern England*, 1370–1600, McIntosh analyzes reports of social misconduct from 267 public courts held in 255 villages, market centers, and hundreds. She classifies conduct that was "regarded as socially harmful or disruptive by jurors" but not expressly against the law into eleven offenses, ten of which she then groups into clusters: the Disharmony cluster (scolding/quarreling, eavesdropping, nightwalking); the Disorder cluster (sexual misconduct, unruly alehouses, being of "bad government" or "evil reputation"); the Poverty cluster (hedgebreaking, vagabondage/living idly, and receiving subtenants) (9–10). McIntosh notes that despite the official jurisdiction of the church courts over sexual offenses, cases of sexual misconduct did appear in the local public courts when they were perceived to threaten "good order within their communities" (70).

18. Renaissance Florence provides an instructive contrast with what I am describing as the informal, indirect social and legal disciplining of sodomy in early modern

England. As Michael Rocke relates in his book *Forbidden Friendships*, in 1432 Florence established the Office of the Night, a "special magistracy" for discovering and prosecuting sodomy (45). The Office of the Night encouraged community participation in its policing efforts by offering rewards to local informants and by guaranteeing their anonymity. In addition, "whole neighborhoods acted at times in collective, informal ways to rid themselves of a sodomite or to convince a neighbor to reform" (83). For instance, in 1468 an informer testified against a mercer whom neighbors caught twice in his shop at night with a boy; the neighbors jeered at him and enjoined him to put an end to his disgraceful behavior. Clearly, the vast differences obtaining between fifteenth-century Florence and late sixteenth-century England—among the most relevant of which might be the particularly vigorous excoriation of the "unnatural" vice of sodomy by the Roman Catholic Church (Rocke 19–20, 36–37)—mean that no simple conclusion can be drawn from this discrepancy in attitudes toward same-sex activity. Nonetheless, the discrepancy does support a conclusion Randolph Trumbach came to in an early essay on "sodomitical subcultures" in early modern Europe, namely, that male same-sex activity in early seventeenth-century England was acknowledged yet not deemed threatening or objectionable enough to warrant public attack ("Sodomitical" 118).

19. On London preachers' use of Sodom as a prophetic warning to English sinners, see Alexandra Walsham, p. 299. Walsham cites eight sermons that treat the destruction of Sodom and Gomorrah, including Milles's *Abrahams Suite for Sodome*.

20. Mark Jordan argues that "there is no text of the Christian Bible that determines the reading of Sodom as a story about same-sex copulation. On the contrary, there is explicit scriptural evidence that the sin of the Sodomites was some combination of arrogance and ingratitude" (32). In the interpretations of medieval Christian exegetes, Sodom does become associated with sexual irregularities generally and with same-sex copulation specifically, but such sexual sins are also identified as the product of the Sodomites' "brazen arrogance bred of opulence" and the "madness of their fleshly appetites" (33, 35).

21. Jurist Edward Coke also mentions the four sins of the Sodomites in his account of the sodomy statute: "The Sodomites came to this abomination by four means: viz. by pride, excess of diet, idleness, and contempt of the poor" (qtd. Borris, *Same-Sex* 98).

22. In his sermon *The Crie of England* (1595), Adam Hill mentions "Sodometrie" and "unnatural lust" as sins that cry out for punishment (24). At the end of the sermon, he explicitly names the four major sins of the Sodomites, referring only obliquely to sodomy as a cause of infertility: "the Sodomites turned the fertilitye of the earth into *pride, fulnesse of bread, idlenesse,* and *unmercifulnes to the poore*: and therefore when this wickednesse was to be punished, it was revenged not with famin, pestilence or sword, but as the wicked had perverted themselves, so the Lord perverted the raine, not to the nourishment of the earth, but to the sterilitie of it; and gave them for dew, brimstone, and for water, fire" (106).

23. The Elizabethan "Sermon against Whoredom and Uncleanness," one of several state-sponsored homilies designed to be read during weekly church services, warns that God destroyed Sodom and Gomorrah for "the filthy sin of uncleanness" (13).

24. The quarto reads "Thou art said to be Achilles' male varlet"; the folio reads "Thou

art thought to be Achilles' male varlet." The quarto's "said" more explicitly attributes Thersites's information to the circulation of rumor.

25. The implication, of course, is that to be a male whore is to be effeminized in relation to another man. In *Common Bodies*, Laura Gowing discusses an extraordinary legal deposition of 1611 that records an incident between two men in an alehouse, John Pulford and Robert Lyle: "Pulford said that Lyle was his whore, and thereupon he took Lyle by the waist and threw him upon the bed, and laying upon him face to face jerked him very grievously . . . and after a while leaving the bed came to the table and there took out Lyle's privities, and rolled them upon the table saying, look what a fine thing (and filthy words) my whore hath" (1). As Gowing comments, these indignities "effeminised Robert Lyle's body. They made him not so much a sodomite, as a whore" (1).

26. I am aware of only one other reference in the drama to a "male varlet," as cited by Gordon Williams in his *Dictionary of Sexual Language and Imagery in Shakespearean and Stuart Literature*. In Dekker's *The Honest Whore, Part One*, the whore Bellafront appears disguised as a page; a servant who registers the discrepancy between the page's feminine appearance (he "has nere a beard") and male clothing describes him as a "male-varlet" (4.1.96–97, 101).

27. For a fuller analysis of effeminacy in *Troilus and Cressida*, see Spear. Spear, however, does not comment on the anomalous gendering of "male varlet."

28. A similar analysis of the composite type of the sodomite might be done of the scene in *Romeo and Juliet* in which Tybalt accuses Mercutio of "consort[ing]" with Romeo. For a reading that begins to unpack Tybalt's deployment of sodomy see Nicholas Radel (93).

29. Alan Stewart discusses the Stafford case in the context of the 1631 sodomy trial of the Earl of Castlehaven ("Queer" 145–46). Gilles Monsarrat mentions Humphrey Stafford in a chapter on stoicism in the writing of Anthony Stafford, Humphrey's younger brother (118–19).

30. In an essay on the politics of women's friendships, Laura Gowing describes an incident from 1605 in which two women were presented to the Bridewell court for "keeping company." Gowing remarks that "'keeping company' was generally used to refer to suspicions of adultery or fornication between men and women." In this case the charge might have referred to suspicion of sex between women or fear that one of the women was tempting the other into some form of unchaste behavior ("Politics" 137). I discuss this incident further in Chapter 5.

31. Whatever the circumstances in which Stafford had sex with these adolescents, because the age of consent under the English buggery law was fourteen, the boys had to accuse Stafford of rape in order to escape the death penalty as willing participants in sodomy. *The Arraignment* gives no further information about the boys, though presumably had they been of gentle status that fact would have been noted.

32. The juridical use of medical evidence of anal penetration is documented on the continent and in texts such as Paolo Zacchia's *Quaestiones Medico-Legales*, first published in 1630, with an added collection of "consultations" and verdicts in the 1661 edition (Rousseau 77–82).

In his "Introduction" to *The Sciences of Homosexuality in Early Modern Europe*, Kenneth Borris discusses Florentine, Venetian, and Luccan legal records that mention medical examinations of the anus (11). The "possibly adverse effects of anal intercourse between males" are also treated in Amato Lusitano's *Curationum Medicinalium Centuriae Septem* (1551), which went through many editions in the sixteenth and seventeenth centuries and presumably would have been available in England (Rousseau 86). Stafford's case appears to be the only extant English example in which a medical examination of the anus factored into a sodomy trial (Borris, "Introduction," 35 n. 61). The explicitness of the account of sexual violence in the Stafford case also seems atypical. Regarding legal depositions concerning the rape of women, Laura Gowing writes that "Rape stories suppressed the act of sex and the trauma of the sexual body" (*Common* 99). On the occlusion of sex acts in legal narratives of the rape of women, see also Garthine Walker, "Rereading Rape and Sexual Violence in Early Modern England."

33. According to Peter Lake, the temptations of "evil company" are linked to the image of London "as a sink of corruption" for "wild young gentlemen drawn to the pleasures and displays of metropolitan life" (123, 114).

34. Mary Bly observes that "Early modern commentators on the fall of Sodom are concerned not only with the individual moral failures of Sodomites, but with a flourishing communal openness" (25).

35. According to Mary Bly, "the infectious qualities of sodomy are often noted in satires" (25).

36. I do not assume that the text reports Stafford's speech accurately; in any case, there is no way to adjudicate accuracy, since no other account of the execution seems to exist. Whenever I refer to what Stafford said, then, it should be understood that I am treating the text as an interested representation of an event to which we have no other access.

37. The wearing of excessive ruffs by apprentices was prohibited in guild and civic ordinances, such as the 1582 ordinance issued by the Lord Mayor of London that forbade ruffs of "more than a yard and a half long" (qtd. Bailey 32). The Elizabethan "Homily Concerning Good Order" anticipates Stafford's image of the ruff as a kind of halter in its complaint that young men "hang their revenues about their necks, ruffling in their ruffs" (qtd. Bailey 47). In Chapter 3, I discuss an image that satirizes the death of a gallant depicted with ruffs and other fashionable items of apparel. Apart from the ruff, Stafford's reference to the "falling band" or "fall" (*OED*, fall *n*1 23a) associates his fall from the gallows with his moral fall.

38. I have added quotation marks to clarify the dialogue in this passage.

39. Alexandra Shepard cites an unusually overt linkage between drinking and same-sex intimacy from B.H.'s *The Glasse of Mans Folly* (1615), which warns readers to "Bee not a sucking Sodomite" (qtd. "Drink Culture," 118). A satirical epigram in I. H.'s *House of Correction* (1619) describes how one Bibens made Lusus drunk, as the "Signe of his familiar love." The epigram ends with a warning that might be taken to refer to sodomitical sex: "*Lusus*, beware, thou'lt finde him in the end / Familier Devill, no familier Friend" (sig. A4r).

40. Shepard, "Drink Culture," 118–19.

41. Lake mentions the Stafford case in his essay on Catholic activism in prisons (215, 219). On Catholic evangelism in prisons, see also Sena (57).

42. I owe this insight to Lowell Gallagher.

43. In "A Society of Sodomites," however, Stewart challenges the assumption, derived from Alan Bray's work, that in Renaissance England "a charge of sodomy meant an attack on Catholicism" (94).

44. Despite what *The Arraignement* claims, it is not likely, considering the danger, that recusants living "out of prison" would be proselytes.

45. Laura Lunger Knoppers reproduces several Post-Reformation illustrations of the Whore of Babylon, largely inspired by the woodcuts in Albrecht Dürer's *Apocalypse* of 1498. On anal sex and the "fantasy of anal birth" in Shakespeare's *Coriolanus*, see Jonathan Goldberg, "The Anus in *Coriolanus*" (183).

46. Considering Stafford's execution for sodomy, Bly's hypothesis that the Whitefriars Theater celebrated a "sodomitical subjectivity" centered on disruptive, bawdy laughter cannot be taken too literally. There is not much to laugh about in early modern legal or theological references to Sodomites.

47. James Grantham Turner describes the early modern notion of education as physical implantation or infusion, "often ascribed to pederastic philosophers" to justify their homoerotic infatuation with young male pupils. Turner notes that mind or *mens*, "in a Latin etymological pun, comes from the *mentula* or penis" (44).

48. This is not to imply that only men attended or enjoyed these plays.

49. By the 1630s, it does seem possible to imagine a community of sodomites. See Goran Stanivukovic's discussion of Benjamin Carrier's *Puritanisme The Mother, Sinne The Daughter. . .* (St. Omer: English College Press, 1633), a Catholic pamphlet that purports to reveal the existence of "a company of *Sodomieticall Persons*," all Puritans, living in London (234).

50. Shepard, *Meanings* 96–113, and "Drink Culture," 112–14.

51. Paul Hammond concurs that "the growth of the molly houses in London would make society at large much more aware of sexual relations between men, and would provoke responses (ranging from mockery to murder) from the guardians of public morality. But this only happens once an imaginable social life with its own idiolect, fashions, and geography has begun to coalesce around the practice of men enjoying sex with one another" (183).

Chapter 2. Fulfilling Venus: Substitutive Logics and the Tribade's Agency

1. As Laurie Shannon has shown, there was in early modern culture an important discourse of the homonormative that organized and valorized same-sex friendships and eroticisms; however, as Shannon's analysis of Emilia's coerced marriage in Shakespeare's *The Two Noble Kinsmen* indicates (90–122), these discourses of homonormativity existed in tension with early modern social institutions and practices that promoted male-female coupling. To claim that married procreative intercourse was a "norm" of female sexuality in early

modern England is not to claim that "heterosexuality" was a normative sexuality. On the problem of the "normative" in the premodern period, see Karma Lochrie, *Heterosyncrasies*.

2. This is not to claim that sex was thought to provide pleasure only to the male partner; to the contrary, see Traub's discussion of female orgasm (*Renaissance of Lesbianism* 77ff.). Traub also comments on the "paradoxical understandings of women's eroticism" in sixteenth-century medical, prescriptive, and obscene discourses, which were split between an authorization of "erotic mutuality and equality" and the "subordination of women . . . within a resolutely patriarchal, reproductive economy" (125). All further citations of Traub in this chapter will come from *Renaissance*.

3. In an analysis of the instability of gender identifications within female same-sex relations that complements my own, Jonathan Goldberg demonstrates how Amelia Lanyer's poem *Salve Deus Rex Judaeorum* (1611) enacts multiple "crossings" across the divides of gender and sexual binaries such as active/passive, male/female, and hetero-/homo-erotic (*Desiring* 16–41). Jessica Tvordi's discussion of female alliance in *Twelfth Night* posits that Maria, despite her "feminine" behavior, "directly challenges masculinist constructs of feminine subjectivity by transgressing accepted boundaries of gender, sexuality, and power" (116).

4. Citing Traub and referring to the "one-sex" anatomical theory of homology between the penis and vagina, Maurizio Calbi similarly argues that "the clitoris turns out to be a double too many, a less-than-reassuring uncanny double of the male penis that also stands side by side the penis duplicate [i.e., the vagina] woman is already alleged to bear within" (92). Calbi is interested not in the gender dynamics of sex between women but in how the clitoris, as a "masculinized bodily part," is represented as both imitating and displacing the penis's role in heterosexual intercourse (93). Kathryn Schwarz's analysis of the figure of the Amazon in early modern England is also instructive here. Schwarz argues that the dominant cultural meaning of the Amazon "is constituted out of an inappropriate relationship between sexed bodies and gendered acts, constructing an identity defined by the agency of sexual choice and by a perception of that choice as inherently perverse" (3). Discussing Sidney's *Arcadia*, in which Pyrocles, disguised as the Amazon Cleophila, falls in love with Philoclea, Schwarz demonstrates that the Amazon/tribade is not simply a figure of imitative masculinity (195): "Cleophila appears in both conventionally masculine and conventionally feminine terms, her impersonation collapsing heterosocial oppositions" (199). Ultimately, female erotic agency reflects back on the male norm, as the "persistence of desire between women revises the meaning of men" (200).

5. Invisibility is one of the dominant tropes of lesbian historiography and literary criticism. Traub writes that "Because the tribade did not function, as the whore arguably did, as a social 'type,' she is far less familiar a figure" (24); she also observes that "nowhere is social significance more visibly and forcibly marked than in the disciplinary apparatus of the law," yet the Elizabethan sodomy statute did not criminalize sex between women, and the same-sex behaviors of women were generally beyond the notice of the law (164). Elizabeth Susan Wahl's *Invisible Relations* aims to illuminate the "less 'visible' forms of female intimacy" in premodern Europe that "have largely been ignored" by scholarship focused on "transgressive categories like hermaphroditism and female-to-male cross-dressing" (4,

8). Likewise, one of Denise Walen's goals in *Constructions of Female Homoeroticism in Early Modern Drama* is the "recovery" of "unknown, neglected, or forgotten" texts that reveal a cultural presence of female homoeroticism where only absence had been assumed (1). On the "sparse evidence for actual lesbian practices" in the middle ages, see Bennett, *History* 110–14; on lesbian invisibility in the eighteenth century, see Castle 1–19. Emma Donoghue claims that her book, *Passions Between Women*, "is not about silence" but about the "wide variety of lesbian types" described in seventeenth- and eighteenth-century texts (3). See also Simons, "Lesbian (In)Visibility in Italian Renaissance Culture."

6. Traub also identifies as metonymy the long cultural history of the "association between the clitoris and tribadism" (190). She cautions that insofar as the tribade's "appropriation of the phallus was interpreted through the rubric of masculine imitation, it comprised part of a colonial, patriarchal history of abjection" (227).

7. Other European trials of "female husbands" for sodomy are described in Puff (31–35) and Dekker and van de Pol (58–63); on the juridical punishment of "masculine" female sodomites in the middle ages, see Benkov (111–16).

8. Kenneth Borris argues that "Whereas Traub sharply distinguishes nonpenetrative erotic relations of apparently 'chaste' feminine friends . . . from definitively 'unnatural' tribadism," these "categories interpenetrated" to a much greater degree well before the late seventeenth century (*Same-Sex* 19); hence he would "define and apply" Traub's categories more loosely (255). For a critique of Traub's taxonomy that focuses on late seventeenth-century pornographic literature, see Toulalan, 138–39.

9. Bettina Mathes argues that early modern anatomical illustrations of the penis might also be interpreted as representations of the enlarged clitoris attributed to the tribade. Although the tribade's clitoris might thus be figured as an "imitation of the original penis" (122), Mathes provides no evidence from her sources that the tribade's partner was regarded as "feminine," in contradistinction to the tribade's phallic masculinity.

10. Similar ambiguities about erotic agency and gender difference characterize medieval discourses about female same-sex activity. In her analysis of medieval penitentials, Edith Benkov finds a "marked lack of elaboration" of exactly which acts constitute sexual "vice" between women, in part because such texts assume a "phallic model of sexuality that denies agency to women." Strikingly for my purposes, Benkov observes that the penitential of Hincmar of Rheims claims that since women cannot penetrate each other (presumably because they lack a penis), they instead make use of "*instruments of diabolical operations to excite desire*" (qtd. 104). Hincmar thus "appears to leave a space for either partner (or both?) to be 'active' within a less rigid sexual relationship" (105). As Benkov explains, Hincmar's was not the dominant notion of female homoeroticism in the Middle Ages; secular legal discourse facilitated the prosecution of women for sodomy by modeling relationships between women on a male ("active")/female ("passive") paradigm, in which the "active" woman was deemed especially culpable (110).

11. On the continent, the recognition that women could engage in non-penetrative sexual activity might have thwarted prosecutions for sodomy. Helmut Puff concludes from an analysis of continental legal cases that "Compared to men suspected of sodomy, women

suspects created confusion for the judges," since their "gender and their manipulation of expected female behavior apparently made the application of sentences to identifiable sexual acts difficult" (33). Puff pointedly ventriloquises the judges' epistemological dilemma: "how could a woman act sodomitically, if the images this term invoked had to do with anal sexuality and penetration?" (35).

12. I first discussed the passage in *Homoerotics* (95–96); see also Bruster (*Shakespeare* 128), Traub (200), Andreadis (4–5), and Walen (26).

13. Douglas Bruster points out that even more romanticized or "innocent" accounts of female-female desire in early modern drama can provide explicit imagery of sexual contact between women that might titillate audiences or readers (*Shakespeare* 131): "However affective and close female-female relationships were portrayed, they were always open to . . . erotic appropriation" (132).

14. The image is reproduced in Borris, *Same-Sex* (352).

15. Lyndal Roper, however, discusses early modern German drawings of women's baths that depict "nude women of various shapes and ages" (144–45). Roper argues that such images were not primarily erotic, but reflected a cultural "obsession" with the "fertile female body" (144).

16. Cf. the erotic references to the pandora and the viol da gamba discussed below in Chapter 5.

17. Deborah Willis argues that whereas continental witchcraft beliefs tended to attribute sexual transgressions to witches, English treatises and trials did not (9). I have come across only one English text that implicates a local witch in what appears to be a tribadic assault. In the published account of a 1582 witchcraft trial in Essex, a local man testifies that his wife and one Elizabeth Bennet, the accused witch, "were lovers and familiar friendes, and did accompanie much together." One day, Elizabeth Bennet "clasped her in her armes, and kissed her: Whereupon presently after her upper Lippe swelled & was very bigge, and her eyes much sunked into her head, and shee hath lien sithence in a very strange case" (W. W., *A true and just Recorde*. . . sigs. B5v–6r). A possible link between witchcraft and tribadic assault appears in a pamphlet of 1595 that describes how a female con artist posing as a fortune-teller tricks a widow into allowing her to cut off a lock of pubic hair. The pamphlet purports to discover whether or not the fortune-teller "trimmed" the widow, "trimmed" connoting "cheating, satirizing, and sex" (Pamela Brown 157). I discuss this text in greater detail in Chapter 5.

18. Traub observes that in the votaress passage "racial differences, erotic possibilities, and gender identifications intersect in an ambivalent coding of bodies and bonds" (69).

19. All citations from *A Midsummer Night's Dream* come from Peter Holland's Oxford edition; further references will be cited parenthetically in the text.

20. Nonetheless, the gossiping of Titania and the votaress might also be taken to epitomize the cultural practices of a larger female community that is associated with Titania elsewhere in the play. In her analysis of the politics of dancing in *A Midsummer Night's Dream*, Skiles Howard argues that Titania and Oberon embody distinctly gendered cultural practices, Titania's being associated with a feminine, oral, popular tradition (331).

21. According to the *OED*, calamus is "some eastern aromatic plant or plants"; spikenard is "an aromatic substance obtained from an eastern plant"; gum arabic is "exuded by certain species of Acacia"; and opobalsamum is "a fragrant oleoresin obtained from the tree *Commiphora opobalsamum* (family Burseraceae) of Arabia and north-east Africa."

22. On female laughter as a vehicle of social power, see Pamela Brown, esp. 27–32.

23. Laughter is here associated with the boundary violations of the female body. Gail Kern Paster observes that for Joubert, laughter involves not simply pleasure, but also the potential for embarrassing exposure: it causes "a violent solicitation from the body below" that overcomes the "will to bodily control" (*Body* 123). Although it is beyond the chronological scope of this chapter, Bernard Capp cites a suggestive description of the corporeal immodesty of women's laughter from a conduct book of 1683: "to laugh as women do sometimes, with their hands on both sides, and with a lascivious agitation of their whole body, is the height of indecency and immodesty" (qtd. Capp, *Gossips* 4).

24. Joubert's *Traité du Ris* was published complete in French in 1579. Thomas Wright, in *The passions of the minde in generall* (1604), also describes laughter as one of the passions that dilates the heart (60–61).

25. According to Trevor Griffiths, nineteenth-century producers of *A Midsummer Night's Dream* were offended not by any intimation of lesbian desire in this passage, but by the lines describing the votaress's pregnant body, which they typically cut (126–27, note to lines 127–35).

26. The sixteenth-century Sienese humanist Alessandro Piccolomini held that "the love between two women clearly cannot be procreative and therefore must be pure" (Eisenbichler 284).

27. In *The Midwives Book* (1671) Jane Sharp writes of the "frequent" sexual abuse of the clitoris by women in "the *Indies*, and *Egypt*" (qtd. Traub 203).

28. In a discussion of the "queer marriage" between Titania and the votaress, Arthur Little makes a similar observation about the reproductive agency of the two female figures (223). Arguing that Titania remains "thoroughly committed to a society of women" (222), Little does not discuss the status and power differences between Titania and her votaress.

29. Ian Moulton discusses a bawdy early modern manuscript poem about a vagina in terms vaguely reminiscent of the votaress passage—although, admittedly, to entertain such a parallel is to open oneself to Stanley Wells's complaint about "lewd interpreters" of Shakespeare (10–37). The manuscript poem describes the vagina as an "engulfing wound" but also as "a locus of pleasure—possibly of autonomous pleasure that has no need for men," as witnessed by a reference to it as "Doctor Dildoes dauncinge schoole" (Moulton 51). Titania's account of her votaress's pregnant body resonates with two attributes of the vagina in the poem: its association with fairies—"Its all (maydes say) that god them sendes / a fayry circle whear inherrittes / nought but Hobgoblins Elves and spirrittes"—and with navigation—it is a "sculler in the Ocean plac't / transporting thinges to the land of wast" (qtd. Moulton 49–50).

30. The hierarchical elements of the relationship between Titania and her nameless "votaress" can be further illuminated by comparison with the relationship between Emilia

and her nameless "Woman" in Shakespeare and Fletcher's *The Two Noble Kinsmen* (Mallette).

31. To gratify the Duchess's longing for grapes, Faustus sends a spirit to fetch the fruit from a warmer region such as "India, Saba, and farther countries in the East" (4.2.25). Unlike the spirits controlled by Dr. Faustus, Titania is not the pliant servant of a human magus but a Fairy Queen who receives devotion from a human servant.

32. Shankar Raman's psychoanalytic, postcolonialist reading of *A Midsummer Night's Dream* identifies a structural homology between Hermia and the Indian Boy as disputed family properties and tokens of exchange (242). Raman regards Titania's reminiscence of her votaress as evidence of an "idealized female community"; at the same time, he notes that Titania uses the "discourse of mercantile colonialism to justify her ownership of the child," who is "the distilled essence of the East" (243–44).

33. In an essay on the illustrated text of Christine de Pizan's *Epistre Othea*, Marilynn Desmond and Pamela Sheingorn argue that Christine's "queer" revision of "the Ovidian obsession with metamorphosis" serves to validate female erotic desire in terms of "transspecies sexuality" (3).

34. Boehrer discusses the juxtaposition of a parrot and an "ethnic servant" in Anthony Van Dyck's *Portrait of William Fielding, First Earl of Denbigh*, which commemorates the earl's visit to Persia and India in 1631–1633 (*Shakespeare* 106–8).

35. Douglas Green posits that Titania's bestial desire for Bottom the ass is a displacement, at least "from Oberon's voyeuristic position," of the "unthinkable (lesbian) love of Titania for her votaress" (376).

36. According to Deborah Willis, the English tended to associate witches less with fantasies about sexuality (tribadic or otherwise) than with fantasies about maternal power (10). Nonetheless, transgressive same-sex intimacies—such as define the groups of witches in Shakespeare's *Macbeth* and Jonson's *Masque of Queens*—metonymically link witches with tribades, and Leontes's designation of Paulina as a "mankind" witch raises the specter of the unnatural in matters of sex and gender. Moreover, "witchcraft" is commonly used in Shakespeare to connote illicit sexual seduction: the word is deployed in this way against Claudius, Othello, Cleopatra, and, in a same-sex context, Sebastian from *Twelfth Night*. In *The Winter's Tale*, the association of witchcraft with perverse sexuality arises when Polixenes accuses Perdita of being a "fresh piece / Of excellent witchcraft" who has seduced Florizel (4.4.419–20).

37. Ironically, when Leontes commands Antigonus to abandon Hermione's "bastard" in some deserted place, his direct threat to the infant's life typifies the "unnatural" rejection of nurture commonly attributed to the witch (2.3.112).

38. Other examples of metonymic substitution between Leontes and Paulina might be adduced, as when the caloric language of Leontes's initial expression of jealousy—"Too hot, too hot!" (1.2.107)—gets inverted in Paulina's rebuke to a servant who blocks her access to Leontes: "Not so hot, good sir" (2.3.32).

39. In my edition of *The Winter's Tale* I briefly discuss John Marston's overtly sexual

version of the Pygmalion myth, which emphasizes the perverse eroticism of a man's desire for a statue (401–5).

40. Helkiah Crooke describes the clitoris as a "small production . . . answerable to the member of the man, from which it differs in the length, the common passage and the want of one paire of muscles" (238).

CHAPTER 3. MINCING MANNERS: THE NARCISSISTIC COURTIER AND THE (DE)FORMATION OF CIVILITY

1. As Lorna Hutson observes in an analysis of "stylistic manliness" in early modern literature, Jonson is "the English humanist whose poetry and drama affords most scope for an exploration of the meaning of civil conversation, and whose prescriptive prose, as it happens, most strikingly and consistently advocates the classical ideal of the virile style" ("Civility" 2). Since Hutson is mainly concerned here with "censorious self-surveillance" as a mark of virile civility, she focuses on Jonson's *Sejanus and Every Man in His Humour* (10). With its mythological framework, *Cynthia's Revels* departs in an important way from the "naturalistic, manly form" of *Every Man in His Humour*, a "drama of everyday life and speech in turn-of-the-century London" (18).

2. Hester Lees-Jeffries suggests that Jonson might also have had in mind the Ovidian myth of Salmacis and Hermaphroditus: "Amorphus is the central figure, and his name surely recalls the fate of Salmacis and Hermaphroditus, as it can also be translated as 'shapeless' or even 'one who changes shape'" (245).

3. A brief plot summary is in order. The play begins with Cupid and Mercury disguising themselves as pages at Cynthia's court. Following Jove's commandment, Mercury allows Echo the opportunity to express her grief over Narcissus's death (1.2). The mythological and courtly plots merge when Amorphus arrives at Narcissus's Fountain of Self-Love, drinks from its waters (1.3), and carries back to court the news of this elixir. From this point, there is little plot to speak of, and the play unfolds as a satiric exposure of the courtiers and ladies who have gathered for Cynthia's revels that evening.

4. The play exists in two versions. It was published in quarto in 1601 under the title *The Fountain of Self-Love. Or Cynthia's Revels.* For the 1616 Folio, Jonson printed an expanded version of the play and called it *Cynthia's Revels, or The Fountain of Self-Love.* Janet Clare attributes the differences between the texts in part to official censorship of Jonson's "unsparing lampoon" of Queen Elizabeth's court entourage (83). Clare points out that the shorter quarto text, "lacking the tedious diversion of the courtship game in Act V, is certainly a more attractive stage version" (85). I am using Wilkes's modern edition of the play based on the 1616 Folio version.

5. "To mince" means to "cut up, subdivide minutely; to tear, smash, etc., to pieces" (*OED*, mincing *v.* 2a).

6. Gary Spear discusses "mincing" as effeminate comportment in Shakespeare's *Troilus and Cressida* (413).

7. The *OED* cites the contemporary derogatory use of "mincing" to describe "a homosexual" as "effeminate, effete" (*OED*, mincing, *adj.* 1.b).

8. In her influential feminist essay "Diana Described," Nancy Vickers argues that the fragmentation of the female body in Petrarchan verse constitutes the poet's defensive response to the threat of emotional dismemberment. The mirrored relationship between the fragmented poet and the fragmented beloved connects the Acteon/Diana myth with the Narcissus myth (273). Altering this paradigm, *Cynthia's Revels* subjects the body of the male courtier to fragmentation by foregrounding the Narcissus myth and its emphasis on male deformity. Vickers elaborates on tropes of "bodily dismemberment" in "Members Only: Marot's Anatomical Blazons," a chapter in *The Body in Parts*, which argues that the body part in early modern texts is afforded the dual status of both subject and object.

9. Interestingly, the immoderate "mincing" that I associate with Jonson's aggressive dramatic strategy in *Cynthia's Revels* is the antithesis of the decorous "mincing" that would seem more appropriate for a play about courtly manners. "To mince"—as in "to mince words"—is to "moderate or restrain (one's language) so as to keep within the bounds of prudence, politeness, or decorum" (*OED*, mince *v* 2d). Amanda Bailey discusses the English state's "investment in a nationalist discourse that placed proper comportment at the centre of the project of English civility" (12). She notes that "Effeminacy signalled the inability to control one's passions, and immoderation in dress was both the cause and the sign of incivility and hence of unmanliness" (48).

10. A lovely youth who scorns his suitors and consequently dies yearning for his own reflection, Narcissus is the Ovidian figure most commonly associated with homosexual desire in our own era. The familiar link between Narcissus and homosexual desire comes from Freudian theory, in which "narcissism" describes the interruption of proper libidinal development supposedly characteristic of homosexual object-choice. For different attempts to theorize "narcissism" in relation to early modern homoeroticism see Traub, *Desire* 104; Blank; Enterline; and Ellis 110–21.

11. Golding, *Shakespeare's Ovid*, Epistle 105–6. Subsequent references to Ovid will come from this edition, and will be cited parenthetically in the text. Jonathan Bate provides a useful overview of Ovid's place in sixteenth-century English literature (1–47).

12. Kinney with Styron, "Ovid Illustrated."

13. In a reading of Edwards's poem as a warning against the seductions of Petrarchan rhetoric, Ellis suggests that, once transformed into a woman, Narcissus "seeks the attention of male admirers" (114).

14. On the Narcissus and Echo myth in *Cynthia's Revels* see Starnes and Talbert, 188–212.

15. D. A. L. Morgan demonstrates that the concept of a politically centralized "court" and attendant "courtiers" begins to emerge in the mid-fifteenth century, eventually replacing the dominant institution of the royal household as "the active nucleus of war enterprise" (68, 35). Malcolm Smuts explains that strictly speaking the court comprised "the monarchs' immediate entourage and those institutions of the royal household responsible for their personal and ceremonial needs," but "a much larger social network always formed around

this relatively compact group" (3). John Turner describes court life as full of "internal tensions caused by the multiplicity of the roles demanded of a courtier; for the court was a complex institution, whose diverse functions often placed baffling and sometimes tragically irreconcilable claims upon its followers, both in their work and in their leisure" (4).

16. When the concept of engrossing is mentioned in *Cynthia's Revels*, it is in the context of sexual courtship: Anaides complains that Hedon "engross[es]" all the ladies for his "own use" (4.2.16–17). Arguing that several developments during the sixteenth century—including the centralization of royal power and the growth in numbers of the landed elite—"altered the contours and dimensions of patronage," Linda Levy Peck concludes that there was increasing concern about court corruption in the early seventeenth century (*Court Patronage* 3).

17. A "gallant," or "man of fashion and pleasure; a fine gentleman" (*OED*), might or might not be a courtier: both Hedon and Anaides are called gallants.

18. Although complaints about the English importation of foreign fashions are common, David Kuchta points out that merchant capitalists complained that the "dearness of prices, not the consumption of imports, was threatening England's social fabric" (43).

19. Ann Rosalind Jones and Peter Stallybrass observe that the "brokers and second-hand clothes dealers of Long Lane and Houndsditch provided dramatists and pamphleteers with an inexhaustible supply of satiric attacks" against the market in used clothes (192).

20. In a brief analysis of Osric, the effeminate courtier in *Hamlet*, Margreta de Grazia describes his "ambition for land" as a "form of self-aggrandizement" (34). The effeminate courtier's "extravagant dress, gestures, and speech are the pretenses" of someone who owns land but is not inherently noble (34). Robert Brustein more fully discusses Osric as the type of the Italianate courtier, in a chapter called "Effemiphobia: The Osric Courtier," though he is not interested in the ideological tensions that I explore arising from the assertion and resistance of sexual norms.

21. On the early modern ideal of friendship and its relation to homoeroticism, see Masten, 28–37.

22. The word "ravish" also informs the homoerotic sparring of the play's Induction, in which one of three boy players protests against being "rape[d]" by the other two (84, 88). See McDermott.

23. On beaver hats as a new luxury item in early seventeenth-century London, see Peck, *Consuming Splendor* (40–43).

24. Early moderns associated both effeminacy and sodomy with the relinquishing of a properly "masculine" self-control. In a chapter on "effeminate persons, Sodomites, and other such like monsters" in his *Theatre of Gods judgements*, Thomas Beard argues that effeminate men and sodomites give free rein to "monstrous" and "unnaturall" passions. Those Roman emperors who wore women's clothing "ranne too much out of frame in their unbridled lusts and affections"; and the biblical Sodomites "gave themselves over with all violence, and without all shame and measure, to their infamous lusts" (360).

25. Attempts to regulate the courtly male body have a long history, as Mary Partridge shows in her analysis of anti-court satire from the eleventh through the sixteenth centuries.

The courtly fop was typically excoriated for his effeminate dress and comportment, including the "enduring association of strange courtly fashions with deformity," "lasciviousness," and sodomy (132–33). Despite Castiglione's effort in *The Courtier* to advocate the virtue of the ideal courtier, anti-courtier texts were still current throughout the sixteenth century. Moreover, "anti-courtier discourse experienced a vigorous renaissance" during the troubled final decade of Elizabeth's reign (249).

26. See also Stephen Orgel's discussion of the difficulty of distinguishing "masculine" from "feminine" courtly attire (*Impersonations* 84–98). Thomas King provides a complex Foucauldian analysis of the shifting meanings of effeminacy in the seventeenth century, during which period, he argues, England shifted from a society based on hierarchical "alliance" to a society based on private "sexuality" (1: 64–88). King argues that in the early seventeenth century "*effeminacy* described not a falsely gendered or sexual subjectivity but a failure of, or lack of access to, the public representativeness of those men and exceptional women who were statesmen, citizens, and householders. . . . Dependent males (slaves, servants, and laborers, for example) would perpetually lack the capacity to command the passions and exercise reason; consequently they remained 'boys.' . . . The effeminate man's excessive pleasures wantonly displayed his desire for subjection" (1: 67–68).

27. See Linda Levy Peck on the conventional metaphor of the fountain in early modern England as a symbol of the monarch's favor (*Court Patronage* 1). In her reading of this passage and of fountain imagery in *Cynthia's Revels*, Hester Lees-Jeffries examines the fountain as "an ancient and complex political symbol," which was "specifically associated with Elizabeth I in subtle, yet increasingly complicated and ambivalent ways" (198). Explicating the common fountain-as-government metaphor, Lees-Jeffries writes that the "fountain's reflecting surface can stand for exemplarity, while its flowing waters are the means by which that exemplarity is to be transmitted. Yet in both these capacities, as Jonson's dedication and his play reveal, the fountain of the prince or the court is vulnerable to distortion or corruption" (200).

28. Amada Bailey devotes a chapter to sartorial excess in *Every Man Out of His Humour*.

29. Bailey argues that the lavish sartorial displays staged at the public theaters enticed non-elite young men into their own public displays of sartorial excess: "by changing and exchanging sumptuous clothes on stage, by renting and selling them off the stage, and by modelling them within the playhouse, company heads, playwrights, and actors created the conditions not only for new disorderly commercial practices but also new disorderly social practices among a particular population" (19).

CHAPTER 4. CALLING WHORE: THE CITIZEN WIFE AND THE EROTICS OF OPEN WORK

1. Moll Frith has been so central to feminist and queer Renaissance criticism that, in an essay of 2004, Reynolds and Segal analyze "the vast amount of criticism published on

The Roaring Girl and Mary/Moll as an avenue through which to examine the preoccupations of recent literary-cultural criticism" (68).

2. Originally published in a 1984 issue of *English Literary Renaissance*, Rose's essay was reprinted in 1986 in the "Renaissance Historicism" special issue of ELR, and then again in the 1987 anthology *Renaissance Historicism: Selections from English Literary Renaissance*. The influence of Rose's essay is evident in the 1991 anthology *The Matter of Difference: Materialist Feminist Criticism of Shakespeare*, in which four of ten essays cite it.

3. By date of publication, these critics include Viviana Comensoli (1987), Marjorie Garber (1991), Jean Howard ("Sex," 1992), Stephen Orgel ("Subtexts," 1992), Susan Krantz (1995), and Lloyd Edward Kermode (1997). The year 1997 might be taken as a watermark in queer Renaissance criticism, as several major studies were published as of that date. A slightly later group of critics focusing on issues of gender and sexuality in *The Roaring Girl* include Craig Rustici (1999), Herbert Heller (2000), Gustav Ungerer (2000), Madhavi Menon (2004), and Heather Hirschfield (2003). An earlier version of this chapter also appeared in 2003.

4. These studies include those by Jodi Mikalachki (1994); Fiona McNeill (1997), later incorporated into her book (2007); Gustav Ungerer (2000); Bryan Reynolds (2002); Miles Taylor (2005); Natasha Korda (2005); and Clare McManus (2006).

5. With the exception of Jo E. Miller (1990), most of these economic interpretations are relatively recent: Valerie Forman (2001), Jonathan Gil Harris (*Sick*, 2004), Natasha Korda (2005), and Aaron Kitch (2007).

6. Miller briefly describes Moll's conflict with the citizen wives as an effect of market competition among women (19–20). Forman includes the wives (particularly Mistress Gallipot) in an account of the commercialism that motivates the gallant/merchant plots (1532–36). Harris sporadically mentions the wives in his remarks about the play's display of luxury goods and its discourse of consumption (*Sick* 178–84). The citizen wives do not play a discernable role in Korda's and Kitch's accounts, though Korda's fascinating essay is less concerned with the play than with the actual Moll Frith's activities as a broker of second-hand clothing.

7. In early modern England, the "middling sort" of people comprised "independent trading households," the work of which ensured the family's "independence from poverty and thus laid the foundation for social, cultural and political independence" (Barry, "Introduction" 2–3). Emphasizing the multiple forms of civic association, Jonathan Barry identifies the "common urban values" and the "collective responses" to the challenges of urban life that shaped bourgeois identity in early modern England ("Bourgeois" 85). In *The Roaring Girl*, the citizens associate with each other not only through the shared space of the urban marketplace—their "three shops" are represented on stage "open in a rank" (2.1.1 *sd*)—but also through shared leisure activities. At the end of 2.1, the citizens close shop and go off to Hoxton, a district north of London, to sport with their water spaniels.

8. Although McNeill briefly discusses the significance in the play of "litigious whore-calling" between women (*Poor* 126), her central focus is not on the working wives but on Moll's notoriety as a poor woman and criminal.

9. Heather Hirschfeld argues that Moll presents an "epistemological challenge" to her community, in that she represents an "unknowable" woman who "simultaneously parades and conceals her social and sexual acumen" (124–25).

10. Scholarship on women and work in premodern England is extensive and varied. However, it seems possible to offer a broad narrative of seventeenth-century developments. During the course of the seventeenth century, the emergence of capitalist forms of commodity production and exchange increasingly relegated women to the domestic sphere, hence restricting their participation in "many productive and skilled employments in which they had previously been engaged" (Chris Middleton 183; see also Cahn 9). Whereas some wives still continued to assist their husbands in a trade or pursued their own trades (Capp, "Separate" 127), the "increasing availability and relative cheapness of wage labor" and the "more complex and stratified division of labor" gradually pushed women out of these productive roles (Cahn 47, 51). At the same time, the expansion of a market economy and the greater availability of goods once considered luxuries made it more economical for women to purchase food, drink, and clothing at the market than to rely on home production (Cahn 42–44). On these historical developments, in addition to Cahn and Middleton, see the work of Bennett; A. Clark; Honeyman and Goodman; Howell; Mendelson and Crawford; and Wiesner.

11. Jean Howard concurs that as population and commerce rapidly expanded in early seventeenth-century London, women "who sold goods could be suspected of also selling themselves, and the city afforded women numerous opportunities to lead public lives that involved being visible to many people, including strangers" (Howard, *Theater* 128). Focusing on Marston's *The Dutch Courtesan*, Garrett Sullivan argues that "city comedy's simultaneous reduction of female labor and alignment of it with prostitution is arguably a response to shifting conceptions of women's roles in a household economy" (34). As female labor was gradually relegated from market production to domestic maintenance, "female visibility" became "increasingly transgressive" (33). However, in her valuable survey of the depiction of shop wives in plays between 1594- 1639, Leslie Thomson concludes that the drama is less complicit in the development of this restrictive ideology than Sullivan suggests. Thomson argues that dramatists repeatedly counter the satirical stereotype of the sexually available shop wife "by showing shop women who are either aware of being used as lures for customers and resist, or who simply behave in such a way as to demonstrate the freedom from masculine control their position evidently gives them" (159). *The Roaring Girl*, I would propose, has it both ways, vindicating Moll's chastity as a unmarried female worker while representing the citizen wives as free to use their sexual and economic agency in potentially transgressive ways.

12. Susan Amussen describes a similar contradiction facing economically productive women: "in the market they should be assertive, at home obedient" (119).

13. In her analysis of the representation of brothels in London comedy, Jean Howard notes how wives "repeatedly defy wifely codes of married chastity, blurring the line between themselves and their explicitly entrepreneurial sisters, the open whores" (*Theater* 124). Coppélia Kahn describes the category slippage between "virgin"/"chaste wife" and

"whore" in the plays of Middleton, including *A Chaste Maid in Cheapside*, *The Changeling*, *The Mayor of Queenborough*, and *The Roaring Girl*, though she discusses only Moll in this context (256).

14. Krantz, 6, 16–17; Mikalachki, 133; Orgel, *Impersonations* 145–47; Rose, "Women" 378; Ungerer, 56–60. For a detailed, insightful analysis of this document and of Mary Frith's encounter with the law, see McNeill, *Poor* 134–41.

15. For the distinction between mimesis and exhibition, see Callaghan, *Shakespeare* 77–78. Miller usefully discusses the metatheatrical self-consciousness generated by Middleton and Dekker's presentation of Moll (17–18). However, Miller's overly broad conclusion that "we are positioned, as audience, in the role of male consumer" flattens the range of possible gendered responses to Moll (18).

16. On the relationship between merchandizing and illicit sexual opportunity, Linda Levy Peck provides the example of a London mercer who, while away on business, "sought to control the sexuality of his customers" and of a female employee; in his absence, his wife and sometimes her mother tended shop (*Consuming* 66–67).

17. A "haunt" can be "a den or place frequented by the lower animals or by criminals" (*OED*, haunt *n.*3).

18. Sexual rivalry between women also informs the tense scene in *Othello* in which Emilia slanders Bianca as a "strumpet" (5.1.123). Iago labels Bianca "trash" (86); earlier in the play he had described her as a "hussy that by selling her desires / Buys herself bread and clothes" (4.1.92–93). Yet not Iago but Emilia, the lawful housewife, openly accuses this single working woman of being a hussy or strumpet. Whereas Bianca does not respond to Iago's insinuations, she immediately refutes Emilia's charge by insisting she is no less virtuous than her accuser: "I am no strumpet, but of life as honest / As you that thus abuse me" (5.1.124–25).

19. Kermode discusses Laxton's and Mistress Openwork's sexual slanders against Moll in this scene (427–29). He concludes, wrongly I think, that the play presents slander specifically as a "man's offense," so that when Mistress Openwork accuses Moll of being a "marriage-breaking whore" she is "practicing male slander" (428). Kermode's gendering of slander as male eliminates precisely the kind of female sexual rivalry that Gowing finds in defamation cases and that I find in the play's depiction of conflict between the citizen wives and Moll.

20. *OED*, wrapped *adj.* (II.5.a.) and (II.6.).

21. *OED*, stitch (*n.*1), back-stitch.

22. *OED*, hemming (*vbl. n.*1, *vbl. n.*2).

23. *OED*, cutwork (*n.*2.b.).

24. Although she does not discuss *The Roaring Girl*, Crane explores the early modern association between "working-class women's wage-earning potential within the home" and "a concomitant sexual independence" (212). Whereas I focus on sexualized representations of women who work in the marketplace, Crane locates a similar anxiety about female sexuality in home production, particularly through "an unspoken analogy between spinning

and marital sexuality" (214). Jones and Stallybrass also discuss the analogy between spinning and female sexuality in early modern texts and prints (126–32).

25. This kind of sexualized dynamic shows up again in the encounter between the con artist Doll Philips and the Tripe-Wife that I discuss below.

26. The two existing versions of the woodcut are discussed by Rustici (159–62) and Ungerer (60, 75–79).

27. McNeill provides an excellent account of Bridewell as an institution dedicated to the discipline of "idle" and masterless women (*Poor* 172–77).

28. According to Michael Roberts, "record-keepers persisted in assuming that women merely 'did' various kinds of work, whereas their husbands were identified by them. . . . Throughout the 1570 Norwich census it was to the husband's name that the phrase 'in work,' or 'not in work' was attached" (139).

29. Natasha Korda argues that the historical Mary Frith might have worked as "both a receiver and broker of second-hand and stolen goods," a trade that could have brought her into contact with Prince Henry's Men and the Fortune theater (76).

30. Mistress Openwork's marriage to a social inferior has some historical basis in the relative shortage of marriageable men to women in the period; as a result, a "woman might be forced to marry a man below her station" (Leinwand 141).

31. As a remarried widow, the Tripe-Wife represents an identifiable demographic in early modern London. Ian Archer observes that high mortality in London meant that "many households, no less than 16 percent in Southward in the 1620s, were headed by women; it also meant that remarriage in the capital was common; no less than 25 percent of the marriages of London tradesmen were to widows " ("Material" 184). Archer suggests that remarried widows would have enjoyed "greater leverage within the household" (185).

32. Rustici analyzes the transgressive connotations of tobacco-smoking in the play and in other early modern texts.

Chapter 5. Making Common: Familiar Knowledge and the Bawd's Seduction

1. *OED*, common, *a*. II. 10a.

2. *OED*, common, *a*. 1. "Common," of course, also signifies low social rank. Karen Newman observes that the "ubiquitous *common*" in the Bridewell depositions about London prostitutes "insists on the preoccupation with status and degree, with hierarchy, that characterized early modern social relations" (138).

3. *OED*, commonplace *n*.: 1. a "passage of general application, such as may serve as the basis of argument"; 5. a "stock theme or subject of remark." On the use of proverbs as a persuasive strategy in *Othello*, see Joseph Mccullen.

4. Early seventeenth-century satiric texts also convey male "suspicion of women meeting together" (Woodbridge 224). Surveying this literature, Linda Woodbridge notes the "fear that marital insubordination was contagious" (232); she concludes that "what literary

husbands feared most from gossips was the wicked tricks women might learn from each other" (231).

5. On the complicated question of when "old age" began for women in early modern England, see Beam; on the same question with regard to early modern Europe more generally, see Campbell 157–62.

6. In *Fictions of Old Age in Early Modern Literature and Culture*, Nina Taunton analyzes three early modern plays that "typecast old women as witches or fraudulent hags" (95). Writing about early modern Germany, Lyndal Roper argues that infertile older women were often associated with witchcraft because they were believed to envy younger women's fertility. Moreover, some women "said they had been seduced into witchcraft by an old woman, who had introduced them to the Devil and had watched while he debauched them. Like a master of a craft, the old woman teaches the younger the secrets of the diabolic trade." In a Würzburg deposition of 1616, one woman recounted how, forty-seven years before when she was only ten years old, the bailiff's wife seduced her into witchcraft (Roper 172–73).

7. Ruth Mazo Karras points to the long tradition of representations of older women teaching younger women how to profit from sex. Referring to a fifteenth-century German text, "Stepmother and Daughter" known in some manuscripts as "How a Mother Teaches Her Daughter Whoring," Karras observes that both "the character of the older woman and the advice to extract wealth from the lover are reminiscent of La Vieille in the *Roman de la Rose* and indeed a whole lineage of similar representations of older women, from Aphrodisia to La Celestina" (134). Aretino's *Ragioniamenti* (1534, 1536), in which two courtesans determine to make a prostitute of one of their daughters, epitomizes this tradition. On Aretino's reputation and influence in England, see Moulton, esp. 119–57. The familiarity of the bawd type in early modern English drama demonstrates that subsequent depictions of older women initiating younger women into sex—a staple of seventeenth- and eighteenth-century pornography—have a prehistory, not only in Aretino and in the older texts discussed by Karras, but on the popular stage.

8. Lynn Botelho's observation that perceptions of old age in early modern England were "determined primarily by cultural considerations, considerations which were, in the deeply iconographic world of early modern England, primarily visual in nature" informs my attention in this chapter to graphic descriptions and images of the bawd's body (43).

9. In his mock-encomium *A Bawd* (1635), John Taylor claims that the bawd embroiders her seductions with the rhetorical colors of socially orthodox concepts: "sometimes with great labour and difficulty shee's forced to perswade mens wives and daughters; all which considered, a *Bawd* doth not get her living with so great ease as the world supposeth; nor is her adventure, paines, charge and perill to be inconsiderately slighted. . . . For *Rhetoricke*, she must have the *Theoricke* and *Practicke*, that though the subject of her Discourse or writing be foule and deformed, yet must shee (like a Medicine-monger, Quack-salver, that covers his bitter pils in Sugar) with the Embroidery of her Eoquence [eloquence], flourish over her immodest pretences, under the inchanting and various colours of pleasure, profit, estimation, love, reputation, and many more the like" (sigs. B2v, 3v). This passage is open

to a dissident reading in its implication that the bawd imitates the spokesmen of social orthodoxy, who use the same rhetorical sugar-coating (concepts such as "profit," "estimation," and "love") to get their audiences to swallow the "bitter pils" of lessons about righteous behavior. Taylor, that is, reveals the mechanisms of ideological mystification.

10. Erasmus's *Adages* in Latin and English were published in editions of 1621 and 1622. In 1627, one I. L. S. published *Flores Regii*, a collection of "proverbes and aphorismes, divine and morall" allegedly spoken "at severall times upon sundry occasions" by King James (title page).

11. In his *Crossing of proverbs* (1616), Nicholas Breton actually makes a "crossed proverb" of the proverbial career path from whore to bawd: "P[roverb]. As the life is, so is the death. C[rossed proverb]. Not so, for she that lived a Whore, may dye a Bawde" (sig. A4r).

12. Shakespeare has one other professional female bawd, Mistress Overdone, who appears briefly in *Measure for Measure*. Mistress Quickly in *The Merry Wives of Windsor* and Juliet's Nurse in *Romeo and Juliet* function in certain ways as bawds. Shakespeare's most famous male bawd, of course, is Pandarus in *Troilus and Cressida*.

13. Paul Griffiths describes the limitations of the Bridewell archive: hardly objective accounts of urban crime, the records are "shot through with moral impulses." Moreover, because the Bridewell governors targeted brothels instead of street prostitutes, the records reveal only "the higher echelons of late Tudor prostitution" and hence "likely to be unrepresentative of the whole milieu of commercial sex in the capital." Finally, it is necessary to take into account "the uneven survival of the records and the process of apprehension and examination" (P. Griffiths 43). See also Archer's discussion of the "intractable problems" posed by the Bridewell documents (*Pursuit* 205; 237–41). Karen Newman points to a methodological limitation in the work of historians such as Griffiths and Archer who use the Bridewell courtbooks to "produce a set of facts and numbers" about prostitution. "Rarely," she remarks, "do they consider questions of language, affect, dress, motivation, desire, or performance" (136). Hence Newman rightly objects to Griffiths's assertion that these legal records bring us "closer to the authentic voice of the bawd and prostitute" than do pamphlets, ballads, or plays (137; P. Griffiths qtd. 41).

14. In early modern England, the word "bawd" was gender-neutral and could refer either to professional panders/brothel-owners or to ordinary people thought to have facilitated fornication. Perhaps because prostitution outside of London was largely informal, Martin Ingram finds in the Wiltshire ecclesiastical court records very few instances of sexual slander cases brought by men or women accused of "keeping bawdy house" (301). As Newman observes, "commercial sex is city sex": organized prostitution that took place in brothels "was a market phenomenon associated with town and, increasingly, city life" (135).

15. Some plays include both male and female procurers. Because the ability to identify a particular character as a "bawd" or "pander" is in some cases more than others a matter of interpretation, these figures should not be taken as absolute. Moreover, Berger, Bradford, and Sondergard's *Index* is not comprehensive, in that it includes under the rubrics of "Bawds" or "Panders" only those characters who are labeled as such in a play's Dramatis Personae or who are overtly identified as such within the play. Consequently, the *Index*'s

entry for "Bawds" does not include Anne Drury from *A Warning for Fair Women* or Livia from *Women Beware Women,* even though these characters do function as sexual procurers.

16. As Faramerz Dabhoiwala cautions regarding the distinction between professional and nonprofessional prostitution, because a "'whore' was any woman who had sexual relations outside marriage," and because a "'bawdy house' was simply any place—a home, tavern or lodging-house—where men and women met to commit sexual immorality," it is "often difficult in legal records to separate prostitution from other forms of sexual immorality" (87).

17. Jean Howard brought the example from Dekker to my attention. In his study of the legal records of the County of Somerset and the Diocese of Bath and Wells, Quaife finds evidence that "Some husbands played an active role as panders for their wives" (151).

18. Gowing cites the case of a father accused of being a bawd to his daughter (*Domestic* 96).

19. I thank Jean Howard for drawing my attention to Sharpham's play.

20. In a chapter on "Pregnant Maids and the New Bastardy Laws," however, Fiona McNeill discusses several seventeenth-century plays that depict the dilemma of the pregnant, unmarried, woman (*Poor* 80–114).

21. Ingram provides examples of twelve men and three women who were accused of harboring pregnant women (286–89).

22. Jean Howard similarly argues that the focus on whores and whorehouses in London comedies allowed playwrights to "examine other troubling or novel aspects of urban life such as the quickening and expansion of the market economy, the feminization of those who became garden variety hucksters in this new market, or the novel positions in which the city places women, complicating their social status" (*Theater* 120).

23. Jennifer Panek explores the motif of the mother as bawd in *A Mad World* and *The Revenger's Tragedy* as a sign of anxiety about maternal authority and as a critique of the sexual definition of woman's value in a patriarchal society ("Mother as Bawd").

24. Originally performed around 1624, the play was first published in the Beaumont and Fletcher folio of 1647.

25. Theophrastus's *Characters* (ca. 319 b.c.) was first translated into English by John Healy in 1593 (Bourassa 85). Joseph Hall's *Characters of vertues and vices* (1608) is generally considered the first English imitation of Theophrastus. Lawrence Manley observes that the vogue for character-writing was influenced by other contemporary genres, including cony-catching pamphlets, verse satires, and city comedies (316–17).

26. A "maquerela" (many variations) is a "procurer or procuress" (*OED*, mackerel, *n.* 2).

27. *OED*, botch, *n.* 2 and 3. *OED* has "bebauch, *v.*" as an alternate form of "debauch."

28. Paul Griffiths finds that professional prostitutes were "mostly single young women . . . [a] high proportion of whom were given the significant age-titles 'maid' or 'servant' in the courtbooks" (49).

29. *Westward Ho* was originally performed around 1604 and published in a quarto of 1607.

30. A similar joke appears in Cooke's play *Greenes Tu quoque*, in which the bawd Sweatman asks the young gallant Spendall to buy her a new forepart: "And will you (sonne) remember me for a new fore-part, by my troth, my old one is worne so bare, I am asham'd any body should see't" (sig. Civ). In *Greenes Tu quoque*, the forepart reference is a joke at the expense of the old bawd; in *Westward Ho* the forepart reference is a tactic of the bawd's seduction.

31. In *As You Like It*, Shakespeare also plays with this conventional wisdom: Rosalind compares ardent "May" wooers to cold "December" husbands, and threatens to use her wit to cuckold Orlando.

32. Richard Dutton refers to these sources in his note on Jonson's use of the German clock analogy in *Epicene* (4.2.88–95). Anthony Fletcher also discusses these iterations of the proverb (70–71). On the comparison between women and German clocks in the larger context of the "horological revolution" in early modern Europe, see Adam Max Cohen (esp. 143–45).

33. Margaret Ferne-seede is supposed to have confessed to a similar strategy for luring wives into prostitution: "some, by perswading them they were not beloved of their husbands, especially if I could at any time have note of any breach or discontent betweene them: others, that their husbands maintained them not sufficiently to expresse their beauty, and according to their owne desarts " (*The Araignement & burning*, sig. B3r).

34. Citing the example of *The Spanish Bawd* (1631), a translation of the Spanish tragicomedy *Celestina*, Denise Walen discusses "the homoerotic potential in the commercial relationships between bawds and prostitutes" (109). Although Walen describes how the bawd Celestina uses her hands to stimulate a woman who is reluctant to take a male sexual partner (111), she does not address the issue of rhetorical seduction.

35. *Malo in consilio feminae vincunt viros* ("women surpass men in evil scheming") is a maxim from the Sententiae of Publilius Syrus. *The Revenger's Tragedy* cites a similar maxim: "Women with women can work best alone," says Gratiana of her plan to act as bawd to her own daughter (2.1.246).

36. In *A Warning for Fair Women* (1599), Roger cites the more typical figure of rhetoric's ability to move stones when expressing his confidence that his mistress, Anne Drury, will persuade Anne Sanders to commit adultery: "yet if you wold wrong her husband your deere frind, me thinks ye have such a sweete tongue as wil supple a stone, and for my life, if ye list to labour, youle win her" (lines 258–61).

37. Birdlime's mention of the "commodity of beauty" that is "not made to lye dead upon any young womans hands" recalls Mistress Openwork's similarly worded complaint against her husband in *The Roaring Girl*, discussed in Chapter 4.

38. Mistress Birdlime is not the only dramatic bawd to apply proverbial knowledge so thickly. In Heywood's *The English Traveller* (1633), a bawd instructs her charge not to devote herself to one man: "Doth the mill grind only when the wind sits in one corner, or ships only sail when it's in this or that quarter? Is he a cunning fencer that lies but at one guard, or he a skilful musician that plays but on one string? Is there but one way to the wood, and but one bucket that belongs to the well? To affect one and despise all other becomes the

precise matron, not the prostitute; the loyal wife, not the loose wanton. Such have I been, as you are now and should learn to sail with all winds, defend all blows, make music with all strings, know all the ways to the wood, and, like a good travelling hackney, learn to drink of all waters" (1.2.159–68).

39. *Women Beware Women* was probably originally performed in 1621–22; it was first published in an octavo of 1657.

40. In my emphasis on Livia's own erotic pleasures, I necessarily disagree with Lisa Hopkins's claim that Livia is motivated by the self-sacrificing pleasure of gratifying others' erotic desires (70). Whereas Kenneth Muir argues that Livia "enjoys manipulating other people" (127), I am arguing that Livia takes particular erotic enjoyment in manipulating other women.

41. Carla Mazzio writes of "the isomorphic relations between the tongue and the penis, that other bodily member with an apparent will of its own" (59).

42. Charles Estienne, in *La Dissection des Parties du Corps Humain* (Latin 1545, French 1546), describes the clitoris as part of woman's "shameful member," "a little tongue [*languette*] . . . at the place of the neck of the bladder" (qtd. Park 176–77).

43. "Coney" or "cony" is "a term of endearment for a woman" (*OED* 5a), or "indecently" (5b), a reference to the female genitalia. The *OED* cites Massinger's *Virgin Martyr* (1622) 2.1: "A pox on your Christian cockatrices! They cry, like poulterers' wives, 'No money, no coney.'" Richard Levin argues that Livia's game is "cunning" because its goal is "entrance into Bianca's 'cun_'" (381).

44. Middleton invents the chess scene. In his Italian source (Celio Malespini's *Ducento Novelle*), the mother-in-law and Bianca visit the Signora Mondragone's palazzo. Signora Mondragone offers to show Bianca her home while the "mother-in-law, who is advanced in years and weak-legged, will stay and rest till we return to her" (qtd. in *Women*, Mulryne, ed., 171).

45. The Semele myth is depicted in the illustration preceding Book Three of George Sandys's *Ovids Metamorphosis Englished* (1632) (see chap. 3, fig. 13). Near the upper right edge of the image, Juno, disguised as an old nurse, advises Semele to see Jove in his divine glory; to the right, Semele burns in her bed.

46. Assuring that we do not miss the reference to the myth, Middleton has Fabritio remark that Isabella "has her lapful" of gold (5.2.122).

47. Julie Sanders analyzes "financially-driven, sceptical readings" of the Danaë myth in plays by Heywood and Jonson ("Danae," para. 3). On the widespread Renaissance interpretation of Danaë as a prostitute, see Cathy Santore.

48. Lorraine Helms proposes the Senecan *controversia* over the Prostitute Priestess as an analogue for the brothel scenes of *Pericles*. The narrative premise of Seneca's rhetorical declamation is the capture of a virgin by pirates, who sell her to a brothel; through eloquent speech, she retains her virginity, but finally kills a soldier who tries to rape her; she is tried, acquitted, and returned to her family, at which point she seeks a priesthood. The declaimers must argue for or against the woman's eligibility legally to become a holy virgin. Whereas

some declaimers argue that she has been polluted by her experiences in the brothel, others argue that her internal purity protects her from defilement.

49. On the objectification of the hymen as a valuable object, see William C. Carroll (290).

50. Theodora Jankowski acknowledges the "queer aura of power" bestowed by Marina's virginity, even as she argues that the preservation of her virginity is ultimately in the service of "protecting male bloodlines and male inheritance patterns"; Marina will maintain her virginity only until she secures a "parentally sanctioned marriage" (*Pure* 134).

51. Although it becomes evident that Marina will eventually be forced to lose her virginity in the brothel, her commitment to chastity is such that she vows to kill herself before working as a prostitute. By force or fraud, the Bawd will never persuade Marina to become a prostitute.

Chapter 6. Making Monsters: The Caroline Favorite and the Erotics of Royal Will

1. In a chapter on "Erotic Favoritism," Perry detects a different, but possibly related, shift in the representation of the favorite from Elizabethan and Jacobean plays (the anonymous *A Knack To Know a Knave*, the anonymous *Charlemagne*, and Fletcher's *The Loyal Subject*) to Caroline plays (Davenant's *The Cruel Brother* and Ford's *Love's Sacrifice*). Unlike the earlier plays, Perry argues, the Caroline plays blame court corruption not on wicked ministers and courtiers, but on the "ruler's overly passionate personal affections" (*Favoritism* 181). My analysis of Caroline plays suggests that court corruption is blamed on wicked ministers as the authorized agents (and sexual intermediaries) of overly passionate rulers.

2. In his account of Buckingham's short-lived popularity following the failure of the Spanish Match in 1623, Thomas Cogswell cites the claim in the anonymous *Cabala* (1624) that a "triumviri" ruled the kingdom, "whereof Buckingham was the first and chiefest, the Prince second, and the King the last" (220). Linda Levy Peck describes the "increased span of the seventeenth-century favourite's control, ranging from law, matters of state, diplomacy and war to foreign plantations, colonies and trade" ("Monopolizing" 60).

3. In his informative essay "Favourites on the English Stage," Blair Worden surprisingly asserts that after the early 1600s, favoritism "though a regular theatrical subject, is never again quite so dominant a one: not even during the supremacy of Buckingham" (172). Beyond citing Massinger's *The Great Duke of Florence* and Ford's *The Broken Heart* as typical of a dramatic trend to "capture the ethical ambivalences of power" (172), Worden has little to say about the many Caroline representations of favoritism.

4. Perry estimates that "there are upwards of fifty extant plays from 1587–1642 that deal centrally with the problem of royal favoritism" (*Favoritism* 3).

5. Even so, Berger, Bradford, and Sondergard's *Index of Characters* provides only a partial list of Caroline plays featuring favorites. For instance, it does not include Lodowick

Carlell's *The Deserving Favorite*, presumably because the text of the play does not overtly identify the title character as a "favorite."

6. Of the more than 40 late Jacobean and Caroline plays I examined for this chapter, seven provide the foundation for the argument that follows; I discuss six additional plays in the text and the notes. I have excluded from discussion plays in which favoritism is of peripheral importance; in which the favorite does not manipulate sexual alliances; in which the favorite is a farcical character; in which the favorite is virtuous (cf. Perry, *Favoritism* 55–94); or in which favoritism is represented as an opposite-sex relationship.

7. Despite important differences in how they define, present, and evaluate the available evidence, many modern scholars have acknowledged James's same-sex attachments. Historian Michael Young articulates the most categorical position: James "did have sex with his male favourites, and it is nonsense to deny it" (135). But even those who have taken a more skeptical view as to actual sexual activity between the king and his favorites concede that "the question of James's sexual nature must be faced" (Maurice Lee, qtd. in Young [1]). Young surveys accounts of James's sexuality by historians and literary scholars including David Bergeron, Caroline Bingham, Alan Bray, Jonathan Goldberg, Tim Hitchcock, Barbara Kiefer Lewalski, Roger Lockyer, Stephen Orgel, Bruce Smith, David Willson, and Jenny Wormald. Accounts of James's sexuality published since Young include Stewart, *The Cradle King*, and Perry, *Favoritism* (esp. 131–37).

8. Roger Lockyer's biography of the Duke explicitly rejects the possibility of an erotic bond between Charles and Buckingham. Similarly, in his authoritative study *The Personal Rule of Charles I*, Kevin Sharpe holds that Charles's love for Buckingham, while intense and sincere, was "not physically expressed" (46).

9. If what provoked resentment during James's reign was the favorite's presence in court, what could provoke resentment after Buckingham's death was the absence of a favorite—or, rather, the fear among some that the queen was fulfilling the role of leading the King astray. In an account of the political impact of Henrietta Maria's theatrical activities, Julie Sanders remarks that William Prynne spoke for those who "feared that the Queen sought to convert the nation [to Catholicism] by seducing it through her feminine wiles and her erotic performances" (33). Describing the intertwined attacks on Marian devotion and Henrietta Maria during the 1630s, Frances Dolan argues that "at the heart of the debates about both Henrietta Maria's and the Virgin Mary's authority and influence was proximity to power and, more dangerous, intimacy" (*Whores* 122): critics alleged that through his affection and dependency, Charles relinquished control to his wife (124). G. F. Sensabaugh describes Henrietta Maria's Platonism as "a system of manners and morals" that challenged Puritan orthodoxies about love and marriage (105–51). On the rise of the queen's faction at court during 1635–1637, see Sharpe, *Personal* 537–41; on her power to bestow "social and political favor" on male courtiers, see Smuts 194–96.

10. During the second half of James's reign, sexual scandals at court and concern over the Duke of Buckingham's ascendancy spurred a "marked growth" of manuscript libel (Perry, "Manuscript" 210), among which were two poems, known as the "Wars of the Gods" and "The King's Five Senses," that used the Ganymede myth to allege sodomitical

relations between James and Buckingham. "The King's Five Senses," for instance, describes the harmful influence of favorites with "smooth or beardless chin / As may provoke or tempt to sin" (qtd. Bellany, *Politics* 259). See also Cogswell (212) and Bellany, "Raylinge" (299–310) and *Politics* (254–61).

11. On Davenant's "searching and incisive" (62) examination of courtly politics through the topics of love and passion, see Sharpe, *Criticism*, 61–68, 75–82.

12. On manuscript libels against Buckingham, see Marotti (107–10) and Gerald Hammond (51–66). The libels I discuss date from the late 1620s.

13. Hubert's *Historie of Edward the Second* exists in three different versions: a manuscript from the late 1590s, a revised Jacobean text surreptitiously published in 1628, and a further revised authorized text published in 1629. Although we cannot know for certain when specific verses were written or revised, Curtis Perry argues that "the Jacobean version" of the poem published in 1628 "owed its readership to avid interest in the controversial career of the Duke of Buckingham toward the end of James's reign and during the early years of Charles's" (*Favoritism* 203–4). Hubert's portrait of Gaveston as a monster "huge and vast" certainly would have resonated for Caroline readers. On the overall importance of the Edward II story for addressing "questions of prerogative and imbalance" (188), see Perry, *Favoritism* 185–228. My argument about the residual type of the favorite as Ganymede gains support from the performance and publication history of Marlowe's *Edward II*, which continued to be performed (in 1609–1619) and published (1622) in the later Jacobean period, but not during the Caroline period (Forker 99).

14. Jonathan Brown argues that Eliot's comparison of Buckingham to the stellion epitomizes the "excesses" of the hostile rhetoric to which Rubens's allegorical painting, *Glorification of the Duke of Buckingham* (1627), constitutes a response (226). Perry also discusses Eliot's charge (*Favoritism* 15, 229–30).

15. "Nor do I use harsher words than nature has made, nor lighter ones than the case demands" (*Proceedings* vol. 3, 289 n. 8).

16. Similarly, Francis Osborne writes that King James's lascivious kissing of his favorites in public "prompted many to image some things done" in private "that exceed my expressions no less then they do my experience" (qtd. Perry, "Access" 1073). Even defenders of favoritism might prudently decline to probe the depths of royal affection. Henry Wotton, for instance, "briefly set down" Charles's affection for Buckingham "without looking beyond the veil of the temple . . . into the secret of high inclinations; since even satirical poets, (who are otherwise of so licentious fancy) are in this point modest enough to confess their ignorance" (7). Writing under James, Edward Forset allegorically compared a prince's favorites to the delightful and satisfying "fantasies of the Soule," adding, "I will refraine to presse the application farther than the well taught Subjects will of themselves conceive" (15).

17. In *Albovine*, Davenant aptly compares treacherous favorites to small worms:

Wise Favourites doe walke

I'th darke, and use false lights. Nay, oft disguize
Their breadth and stature; seeme lesser then they are:

> For know, the slender Worme, or nimble Grig,
> May wriggle downe into th'oblique, and low
> Descent o'th narrow hole; whilst th'oregrowne Snake
> Peepes at the brimme, but ne're can view the bottome. (sigs. E1v–2r)

18. Martin Butler observes a "powerful sentiment" during the 1630s that "men of real worth and fidelity are being deliberately, calculatedly excluded and abused, while the basest parasites are graced as though they only were faithful and true" (209). He supports this point through an analysis of favoritism in the unprinted play *The Wasp* (1630).

19. Albert Tricomi (156–64), Margot Heinemann (239–40, 253–61), Ira Clark (*Moral* 87–92; *Professional* 45–46), and Robert Turner (376–79) discuss the oppositional stance to royal absolutism conveyed by Massinger's portrayals of favoritism throughout the 1620s. Originally performed in 1621–22, *The Maid of Honor* is strictly not a "Caroline" play; however, it remained popular throughout the 1630s, was published in 1632, and according to its editors "may have remained in the repertory of successive companies at the Phoenix or Cockpit for about 18 years" (Massinger, *Maid* 113). *The Great Duke of Florence* was first performed in 1627 and published in 1636.

20. See Lawrence Venuti's astute discussion of the "discontinuous characterization of tragicomedy" in *The Maid of Honor*, which allows characters such as the King and Camiola to articulate ideological positions in conflict with their social stations (80). Venuti observes that Camiola's resistance to Roberto expresses an ideology of "bourgeois individualism" that conflicts with her earlier stance as the protector of an "aristocratic code of honor" (84).

21. Sanazarro's image recalls that walking barefoot across hot plowshares was an ancient form of trial by ordeal, in which innocence was usually proven by quick healing of the wounds.

22. The plays are roughly contemporaneous: *Claricilla* was first performed around 1636 and published in 1641; *The Royal Master* was first performed and published in 1638.

23. Ira Clark argues that, although a monarchist, Shirley typically identifies threats posed to political order by irresponsible princes and the corrupt ministers they authorized (*Professional*, 120–21).

24. Another play that might be considered in this light is Davenant's tragedy *The Unfortunate Lovers* (performed in 1638, published in 1643), in which a "politick stout ambitious favorite" named Galeotto schemes to marry his daughter to the Duke Altophil: "By his alliance so confirme my family, / That I shall need to feare no change of time, / No angrie fate, but from your Princelly selfe" (dramatis personae; 3). Seeking to ruin the Duke's mistress, Galeotto slanders her chastity, for which treachery the prince banishes him. Galeotto then helps a neighbor king conquer the prince and finally tries to coerce the prince himself into marrying his daughter.

25. Whereas Killigrew's king tries to prevent his favorite from marrying into the royal family, Thomas Drue's *The Bloody Banquet* (1639) and Harding's *Sicily and Naples* explore the tragic results of a king allowing an untrustworthy favorite to marry into the royal family. In *The Bloody Banquet*, the King inadvertently encourages rebellious thoughts in his

favorite when he permits him to court his daughter. Regarding the princess as his path to the crown, the favorite ends up destroying the royal family through his schemes to possess her. In *Sicily and Naples*, when the king promises his niece to his favorite, the favorite plots to kill the king and to legitimize his seizure of power through this royal marriage.

26. *The Traitor* was first performed in 1631 and published in 1635.

27. Shirley would continue to depict the consequences of monarchical disorder via the figure of a sexually scheming favorite. In *The Politician* (performed in 1639, published in 1655), the King of Norway marries the widow Marpisa but also courts Albina, the wife of his minion, Gotharius. As the queen's lover, Gotharius plots to murder the king's sole heir and to take control of the kingdom. *The Politician* corroborates Martin Butler's claim that "plays about princes in love provided useful devices to enable discussion of the problem of a king whose resources and popularity were, in the late 1630s, coming to look increasingly limited" (56).

EPILOGUE

1. In addition to the anthology *Shakespeare and Character* (2009), discussed below, the surge of interest in early modern character studies is suggested by several publications since 2005: J. L. Simmons, "From Theatre to Globe: The Construction of Character in *Julius Caesar*" (2005); R. A. Foakes, "Reviving Shakespeare Character Criticism" (2005); the six contributors to the forum "Is There Character After Theory?" in *Shakespeare Studies* (2006); Mustapha Fahmi, "Man's Chief Good: The Shakespearean Character as Evaluator" (2008); Travis Curtwright, "'Falseness Cannot Come from Thee': Marina as Character and Orator in Shakespeare's *Pericles*" (2009); and Bruce Boehrer, "Animal Studies and the Deconstruction of Character" (2009). One might also include as a contribution to character studies Gail Kern Paster's *Humoring the Body* (2004).

2. Yachnin and Slights provide an excellent survey of Shakespearean character criticism since the late seventeenth century ("Introduction"). Having reached its modern apex in A. C. Bradley's *Shakespearean Tragedy* (1904), character studies fell out of favor with the shift to New Criticism and structuralism (1930s–1960s), with post-structuralist and materialist critics of the 1980s and 1990s striking decisive blows against the notion of Shakespeare's characters as coherent and autonomous individuals. For more on this history, see Alan Sinfield, "From Bradley to Cultural Materialism."

3. Lorna Hutson more pointedly observes the extent to which "the notion of character is itself the historical legacy of Shakespearean drama" ("*Ethopoeia*" 140).

4. For more on Shakespearean characters as textual inscriptions, see Goldberg, "Shakespearean Characters."

5. Here I'm borrowing Judith Butler's notion of a gender norm as a cultural ideal that exists only through its instantiations. For Butler, a norm functions as a positive ideal, in the sense that it offers a culturally dominant model of those forms of embodiment required to achieve a valorized subjectivity (e.g., "masculinity" for men, "femininity" for women). A

sexual type might be considered a "negative norm" in that it provides a culturally dominant model of those forms of embodiment that must be avoided in order to achieve a valorized subjectivity (e.g., men should avoid "effeminacy").

6. Whether or not particular audience members will recognize, accept, or resist the critical opportunities offered by this open space is impossible to determine. For recent attempts to understand the dynamics of audience response to early modern drama, see Charles Whitney, *Early Responses to Renaissance Drama*, and Jeremy Lopez, *Theatrical Convention and Audience Response in Early Modern Drama*.

7. As is the case with most of the characters in my study, it is difficult to test any theories about a character's theatrical effects on a present-day audience, since the plays of Shirley, Fletcher, Massinger, and others are so rarely produced. It might be that the reality effect of Shakespeare's characters is enhanced by the fact that we can actually experience those characters as "persons" through live performances.

Bibliography

PRIMARY TEXTS

Africanus, Leo. *A geographical historie of Africa*. Trans. John Pory. London, 1600.

Albee, Edward. The American Dream *and* The Zoo Story: *Two Plays by Edward Albee*. New York: Signet, 1959–1961.

Alciati, Andrea. *Emblemata*. Lyons, 1550. Trans. and anno. Betty I. Knott. Aldershot: Scolar, 1996.

Alley, Hugh. *Hugh Alley's Caveat: The Markets of London in 1598. Folger Ms V. a. 318*. Ed. Ian Archer, Caroline Barron, and Vanessa Harding. London Topographical Society Publication 137. London: London Topographical Society, 1988.

The Araignement & burning of Margaret Ferne-seede. London, 1608.

Aretino, Pietro. *Dialogues*. Trans. Raymond Rosenthal, pref. Alberto Moravia, intro. Margaret F. Rosenthal. Toronto: University of Toronto Press, 2005.

The Arraignement, Judgement, Confession, and Execution of Humfrey Stafford Gentleman. London, 1607.

Barlow, William. *A Brand*. London, 1607.

Barnes, Barnabe. *The Divils charter*. London, 1607.

Baron, Robert. *Mirza*. London, 1630.

Bartholin, Thomas. *Bartholinus Anatomy*. London, 1668.

Batman, Stephen. *A christall glasse of christian reformation*. London, 1569.

———. *The new arival of the three gracis, into Anglia. Lamenting the abusis of this present age*. London, 1580.

Beard, Thomas. *The theatre of Gods judgements*. London, 1597.

The Bloudie Booke. London, 1605.

Botero, Giovanni. *An historicall description of the most famous kingdomes and common-weales in the worlde*. London, 1603.

Brathwaite, Richard. *The Golden Fleece. Whereto bee annexed two Elegies, Entitled Narcissus Change and Aesons Dotage*. London, 1611.

Breton, Nicholas. *Crossing of proverbs. The second part*. London, 1616.

————. *The Good and The Badde*. London, 1616.

The brideling, sadling and ryding, of a rich churle in Hampshire . . . London, 1595.

Bruto, Giovanni Michele. *The . . . Education of a yong Gentlewoman*. Trans. W. P. London, 1598.

Burton, Robert. *The Anatomy of Melancholy*. 1621. Vol. 1. Ed. Thomas C. Faulkner, Nicholas K. Kiessling, and Rhonda L. Blair, intro. J. B. Bamborough. Oxford: Clarendon Press, 1989.

Camden, William. *Remaines concerning Britaine*. London, 1614.

Cawdry, Robert. *A Table Alphabeticall, conteyning and teaching the true writing, of hard usual English wordes* . . . London, 1604.

Chapman, George. *May-Day*. London, 1611.

Cocles, Bartolommeo. *The Contemplation of Mankinde*. . . . 1504. Trans. Thomas Hill. London, 1571.

Comenius, Johann Amos. *Orbis Sensualium Pictus*. London, 1659.

Cooke, Jo. *Greenes Tu quoque*. London, 1614.

Cooper, Thomas. *Thesaurus linguæ Romanæ & Britannicæ*. London, 1565.

Crooke, Helkiah. *Mikrokosmographia*. London, 1615.

Daborne, Robert. *The Poor-Mans Comfort*. London, 1655.

Davenant, William. *The Tragedy of Albovine, King of the Lombards*. London, 1629.

————. *The Unfortunate Lovers*. London, 1643.

Dekker, Thomas. *Match Me in London*. 1631. In *The Dramatic Works of Thomas Dekker*. Ed. Fredson Bowers. Vol. 3. Cambridge: Cambridge University Press, 1958.

Dekker, Thomas, John Ford, and William Rowley. *The Witch of Edmonton*. 1621. In *Three Jacobean Witchcraft Plays*, ed. Peter Corbin and Douglas Sedge. Manchester: Manchester University Press, 1986.

Dekker, Thomas, and Thomas Middleton. *The Honest Whore, Part One*. 1604. In *The Dramatic Works of Thomas Dekker*. Ed. Fredson Bowers. Vol. 2. Cambridge: Cambridge University Press, 1955.

Dekker, Thomas, and John Webster. *Westward Ho*. 1607. In *The Dramatic Works of Thomas Dekker*. Ed. Fredson Bowers. Vol 2. Cambridge: Cambridge University Press, 1955.

Du Laurens, André (Andreas Laurentius). *Historia Anatomica Humani Corporis et singularum eius partium multis*. Paris, 1595.

Earle, John. *Microcosmography*. London, 1628.

Edwards, Thomas. *Cephalus and Procris. Narcissus*. 1595. Ed. W. E. Buckley. London, 1882.

Erasmus, Desiderius. *Adagia in Latin and English*. London, 1621 and 1622.

Fairholt, F. W., ed. *Poems and Songs Relating to George Villiers, Duke of Buckingham*. . . . 1850.

Fletcher, John. *The Loyal Subject*. 1647. In *The Dramatic Works in the Beaumont and Fletcher Canon*, ed. Fredson Bowers. Vol. 5. Cambridge: Cambridge University Press, 1982.

————. *A Wife for a Month*. 1647. In *The Dramatic Works in the Beaumont and Fletcher Canon*, ed. Fredson Bowers. Vol. 6. Cambridge: Cambridge University Press, 1985.

Ford, John. *'Tis Pity She's a Whore*. 1633. In *'Tis Pity She's a Whore and Other Plays*, ed. Marion Lomax. Oxford: Oxford University Press, 1995.

Forset, Edward. *A comparative discourse of the bodies natural and politique*. London, 1606.

Gainsford, Thomas. *The Rich Cabinet*. London, 1616.

Golding, Arthur. *Shakespeare's Ovid: Being Arthur Golding's Translation of the Metamorphoses*. Ed. W. H. D. Rouse. Carbondale: Southern Illinois University Press, 1961.

Gough, J. *The Strange Discovery*. London, 1640.

H., I. *House of Correction*. London, 1619.

Harding, Samuel. *Sicily and Naples*. Oxford, 1640.

Heywood, Thomas. *The English Traveller*. 1633. In *Thomas Heywood: Three Marriage Plays*, ed. Paul Merchant. Manchester: Manchester University Press, 1996.

———. *The Royall King, and The Loyall Subject*. London, 1637.

———. *The Wise-woman of Hogsdon*. 1638. In *Thomas Heywood: Three Marriage Plays*, ed. Paul Merchant. Manchester: Manchester University Press, 1996.

Hill, Adam. *The Crie of England*. London, 1595.

Hubert, Francis. *The Historie of Edward the Second*. 1629. In *The Poems of Sir Francis Hubert*. Ed. and intro. Bernard Mellor. Hong Kong: Hong Kong University Press, 1961.

Jonson, Ben. *Cynthia's Revels: Or the Fountain of Self-Love*. 1616. In *The Complete Plays of Ben Jonson*, ed. G. A. Wilkes. Vol. 2. Oxford: Clarendon Press, 1981.

———. *Cynthia's Revels, or the Fountain of Self-love*. Ed. Alexander Corbin Judson. New York: Henry Holt, 1912.

———. *Epicene, or The Silent Woman*. 1609. Ed. Richard Dutton. Manchester: Manchester University Press, 2003.

———. *Volpone; or, The Fox*. 1607. Ed. R. B. Parker. Manchester: Manchester University Press, 1983.

Joubert, Laurent. *Treatise on Laughter. Traité du Ris*, 1579. Trans. and anno. Gregory David de Rocher. University: University of Alabama Press, 1980.

Killigrew, Thomas. *Claricilla*. 1641. Ed. William T. Reich. New York: Garland, 1980.

Lee, Maurice, Jr. *Dudley Carleton to John Chamberlain 1603–1624, Jacobean Letters*. New Brunswick, N.J.: Rutgers University Press, 1972.

Lenton, Francis. *Characterismi: or Lenton's Leisures*. London, 1631.

The London Surveys of Ralph Treswell. Ed. John Schofield. London Topographical Society Publication 135. London: London Topographical Society, 1987.

The Manner of the Cruell Outragious Murther of William Storre. London, 1603.

Marlowe, Christopher. *Doctor Faustus*. 1604 and 1616. Ed. David Bevington and Eric Rasmussen. Revels Plays. Manchester: Manchester University Press, 1993.

———. *Ovid's Elegies*. 1603. *In The Complete Works of Christopher Marlowe*. Vol. 2. Ed. Fredson Bowers. 2nd ed. Cambridge: Cambridge University Press, 1981.

Marmion, Shackerley. *Hollands leaguer*. London, 1632.

Marston, John. 1599. *Antonio and Mellida*. Ed. G. K. Hunter. Lincoln: University of Nebraska Press, 1965.

———. *The Dutch Courtesan*. 1605. Ed. David Crane. New York: Norton, 1997.

———. *The Malcontent*. 1604. Ed. W. David Kay. New York: Norton, 1998.

Massinger, Philip. *The Duke of Milan*. 1623. In *The Plays and Poems of Philip Massinger*. Ed. Philip Edwards and Colin Gibson. 5 vols. Vol. 1. Oxford: Clarendon Press, 1976.

———. *The Great Duke of Florence*. 1636. In *The Plays and Poems of Philip Massinger*. Ed. Philip Edwards and Colin Gibson. Vol. 3. Oxford: Clarendon Press, 1976.

———. *Three New Playes; viz. The Bashful Lover, The Guardian, The Very Woman*. London, 1655.

———. *The Maid of Honor*. 1632. In *The Plays and Poems of Philip Massinger*. Ed. Philip Edwards and Colin Gibson. Vol. 1. Oxford: Clarendon Press, 1976.

———. *The Unnaturall Combat*. London, 1639.

Middleton, Thomas. *A Mad World, My Masters*. London, 1608.

———. *Michaelmas Term*. 1607. Ed. Richard Levin. Lincoln: University of Nebraska Press, 1966.

———. *Women Beware Women*. 1657. Ed. J. R. Mulryne. Manchester: Manchester University Press, 1975.

Middleton, Thomas, and Thomas Dekker. *The Roaring Girl*. 1611. Ed. Paul A. Mulholland. Revels Plays. Manchester: Manchester University Press, 1987.

Milles, Robert. *Abrahams Suite for Sodome*. London, 1612.

Nabbes, Thomas. *The Unfortunate Mother*. London, 1640.

Narcissus, A Twelfe Night Merriment. 1602. Ed. Margaret L. Lee. London: David Nutt, 1893.

Nicolay, Nicholas de. *The navigations, peregrinations and voyages, made into Turkie*. Trans. T. Washington. London, 1585.

Oat-meale, Oliver. *A quest of enquirie . . .* London, 1595.

Overbury, Sir Thomas. *Sir Thomas Overbury his Wife with New Elegies upon his Untimely Death: Whereunto are Annexed, New News and Characters*. London, 1616.

Paradin, Claude. *The heroicall devises of M. Claudius Paradin*. Trans. P. S. London, 1591.

———. *The true and lyvely historyke purtreatures of the woll Bible*. Trans. Peter Derendel. Lyons, 1553.

Peacham, Henry. *Minerva Britanna*. 1612. Leeds: Scolar, 1966.

Peyton, Edward. *The divine catastrophe of the kingly family of the house of Stuarts. . . .* 1652. In *Secret History of the Court of James the First*, ed. Walter Scott. Edinburgh: Ballantyne, 1811.

Proceedings in Parliament, 1626. Ed. William B. Bidwell and Maija Jansson. Vols. 1 (House of Lords) and 3 (House of Commons). 4 vols. New Haven, Conn.: Yale University Press, 1991–1996.

The Revenger's Tragedy. 1607. Ed. Brian Gibbons. New York: Norton, 1991.

Rowley, William. *All's lost by Lust*. London, 1633.

S., I. L. *Flores Regii*. London, 1627.

Sandys, George. *Ovids Metamorphosis Englished, mythologiz'd, and represented in figures*. London, 1632.

"A Sermon against Whoredom and Uncleanness." 1623. In *Sexuality and Gender in the English Renaissance: An Annotated Edition of Contemporary Documents*, ed. Lloyd Davis. New York: Garland, 1998.

Shakespeare, William. *A Midsummer Night's Dream*. 1600. Ed. Peter Holland. Oxford: Oxford University Press, 1998.

————. *The Norton Shakespeare.* Ed. Stephen Greenblatt. New York: Norton, 1997.

————. *The Winter's Tale.* 1623. Ed. Stephen Orgel. Oxford: Oxford University Press, 1996.

Sharpham, Edward. *Cupids Whirligig.* London, 1607.

————. *The Fleire.* London, 1607.

Shirley, James. *The Duke's Mistress.* 1638. In *The Dramatic Works and Poems of James Shirley.* Ed. William Gifford and Alexander Dyce. 6 vols. Vol. 4. 1833. New York: Russell and Russell, 1966.

————. *The Royal Master.* 1638. In *The Dramatic Works and Poems of James Shirley.* Ed. William Gifford and Alexander Dyce. Vol. 4. 1833. New York: Russell and Russell, 1966.

————. *The Traitor.* 1635. Ed. John Stewart Carter. Lincoln: University of Nebraska Press, 1965.

Sidney, Sir Philip. *The Defence of Poesy.* London, 1595.

Taylor, John. *A Bawd.* London, 1635.

————. *A Juniper Lecture.* London, 1639.

Tilney, Edmund. *The Flower of Friendship: A Renaissance Dialogue Contesting Marriage.* 1568. Ed. and intro. Valerie Wayne. Ithaca, N.Y.: Cornell University Press, 1992.

Tittle-Tattle: Or, the Several Branches of Gossipping. London, ca. 1600.

Topsell, Edward. *The historie of serpents.* London, 1608.

van de Passe the Elder, Crispijn. *The Gunpowder Plot Conspirators.* 1605.

W., W. *A true and just Recorde, of the Information, Examination and Confession of all the Witches, taken at S. Oses . . .* London, 1582.

A Warning for Fair Women. 1599. Ed. Charles Dale Canon. The Hague: Mouton, 1975.

Webster, John. *The Duchess of Malfi.* 1623. Ed. John Russell Brown. Manchester: Manchester University Press, 1974.

Whately, William. *A Bride-Bush: Or, a Direction for Married Persons.* 1617. In *Sexuality and Gender in the English Renaissance: An Annotated Edition of Contemporary Documents,* ed. Lloyd Davis. New York: Garland, 1998. 245–76.

Whitney, Geffrey. *A choice of emblemes.* Leyden, 1586.

Wilkinson, Robert. *The merchant royall.* 1607. Intro. Stanley Pargellis. Herrin, Ill.: Trovillion Press, 1945.

Wotton, Henry. *The Characters of Robert Devereux, Earl of Essex; and George Villiers, Duke of Buckingham: Compared and Contrasted.* 1641. Ed. Sir Egerton Brydges. Lee Priory, 1814.

Wright, Thomas. *The passions of the minde in generall.* London, 1604.

SECONDARY TEXTS

Amussen, Susan Dwyer. *An Ordered Society: Gender and Class in Early Modern England.* New York: Columbia University Press, 1988.

Andreadis, Harriette. *Sappho in Early Modern England: Female Same-Sex Literary Erotics 1550–1714.* Chicago: University of Chicago Press, 2001.

Archer, Ian W. "Material Londoners?" In *Material London, ca. 1600*, ed. Lena Cowen Orlin. Philadelphia: University of Pennsylvania Press, 2000. 174–92.

———. *The Pursuit of Stability: Social Relations in Elizabethan London.* Cambridge: Cambridge University Press, 1991.

Arendt, Hannah. "Introduction." In Walter Benjamin, *Illuminations.* Ed. and intro. Hannah Arendt, trans. Harry Zohn. New York: Schocken, 1969. 1–55.

Aughterson, Kate, ed. *Renaissance Woman: Constructions of Femininity in England.* London: Routledge, 1995.

Bach, Rebecca Ann. "Manliness Before Individualism: Masculinity, Effeminacy, and Homoerotics in Shakespeare's History Plays." In *A Companion to Shakespeare's Works: The Histories.* Vol. 2. 4 vols. Ed. Richard Dutton and Jean E. Howard. Malden, Mass.: Blackwell, 2003. 220–45.

Bailey, Amanda. *Flaunting: Style and the Subversive Male Body in Renaissance England.* Toronto: University of Toronto Press, 2007.

Barry, Jonathan. "Bourgeois Collectivism? Urban Association and the Middling Sort." In *The Middling Sort of People: Culture, Society and Politics in England, 1550–1800*, ed. Jonathan Barry and Christopher Brooks. New York: St. Martin's, 1994. 84–112.

———. "Introduction." In *The Middling Sort of People: Culture, Society and Politics in England, 1550–1800*, ed. Jonathan Barry and Christopher Brooks. New York: St. Martin's, 1994. 1–27.

Bartels, Emily. *Speaking of the Moor: From "Alcazar" to "Othello."* Philadelphia: University of Pennsylvania Press, 2008.

Bate, Jonathan. *Shakespeare and Ovid.* Oxford: Clarendon, 1994.

Beam, Aki C. L. "'Should I as Yet Call You Old?' Testing the Boundaries of Female Old Age in Early Modern England." In *Growing Old in Early Modern Europe: Cultural Representations*, ed. Erin Campbell. Burlington, Vt.: Ashgate, 2006. 95–116.

Bellany, Alastair. *The Politics of Court Scandal in Early Modern England: News Culture and the Overbury Affair, 1603–1660.* Cambridge: Cambridge University Press, 2002.

———. "'Rayling e Rymes and Vaunting Verse': Libellous Politics in Early Stuart England, 1603–1628." In *Culture and Politics in Early Stuart England*, ed. Kevin Sharpe and Peter Lake. Stanford, Calif.: Stanford University Press, 1993. 285–310.

Benkov, Edith. "The Erased Lesbian: Sodomy and the Legal Tradition in Medieval Europe." In *Same-Sex Love and Desire Among Women in the Middle Ages*, ed. Canadé Sautman and Pamela Sheingorn. New York: Palgrave, 2001. 101–22.

Bennett, Judith M. *History Matters: Patriarchy and the Challenge of Feminism.* Philadelphia: University of Pennsylvania Press, 2006.

———. "Medieval Women, Modern Women: Across the Great Divide." In *Culture and History, 1350–1600: Essays on English Communities, Identities and Writing*, ed. David Aers. Detroit: Wayne State University Press, 1992. 147–75.

Berger, Thomas L., William C. Bradford, and Sidney L. Sondergard, eds. *An Index of*

Characters in Early Modern English Drama: Printed Plays, 1500–1660. Rev. ed. Cambridge: Cambridge University Press, 1998.

Bergeron, David M. *King James and Letters of Homoerotic Desire.* Iowa City: University of Iowa Press, 1999.

Bingham, Caroline. *James I of England.* London: Weidenfeld and Nicolson, 1981.

Blank, Paula. "Comparing Sappho to Philaenis: John Donne's 'Homopoetics.'" *PMLA* 110 (1995): 358–68.

Bloom, Harold. *Shakespeare: The Invention of the Human.* New York: Riverhead, 1998.

Bly, Mary. *Queer Virgins and Virgin Queans on the Early Modern Stage.* New York: Oxford University Press, 2000.

Boehrer, Bruce. "Animal Studies and the Deconstruction of Character." *PMLA* 124 (2009): 542–47.

———. *Shakespeare Among the Animals: Nature and Society in the Drama of Early Modern England.* New York: Palgrave, 2002.

Borris, Kenneth, "Introduction: The Prehistory of Homosexuality in the Early Modern Sciences." In *The Sciences of Homosexuality in Early Modern Europe*, ed. Kenneth Borris and George Rousseau. London: Routledge, 2008. 1–40.

———, ed. *Same-Sex Desire in the English Renaissance: A Sourcebook of Texts, 1470–1650.* New York: Routledge, 2004.

Botelho, Keith M. *Renaissance Earwitnesses: Rumor and Early Modern Masculinity.* New York: Palgrave Macmillan, 2009.

Botelho, Lynn. "Old Age and Menopause in Rural Women of Early Modern Suffolk." In *Women and Ageing in British Society Since 1500*, ed. Lynn Botelho and Pat Thane. London: Longman, 2001. 43–65.

Bourassa, André G. "Personnage: History, Philology, Performance." In *Shakespeare and Character: Theory, History, Performance, and Theatrical Persons*, ed. Paul Yachnin and Jessica Slights. New York: Palgrave Macmillan, 2009. 83–97.

Bray, Alan. *The Friend.* Chicago: University of Chicago Press, 2003.

———. "Homosexuality and the Signs of Male Friendship in Elizabethan England." In *Queering the Renaissance*, ed. Jonathan Goldberg. Durham, N.C.: Duke University Press, 1994. 40–61.

———. *Homosexuality in Renaissance England.* London: Gay Men's Press, 1982.

Bredbeck, Gregory W. *Sodomy and Interpretation: Marlowe to Milton.* Ithaca, N.Y.: Cornell University Press, 1991.

Breitenberg, Mark. *Anxious Masculinity in Early Modern England.* Cambridge: Cambridge University Press, 1996.

Bristol, Michael. "Confusing Shakespeare's Characters with Real People: Reflections on Reading in Four Questions." In *Shakespeare and Character: Theory, History, Performance, and Theatrical Persons*, ed. Paul Yachnin and Jessica Slights. New York: Palgrave Macmillan, 2009. 21–40.

Bromham, A. A. "*Women Beware Women*: Danae, and Iconographic Tradition." *Notes and Queries* n.s. 50.1 (2003): 74–76.

Brooten, Bernadette J. *Love Between Women: Early Christian Responses to Female Homoeroticism*. Chicago: University of Chicago Press, 1996.

Brotton, Jerry. *The Renaissance Bazaar: From the Silk Road to Michelangelo*. Oxford: Oxford University Press, 2002.

Brown, Jonathan. "'Peut-on assez louer cet excellent ministre?' Imagery of the Favourite in England, France, and Spain." In *The World of the Favourite*, ed. J. H. Elliott and L. W. B. Brockliss. New Haven, Conn.: Yale University Press, 1999. 223–38.

Brown, Pamela Allen. *Better a Shrew Than a Sheep: Women, Drama, and the Culture of Jest in Early Modern England*. Ithaca, N.Y.: Cornell University Press, 2003.

Brustein, Robert. *The Tainted Muse: Prejudice and Presumption in Shakespeare and His Time*. New Haven, Conn.: Yale University Press, 2009.

Bruster, Douglas. *Drama and the Market in the Age of Shakespeare*. Cambridge: Cambridge University Press, 1992.

———. *Shakespeare and the Question of Culture: Early Modern Literature and the Cultural Turn*. New York: Palgrave, 2003.

Bryson, Anna. *From Courtesy to Civility: Changing Codes of Conduct in Early Modern England*. Oxford: Oxford University Press, 1998.

Butler, Judith. *Undoing Gender*. New York: Routledge, 2004.

Butler, Martin. *Theatre and Crisis 1632–1642*. Cambridge: Cambridge University Press, 1984.

Cady, Joseph. "'Masculine Love,' Renaissance Writing, and the 'New Invention' of Homosexuality." In *Homosexuality in Renaissance and Enlightenment England: Literary Representations in Historical Context*, ed. Claude J. Summers. Binghamton, N.Y.: Harrington Park Press, 1992. 9–40.

Cahn, Susan. *Industry of Devotion: The Transformation of Women's Work in England, 1500–1660*. New York: Columbia University Press, 1987.

Calbi, Maurizio. *Approximate Bodies: Gender and Power in Early Modern Drama and Anatomy*. London: Routledge, 2005.

Callaghan, Dympna. "Do Characters Have Souls?" *Shakespeare Studies* 34 (2006): 41–45.

———. *Shakespeare Without Women: Representing Gender and Race on the Renaissance Stage*. London: Routledge, 2000.

Campbell, Erin J. "'Unenduring' Beauty: Gender and Old Age in Early Modern Art and Aesthetics." In *Growing Old in Early Modern Europe: Cultural Representations*, ed. Erin Campbell. Burlington, Vt.: Ashgate, 2006. 153–68.

Capp, Bernard. "Separate Domains? Women and Authority in Early Modern England." In *The Experience of Authority in Early Modern England*, ed. Paul Griffiths, Adam Fox, and Steve Hindle. New York: St. Martin's, 1996. 117–45.

———. *When Gossips Meet: Women, Family, and Neighborhood in Early Modern England*. Oxford: Oxford University Press, 2003.

Carroll, William C. "The Virgin Not: Language and Sexuality in Shakespeare." In *Shakespeare and Gender: A History*, ed. Deborah E. Barker and Ivo Kamps. London: Verso, 1995. 283–301.

Castle, Terry. *The Apparitional Lesbian: Female Homosexuality and Modern Culture*. New York: Columbia University Press, 1993.

Charnes, Linda. *Notorious Identity: Materializing the Subject in Shakespeare*. Cambridge, Mass.: Harvard University Press, 1993.

Clare, Janet. *"Art Made Tongue-Tied by Authority": Elizabethan and Jacobean Dramatic Censorship*. Manchester: Manchester University Press, 1990.

Clark, Alice. *Working Life of Women in the Seventeenth Century*. Intro. Miranda Chaytor and Jane Lewis. London: Routledge, 1982.

Clark, Ira. *The Moral Art of Philip Massinger*. Lewisburg, Pa.: Bucknell University Press, 1993.

———. *Professional Playwrights: Massinger, Ford, Shirley, and Brome*. Lexington: University Press of Kentucky, 1992.

Clark, Sandra. "Spanish Characters and English Nationalism in English Drama of the Early Seventeenth Century." *Bulletin of Hispanic Studies* 84, 2 (2007): 131–44.

Cogswell, Thomas. "The People's Love: The Duke of Buckingham and Popularity." In *Politics, Religion and Popularity in Early Stuart Britain,* ed. Thomas Cogswell, Richard Cust, and Peter Lake. Cambridge: Cambridge University Press, 2002. 211–34.

Cohen, Adam Max. *Shakespeare and Technology: Dramatizing Early Modern Technological Revolutions*. New York: Palgrave Macmillan, 2006.

Comensoli, Viviana. "Play-Making, Domestic Conduct, and the Multiple Plot in *The Roaring Girl.*" *SEL: Studies in English Literature, 1500–1900* 27 (Spring 1987): 249–66.

Corum, Richard. "Henry's Desires." In *Premodern Sexualities*, ed. Louise Fradenburg and Carla Freccero. New York: Routledge, 1996. 72–97.

Crane, Mary Thomas. "'Players in Your Huswifery, and Huswives in Your Beds': Conflicting Identities of Early Modern English Women." In *Maternal Measures: Figuring Caregiving in the Early Modern Period*, ed. Naomi J. Miller and Naomi Yavneh. Burlington, Vt.: Ashgate, 2000. 212–23.

Cressy, David. *Birth, Marriage, and Death: Ritual, Religion, and the Life-Cycle in Tudor and Stuart England*. Oxford: Oxford University Press, 1997.

Crewe, Jonathan. "Reclaiming Character?" *Shakespeare Studies* 34 (2006): 35–40.

Cunningham, Karen. *Imaginary Betrayals: Subjectivity and the Discourses of Treason in Early Modern England*. Philadelphia: University of Pennsylvania Press, 2003.

Curtwright, Travis. "'Falseness Cannot Come from Thee': Marina as Character and Orator in Shakespeare's *Pericles*." *Literary Imagination* 11, 1 (2009): 99–110.

Dabhoiwala, Faramerz. "The Pattern of Sexual Immorality in Seventeenth- and Eighteenth-Century London." In *Londinopolis: Essays in the Cultural and Social History of Early Modern London*, ed. Paul Griffiths and Mark S. R. Jenner. Manchester: Manchester University Press, 2000. 86–106.

Daileader, Celia R. *Eroticism on the Renaissance Stage: Transcendence, Desire, and the Limits of the Visible*. Cambridge: Cambridge University Press, 1998.

D'Amico, Jack. *The Moor in English Renaissance Drama*. Tampa: University of South Florida Press, 1991.

Dawson, Anthony B. "*Women Beware Women* and the Economy of Rape." *SEL: Studies in English Literature, 1500–1900* 27 (1987): 303–20.

de Grazia, Margreta. Hamlet *Without Hamlet*. Cambridge: Cambridge University Press, 2007.

Dekker, Rudolph M., and Lotte C. van de Pol. *The Tradition of Female Transvestism in Early Modern Europe*. New York: St. Martin's, 1989.

Desmet, Christy. "The Persistence of Character." *Shakespeare Studies* 34 (2006): 46–55.

Desmet, Christy, and Robert Sawyer, eds. *Harold Bloom's Shakespeare*. New York: Palgrave, 2001.

Desmond, Marilynn, and Pamela Sheingorn. "Queering Ovidian Myth: Bestiality and Desire in Christine de Pizan's *Epistre Othea*." In *Queering the Middle Ages*, ed. Glenn Burger and Steven F. Kruger. Minneapolis: University of Minnesota Press, 2001. 3–27.

DiGangi, Mario. *The Homoerotics of Early Modern Drama*. Cambridge: Cambridge University Press, 1997.

———, ed. *The Winter's Tale: Texts and Contexts*. By William Shakespeare. Boston: Bedford-St. Martin's, 2008.

Dodd, William. "Character as Dynamic Identity: From Fictional Interaction Script to Performance." In *Shakespeare and Character: Theory, History, Performance, and Theatrical Persons*, ed. Paul Yachnin and Jessica Slights. New York: Palgrave Macmillan, 2009. 62–79.

Dodson, Daniel. "Middleton's Livia." *Philological Quarterly* 27 (1948): 376–81.

Dolan, Frances E. *Dangerous Familiars: Representations of Domestic Crime in England, 1550–1700*. Ithaca, N.Y.: Cornell University Press, 1994.

———. *Whores of Babylon: Catholicism, Gender and Seventeenth-Century Print Culture*. Ithaca, N.Y.: Cornell University Press, 1999.

Dollimore, Jonathan. *Radical Tragedy: Religion, Ideology and Power in the Drama of Shakespeare and His Contemporaries*. Chicago: University of Chicago Press, 1984.

Donoghue, Emma. *Passions Between Women: British Lesbian Culture 1668–1801*. New York: HarperCollins, 1993.

Eisenbichler, Konrad. "'Laudomia Forteguerri Loves Margaret of Austria.'" In *Same-Sex Love and Desire Among Women in the Middle Ages*, ed. Canadé Sautman and Pamela Sheingorn. New York: Palgrave, 2001. 277–304.

Elias, Norbert. *The Civilizing Process*. Trans. Edmund Jephcott. Oxford: Blackwell, 1994.

Ellis, Jim. *Sexuality and Citizenship: Metamorphosis in Elizabethan Erotic Verse*. Toronto: University of Toronto Press, 2003.

Enterline, Lynn. *The Tears of Narcissus: Melancholia and Masculinity in Early Modern Writing*. Stanford, Calif.: Stanford University Press, 1995.

Fahmi, Mustapha. "Man's Chief Good: The Shakespearean Character as Evaluator." *Shakespearean International Yearbook* 8 (2008): 119–35.

Falco, Raphael. "Forum: Is There Character After Theory?" *Shakespeare Studies* 34 (2006): 21–24.

Fisher, Will. *Materializing Gender in Early Modern English Literature and Culture.* Cambridge: Cambridge University Press, 2006.

———. "Queer Money." *ELH 66* (1999): 1–24.

Fletcher, Anthony. *Gender, Sex, and Subordination in England 1500–1800.* New Haven, Conn.: Yale University Press, 1995.

Foakes, R. A. "Reviving Shakespeare Character Criticism." In *In the Footsteps of William Shakespeare*, ed. Christa Jansohn. Münster: Lit Verlag, 2005: 190–204.

Forker, Charles R., ed. *Edward the Second.* By Christopher Marlowe. Manchester: Manchester University Press, 1994.

Forman, Valerie. "Marked Angels: Counterfeits, Commodities, and *The Roaring Girl.*" *Renaissance Quarterly* 54 (Winter 2001): 1531–60.

Fowler, Elizabeth. *Literary Character: The Human Figure in Early English Writing.* Ithaca, N.Y.: Cornell University Press, 2003.

———. "Shylock's Virtual Injuries." *Shakespeare Studies* 34 (2006): 56–64.

Garber, Marjorie. "The Logic of the Transvestite: *The Roaring Girl.*" In *Staging the Renaissance: Essays on Elizabethan and Jacobean Drama*, ed. David Scott Kastan and Peter Stallybrass. New York: Routledge, 1991.

Gill, Roma, ed. *Women Beware Women.* By Thomas Middleton. New York: Hill and Wang, 1969.

Ginzburg, Carlo. "Titian, Ovid, and Sixteenth-Century Codes for Erotic Illustration." In *Myths, Emblems, Clues.* Trans. John Tedeschi and Anne C. Tedeschi. London: Hutchison Radius, 1990. 77–95.

Goldberg, Jonathan. "The Anus in Coriolanus." In *Shakespeare's Hand.* Minneapolis: University of Minnesota Press, 2003. 176–85.

———. *Desiring Women Writing: English Renaissance Examples.* Stanford, Calif.: Stanford University Press, 1997.

———. *James I and the Politics of Literature: Jonson, Shakespeare, Donne, and Their Contemporaries.* Stanford, Calif.: Stanford University Press, 1989.

———. "Shakespearean Characters: The Generation of Silvia." In *Shakespeare's Hand.* Minneapolis: University of Minnesota Press, 2003. 10–47.

———. *Sodometries: Renaissance Texts, Modern Sexualities.* Stanford, Calif.: Stanford University Press, 1992.

———, ed. *Queering the Renaissance.* Durham, N.C.: Duke University Press, 1994.

Gowing, Laura. *Common Bodies: Women, Touch and Power in Seventeenth-Century England.* New Haven, Conn.: Yale University Press, 2003.

———. *Domestic Dangers: Women, Words, and Sex in Early Modern London.* Oxford: Oxford University Press-Clarendon, 1996.

———. "The Politics of Women's Friendship in Early Modern England." In *Love, Friendship, and Faith in Europe, 1300–1800*, ed. Laura Gowing, Michael Hunter, and Miri Rubin. New York: Palgrave Macmillan, 2005. 131–49.

Green, Douglas E. "Preposterous Pleasures: Queer Theories and *A Midsummer Night's*

Dream." In *A Midsummer Night's Dream: Critical Essays*, ed. Dorothea Kehler. New York: Routledge, 2001. 369–400.

Greenblatt, Stephen. "Fiction and Friction." In *Shakespearean Negotiations: The Circulation of Social Energy in Renaissance England*. Berkeley: University of California Press, 1988.

Griffiths, Paul. "The Structure of Prostitution in Elizabethan London." *Continuity and Change* 8, 1 (1993): 39–63.

Griffiths, Trevor R., ed. *Shakespeare in Production: A Midsummer Night's Dream*. Cambridge: Cambridge University Press, 1996.

Gross, Kenneth. *Shakespeare's Noise*. Chicago: University of Chicago Press, 2001.

Grosz, Elizabeth. *Volatile Bodies: Toward a Corporeal Feminism*. Bloomington: Indiana University Press, 1994.

Hall, Kim F. *Things of Darkness: Economies of Race and Gender in Early Modern England*. Ithaca, N.Y.: Cornell University Press, 1995.

Halperin, David M. *How to Do the History of Homosexuality*. Chicago: University of Chicago Press, 2002.

Halpern, Richard. *Shakespeare's Perfume: Sodomy and Sublimity in the Sonnets, Wilde, Freud, and Lacan*. Philadelphia: University of Pennsylvania Press, 2002.

Hammond, Gerald. *Fleeting Things: English Poets and Poems, 1616–1660*. Cambridge: Harvard University Press, 1990.

Hammond, Paul. *Figuring Sex Between Men from Shakespeare to Rochester*. Oxford: Clarendon, 2002.

Harris, Jonathan Gil. "'Narcissus in Thy Face': Roman Desire and the Difference It Fakes in *Antony and Cleopatra*." *Shakespeare Quarterly* 45 (1994): 408–25.

———. *Sick Economies: Drama, Mercantilism, and Disease in Shakespeare's England*. Philadelphia: University of Pennsylvania Press, 2004.

Haynes, Jonathan. *The Social Relations of Jonson's Theater*. Cambridge: Cambridge University Press, 1992.

Heinemann, Margot. "Drama and Opinion in the 1620s: Middleton and Massinger." In *Theatre and Government Under the Early Stuarts*, ed. J. R. Mulryne and Margaret Shewring. Cambridge: Cambridge University Press, 1993. 237–65.

Heller, Herbert Jack. *Penitent Brothellers: Grace, Sexuality, and Genre in Thomas Middleton's City Comedies*. Newark: University of Delaware Press, 2000.

Helms, Lorraine. "The Saint in the Brothel: Or, Eloquence Rewarded." *Shakespeare Quarterly* 41, 3 (1990): 319–32.

Henderson, Katherine Usher, and Barbara F. McManus, eds. *Half Humankind: Contexts and Texts of the Controversy About Women in England, 1540–1640*. Urbana: University of Illinois Press, 1985.

Hendricks, Margo. "'Obscured by Dreams': Race, Empire, and Shakespeare's *A Midsummer Night's Dream*." *Shakespeare Quarterly* 47 (1996): 37–60.

Hirschfeld, Heather. "What Do Women Know? *The Roaring Girl* and the Wisdom of Tiresias." *Renaissance Drama* n.s. 32 (2003): 123–46.

Hitchcock, Tim. *English Sexualities, 1700–1800*. London: Macmillan, 1997.

Hoenselaars, A. J. *Images of Englishmen and Foreigners in the Drama of Shakespeare and His Contemporaries: A Study of Stage Characters and National Identity in English Renaissance Drama, 1558–1642*. Cranbury, N.J.: Associated University Press, 1992.

Holmes, Morgan. "A Garden of Her Own: Marvell's Nymph and the Order of Nature." In *Ovid and the Renaissance Body*, ed. Goran V. Stanivukovic. Toronto: University of Toronto Press, 2001. 77–93.

Honeyman, Katrina, and Jordan Goodman. "Women's Work, Gender Conflict, and Labour Markets in Europe, 1500–1900." In *Gender and History in Western Europe*, ed. Robert Shoemaker and Mary Vincent. London: Arnold, 1998.

Hopkins, Lisa. "Middleton's *Women Beware Women* and the Mothering Principle." *Journal of Gender Studies* 7 (1998): 63–72.

Howard, Jean E. "Sex and Social Conflict: The Erotics of *The Roaring Girl*." In *Erotic Politics: Desire on the Renaissance Stage*, ed. Susan Zimmerman. New York: Routledge, 1992. 170–90.

———. *Theater of a City: The Places of London Comedy, 1598–1642*. Philadelphia: University of Pennsylvania Press, 2007.

———. "Women, Foreigners, and the Regulation of Urban Space in *Westward Ho*." In *Material London, ca. 1600*, ed. Lena Cowen Orlin. Philadelphia: University of Pennsylvania Press, 2000. 150–67.

Howard, Skiles. "Hands, Feet, and Bottoms: Decentering the Cosmic Dance in *A Midsummer Night's Dream*." *Shakespeare Quarterly* 44 (1993): 325–42.

Howell, Martha. *Women, Production, and Patriarchy in Late Medieval Cities*. Chicago: University of Chicago Press, 1986.

Hutson, Lorna. "Civility and Virility in Ben Jonson." *Representations* 78 (Spring 2002): 1–27.

———. "*Ethopoeia*, Source-Study and Legal History: A Post-Theoretical Approach to the Question of 'Character' in Shakespearean Drama." In *Post-Theory: New Directions in Criticism*, ed. Martin McQuillian, Graeme MacDonald, Robin Purves, and Stephen Thomson. Edinburgh: Edinburgh University Press, 2000. 139–60.

———. *The Usurer's Daughter: Male Friendship and Fictions of Women in Sixteenth-Century England*. London: Routledge, 1994.

Ingram, Martin. *Church Courts, Sex and Marriage, 1570–1640*. Cambridge: Cambridge University Press, 1987.

Jankowski, Theodora A. ". . . in the Lesbian Void: Woman-Woman Eroticism in Shakespeare's Plays." In *A Feminist Companion to Shakespeare*, ed. Dympna Callaghan. Malden, Mass.: Blackwell, 2000. 299–319.

———. *Pure Resistance: Queer Virginity in Early Modern English Drama*. Philadelphia: University of Pennsylvania Press, 2000.

Jardine, Lisa. *Still Harping on Daughters: Women and Drama in the Age of Shakespeare*. 2nd ed. New York: Columbia University Press, 1989.

Jones, Ann Rosalind. "Italians and Others: Venice and the Irish in *Coryat's Crudities* and *The White Devil*." *Renaissance Drama* 18 (1987): 101–19.

Jones, Ann Rosalind, and Peter Stallybrass. *Renaissance Clothing and the Materials of Memory*. Cambridge: Cambridge University Press, 2000.

Jones, Malcolm. "Print of the Month. No. 13, September 2007." In *British Printed Images to 1700*. British Museum. http://www.bpi1700.org.uk/printsMonths/september2007.html

Jordan, Mark D. *The Invention of Sodomy in Christian Theology*. Chicago: University of Chicago Press, 1997.

Kahn, Coppélia. "Whores and Wives in Jacobean Drama." In *In Another Country: Feminist Perspectives on Renaissance Drama*, ed. Dorothea Kehler and Susan Baker. Metuchen, N.J.: Scarecrow Press, 1991. 246–60.

Kaplan, M. Lindsay. *The Culture of Slander in Early Modern England*. Cambridge: Cambridge University Press, 1997.

Kaplan, Morris B. *Sexual Justice: Democratic Citizenship and the Politics of Desire*. New York: Routledge, 1997.

Karras, Ruth Mazo. "Sex and the Singlewoman." In *Singlewomen in the European Past, 1250–1800*, ed. Judith M. Bennett and Amy M. Froide. Philadelphia: University of Pennsylvania Press, 1998. 127–45.

Kermode, Lloyd Edward. "Destination Doomsday: Desires for Change and Changeable Desires in *The Roaring Girl*." *English Literary Renaissance* 27 (1997): 421–42.

King, Thomas A. *The Gendering of Men, 1600–1750*. Vol. 1, *The English Phallus*. Madison: University of Wisconsin Press, 2004.

Kinney, Arthur F., and Dan S. Collins, eds. *Renaissance Historicism: Selections from* English Literary Renaissance. Amherst: University of Massachusetts Press, 1987.

Kinney, Daniel, with Elizabeth Styron. "Ovid Illustrated: The Reception of Ovid's *Metamorphoses* in Image and Text." University of Virginia. http://etext.virginia.edu/latin/ovid/posthius1–7.html

Kitch, Aaron. "The Character of Credit and the Problem of Belief in Middleton's City Comedies." *SEL: Studies in English Literature, 1500–1900* 47 (Spring 2007): 403–26.

Knoppers, Laura Lunger. "'The Antichrist, The Babilon, The Great Dragon': Oliver Cromwell, Andrew Marvell, and the Apocalyptic Monstrous." In *Monstrous Bodies/Political Monstrosities in Early Modern Europe*, ed. Laura Lunger Knoppers and Joan B. Landes. Ithaca, N.Y.: Cornell University Press, 2004. 93–123.

Knowles, James. "Sexuality: A Renaissance Category?" In *A Companion to English Renaissance Literature and Culture*, ed. Michael Hattaway. Oxford: Blackwell, 2000. 674–89.

Korda, Natasha. "The Case of Moll Frith: Women's Work and the 'All-Male Stage.'" In *Women Players in England, 1500–1660: Beyond the All-Male Stage*, ed. Pamela Allen Brown and Peter Parolin. Aldershot: Ashgate, 2005. 71–87.

Krantz, Susan E. "The Sexual Identities of Moll Cutpurse in Dekker and Middleton's *The Roaring Girl* and in London." *Renaissance and Reformation* 19, 1 (1995): 5–20.

Kuchta, David. *The Three-Piece Suit and Modern Masculinity: England 1550–1850*. Berkeley: University of California Press, 2002.

Lake, Peter, with Michael Questier. *The Anti-Christ's Lewd Hat: Protestants, Papists and Players in Post-Reformation England*. New Haven, Conn.: Yale University Press, 2002.

Lamb, Mary Ellen. "Taken by the Fairies: Fairy Practices and the Production of Popular Culture in *A Midsummer Night's Dream*." *Shakespeare Quarterly* 51 (2000): 277–312.

Lee, Maurice, Jr. *Great Britain's Solomon: James VI and I in His Three Kingdoms*. Urbana: University of Illinois Press, 1990.

———, ed. and intro. *Dudley Carleton to John Chamberlain, 1603–1624: Jacobean Letters*. New Brunswick, N.J.: Rutgers University Press, 1972.

Lees-Jeffries, Hester. *England's Helicon: Fountains in Early Modern Literature and Culture*. Oxford: Oxford University Press, 2007.

Leinwand, Theodore B. *The City Staged: Jacobean Comedy, 1603–13*. Madison: University of Wisconsin Press, 1986.

"Lesbian Historiography Before the Name?" *GLQ: A Journal of Lesbian and Gay Studies* 4 (1998): 557–630.

Levin, Richard A. "If Women Should Beware Women, Bianca Should Beware Mother." *Studies in English Literature, 1500–1900* 37 (1997): 371–89.

Lewalski, Barbara Kiefer. *Writing Women in Jacobean England*. Cambridge, Mass.: Harvard University Press, 1993.

Lieblein, Leanore. "Embodied Intersubjectivity and the Creation of Early Modern Character." In *Shakespeare and Character: Theory, History, Performance, and Theatrical Persons*, ed. Paul Yachnin and Jessica Slights. New York: Palgrave Macmillan, 2009. 117–35.

Linton, Joan Pong. *The Romance of the New World: Gender and the Literary Formations of English Colonialism*. Cambridge: Cambridge University Press, 1998.

Little, Arthur L., Jr. "'A Local Habitation and a Name': Presence, Witnessing, and Queer Marriage in Shakespeare's Romantic Comedies." In *Presentism, Gender, and Sexuality in Shakespeare*, ed. Evelyn Gajowski. New York: Palgrave Macmillan, 2009. 207–36.

Lochrie, Karma. *Heterosyncrasies: Female Sexuality When Normal Wasn't*. Minneapolis: University of Minnesota Press, 2005.

Lockyer, Roger. *Buckingham: The Life and Political Career of George Villiers, First Duke of Buckingham, 1592–1628*. London: Longman, 1981.

Loomba, Ania. "The Great Indian Vanishing Trick—Colonialism, Property, and the Family in *A Midsummer Night's Dream*." In *A Feminist Companion to Shakespeare*, ed. Dympna Callaghan. Malden, Mass.: Blackwell, 2000. 163–87.

———. *Shakespeare, Race, and Colonialism*. Oxford: Oxford University Press, 2002.

Lopez, Jeremy. *Theatrical Convention and Audience Response in Early Modern Drama*. Cambridge: Cambridge University Press, 2003.

Mallette, Richard. "Same-Sex Erotic Friendship in *The Two Noble Kinsmen*." *Renaissance Drama* 26 (1995): 29–52.

Manley, Lawrence. *London in the Age of Shakespeare: An Anthology*. University Park: Pennsylvania State University Press, 1986.

Marotti, Arthur F. *Manuscript, Print, and the English Renaissance Lyric*. Ithaca, N.Y.: Cornell University Press, 1995.

Masten, Jeffrey. *Textual Intercourse: Collaboration, Authorship, and Sexualities in Renaissance Drama*. Cambridge: Cambridge University Press, 1997.

Mathes, Bettina. "As Long as a Swan's Neck? The Significance of the 'Enlarged' Clitoris for Early Modern Anatomy." In *Sensible Flesh: On Touch in Early Modern Culture*, ed. Elizabeth D. Harvey. Philadelphia: University of Pennsylvania Press, 2003. 103–24.

Mazzio, Carla. "Sins of the Tongue." In *The Body in Parts: Fantasies of Corporeality in Early Modern Europe*, ed. David Hillman and Carla Mazzio. New York: Routledge, 1997. 53–79.

Mccullen, Joseph T. "Iago's Use of Proverbs for Persuasion." *SEL: Studies in English Literature, 1500–1900* 4 (1964): 247–62.

McDermott, Kristen. "'He May Be Our Father, Perhaps': Paternity, Puppets, Boys, and *Bartholomew Fair*." In *Critical Essays on Ben Jonson*, ed. Robert N. Watson. New York: G.K. Hall, 1997. 60–81.

McIntosh, Marjorie Keniston. *Controlling Misbehavior in Early Modern England, 1370–1600*. Cambridge: Cambridge University Press, 1998.

———. *Working Women in English Society, 1300–1620*. Cambridge: Cambridge University Press, 2005.

McManus, Clare. "*The Roaring Girl* and the London Underworld." In *Early Modern English Drama: A Critical Companion*, ed. Garrett A. Sullivan, Jr., Patrick Cheney, and Andrew Hadfield. New York: Oxford University Press, 2006. 213–24.

McNeill, Fiona. "Gynocentric London Spaces: (Re)Locating Masterless Women in Early Stuart Drama." *Renaissance Drama* n.s. 28 (1997): 195–244.

———. *Poor Women in Shakespeare*. Cambridge: Cambridge University Press, 2007.

Mendelson, Sara, and Patricia Crawford. *Women in Early Modern England, 1550–1720*. Oxford: Oxford University Press, 1998.

Menon, Madhavi. *Wanton Words: Rhetoric and Sexuality in English Renaissance Drama*. Toronto: University of Toronto Press, 2004.

Middleton, Chris. "Women's Labour and the Transition to Pre-Industrial Capitalism." In *Women and Work in Pre-Industrial England*, ed. Lindsey Charles and Lorna Duffin. London: Croom Helm, 1985.

Mikalachki, Jodi. "Gender, Cant, and Cross-Talking in *The Roaring Girl*." *Renaissance Drama* 25 (1994): 119–43.

Miller, Jo E. "Women and the Market in *The Roaring Girl*." *Renaissance and Reformation* 26, 1 (1990): 11–23.

Mohler, Christina. "'What Is Thy Body But a Swallowing Grave . . . ?': Desire Underground in *Titus Andronicus*." *Shakespeare Quarterly* 57 (2006): 23–44.

Monsarrat, Gilles D. *Light from the Porch: Stoicism and English Renaissance Literature*. Paris: Didier-Érudition, 1984.

Morgan, D. A. L. "The House of Policy: The Political Role of the Late Plantagenet

Household." In *The English Court: From the Wars of the Roses to the Civil War*, ed. David Starkey. London: Longman, 1987. 25–70.

Moulton, Ian Frederick. *Before Pornography: Erotic Writing in Early Modern England*. Oxford: Oxford University Press, 2000.

Muir, Kenneth. "The Role of Livia in *Women Beware Women*." In *Shakespeare: Contrasts and Controversies*. Norman: University of Oklahoma Press, 1985. 127–42.

Newman, Karen. *Cultural Capitals: Early Modern London and Paris*. Princeton, N.J.: Princeton University Press, 2007.

Orgel, Stephen. *Impersonations: The Performance of Gender in Shakespeare's England*. Cambridge: Cambridge University Press, 1996.

———. "The Subtexts of The Roaring Girl." In *Erotic Politics: Desire on the Renaissance Stage*, ed. Susan Zimmerman. New York: Routledge, 1992. 12–26.

Orlin, Lena Cowen. "Three Ways to Be Invisible in the Renaissance: Sex, Reputation, and Stitchery." In *Renaissance Culture and the Everyday*, ed. Patricia Fumerton and Simon Hunt. Philadelphia: University of Pennsylvania Press, 1999. 183–203.

Panek, Jennifer. "The Mother as Bawd in *The Revenger's Tragedy* and *A Mad World, My Masters*." *SEL: Studies in English Literature, 1500–1900* 43 (2003): 415–37.

———. *Widows and Suitors in Early Modern English Comedy*. Cambridge: Cambridge University Press, 2004.

Park, Katherine. "The Rediscovery of the Clitoris: French Medicine and the Tribade, 1570–1620." In *The Body in Parts: Fantasies of Corporeality in Early Modern Europe*, ed. H. David Hillman and Carla Mazzio. New York: Routledge, 1997. 171–93.

Partridge, Mary. "Images of the Courtier in Elizabethan England." Ph.D. Thesis, University of Birmingham, 2008. University of Birmingham eTheses Repository. http://etheses.bham.ac.uk/168/1/Partridge08PhD.pdf

Paster, Gail Kern. *The Body Embarrassed: Drama and the Disciplines of Shame in Early Modern England*. Ithaca, N.Y.: Cornell University Press, 1993.

———. *Humoring the Body: Emotions and the Shakespearean Stage*. Chicago: University of Chicago Press, 2004.

Patterson, Annabel. *Censorship and Interpretation: The Conditions of Writing and Reading in Early Modern England*. Madison: University of Wisconsin Press, 1984.

Peck, Linda Levy. *Consuming Splendor: Society and Culture in Seventeenth-Century England*. Cambridge: Cambridge University Press, 2005.

———. *Court Patronage and Corruption in Early Stuart England*. London: Routledge, 1990.

———. "Monopolizing Favour: Structures of Power in the Early Seventeenth-Century English Court." In *The World of the Favourite*, ed. J. H. Elliott and L. W. B. Brockliss. New Haven, Conn.: Yale University Press, 1999. 54–70.

Perry, Curtis. "'If Proclamations Will Not Serve': The Late Manuscript Poetry of James I and the Culture of Libel." In *Royal Subjects: Essays on the Writings of James VI and I*, ed. Daniel Fischlin and Mark Fortier. Detroit: Wayne State University Press, 2002. 205–32.

————. *Literature and Favoritism in Early Modern England.* Cambridge: Cambridge University Press, 2006.

————. "The Politics of Access and Representations of the Sodomite King in Early Modern England." *Renaissance Quarterly* 53 (2000): 1054–83.

Piesse, A. J. "Identity." In *A Companion to English Renaissance Literature and Culture*, ed. Michael Hattaway. Oxford: Blackwell, 2000. 634–43.

Puff, Helmut. *Sodomy in Reformation Germany and Switzerland, 1400–1600.* Chicago: University of Chicago Press, 2003.

Quaife, G. R. *Wanton Wenches and Wayward Wives: Peasants and Illicit Sex in Early Seventeenth-Century England.* New Brunswick, N.J.: Rutgers University Press, 1979.

Rackin, Phyllis. "Foreign Country: The Place of Women and Sexuality in Shakespeare's Historical World." In *Enclosure Acts: Sexuality, Property, and Culture in Early Modern England*, ed. Richard Burt and John Michael Archer. Ithaca, N.Y.: Cornell University Press, 1994. 68–95.

Radel, Nicholas F. "Queer Romeo and Juliet: Teaching Early Modern 'Sexuality' in Shakespeare's 'Heterosexual' Tragedy." In *Approaches to Teaching Shakespeare's Romeo and Juliet*, ed. Maurice Hunt. New York: MLA, 2000. 91–97.

Raman, Shankar. *Framing "India": The Colonial Imaginary in Early Modern Culture.* Stanford, Calif.: Stanford University Press, 2001.

Reynolds, Bryan. *Becoming Criminal: Transversal Performance and Cultural Dissidence in Early Modern England.* Baltimore: Johns Hopkins University Press, 2002.

Reynolds, Bryan, and Janna Segal. "The Reckoning of Moll Cutpurse: A Transversal Enterprise." In *Rogues and Early Modern English Culture*, ed. Craig Dionne and Steve Mentz. Ann Arbor: University of Michigan Press, 2004. 62–97.

Ricks, Christopher. "Word-Play in *Women Beware Women.*" *Review of English Studies* n.s. 12 (1961): 238–50.

Roberts, Jeanne Addison. "The Crone in English Renaissance Drama." *Medieval and Renaissance Drama in England* 15 (2002): 116–37.

Roberts, Michael. "'Words They Are Women, and Deeds They Are Men': Images of Work and Gender in Early Modern England." In *Women and Work in Pre-Industrial England*, ed. Lindsey Charles and Lorna Duffin. London: Croom Helm, 1985.

Rocke, Michael. *Forbidden Friendships: Homosexuality and Male Culture in Renaissance Florence.* New York: Oxford University Press, 1996.

Roper, Lyndal. *Witch Craze: Terror and Fantasy in Baroque Germany.* New Haven, Conn.: Yale University Press, 2004.

Rose, Mary Beth. "Women in Men's Clothing: Apparel and Social Stability in *The Roaring Girl.*" *English Literary Renaissance* 14, 3 (1984): 367–91.

Rousseau, George. "Policing the Anus: Stuprum and Sodomy According to Paolo Zacchia's Forensic Medicine." In *The Sciences of Homosexuality in Early Modern Europe*, ed. Kenneth Borris and George Rousseau. London: Routledge, 2008. 75–91.

Rustici, Craig. "The Smoking Girl: Tobacco and the Representation of Moll Frith." *Studies in Philology* 92 (1999): 159–79.

Sanders, Julie. *Caroline Drama: The Plays of Massinger, Ford, Shirley and Brome.* Plymouth: Northcote House, 1999.

———. "'Powdered with Golden Rain': The Myth of Danae in Early Modern Drama." *Early Modern Literary Studies* 8, 2 (September 2002): 1–23. http://extra.shu.ac.uk/emls/08-2/sanddane.htm.

Santore, Cathy. "Danaë: The Renaissance Courtesan's Alter Ego," *Zeitschrift für Kunstgeschichte* 54, 3 (1991): 412–27.

Saunders, Ben. *Desiring Donne: Poetry, Sexuality, Interpretation.* Cambridge, Mass.: Harvard University Press, 2006.

Sawday, Jonathan. *The Body Emblazoned: Dissection and the Human Body in Renaissance Culture.* New York: Routledge, 1995.

Schwarz, Kathryn. *Tough Love: Amazon Encounters in the English Renaissance.* Durham, N.C.: Duke University Press, 2000.

Sena, Margaret. "William Blundell and the Networks of Catholic Dissent in Post-Reformation England." In *Communities in Early Modern England: Networks, Place, Rhetoric,* ed. Alexandra Shepard and Phil Withington. Manchester: Manchester University Press, 2000. 54–75.

Sensabaugh, G. F. *The Tragic Muse of John Ford.* New York: Blom, 1944.

Shannon, Laurie. *Sovereign Amity: Figures of Friendship in Shakespearean Contexts.* Chicago: University of Chicago Press, 2002.

Shapiro, Michael. *Gender in Play on the Shakespearean Stage: Boy Heroines and Female Pages.* Ann Arbor: University of Michigan Press, 1995.

Sharpe, Kevin. *Criticism and Compliment: The Politics of Literature in the England of Charles I.* Cambridge: Cambridge University Press, 1987.

———. *The Personal Rule of Charles I.* New Haven, Conn.: Yale University Press, 1992.

Shepard, Alexandra. *Meanings of Manhood in Early Modern England.* Oxford: Oxford University Press, 2003.

———. "'Swil-bols and Tos-pots': Drink Culture and Male Bonding in England, c. 1560–1640." In *Love, Friendship, and Faith in Europe, 1300–1800,* ed. Laura Gowing, Michael Hunter, and Miri Rubin. New York: Palgrave Macmillan, 2005. 110–30.

Shepherd, Simon. "What's So Funny About Ladies' Tailors? A Survey of Some Male (Homo)sexual Types in the Renaissance." *Textual Practice* 6 (1992): 17–30.

Simmons, J. L. "From Theatre to Globe: The Construction of Character in *Julius Caesar.*" In *"Julius Caesar": New Critical Essays,* ed. Horst Zander. New York: Routledge, 2005. 155–63.

Simons, Patricia. "Lesbian (In)Visibility in Italian Renaissance Culture: Diana and Other Cases of *donna con donna.*" In *Gay and Lesbian Studies in Art History,* ed. Whitney Davis. New York: Routledge, 1994. 81–122.

Sinfield, Alan. "From Bradley to Cultural Materialism." *Shakespeare Studies* 34 (2006): 25–34.

Singh, Jyotsna. "The Interventions of History: Narratives of Sexuality." In *The Weyward*

Sisters: Shakespeare and Feminist Politics, ed. Dympna C. Callaghan, Lorraine Helms, and Jyotsna Singh. Oxford: Blackwell, 1994. 7–58.

Smith, Bruce R. *Homosexual Desire in Shakespeare's England: A Cultural Poetics*. Chicago: University of Chicago Press, 1991.

———. *Shakespeare and Masculinity.* Oxford: Oxford University Press, 2000.

Smuts, R. Malcolm. *Court Culture and the Origins of a Royalist Tradition in Early Stuart England*. Philadelphia: University of Pennsylvania Press, 1987.

Spear, Gary. "Shakespeare's 'Manly' Parts: Masculinity and Effeminacy in *Troilus and Cressida.*" *Shakespeare Quarterly* 44, 4 (1993): 409–22.

Stanivukovic, Goran V. "Between Men in Early Modern England." In *Queer Masculinities, 1550–1800: Siting Same-Sex Desire in the Early Modern World*, ed. Katherine O'Donnell and Michael O'Rourke. New York: Palgrave Macmillan, 2006. 232–51.

Starkey, David. "Introduction: Court History in Perspective." In *The English Court: From the Wars of the Roses to the Civil War*, ed. David Starkey. London: Longman, 1987. 1–24.

Starnes, Dewitt T., and Ernest William Talbert. *Classical Myth and Legend in Renaissance Dictionaries*. Westport, Conn.: Greenwood Press, 1955.

Steinberg, Leo. "Michelangelo's Florentine *Pietà*: The Missing Leg." *Art Bulletin* 50, 4 (1968): 343–53.

Stewart, Alan. "Bribery, Buggery, and the Fall of Lord Chancellor Bacon." In *Rhetoric and Law in Early Modern Europe*, ed. Victoria Kahn and Lorna Hutson. New Haven, Conn.: Yale University Press, 2001. 125–42.

———. *The Cradle King: The Life of King James VI and I, the First Monarch of a United Great Britain*. New York: St. Martin's, 2003.

———. "Queer Renaissance Bodies? Sex, Violence, and the Constraints of Periodisation." In *In a Queer Place: Sexuality and Belonging in British and European Contexts*, ed. Kate Chedgzoy, Emma Francis, and Murray Pratt. Aldershot: Ashgate, 2002. 137–54.

———. "A Society of Sodomites: Religion and Homosexuality in Renaissance England." In *Love, Friendship, and Faith in Europe, 1300–1800*, ed. Laura Gowing, Michael Hunter, and Miri Rubin. New York: Palgrave Macmillan, 2005. 88–109.

Sullivan, Garrett A., Jr. "'All Things Come into Commerce': Women, Household Labor, and the Spaces of Marston's *The Dutch Courtesan.*" *Renaissance Drama* 27 (1996): 19–46.

Taunton, Nina. *Fictions of Old Age in Early Modern Literature and Culture*. New York: Routledge, 2007.

Taylor, Miles. "'Teach Me This Pedlar's French': The Allure of Cant in *The Roaring Girl* and Dekker's Rogue Pamphlets." *Renaissance and Reformation* 29 (Fall 2005): 107–24.

Taylor, Neil, and Bryan Loughrey. "Middleton's Chess Strategies in *Women Beware Women.*" *Studies in English Literature, 1500–1900* 24 (1984): 341–54.

Thomson, Leslie. "'As Proper a Woman as Any in Cheap': Women in Shops on the Early Modern Stage." *Medieval and Renaissance Drama in England* 16 (2003): 145–61.

Toulalan, Sarah. *Imagining Sex: Pornography and Bodies in Seventeenth-Century England.* Oxford: Oxford University Press, 2007.

Traub, Valerie. "The Present Future of Lesbian Historiography." In *A Companion to Lesbian, Gay, Bisexual, Transgender, and Queer Studies*, ed. George E. Haggarty and Molly McGarry. Chichester: Wiley-Blackwell, 2007. 124–45.

———. *The Renaissance of Lesbianism in Early Modern England.* Cambridge: Cambridge University Press, 2002.

Tricomi, Albert H. *Anticourt Drama in England, 1603–1642.* Charlottesville: University of Virginia Press, 1989.

Trumbach, Randolph. *Sex and the Gender Revolution: Heterosexuality and the Third Gender in Enlightenment London.* Chicago: University of Chicago Press, 1998.

———. "Sodomitical Subcultures, Sodomitical Roles, and the Gender Revolution of the Eighteenth Century: The Recent Historiography." In *'Tis Nature's Fault: Unauthorized Sexuality During the Enlightenment*, ed. Robert Purks Maccubbin. Cambridge: Cambridge University Press, 1987.

Turner, James Grantham. *Schooling Sex: Libertine Literature and Erotic Education in Italy, France, and England 1534–1685.* Oxford: Oxford University Press, 2003.

Turner, John. "Introduction." In *Shakespeare, Out of Court: Dramatizations of Court Society*, ed. Graham Holderness, Nick Potter, and John Turner. New York: St. Martin's, 1990. 1–12.

Turner, Robert Y. "Giving and Taking in Massinger's Tragicomedies." *SEL: Studies in English Literature, 1500–1900* 35 (1995): 361–81.

Tvordi, Jessica. "Female Alliance and the Construction of Homoeroticism in *As You Like It* and *Twelfth Night*." In *Maids and Mistresses, Cousins and Queens: Women's Alliances in Early Modern England*, ed. Susan Frye and Karen Robertson. New York: Oxford University Press, 1999. 114–30.

Ungerer, Gustav. "Mary Frith, Alias Moll Cutpurse, in Life and Literature." *Shakespeare Studies* 28 (2000): 42–84.

Varholy, Cristine Mari. "Representing Prostitution in Tudor and Stuart England." Ph.D. Dissertation, University of Wisconsin-Madison, 2000. *ProQuest Digital Dissertations.*

Venuti, Lawrence. *Our Halcyon Dayes: English Prerevolutionary Texts and Postmodern Culture.* Madison: University of Wisconsin Press, 1989.

Vickers, Nancy J. "Diana Described: Scattered Woman and Scattered Rhyme." *Critical Inquiry* 8 (1981): 265–79.

———. "Members Only: Marot's Anatomical Blazons." In *The Body in Parts: Fantasies of Corporeality in Early Modern Europe*, ed. David Hillman and Carla Mazzio. New York: Routledge, 1997. 3–21.

Vinge, Louise. *The Narcissus Theme in Western European Literature Up to the Early 19th Century.* Lund: Gleerups, 1967.

Vitkus, Daniel. *Turning Turk: English Theater and the Multicultural Mediterranean, 1570–1630.* New York: Palgrave, 2003.

Wahl, Elizabeth Susan. *Invisible Relations: Representations of Female Intimacy in the Age of Enlightenment*. Stanford, Calif.: Stanford University Press, 1999.

Walen, Denise A. *Constructions of Female Homoeroticism in Early Modern Drama*. New York: Palgrave, 2005.

Walker, Garthine. "Rereading Rape and Sexual Violence in Early Modern England." *Gender & History* 10, 1 (April 1998): 1–25.

Walsham, Alexandra. *Providence in Early Modern England*. Oxford: Oxford University Press, 1999.

Wayne, Valerie, ed. *The Matter of Difference: Materialist Feminist Criticism of Shakespeare*. Ithaca, N.Y.: Cornell University Press, 1991.

Wells, Stanley. *Looking for Sex in Shakespeare*. Cambridge: Cambridge University Press, 2004.

Whigham, Frank. *Ambition and Privilege: The Social Tropes of Elizabethan Courtesy Theory*. Berkeley: University of California Press, 1984.

Whitney, Charles. *Early Responses to Renaissance Drama*. Cambridge: Cambridge University Press, 2006.

Wiesner, Merry E. "Spinning Out Capital: Women's Work in the Early Modern Economy." In *Becoming Visible: Women in European History*. 2nd ed., ed. Renate Bridenthal, Claudia Koonz, and Susan Mosher Stuard. Boston: Houghton Mifflin, 1987.

Wigler, Stephen. "Parent and Child: The Pattern of Love in *Women Beware Women*." In *"Accompaninge the Players": Essays Celebrating Thomas Middleton, 1580–1980*, ed. Kenneth Friedenreich. New York: AMS, 1983. 183–201.

Willen, Diane. "Women in the Public Sphere in Early Modern England: The Case of the Urban Working Poor." In *Gendered Domains: Rethinking Public and Private in Women's History*, ed. Dorothy O. Helly and Susan M. Reverby. Ithaca, N.Y.: Cornell University Press, 1992. 183–98.

Willis, Deborah. *Malevolent Nurture: Witch-Hunting and Maternal Power in Early Modern England*. Ithaca, N.Y.: Cornell University Press, 1995.

Willson, David H. *King James VI and I*. London: Jonathan Cape, 1956.

Wiltenburg, Robert. *Ben Jonson and Self-Love: The Subtlest Maze of All*. Columbia: University of Missouri Press, 1990.

Woodbridge, Linda. *Women and the English Renaissance: Literature and the Nature of Womankind, 1540–1620*. Urbana: University of Illinois Press, 1984.

Worden, Blair. "Favourites on the English Stage." In *The World of the Favourite*, ed. J. H. Elliott and L. W. B. Brockliss. New Haven, Conn.: Yale University Press, 1999. 159–83.

Wormald, Jenny. "James VI and I: Two Kings or One?" *History* 68 (June 1983): 187–209.

Wright, Louis B. *Middle-Class Culture in Elizabethan England*. 1935. New York: Farrar, Straus, and Giroux-Octagon, 1980.

Yachnin, Paul, and Jessica Slights. "Introduction." In *Shakespeare and Character: Theory,*

History, Performance, and Theatrical Persons, ed. Paul Yachnin and Jessica Slights. New York: Palgrave Macmillan, 2009. 1–18.

———, eds. *Shakespeare and Character: Theory, History, Performance, and Theatrical Persons*. New York: Palgrave Macmillan, 2009.

Young, Michael B. *King James and the History of Homosexuality*. New York: New York University Press, 2000.

Index

Acknowledgments

While writing this book, I was fortunate to have the friendship, wisdom, and support of Mary Bly, Julie Crawford, Will Fisher, and Natasha Korda, who read and incisively critiqued a good deal of it. I also benefitted from the advice of Lowell Gallagher, Jean Howard, Jenn Holl, Michael Plunkett, Nick Radel, and Emily Sherwood. For their generous and rigorous comments, I am indebted to my readers at the University of Pennsylvania Press, one anonymous; the second, Valerie Traub, provided invaluable guidance. I could not have asked for a more supportive editor than Jerome Singerman; it has been a pleasure working closely with Caroline Winschel.

I am also grateful for the support and input of conference organizers, audience members, and seminar members at the following venues: the SAA Seminar on "Domesticities/Sexualities/Work" (1998), organized by Wendy Wall; the Columbia University Shakespeare Seminar (1998); the Queer Masculinities conference, Dublin (2001); the Penn Medieval and Renaissance Studies Group (2002); the SAA Seminar on "Lesbianism in the Renaissance: Questions of Methodology and Purpose," organized by Valerie Traub (2002); Pam Brown, who invited me to speak at the University of Connecticut (2002); the Group for Early Modern Cultural Studies conference (2003); the Early Modern Studies Working Group at the University of California, Berkeley (2003); the Society for the Study of Women in the Renaissance, CUNY (2003); the SAA Seminar on "Localizing Caroline Drama" (2004), organized by Alan B. Farmer and Adam Zucker; the Columbia Early Modern Seminar (2006); the "Processing Gender in Law and Other Literatures" conference at UCLA (2008), organized by Lowell Gallagher and Karen Cunningham; and the Seminar on Women and Culture in the Early Modern World at Harvard University (2008).

My research has been generously supported by a George N. Shuster

Fellowship at Lehman College, and a PSC-CUNY Award, which funded a very productive summer at the Folger Shakespeare Library.

A portion of Chapter 2 was published as "How Queer Was the Renaissance?" in *Love, Sex, Intimacy, and Friendship Between Men, 1550–1800*, ed. Michael O'Rourke and Katherine O'Donnell (London: Palgrave Macmillan, 2002), reproduced by permission of Palgrave Macmillan. An earlier version of Chapter 4 appeared as "Sexual Slander and Working Women in *The Roaring Girl*," *Renaissance Drama* 32 (2003): 240–88, reproduced by permission of Northwestern University Press. Part of Chapter 5 appears in "'Male Deformities': Narcissus and the Reformation of Courtly Manners in *Cynthia's Revels*," in *Ovid and the Renaissance Body*, ed. Goran Stanivukovic (Toronto: University of Toronto Press, 2001), reproduced by permission of University of Toronto Press. A portion of Chapter 7 was published as "'A Beast So Blurred': The Monstrous Favorite in Caroline Drama," in *Localizing Caroline Drama: Politics and Economics of the Early Modern English Stage, 1625–1642*, ed. Adam Zucker and Alan B. Farmer (New York: Palgrave, 2006), reproduced by permission of Palgrave Macmillan. I am grateful for permission to reprint these materials.